The New Farmers' Market

Farm-Fresh Ideas for Producers, Managers & Communities

Vance Corum, Marcie Rosenzweig and Eric Gibson

New World Publishing
Auburn, California

The New Farmers' Market:

Farm-Fresh Ideas for Producers, Managers & Consumers

by Vance Corum, Marcie Rosenzweig and Eric Gibson

Supported in part by USDA's Sustainable Agriculture Network (SAN), the national outreach arm of USDA-SARE.

Cover painting, "Santa Barbara Farmers' Market," by Ralph Auf Der Heide, Santa Barbara, California

Publisher's Cataloging-in-Publication

(Provided by Quality Books, Inc.)

Corum, Vance.
    The new farmers' market : farm-fresh ideas for producers, managers
  & communities / Vance Corum, Marcie Rosenzweig
  and Eric Gibson. -- 1st ed.
    p. cm.
    Includes bibliographical references.
    LCCN: 00-110757
    ISBN: 0-9632814-2-9

    1. Farm produce--Marketing. 2. Farmers' markets.
I. Rosenzweig, Marcie A. II. Gibson, Eric (Eric L.)
III. Title.

HD9000.5.C67 2001   635'.068'8
                  QBI00-1077

New World Publishing
11543 Quartz Dr. #1
Auburn, CA 95602

Contents

Part I: Selling At The Market

Part II: Starting, Managing & Promoting The Market

Part III: The New Farmers' Market

Preface

This book had its origins in my earlier book, *Sell What You Sow!* While researching farmers' markets for that book, I noticed the unusual enthusiasm associated with farmers' markets among both producers and managers. I, too, got caught up in in the colorful, celebratory world of farmers' markets. Hundreds of interviews later, I found myself in a sprawling landscape of ideas, tips, advice and opinions about farmers' markets. Farmers' markets are unique and diverse; yet I also felt there was lacking some governing philosophy or unity which I as a journalist felt unprepared to render. It was like having a parking lot of farmers' market booths without a manager!

Enter Marcie and Vance, friends whom I feel are among the most knowledgeable farmers' markets people around. Marcie is the primary author of the first part of the book, and Vance the second and third parts, and of course there is overlap. To Marcie and Vance, my special thanks, as well as to the thousands of farmers and market managers everywhere who share a love of farmers' markets.

A note about reading this book: Occasionally a writer says "We," or "I." In the first part of the book this will refer to Marcie; in the second and third parts, Vance.

Acknowledgments

Our overwhelming gratitude to the many farmers and market managers who graciously gave of their time, wisdom and experience in being interviewed for this book. Their generosity reflects the bountiful spirit of farmers' markets, and we dedicate this book to them.

Our appreciation also to the folks who spent their valuable time and energy reviewing this work: Janet Bachman and Holly Born (both with ATTRA — see Resources); Gretchen Hoyt, co-owner of Alm Hill Gardens in Everson, Washington; Marion Kalb, co-director of the Southland Farmers Market Association; and Sandra Zak, manager of the Soulard Market in St. Louis.

My personal acknowledgements to several generous people who have been an ongoing source of advice and help in my writing about farmers' markets: Lynn Bagley, director of the Golden Gate Farmers' Market Association in Novato, California; Marion Kalb; Randii MacNear, manager of the Davis Farmers' Market; Pam Roy, executive director of the Friends of the Farmers' Markets in Santa Fe; Diane Eggert, director of the Farmers' Market Federation of New York; Bob Chorney, executive director of Farmers' Markets Ontario; and Tony Manetta, director of New York City's Greenmarket.

Special thanks also to Ralph Auf der Heide, the Santa Barbara artist and farmers' market aficionado who graciously contributed the cover art; to Vance Corum, Randii MacNear and Garth Veerkaamp for the generous use of their slides; and to Nancy Campbell of Campbell Creations for scanning our slides and getting them ready for publication.

—*Eric Gibson*

Working with other knowledgable, strong-willed authors is always an exciting challenge. Nevertheless, we perservered, honored each other, and, in the end, came out with a much better book. This was a work of the heart for all three of us and I'm grateful to be in such company.

My gratitude also to my many Placer County farmer/teachers over the years, especially to Jan and Francis Thompson, Eric, Yarda and Randy Hansen, Kay and Martha Miyamura, Alex and Bonnie Ferreira who welcomed a flatlander into the farming circle and their collective dreams for continuing agriculture in a rapidly urbanizing county. To the Ag Commissioners John Wilson, Griff Yamamoto and now Christine Turner, who helped all of us through the regulatory maze; UC Cooperative Extension farm advisor Roger Ingram and County Director Sharon Junge, who taught us to be better producers, marketers, and consumer educators so we could succeed in a strange landscape; and Joanne Neft, our first market manager — Farmers' Markets have many parents and you are some of the best.

Finally, to Garth Veerkamp, my mentor and friend, who taught me to be a better farmer, encouraged me to teach, and allowed me to write and get credit for it. You have been the essense of what good farm advisors should be. Family farmers need more, not fewer, like you.

— *Marcie A. Rosenzweig*

There are a couple thousand farmers I thank for a multitude of learning experiences over the last 22 years, especially the pioneers who dared to believe we could create a farmers' market in Los Angeles County, including Tony Thacher, Dale Reaser, George and Jim Tamai, the Rodarte family and the many who followed as we built new markets.

My thanks go as well to countless new managers and community leaders who believed in this work, including Betty Hamilton, Gretchen Sterling, Harry Brown-Hiegel, Laura Avery, Fanny & Bill Earl, Therese Condon, Craig Mosbaek, Ginger Rapport, Joe Mann, and Doug Thompson.

With them and many others, including Mack Warner, Mark Wall, Tom Haller, Lynn Bagley, Mark Sheridan, Randii MacNear, John Vlcek, Camille Valley, Pam Roy, Brent Warner, Sam Earnshaw and Bob Lewis, a whirlwind of inspiration, I have treasured long conversations that stimulated better ideas. These and so many others have made work rewarding and life rich.

Thanks to the dedicated staff of the Direct Marketing Program at the California Department of Food and Agriculture back in the 1980s, and our director Les Portello, who always showed respect and support through his challenging reflections on our place in agriculture. He has been all that one could ask of a mentor and even more as a friend.

I can't think of any work and people that could have been more satisfying.

— *Vance Corum*

*I*NTRODUCTION

"The people love the market and the vendors love the customers. It's the relationship with the growers that draws the customers."
— Margaret Carroll, Mgr., Palo Alto Farmers' Market, California

Living in a society where a baseball player signs a quarter-billion dollar contract makes it difficult to imagine public intrigue with the by-gone days of buying fresh produce straight from farmers. Yet these two realities co-exist.

Farmers' markets reassert our faith in the importance of learning about crops and soil, recipes and toil — about farming, food and right livelihood. As the mission statement of The Land Institute in Kansas says, "When people, land and community are as one, all three prosper; when they relate not as members but as competing interests, all three are exploited."

Consumers have lost touch with those who grow their food as sadly as farmers have lost contact with those who eat their food. When a customer says, "You grow the best sweet corn I've ever tasted," she reconnects to historical food roots and inspires a renewed sense of pride in the farmer.

In 1970 a loaf of bread cost 27 cents, of which a farmer received 3 cents, or 11%. In 2000 a loaf of bread cost 86 cents, of which a farmer received 4 cents, or 4%. Farmers have been getting a constantly smaller share of the retail food dollar as greater processing, longer shipping and more handling eat up the lion's share. With liberalized trade agreements, the global farm is at our market door. Growers feeling the price squeeze are tempted by the lure of development money as farmland values vault skyward. These fac-

tors and others have led to the loss of nearly one-half million people from the farm population annually over 40 years beginning in 1950. Today, less than two percent of the American populace lives on farms.

Meanwhile the consumer is consumed with price savings. In 1956 Americans spent 18.6% of household income on food. In 1997 they spent half that, only 9.2%, on food, almost an equal amount on gambling, $8 Billion on cosmetics, $150 Billion on illegal drugs for recreational use, $103 Billion on fast food. Our priorities are clearly with cheap food — an artifice of a petrochemical subsidy — and wasteful personal spending choices. Even so, we have been unwilling to commit to a Food Quality Protection Act that would cost the average consumer $6-8 per year to care for our food and the environment.

Farmers have suffered economically and consumers nutritionally. Instead of food choices based on neighbors sharing recipes and home preserves, we are subjected to the blur of fast food and snack food advertisements dominating our average four hours per day of TV-watching. It is small wonder that America is becoming obese and attendant diseases are on the rise.

Ultimately, there are two components essential to a solution. Farmers must be passionately committed to practicing their craft and consumers must be prepared to pay a higher price for their food. To remain on the farm may require a shift to higher value, highly perishable, specialty crops. Gerald Bentryn, a farmer on Washington's Bainbridge Island, poignantly states that customers must support the island's remaining farmers or they will go out of business. The 18,000 residents may be more able to envision the impact of their personal buying decisions because they live on an island with wonderful remaining views. On the mainland the challenge is less visible but no less ironic: support local farms or lose the rural beauty you love, and your current home value.

The USDA reported that there were 2,863 farmers' markets operating in 2000, up 63% from the 1,755 markets just six years earlier. They estimate more than 20,000 farmers are involved, a fraction of U.S. farmers but significant nevertheless for those particular farmers and for their customers.

The farmers' market renaissance over the last 30 years has revived a rich tradition of vibrant, entrepreneurial culture. It is happening as communities seek to reconnect with their roots, revitalize the local farm scene, provide fresh produce to urban populations, gain access to organic products, and create vibrant communities. Farmers' markets are bringing a farm and quality food consciousness into the minds of millions of people. With seniors we are renewing the connection to agriculture they may have had as part of a farm family. With baby boomers we are reacquainting them to an agriculture they may have heard glamorized by their parents. With each generation of youngsters, we are educating them that just because Old McDonald had a farm doesn't mean he sells under the name McDonald's.

Market founders are imitators in a long line of historically critical socializers and civilizers. Indeed, civilization comes from cities that sprang up from marketplaces. Markets are at the heart of great cities and small towns. They are the birthplace of democracy and politics, if we consider ancient Greece. Democracy and economic freedom are connected to the encouragement of markets by government in certain times. When markets were banned and destroyed, during the Roman Era and the Mercantile Era in

Europe, the result was monopoly, inefficiency, loss of quality and a decline in the quality of life.

The decline has recycled in our era along with the growth in mass production for an urbanized population. America has changed from a substantially small, local business culture to a corporate chain culture. Most economic activity ends up in the hands of a few thousand, even a few hundred major retailers. We have largely lost our regional cultures in favor of a homogenized experience wherever we go.

It is little wonder that 10 million people visit Pike Place Market every year. Bored with the familiar, we seek a novel or even bizarre shopping experience. We strive for a sense of local culture.

Ten years ago while traveling from market to market throughout Europe, I visited Bourg-en-Bresse, France. Entering this small city, I was overwhelmed by hundreds of market stalls overflowing the central plaza. Unbridled competition filled my senses. At the mushroom hut residents brought foraged mushrooms for inspection. Every sight proved that this Wednesday market was the community center for food health, food education and social interaction.

The scene was much the same in Turin, Italy, where farmers spilled out of market sheds to fill an intersection among high-priced retail shops. In Germany, street signs pointed me to the Viktualienmarkt, the food market in the heart of Munich. A huge plaza is filled with a mix of permanent vendor buildings, large canopies that are encased in metal sheathings at night, and painted cobblestones marking open farmer stalls. Public market space clearly is a priority. To the north in Nurnberg, the market winds from a huge square surrounded by residential housing through pedestrian streets with large sculptures. Similar streets are filled with farmers in Chengdu, China, allowing the small vehicle to wind its way through the throngs at a snail's pace.

All the lessons and the public commitment come together in Barcelona, where for 160 years the municipality has built and operated public food markets around the city. Community food security achieves new meaning here with more than 40 market halls serving each neighborhood, architectural marvels that complement churches as the central elements of community life and culture.

I sense the influence of European architectural influence on markets from Guanajuato, Mexico to Cuzco, Peru, perhaps a result of past world expositions. In both design and function, each market reflects the depth of economic and cultural roots within the local food community.

Many of our communities seek similar life. Strangled by new highways and new malls, downtowns are developing markets to attract visitors. They are markets planned for quality — quality produce, activities, musicians, and relationships. They reinforce old varieties that have flavor rather than the structural integrity necessary for shipping. As the gap between rich and poor grows, these markets "teach a person to fish" rather than become a societal dependent. They preserve a place where an individual's food choice can make a difference in one more small grower maintaining his share of the market and a place in the community. They give meaningful life to all. As Oxnard farmer Jim Tamai said to me years ago, "I started in farmers' markets for the cash, but I stayed for the people."

Wendell Berry states in *Conserving Communities* that "no food economy can be, or ought to be, only local. But the orientation of agriculture to local needs, local possibilities, and local limits is simply indispensable to the health of both land and people, and undoubtedly to the health of democratic liberties as well."

If wisdom prevails, people will develop programs to encourage market expansion in response to the consumer, farmer and community call. They will inject new funds into educational programs with Cooperative Extension, 4-H and Ag in the Classroom. Youth and community gardens, prison farms and gardens, school lunch programs, student chef demonstrations, and other programs will be expanded and connected to farmers' markets. It is our hope that the practices and programs shared in this book will give people the tools to strengthen local farms and establish a new model for local food security as we build healthy community economies.

It's been said: "Luck is when preparation meets opportunity." A farmer at the Santa Barbara Farmers' Market in California found that his farm is making 95% of its profit from only 20% of its production. A Louisiana citrus grower finally came to the Crescent City Farmers' Market after repeated calls from the manager. Selling out within an hour, he called his wife to bring more fruit, "Oh my God, I've been doing it all wrong!" Planning with integrity and implementing with enthusiasm, we wish you luck in doing it right.

— *Vance Corum, January 2001*

PORTRAIT OF A FARMER   1

"Our rules can't work for every farm — nor should they. But they worked for us because they helped make the most of limited resources and drew attention to us in the marketplace."
— Cass Peterson, Flickerville Mountain Farm

For our "farmer portrait," we have selected Cass Peterson and Ward Sinclair, who ran Flickerville Mountain Farm and Groundhog Ranch in Maryland from 1983 until 1999. After Ward's death in 1995, Cass continued on her own for five more years. Cass and Ward left behind a wonderful legacy of resourcefulness and creativity, as well as a rich expression of their farming experience. Thanks, Cass and Ward!

Background

In '93, after their first six-figure sales season, Ward Sinclair observed that their farm was little more than a flyspeck on the map of American agriculture, "suggesting a garden that got too big for its britches." Their gross sales of more than $103,000 put them in the top 15% of U.S. farms that year, however, and provided enough profit that "neither of us is even thinking about returning to our old city jobs and the rat race."

The farm never lost money after its first five years, and Ward and Cass lived comfortably (not luxuriously) on its proceeds. Gross sales were up to $130,000/yr. in 1999, the farm's final year, most of the increase attributable to plant sales from a greenhouse which amounted to almost $40,000. "The most Ward and I ever made on the farm was $25,000 after taxes," Cass says. "That's not bad — with all the busi-

ness expenses and such, we figured it was the equivalent of a $50,000 city family income."

Peterson and Sinclair purchased Flickerville Farm in '83. The couple retained their jobs as reporters for The Washington Post and commuted to the farm on weekends until Ward quit to farm full-time in '88 and Cass followed the next year.

They rung up just $25 in sales their first day at the Hagerstown, MD, farmers' market in '85. The pair faced a steep learning curve, but through careful attention to customers' needs and good record keeping, they soon discovered which crops were profitable, how to grow them, and most importantly, how to sell them while avoiding the middleman.

"It's not like we were working excellent farmland," says Peterson. "The soil is a light, shaley loam that dries out quickly during droughts. The fields are rolling and would make OK pasture. They were not ideal for growing vegetables."

Thirty of the farm's 65 acres were in woods. Much of the rest was too steep to crop, not fenced to keep out deer, or too remote to irrigate, leaving the couple with just 12 to 14 acres in production.

The farm's location was not ideal for direct marketing either. Their markets in the Washington, D.C. area were a five-hour round trip.

Concepts

Several key concepts guided the Flickerville Farm: lots of record-keeping, micromanagement, succession plantings, reading, listening to customers and constant attention to making lemonade out of lemons. Among the rules Cass and Ward followed:

✧ Avoid wholesaling.

✧ Constantly seek variety, but quickly drop what doesn't work or doesn't pay.

✧ Ignore the experts, especially when they tell you to grow the same old veggies. "We grow unusual stuff. Then we sell it by helping customers understand what it is and how to use it."

✧ Establish planting patterns that allow a single patch to yield two, three or even four different crops each season. Don't plant more than your retail markets can absorb.

✧ Sell everything that grows, from Grade A Fancy to undersized culls, even if they require special labeling and handling.

Finding Their Niche

Innovative marketing is what really made Flickerville Farm stand out from the pack. Most of the couple's income came from selling at farmers' markets, with the rest coming from sales to upscale restaurants where chefs appreciate the fresh, high-quality items they can't find anywhere else. With the exception of some tomatoes marketed through Fresh Fields Whole Food Market, nothing was sold wholesale.

While Peterson and Sinclair worked for The Washington Post, they also maintained a subscription farming clientele made up primarily of fellow Post employees. "The return wasn't great so we gave it up to focus on supplying restaurants," notes Peterson. "But subscription farming is a good experience to teach

Ward Sinclair & Cass Peterson

you how to meet your customers' needs and how to do succession planting to stretch your growing season."

"Early in the game, we realized there are two equally important sides to this kind of farming," Cass says. "One was learning what to grow and how to grow it. The other was selling it. Very quickly we found out that a farm of this size could not succeed by wholesaling. Even for organically grown stuff, the price just wasn't there.

"We also decided it didn't make sense to compete with standard items such as sweet corn and melons. Even if our Chevy van could handle the weight of a load of melons, they could never hold a candle to a truckload of cantaloupes from Maryland's Eastern Shore.

"When we were city consumers, we acquired a deep-seated bias against the commercial tomatoes sold in supermarkets. Once we began farming, we swore we would not grow these varieties, but many of our competitors do grow them. As a result, there is a huge unmet demand at farmers' markets for varieties with that coveted 'oldtimey' flavor, even during peak tomato season.

"One year, almost as a lark, we decided to grow the Arkansas Traveler (maybe to be politically correct in the Washington area). Our sign for that one had a picture of Bill Clinton and said, 'Hail to the Chef.' It turned out the Arkansas Traveler was one of the best tasting and best-selling tomatoes we grew that year."

"Sleeper Vegetables"

Flickerville Farm became famous for its unique offerings at farmers' markets. The key, says Peterson, is to sell things that no one else sells, or offer a higher quality product than the competition. "For example, everyone sold salad mixes. We stayed ahead by adding new greens. Our mix typically had a dozen to 20 different ingredients." Most farmers only offered lettuce for a few weeks during spring. Cass and Ward developed cultural practices that allowed them to harvest lettuce from the end of April until late fall, drawing lettuce-lovers to their booth throughout the season.

Peterson and Sinclair grew an amazing cornucopia of products that included more than 70 varieties of vegetables and 50 kinds of flowers, including many heirloom varieties that are not available elsewhere. Vegetables and flowers were packaged and promoted in fun ways to entice customers to try and buy. "We found that this is far more effective than getting into price wars with other growers on standard items," Cass says.

Some ideas that paid off included:

✧ Heirloom tomatoes, usually 50 or more varieties each season, kept customers coming to their stand when markets were flooded with common varieties. Peterson and Sinclair also sold several thousand heirloom tomato plants in spring in four-packs and four-inch pots. "There were years we made more on tomato plants than tomatoes," she says.

✧ Variety packs of hot peppers (up to 20 varieties each season) and cherry tomatoes (a dozen or so varieties).

✧ Easy-to-grow "sleeper" crops such as kale, beets, chard, parsnips and rhubarb that take up little space in the field and on the van to market, but produce big returns.

✧ "Making lemonade from lemons." For example, when drought in '91 left the couple swamped with golfball-sized potatoes, they promoted them as gourmet "PeeWee Potatoes" in $2 pint boxes. The lemonade theory worked in other ways, too. They put 8 to 10 peppers of various colors that were too small to sell individually into $1 "Bag O' Peppers." "They almost always sold out," Peterson notes.

✧ Prepackaged kits. Peterson and SInclair sold small but perfectly good peppers, tomatoes, onions and garlic packaged together with basil, oregano and a recipe card as the "Flickerville Spaghetti Kit" until too many other farmers got into the act and flooded the market with similar kits. "They take a lot of labor and you can't afford to bring them back unsold," Cass notes.

All items were attractively presented at the market with entertaining and informative signs, and recipe cards with instructions on how to prepare unusual items.

Free samples were another way to keep interest high and stimulate sales. "We promoted virtually every vegetable or fruit that can be eaten raw on sample trays. Our best example was garlic pesto, made from the leaves and flowerscapes of garlic plants. Offering pesto samples on snack crackers one year helped us sell $933 worth of garlic tops and leaves — items that most farmers wouldn't think of taking to market."

Peterson expanded her greenhouse production of bedding plants and vegetable starts to sell directly from the farm and to bolster early farmers' market sales.

"Keeping detailed records requires effort," Peterson says. "But it also helped us make discoveries that influenced our planting decisions. We learned that we grossed far more on our 'sleeper' vegetables than we did even on tomatoes — and with far less investment in time, space and labor.

"We learned that the huge diversity in our fields is probably our best crop insurance. For us, a tomato crop failure wasn't the catastrophe it might be on another farm, because tomatoes accounted for less than 10% of our gross.

"The importance of that diversity could be seen when our farmers' market stand was stacked to overflowing. The displays were intended to overwhelm customers with choices, different colors — shapes and sizes that we hope will be irresistible. The idea is to beguile with varieties that are available nowhere else, not even in specialty shops.

"To complete the still-life that we tried to paint at each market, we placed our prebunched flowers all around the stand. They were our most labor-intensive product, but they also brought in more than $10,000 one year from less than three quarters of an acre — making them our single biggest sales item. By attracting beneficial insects to our fields, they helped pay their way even before we picked them.

"We were constantly searching the catalogs and the literature for more varieties and more information on what might work for us. Because we could only manage so much, we were always ready to drop crops that didn't pay their way or satisfy customers. Varieties that didn't work — like 80% of the flowers that we tried and found unsuitable for one reason or another — were jettisoned. Varieties that didn't meet our taste standard became history. Varieties that bothered our customers — like the Japanese turnip that tasted like 'piano wire,' as one woman put it — also were abandoned.

"As former newspaper people, we were trained to listen to other people's ideas and then run with them. We subscribed to scads of food magazines and always read newspaper food pages. One article led us to mizuna, a Japanese mustard that one year brought in $875. Our cookbook shelf quadrupled in size. We visited specialty stores and talked with chefs to keep up with and adjust to cooking trends.

"It was a lot of work," admits Peterson. "You have to run constantly just to stay in place. Every time you come up with a winning marketing idea, other growers copy it. Then the next thing you know it's available wholesale from California."

Fun Signs Sell

Given their journalism background, it comes as no surprise that Peterson and Sinclair brought an unmatched flair to the art of making signs for their farmers' market products.

"One of the keys to marketing is making your product look good," Cass notes. "It must be visible and attractive and you have to teach customers how to use the weird and the unusual. (We supplied recipe cards with some less-common items.) We made sure all items were clearly priced and promoted with signs intended to entertain as well as inform. The idea was to make doing business with us fun.

"A Flickerville rutabaga sign said: 'A favorite of Norwegian Olympians,' (not researched, but a pretty good bet). The kohlrabi sign called it 'The UFO vegetable.' A sign for healthy-sized heads of pak choi said they can be stir-fried, made into soup, eaten raw or 'used as a doorstop.'

"We dubbed our celtis, which we grew only one year, 'The Vegetable From Hell.' Our sign invited customers to name their own price, because we had no notion what to charge. Around the 4th of July we packed pints of red, white and blue minipotatoes and called them our 'Firecracker Special.'

"When there was an overabundance of peas, tomatoes or peppers, we marketed them at a discount in half-peck or peck quantities as 'Freezer Pleasers.' We've even bagged up Oriental greens and sold them as the 'Flickerville StirFry Kit.' Convenience packaging, if you will."

Cass' Parting Advice

"Specialty crops continue to be big. Varieties are still big. Farmers still need to read the trade and popular press. Failing that (actually, even better than that), they should try new crops every year, taste-test them at home and at market, and push what's really good. Don't count on the supplier to tell you what's good. They're only selling seeds. You're selling produce.

"A great way for a farmer to cultivate expertise (and also steady customers) is to identify the 'foodies' among your customers. Give them samples, frequently, as you would a chef you're trying to impress. Let them experiment and report back. You will reap magnificently for your munificence."

— Reprinted with permission from:
"Mini-Farm, Maxi-Profits," *The New Farm Magazine,* Mar/April 1994, © 1994, The Rodale Institute, Kutztown, PA.
"1,000 Ways to Sustainable Farming," by Craig Cramer, Project Consultant. (cdcramer@clarityconnect.com) ©1999, January 25, 1999. (To see more profiles written as part of a project sponsored by USDA-SARE, go to www.sare.org and click on "The New American Farmers.") ✿

*G*ETTING READY FOR MARKET   2

"Our marketing plan called for us to diversify markets, just as we had in crops, to increase income and decrease risk. Farmers' markets were the most fun and we couldn't beat them for instant customer surveys."

— Marcie Rosenzweig, Full Circle Organic Farm, Auburn, CA

DO FARMERS' MARKETS FIT INTO YOUR MARKETING PLAN?

Are farmers' markets a viable outlet for your produce or value-added product? Who should consider selling at a farmers' market?

✧ Small-acreage farmers and market gardeners who grow high-value, low-volume crops and need high per-acre returns.

✧ Those tired of being price-takers in the wholesale distribution system who want to take on the additional responsibilities to become price-makers.

✧ Growers, such as CSA (Community Supported Agriculture) farmers, who wish to supplement their other marketing methods. A grower whose farm is located in a rural area and who has not established a farm stand, for example, or a farm stand operator whose stand is not busy at certain times of the week.

✧ New or established farm stands wanting to do outreach for their farm among city folks.

✧ New or established (small or large) growers who can use the farmers' markets to test their product line.

✧ Anyone who likes to grow fruits and vegetables, wishes to supplement his or her income, and enjoys meeting people.

The Start-up

"A farmers' market is the only business I know where you can show up with a case of produce and you're in business."

— Frank Beckwith, Beckwith Gardens, Yarmouth, ME

For beginning or small-acreage farmers with little access to established marketing channels or with small amounts of produce to sell, farmers' markets are a great way to get started in farming. As one farmer said, "All you need is a vehicle, a table and insurance."

Another grower said: "I recommend that all beginning farmers start at the farmers' markets. It takes years and years to develop the uniformity you need to sell to wholesalers."

Farmers' markets offer:

✧ minimal marketing start-up costs — requires only truck and selling area;

✧ exemption from standard size and pack regulations (at most markets);

✧ little or no packaging, advertising and promotion costs — farmers' markets are usually well established and centrally located;

✧ better prices — substantially higher than wholesale; and

✧ immediate, direct feedback. Customers are the best ones to tell you about price, quality, variety preferences, and ideas for other crops to plant.

Farmers' markets are an instant market and they save the overhead of opening a retail outlet with on-farm buildings and high-cost liability insurance. You'll probably need to carry liability insurance for farmers' market participation, but it's usually less than for an on-farm market.

Advertising and other marketing costs are generally borne by the market rather than by individual growers as are the costs of providing site amenities like parking and restrooms. At most farmers' markets, sponsoring groups work through local regulations and restrictions — zoning, sign, health department, business license and site insurance — which take considerable time and effort to comply with for a roadside stand or stall.

The small-acreage farmer

Farmers' markets are especially suited for the smaller grower. Small lots and lack of uniformity often preclude wholesale trade. In farmers' markets, while crop quality must be

Carole Laity of Your Kitchen Garden is doing constant upkeep to her small display baskets as people follow instructions to "Taste the tomatoes!" at the Portland FM, OR.

maintained, small growers can market crops "field run" — picked directly into boxes or containers and taken to market — eliminating the need to repack crops. Almost anyone with a few acres and the ability to grow quality crops can become involved in selling at farmers' markets.

Advantages of Selling at a Farmers' Market

Profits!

By eliminating or taking over some mid-level marketing activities such as transportation, brokerage and handling, growers get better-than-wholesale prices by selling direct at farmers' markets. Also, farmers' market exemptions on packing, labeling, and containers save money.

Jay Visser of J-N-A Produce near Manhattan, MT, grows market vegetables, herbs and bedding plants on six acres. He goes to the Bozeman Farmers' Market once a week, and usually takes in about $1500 each market day. Visser also markets his produce to restaurants, a few chain stores, a local independent supermarket and a restaurant distributor. The main advantage of the farmers' markets, Visser says, is the price. Only a quarter of the farm's volume is sold through farmers' market, but it accounts for half the farm's gross income. "This is a big difference," Visser says. "We try to sell as much as we can at the farmers' market!"

Cash flow

Another advantage of farmers' markets is ready cash. As one grower said: "You get the highest dollar for your produce, often higher than grocery stores, and you get it today, not in 30 or 90 days." Immediate payment is especially helpful for small or startup growers whose capital is limited.

How much money are growers actually bringing home from markets? In 1999, Zachary Lyons, director of the Washington State Farmers' Market Association said: "It's hard to track daily sales of individual vendors. There are markets where some vendors gross $500-1500 per day, and others where they're doing $200 a day or less." The Southland Farmers' Market Association indicates market day sales average $894.

Chris Burke, president of the Colorado Farmers' Market Association, says micro-farmers selling at Colorado markets can gross $10,000-15,000/acre yearly, while some larger acreage producers (10-200 ac.) easily gross $2,000-5,000/market day. "It helps if you have a greenhouse to extend seasons or to develop specific niches such as growing unique bedding plants, hanging baskets of flowers, or heirloom tomatoes," Burke says.

A pototo tasting, sponsored by the Auburn, CA, Farmers' Market and Cooperative Extension, served two functions, that of an event within the market and that of a consumer preference survey.

Promote your farm and your products

Farmers' markets allow you to talk with and educate people about your farm and your growing techniques. You get to pitch your product face-to-face with the buyer. One Southern California farmer was considering pulling out his exotic chocolate fuyu persimmon trees, but when he tried selling them at the Santa Monica Farmers' Market, at least 80% of those who tried his samples bought a bag! Instead of ten flats a week on the wholesale market, he was moving a full truckload because of direct consumer contacts and aggressive sampling.

Farmers selling both wholesale and at farmers' markets, in fact, often find that new or exotic varieties sell well for them at the market. By market-testing new products such as bok choy and Chinese cabbage, or arugula at the farmers' market, farmers have then been able to convince wholesale buyers to try them in wholesale channels.

As Doug Cross, Canter-Berry Farm, Auburn, WA, said: "You get a crowd at the farmers' markets. Instead of 100 people a day coming by your roadside stand, there may be thousands coming by at the larger farmers' markets. We do a robust amount of business with 10,000 people on our mailing list for our pick-your-own, and most of our customers originated at the farmers' markets."

Customer feedback and test marketing

Farmers' markets give farmers an opportunity to test new crops and get valuable feedback from customers. By chatting with customers, you can gain new product and marketing ideas, suggestions for packaging and immediate response to new products.

Growers can give unusual items a try at the markets while getting in on the ground floor of coming trends in produce. Talk about your product, share growing and cooking tips, give samples — these are great ways to educate customers about new products, and increase demand for unusual or high-quality items. Once only available at farmers' markets, gourmet lettuce blends, Asian pears, and fresh herbs are now standard in many supermarkets.

According to Karen Durham, manager of the Bellingham Farmers' Market, WA, "One grower used the market to test-market unusual, designer potatoes. He came in with gold and blue potatoes, and worked with the chef in the market to develop potato recipes. He also worked with the customers: 'Would you like to try this?' He asked them if they would buy them in the market and he kept records of their responses. Then he went to the wholesalers and told them: 'I think you can sell these in the supermarkets.'"

Personal satisfaction and social contact

Farmers' markets are fun! Farmers enjoy talking to people about their products and how they're grown. Growers who are used to wholesalers talking down their product in order to pay lower prices are especially grateful for the positive feedback they get from customers who enjoy their produce! As Sue McEvoy, Sue Mac Farm & Herbary in Washington, NJ, says, "I enjoy the people — this is necessary if you want to go to farmers' markets. Customers have known us for years, and we exchange Christmas cards and notes."

Many markets also report a special camaraderie among market vendors. Valerie Schooler, manager of the Wenatchee Farmers' Market, WA: "We have a friendly bunch of guys here at the market. They work their butts off during the week and this is their social outing."

"I enjoy getting off the farm. The farmers' markets keep me in touch and I don't feel so farm-bound. Going to the farmers' market is like a one-day vacation both socially and physically!"
— Gretchen Hoyt, Alm Hill Gardens, Everson, WA

Farmers' markets are also a great family activity. According to Paul Nelson, Untiedt's Vegetable, Waverly, MN: "The farmers' markets help keep our family together. Each family member has their own job at markets and the kids help out. Our grandparents sell with us on the weekends and it's a family get-together. We all grew up in the business — it teaches good family values and let's the kids learn to deal with people."

Disadvantages of Selling at a Farmers' Market

Limited sales volume

While farmers' markets may have many people coming through them, the farmer must be involved personally in each sale. These are one-to-one sales ratios rather than one-to-many. You'll spend greater time dealing with people and a higher proportion of time marketing for the volume achieved versus other methods of moving your product. Since produce is highly perishable and must be marketed quickly, farmers' market sales may be insufficient to absorb all of your production, and other marketing outlets may be necessary. Farmers' markets are most profitable for small volume, high-value crops.

Time involved

Be prepared for long hours spent in loading, traveling to the market, setting up, unloading, and the reverse at the end of the day. A typical 4-hour market just 30 minutes away from the farm can easily take eight or more hours out of the day. All these hours and the value of your time should be taken into account when deciding whether or not a farmers' market is profitable for your farm.

Sue McEvoy picks on Friday for Saturday market. The produce goes into a big walk-in cooler and gets loaded in the truck at 5 a.m. for the market's opening at 9 a.m. The couple is home by 2:30 p.m.

on Saturday and pick till 8 or 9 p.m. for the Sunday market. "We're often prepping and bunching cutflowers in the dark," Sue says. "Then it's up at 5 a.m. for market and we're home Sunday by 4 p.m. And that's IT for Sunday night!"

For Gretchen Hoyt, a day in the life of a farmers' market seller is also not easy. She's up at 4 a.m., driving to the Seattle farmers' market two hours away and delivering to two grocery stores enroute. "Try to have the farmers' markets be part of a route," Hoyt adds. "Make it pay for delivering to grocery stores, etc. on the way."

As another grower said: "I have to spend a lot more hours selling at the farmers' markets than if I just did wholesale because even if you send employees to the markets, you've got to be there to see that things get done right."

Special considerations

There may be waste unless you have secondary markets lined up. Cold, rainy days or even bright, sunny days may keep customers away. Marketing through farmers' markets is a seasonal business with fluctuations in labor requirements and cash flow.

Depending on the individual market, there may be space limitations, product limitations, a few irritating rules, bureaucratic policies and politics to deal with.

Special costs involved in farmers' markets include carrying liability insurance, paying and supervising employees or spending time at the markets yourself.

A different skill set

Retailing skills. At farmers' markets the farmer becomes a retailer and needs to know about merchandising, display, quality control, pricing, packaging and so on.

People skills. Dealing with customers requires a friendly, outgoing personality, patience and product knowledge. You need to enjoy being around people and be OK working long hours, generally on weekends. If what you really enjoy about farming is the quiet solitude of growing your crop, selling at farmers' markets probably won't work for you!

Production planning and management skills. Can you coordinate production with marketing? Estimating how much to pick for market takes planning and finesse. It helps to watch the blips caused by holidays.

Unless you have an impressive amount of a highly sought-after crop, like a truckload of sweet corn or specialty melons, you should have a variety of produce to sell and sufficient quantity to make the stall look full. The perception of choice and bounty are important; few customers will stop if there are only one or two pieces of each product.

To optimize your investment of time and energy in the farmers' market, you'll want to be in the market as much of the season as possible. Learn and use season extension techniques like succession plantings of early and late season varieties; use row crop covers, tunnels, greenhouses or cold frames and shade cloth to grow beyond the weather; investigate short-season varieties for planting on either side of your main crop. Use timelines to plan when to plant so you don't have weeks in the middle of the market when you have nothing to sell. Customers are creatures of habit. If you help them break their habit of coming to you by not being in the market, you'll spend three times the energy to get them back.

However, even if you have a short-season crop — just three weeks of berries or 10 days of a special peach — you can still build a reputation. Ask the market manager to put out a sign announcing boysenberries, local strawberries or donut peaches coming next week. Then reinforce with your customers that you only have two weeks at the market so that they make the impulse decision.

CHECKING OUT THE MARKETS

"Look at what the market will bear before you even grow the product."
— Gretchen Hoyt, Alm Hill Gardens, Everson, WA

The first question to ask about a new crop or product is: "Is there a market?" Ideally, as part of your business plan, you'll research all marketing possibilities before you put any seed in the ground. If you're already in business and looking to diversify your marketing outlets, your research is more product-specific. In either case, you're trying to identify the market, in the broad sense, for your product. Simply defined, a "market" is a group of people who are, or will be, your customers.

As you check out farmers' markets, look for whether your potential customers are there and whether they're already getting the product and service you want to provide. If your product is mainstream, are there mainstream shoppers in that market? If your product is up-scale or trendy, are there those shoppers in the market? If you have or can generate volume to keep your prices low, are there customers who need and look for that in the market?

Start with farmers' markets in your immediate area. To find them ask your county extension agent and get a Farmers' Market Directory from your state department of agriculture. Many states now have websites devoted to their farmers' market efforts. The USDA has a website listing farmers' markets in each state at:

www.ams.usda.gov/farmersmarkets.

Just click the state on the map.

Some market associations also have websites, like the California Federation of Certified Farmers' Markets at:

http://farmersmarket.ucdavis.edu.

Size, Seasonality & Location

Each market is unique and there can be a big difference in the ambiance. Some markets are large, structured and more competitive. Others are small, loosely confederated and more laid back. Find the market that feels most comfortable to you and caters to your customer base.

Larger, more established markets often fill as early as October of the previous year. Smaller markets may not have any requirements at all. Either way, you should contact the market manager in advance to learn the ground rules.

Some markets may operate only in the height of summer while others may be open from April through December or even year-round. By and large, the earlier in the season you can start at market, the sooner you'll build a loyal clientele who will carry you through the season. However, if the market does a "soft" opening without much fanfare, you may be wise to wait for their summer publicity campaign.

Other criteria necessary for a good market are a good location with adequate parking for customers and adequate population density nearby. Markets that are poorly located may not attract consumers. Also, adequate density may be difficult to achieve in a small-town market.

Stop 'n Shop

Visit the markets

Perhaps the best way to get to know a farmers' market is to shop it. Hang around as a customer for a while, talk to vendors and listen to patrons. Are shoppers enjoying the experience? Are they meeting and greeting friends and still buying produce? Do they mutter about prices as they leave the lot? Are the vendors generally happy? Do they greet customers like old friends? Are they in their stalls selling or in their neighbor's stall complaining about the market or its management?

Go early, go late, go at different times of the season to get a feel for the market as a totality. Is this market a going proposition in the early season but a dud when other, near-by markets open? Conversely, does this market pick up in the fall as other, shorter season markets close? Spend enough time to get a feel for what kind of volume the growers are moving. Check the prices. Can you be competitive and still make a profit?

How well you do depends on the market's overall volume and the need for your product. Are many other growers offering the same product or variety of products you like to grow? In some cases you may do well simply by going to a small market where you have a relative monopoly. Yet at strong volume markets, you may do even better with six or seven competitors.

Study the market's clientele. Are they the right group for your products? It may be worth traveling to a market farther away to maintain a premium price.

Other things to look for. Remember that customers want quality, freshness, selection and variety, restrooms, and easy parking. Also evaluate services offered to vendors, such as stall size, rainy-weather shelter, restrooms, and water for drinking or washing produce. Are these available at the market(s) you're considering?

Does the market fit your schedule?

Consider whether the market's days and hours of operation meet your work schedule. Market hours are controlled by the market organization and may not be ideal for all producers.

Many vendors and managers feel that weekend markets are the best attended and attract more of a food-buying crowd than a weekday market. Weekday evening markets tend to be festival markets where you have crafts, pony rides, etc., which may distract from the farmers. Farmers may have fewer, smaller sales in this environment unless they can match the festive tone.

According to Mary Lou Weiss, manager of the farmers' market in Torrance, California, her Tuesday market caters to seniors and mothers with strollers, and vendors average about $500. The Saturday market is a "family day," and vendors' sales average about $900. Both days are viable for those farmers.

Market promotion

Is the market well promoted? Does the market attract enough customers? Are advertising and promotion, or the lack of them, controlled by the market?

Does the market's advertising and promotion timing coincide with the availability of your products? Look for

The Oregonian provides sponsorship through in-kind advertising for this festival promotion.

signs of active promotion, like prominent signs and banners, or flyers placed on windshields and store windows. Don't waste your time and resources in a market that's not actively promoted.

Do the markets allow sampling? Sampling increases sales! Find what's necessary to do sampling, i.e., can you prepare greens at the table or do you need to have a food handler's permit? Must samples be cut in a certified kitchen and then covered at the market? One creative way around this may be to have a local chef demonstrate a dish using your product.

Does the market accept food stamps? This also helps increase sales.

Once you've narrowed down the choice to markets that fill the bill in terms of clientele, ambiance, promotion, and timing, take a look at some of the less obvious qualifiers.

Market rules & regulations

Rules and regulations vary from state to state and local rules may vary market to market within the state, so check with the market manager before you sign up to sell. There may be requirements for using only certified scales, labeling, sales tax reporting, vehicle permits, and provisions for the food stamp and food coupon programs. In many markets, processed foods can't be sold. You may also need a health permit from each county in which you sell your product.

Request a written copy of the market rules and regulations from the market manager to learn if they correspond with your plans. Make sure you can comply with them and that the market serves your needs.

Find out how much it will cost you to sell at the market — stall fees, promotion fees and insurance assessments. Most markets charge a fee to participate. This may be in addition to association dues or stall fees may be higher for non-association members.

Fees may be collected daily, weekly, monthly or seasonally. The most common are space or percent based, usually about 6-10%. Many markets track sales volumes by requiring that the vendor provide a "load list" for each day of sales. This list tracks what's brought into the market and what's taken back to the farm; fees are calculated on sales per the load list.

What you are permitted to sell at each market can vary based on the organization's rules. Some market rules define precisely how many people can sell produce, how many can specialize in herbs, how many craftspeople can participate, and what geographic area participants must come from. Other small, unstructured markets may require that you simply show up on Saturday morning.

Can you abide by a strict "farmer-grown" policy? At most markets, a farmer can sell only produce grown on his or her farm. Other markets may allow you to sell other growers' items in limited quantities.

Look for a market that guarantees you the same stall site for the season rather than assigning stalls on a first-come, first-serve basis. Selling from the same spot every week helps develop loyal, repeat customers. As one grower said: "If I get there late and am down two spots, my regular customers think I'm not there." On the other hand, if you only want to sell a few months out of the year, renting a stall by the season would work against you and the market.

Insurance. Check to see if you need to carry individual insurance for accidents at the market or for food product liability. Farmers' markets usually have insurance but it may not cover individual sellers. [See Appendix]

Market organization

Is the market well-organized and professionally run? Have you seen or heard publicity about it? Are they open about finances, rules and problems? Is the market sponsored by an active, supportive farmers' market association including farmers and community members or is it the work of one individual?

Can you reach the manager or organizer at home or only during "office hours?" Does s/he live in or near the community? Does s/he know the area well enough to explain the ethnic and income mix of shoppers at the market? Does the manager/organizer admit to mistakes or does s/he always say "not to worry" or "no problem" when asked specific, tough questions?

Do the organizers or manager have a positive community reputation or track record? Is the market working with other markets, especially regarding choice of day and/or hours; i.e., are the sponsors concerned about markets in general, not just theirs?

Becoming a Seller

Now that you've chosen a market, the first step is procuring a space before the season actually begins. Some established markets have waiting lists or on-farm inspections that must be done before you can sell. It is important not to plant until you know exactly where and how you will be selling. Know your markets first!

Contact the market manager to learn if there's room for another grower and for what type of produce. Ask what items are needed in that market and then consider adding them to your product line.

How can you get into market if there is a waiting list? Create a niche. If you know you've got a "hot and happening" item, like Sweet William bouquets on Mother's Day, and other growers are selling it, then do something different — decorate it, put it up in a different size; don't just go with the flow.

The fundamentals of selling at market are pretty straightforward, but nuances can take years to learn. It is important for growers to select markets wisely. New growers are often better off getting into bigger, more established markets first, where things tend to sell faster.

If your farm or crop is quite small, consider alternatives. Could you consign your produce to a regular participant? Check market regulations to see if this is allowed. Maybe another small-acreage grower would share a stall with you.

Keep records. If you're going to 12 markets, but 85% of your income comes from eight of those, cut the bottom four! You'll do a better job and profit just as much. Don't forget the time and costs involved in traveling to a more distant market. Your prices at that market should reflect your greater costs. [See Chapter 3]

Santa Barbara Pistachio has diversity within a crop by marketing many flavors of pistachios, shell and shelled. Note also the eye-catching sign above the crowd.

CHOOSING CROPS & PRODUCTS FOR FARMERS' MARKETS

Diversity vs. Specialization

"I see at least two models for farmers' markets here: one for the large cities, where the small acreage producer can bring lots of different things to a varied market. Truck gardens can work in a large city market. In small town mid-America, however, it's hard to introduce new products like organic, or specialty fruits and vegetables. Bok choy or Swiss chard just sit there. Corn, lettuce, tomatoes, green beans and melons are the big tickets. Find out if the consumer demand is there in your particular market before committing yourself!"
—Charlie Springer, Mgr., Richmond FM, IN

Should you specialize, or offer a wide choice of products?

In a small rural market, you may want to offer one-stop shopping with a wide array of familiar produce. In larger, more competitive markets, you might specialize in fewer but higher value items like honey or berries. If you offer only a few items, create diversity with a line of products. Say you specialize in almonds: Offer raw, roasted, smoked, blanched and slivered almonds, almond butter,and almond oil in a variety of packages and sizes.

"Consider the convenience of customers. We take a big variety of vegetables to market. Some people say they don't have to go anywhere else because they can get everything from me."
— Eydie Ridder, Baraboo FM, WI

Having familiar traditional produce encourages one-stop shopping, but what differentiates your stall from the supermarket besides your pricing? Offer products supermarkets can't handle: in-season, tree- or vine-ripened, fresh-picked and organic. Bring at least one very unusual item. People will stop and ask: "What is it? How do you cook it?"

"The key to farmers' market success is to offer both diversity and 'something special.' If you can establish a following by offering something special such as certified organic, you can develop a loyal clientele. If you sell lettuce that no one else does your lettuce buyers will also buy your tomatoes. We offer 15-20 different items at the market at the height of the season, and several varieties of each item."
— Lisa Bloodnick, Bloodnick Family Farm, Apalachin, NY

Carry a few colorful impulse items like cut flowers, herbs, or a specialty produce item. These attract people to your stand, and having something new each week encourages repeat visits by your "regulars." Don't try so many items that you only bring a little of each. Remember: the higher the heap, the better it sells. Whatever you do, don't take local crops to a glutted market. This embodies the old expression "Bringing coals to Newcastle" — like strawberries or artichokes to the Watsonville, CA, market or citrus to Orange County, FL. Then again, they do use a certain amount of coal in Newcastle. Everyone eats and you want them to buy locally-produced food.

Making Your Niche

"I plant a couple rows of something new each year. Taste and appearance are what sells at the market, and farmers' market varieties are often completely different varieties of the same crop than you would sell on the wholesale market."
— John Paul Barbagelata, Barbagelata Farms, Linden, CA

Successful growers at farmers' markets participate in the market regularly, have a diverse mix of products within their stall or contribute to the overall product mix in the market, and have sufficient, continuous supplies throughout the season or year. Trends in farmers' markets are toward product diversification, unusual or organic products, and value-added items that can increase profit margins.

"Look for something unique and novel to bring to the market. Bring unusual varieties of peppers or heirloom tomatoes — don't come in with a half acre of corn. Go through a seed catalog and if it's something you don't see in the grocery store, it might be a possibility."
— Dan Best, Mgr., Sacramento FMs, CA

The key to farmers' market success is to offer something customers can't find in supermarkets. Customers often perceive produce quality at farmers' markets to be superior to supermarkets. They look for varieties not found in the supermarkets and the greater availability of organics at the farmers' markets.

On the other hand, farmers' market varieties could be the same as their wholesale cousins — just picked later. As John Paul Barbagelata says, "A tomato picked vine-ripened for the farmers' market is a totally different tomato than one picked green for the wholesale market."

Continued on page 16...

Phil Smith of Westwind Gardens built this chili roaster for the 1998 Salsa Festival in Beaverton and used it to increase pepper sales at several Oregon markets. Roasted peppers is Phil's niche.

Hot products: Fresh and Value-Added.

Over the past five years, Eric has had an unusual hobby, asking dozens of growers or market managers: "What are the hottest fresh products being sold in your market?"

Fresh products

"Tree- or vine-ripened is the reason people come to the markets."

"Fresh-from-the-farm, in-season, mainstay fruits and vegetables."

"Whatever is in season! From rhubarb in the spring to cauliflower in the fall."

"The strongest items consistently are 'early'... sweet corn, cuc's, zucchini, tomatoes, peppers and melons."

"Staples are still the big item here. Specialties are just starting to emerge. Our market traditionally serves older customers — it's really a 'beans and 'taters' audience."

Specialty items not found in supermarkets.

"Anything unusual sells here."

"We offer eight different varieties of cherries here, not just a Bing!"

"Growing different varieties of sweet and hot peppers is a great niche, since they are an important ingredient in salsa, an expanding product line."

Heirloom varieties

" 'Old' is 'in.' Old fashioned, heirloom varieties of roses, for example, like your grandmother grew. We have one grower who grows over 80 varieties of roses, with their names all on labels. We have other rose growers in the market, but there's always people in line for hers. Most of the other roses are bred for long stems and visual appearance, not smell. The old heirlooms look fantastic, and they also smell great."

— Mark Sheridan, Mgr., Santa Barbara FM, CA

"Some of the specialty organic heirloom varieties are showing up in the Austin and Dallas-Fort Worth areas."

"Some of the old apple varieties, like Winesap, Arkansas Black or Northern Spy that you won't find in the supermarkets."

Salad mix

"The mesclun craze just doesn't seem to bottom out. The more farmers are getting into it, the more customers, and each farmer seems to have a different mix with each one tasting different."

"One interesting variation on mesclun mixes is a farmer here selling mixed bunches of vegetables, rainbow mixes of radishes or chiogga beets."

"Due to the competition, we give our mixes names and we offer different 'flavors' with different ingredients."

"My salad mix has large leaves instead of baby leaves and I can sell my product for 50 percent cheaper. I found a niche of people willing to pay $3 a pound for salad mix instead of $6 a pound."

"We sell head lettuce with roots on (washed) as 'live.'"

Herbs

Herbs are a great farmers' market niche item, and also lend themselves to great value-added items like herbal vinegars.

Ethnic

"It's a combination of more ethnic buyers coming to the market and other people liking the ethnic foods."

Organic items

"There's a trend toward organic here (New York) at the markets. People are still shopping primarily for price on the East Coast, though, and only a certain percentage of people will pay extra for organics."

"The consumers are more educated now. People are starting to take care of themselves a lot better and they're searching for organic."

Fresh flowers

"There's a lot of competition in the market for flowers. You have to stay ahead of the competition. This means reading a lot of flower and gardening magazines and being a member of the Association of Specialty Cut Flower Growers."

Also mentioned:

Products for canning, vegetable seedlings, bedding plants, maple syrup, nuts, baby vegetables and greenhouse tomatoes.

"We sell compost, which we make from leaves and grass clippings (green waste) from the city of Boulder, and sell it in 40-pound bags at the market to home gardeners. Another good draw is our tomato plants. We grow 20 different varieties, which are purchased by home gardeners to plant themselves. With each plant, we hand out an information sheet on how to grow tomatoes."

—John Ellis, Farmer John's, Boulder, CO

Value-added products

Here are some comments we heard about value-added products at farmers' markets:

"Garlic sells for $1 a bunch, but sell it with dried herb flowers and two cayenne peppers and it sells for $10 a bunch!"

"Make your product attractive! Dress up your product by tying it with ribbon, or bundling different items together! If you are selling items in jars, cover the lid with a small circle of fabric, etc."

"Value-added is little more work out on the farm but gets premium prices. A few years ago you could bring sunflowers and sell them, but now they have to be put in with other flowers in an arrangement. You can't just bring things, put them on the table and expect them to sell. It takes a better job of presentation."

"The market for dehydrated vegetables is really taking off! The 'country kitchen' look is really in. The key is to use down-home, pretty packaging."

"Items for fast preparation. People are uneducated in cooking and in prepping food or produce."

"Value-added takes us away from the concept of fresh and direct! We have to differentiate as much as possible from grocery stores."

Here are some of the many value-added items growers are selling in farmers' markets:

- Baby food (organic)
- Bakery items, including bread, cookies, scones, fruit cobblers, apple dumplings, fruit pies
- Baskets, including fruit baskets
- Canned items, including roasted garlic, vegetables
- Corn shocks
- Crafts
- Dog biscuits (vegetarian)
- Dried fruit, including exotic dried fruit like dried persimmons, fruit squares
- Dried vegetables, including tomatoes
- Flowers, including cut flower arrangements, dried flowers
- Garlic braids
- Gourds
- Greenhouse items
- Herbal products, including braids, crafts, lotions, balms, soaps, oils, teas, bath herbs, dried herbs, lip gloss, salve, massage oils
- Hickory chips
- Honey, including flavored
- Jams, jellies and preserves, including low- or no-sugar, cactus apple, fig jam jelly, pomegranate jelly, rhubarb preserves
- Juices, including fresh, exotic juices like pomegranate
- Lettuce, mixed 6-pack as veggie starts
- Marinated fruits and vegetables and syrups (wild cherry)
- Molasses
- Nursery stock
- Nuts, salted and flavored
- Oil, including jojoba, olive, organic
- Pastas
- Pepper braids
- Pesto, all kinds
- Pickled vegetables
- Popcorn
- Posole (corn soaked in lime and dried) from colored corn
- Potpourri
- Prepared foods, including bagels, pizza relish, onion rhubarb salsa, including tomato, salsa verde mix with tomatilloes, onion, garlic, chilies, cilantro
- Soaps, generally handmade
- Spices
- "Squirrel corn" (field corn put in packages with a feeder stand)
- Vinegar, including gourmet, with fancy labeling and special ingredients like meyer lemons, habanero peppers, berries or edible flowers. ✿

Continued from page 13

Finding the missing link

"Stroll through the local supermarket. What doesn't travel well or is NOT on the shelf is a good item to grow and sell. Why sell what is cheap and in mass at the supermarket? Finding your niche means selling what is not available anywhere else."
— Diane Green, Greentree Naturals, Sandpoint, ID

Not every opening is an opportunity. Do your homework and know what your farm can handle. The first question to ask about a new product is: "Is there a market?" As Jane Desotelle, manager of the Adirondack Farmers' Market Co-op in New York, relates: "We're in a remote rural area and the unusual veggies are a hard sell here."

As Gretchen Hoyt of Alm Hill Gardens says: "Look at what the market will bear before you even grow the product. We've been invited to grow gooseberries for restaurants, for example, but they don't pay enough to even consider growing them. Some products just draw customers to your stand! One grower sold a new super-sweet corn at his roadside stand for 50 cents an ear!"

"We've cut out things like sweet corn where we were competing with larger growers. It just wasn't practical on a small scale. Now we concentrate on the items that the bigger growers don't grow, like heirlooms and specialty varieties, where the yields aren't as high but the flavor is outstanding."
— Lisa Bloodnick, Bloodnick Family Farm, Apalachin, NY

With the maturing of farmers' markets in some areas, it has become more difficult for the entry-level grower to find a market opening. Standard varieties and "the usual suspects," i.e., tomatoes, sweet corn, watermelons, summer squash, green peppers, etc., are probably already spoken for. You may still be able to grow these mainstream items if you can differentiate your product from what's already available. Grow what you love in all its splendor, package it for the market of today, and display it in a way that stops traffic in the marketplace — that's how you'll make your niche.

A Vermont maple syrup producer at New York City's Union Square Greenmarket has diversity within a crop, with various sizes & packages of syrup from utilitarian to gift as well as sugar and sugar candy. The sign is great, but if a crowd develops the sign won't be visible.

Diversifying Within a Crop

"Chip and Susan Planck of Wheatland Vegetable Farms, Purcellville, PA, may grow only 18 categories of vegetables and small fruits, but they offer a lot of choices within those categories. For example, they grow 25 varieties of tomatoes, five of eggplant, six of beans and 15 kinds of greens. 'A new crop complicates your life,' Chip says. 'Diversity within a crop is easy to achieve.' At market, they promote the different varieties by name and offer samples of each. 'People aren't coming to buy tomatoes any more,' Chip says. 'They're coming to buy Brandywine or Early Girl. They've discovered over the seasons which varieties they like best.'"
— *Growing for Market*, Dec. 1995.

If your farm is set up for raspberries, grow early, midseason and late varieties. Grow some golden, purple and black as well as the red. Grow some that freeze well and promote that. Consider adding other cane berries like boysenberries, loganberries, and blackberries.

Look at different packaging sizes for diversity or different forms of the product.

Selling to Ethnic Groups

Cater to neighborhood demographics. If you sell in a larger population center, consider tailoring your product line for the market's neighborhood by growing crops used in the foods of that culture, i.e., Jamaican,

Growing for Market: How One Grower Does It

On Honey Crisp Farms, a small, 17-acre farm near Reedley, California, owner Art Lange raises 3,000-5,000 boxes of fruit per year from over 200 varieties of fruits ("about everything that grows in California"). He is able to plant so many varieties on small acreage by utilizing "hedgerow" planting of dwarf-size trees. "To stay in the market from mid-May until mid-September, we need peaches, plums, and nectarines that ripen at different times," Lange says.

About half of Lange's fruit is sold to high-end restaurant distributors who can resell tree-ripe fruit, and the other half is sold though farmers' markets. "Everybody advertises tree-ripe but I consider tree-ripe ready to eat," Lange says. "When you buy from me you can take a bite out of it and it tastes good!"

"One of the grower's major problems is that you can't always tell just when the fruit will ripen. Sometimes the fruit you bring to market is too green or too ripe. Selling directly to the consumer has its drawbacks: It is expensive in time, labor, and transportation. We have determined that it costs us about a $1 per pound to produce and sell our fruit. Consumers want fresh fruit, but they prefer to pay less than 17% of their income for food."

"Our expenses for picking are phenomenal," Lange says, "but our quality is also phenomenal!" Pickers go up and down the rows looking for the right degree of ripeness. Since fruit is picked commercially up to a week to 10 days early for supermarkets, Lange's neighboring growers often pick the same variety ten days earlier than he does.

Among Lange's specialties are heirloom varieties of white peaches and nectarines that he says are extremely good but very fragile. He plants old, high-quality varieties like Hale, Elberta, and Santa Rosa as well as new, good tasting ones like Snow Candy and Snow Dance peaches, Arctic Pride nectarine, and the Arctic Star white nectarine. "The sweetness is phenomenal on some of the new experimental varieties," Lange says.

The trees are planted close together because it saves on labor and land. The trees are short and open to light. They are fertilized, irrigated, and thinned heavily to get larger fruit.

The fruit is packed in the field and it is not washed. Nor is the fruit machine-sized, graded, or defuzzed, so no one handles the fruit after it is picked until the customer buys it.

The fruit is packed in single-layer boxes and transported to the market on four- to six-inch Styrofoam pads. "This seems extreme, but it enables us to bring our fruit in the best possible shape to the customers."

The fruit is cooled in a small cold room at 45° F to make it last a few more days in the market.

"We arrive at the market early to set up," Lange says. "We let the manager know the quality of the produce we have for sale. It is important to the market and to us that the market have good-quality produce. There are many farmers who want to sell at farmers' markets but want to sell only their culls. This does not help build markets because the quality is not good enough."

Since California's Central Valley is a big fruit growing region and there is heavy competition from many local growers and homeowners at the local farmers' markets, Lange travels long distances to find more profitable markets as far away as San Francisco, Santa Monica, and San Diego.

"It is hard to establish yourself in a new market. When your customers get to know you, they will come back. It is pretty tough to sell your product the first time. The second time it is easier. Having a number of varieties ripening at different times is very helpful because your selling season will be longer." ✿

Italian, Hispanic, etc. Large chain supermarkets have replaced the mom-and-pop stores in many areas and their system of central purchasing provides a homogenized product mix aimed at the largest number of buyers. This means that items like a variety of fresh chilies, specialty eggplants, various Asian vegetables, and fresh herbs could provide an opportunity for the small-acreage farmer. Many peoples from ethnic backgrounds are a "natural" for farmers' markets since they're used to purchasing in open-air, bulk-selling markets in their home countries.

Do your homework first. Talk to customers and scout the neighborhood to make sure this need truly exists. Intent is important here. You must want to provide a service. If all you find interesting in this group of customers is their money, don't do it — you won't succeed. Don't just jump into this market. Some cultures may be accustomed to haggling and purchasing food at low prices. As a trial balloon, grow a couple of "ethnic" varieties of crops you already produce, say a Russian tomato or a Puerto Rican pepper.

Introducing New Products Again and Again

"When Asian pears first came out, everyone saw the first ones who sold them make money, so the rest went out and planted them and lost money as the market got saturated. Now the same thing is happening with pluots!"
— Mary Lou Weiss, Mgr., Torrance FM, CA

Check seed catalogs, check nursery catalogs for something new, and be the first one to present this product in a market. It doesn't work to walk through the market and copy others: Be an innovator! When you are, you'll get the higher price if you educate the consumer with samples, recipes and background.

According to John Ellis, Farmer John's, Boulder, CO, "You need to be ahead of the curve. If you see a crop that's becoming more popular with the chefs, try to plant more of it. My restaurant distributor also keeps me informed about what leading edge chefs are looking for. I also make notes at the end of the year about the good sellers in the market for myself and for other vendors."

You're in the food business. Read about food. Listen about food. If you don't take magazines like *Gourmet* or *Cooking Light,* at least go to the library and read them. Watch the morning news shows, at least the day of the cooking segment. Talk to local chefs. Is there something they see on the horizon? Pay attention to trade shows for related industries like the deli and specialty foods. Try to get a feel for what's coming and what's waning.

"Remember that most new products are short term advantages for only two to three years in the competitiveness of the farmers' markets. Their advantages usually disappear as fellow vendors turn on to your new product. Many of the growers have been doing the same thing for years and wonder why their sales are decreasing when the overall market sales are increasing."
— Rebecca Landis, Mgr., Corvallis-Albany FM, OR

"The economy is so good that people tend to eat out in restaurants more. They tend to cook less at home, have unique preferences, and want specific items, like unique vegetables they read about in cookbooks or magazines, or have a preference for organic. You can't grow for all people, so you have to learn what most of your customers want and grow for them."
— Kathy Rhoads, Rhoads Farm Market, Columbus, OH

Continuous Supply and Extending the Season

Season Extension. Selling transplants at the market is a good way to extend your season.

Make small frequent plantings so everything goes to market at peak maturity. One San Diego County farmer makes 60 plantings of corn, a few rows every other day. And that's just the corn!

To bring fresh-picked broccoli to the farmers' markets, Larry Thompson of Thompson Farms, Boring, OR, plants half an acre every two weeks. When he sold wholesale, Thompson planted broccoli in 5-acre blocks. Instead of the three crops he planted for the wholesale market, he's now planting 25 crops for the farmers' markets. He does a lot of transplanting so he can time the crops exactly. "Consistency is important in farmers' markets," Thompson says. "You can't run out of product or you will lose customers."

Unlike many farmers' market sellers who try to capture early or late season profits, Thompson feels it compromises crops by pushing them beyond their normal growing season. "Each crop seems to have an optimum time, and I feel they don't taste as good when they're pushed," he said.

Still, one of the challenges of farmers' market is to choose products to stretch the season from, say, June until November to maximize returns and keep your customer base.

> "You need to have something to offer all that time. In summer, our main draw is our herbal plants. We sell about 80 varieties in 3-inch pots. This takes us 'til August; our vegetables carry us through August and September, while October is big with mums, cornstalks, winter squash and gourds, and potatoes. Another way we stretch the season is with our homemade herbal soaps."
> — Sue McEvoy, Sue Mac Farm & Herbary, NJ

Try to have crops available as early in the season as possible. If you consistently supply desired produce before other growers, consumers will learn to look for the products they want at your stall. According to Cheryl Boden, West Union Gardens, Hillsboro, OR, "One of the biggest windows of profit is early season crops. Look for early varieties, or get plants to come on early by using floating mulches, row covers, or transplants to capture the early markets. People are hungry for fresh produce when they come to the market in June, and early season customers often keep coming back throughout the season."

Adjunct products can keep you in the marketplace beyond your normal cropping period. Plant the "too small" cloves of your seed garlic in 4-inch pots and sell them for snipping.

Our friend Jan Thompson of Twin Brooks Farm, Loomis and Newcastle Produce, Newcastle, CA, clips the greens from young spring garlic that won't make a decent head, and makes garlic pesto from them for the deli in her store.

California, with its multiple and varied climates, has longer market seasons than most other parts of the country — many year-round. This can be particularly challenging for the smaller-acreage, seasonal grower. At Full Circle Organic Farm in Auburn, CA (co-owned by author Marcie), we planted extra heirloom tomato, eggplant and pepper starts to make sure we had something to sell when the farmers' market opened in May. Sometimes we also had greens, peas, and potatoes but the transplants gave us an early presence and cashflow in years when harsh spring weather had kept us out of the fields. On the flip side of the season, late October and into November, we'd pick the remaining large-fruited tomatoes that wouldn't turn and sell them with recipes for Fried Green Tomatoes.

Selling Everything

Non-food agricultural products may be a niche for you. Try gourds for crafters and/or to make into value-added products: curly willow branches for flower arrangers, dried chilies in various colors for wreath makers, or pumpkins and decorative gourds in fall. Cut flowers are often the biggest money maker in the market. A grower in Edmonton, Canada, sells bunches of cedar boughs for $4 a piece. People love to decorate!

One October when the pumpkins from Dehn's Gardens, Andover, MN, came down with spotted little speckles from a hailstorm, Bonnie Dehn dressed up as a scarecrow to sell the pumpkins as freckled pumpkins! Some corn growers we know plant a small plot of multi-colored decorative popcorn. They sell some in the husk with just a strip peeled back, some with the whole husk peeled back, and some tied to a paper bag with popping instructions. Around Halloween and to a lesser extent at Thanksgiving, they bundle up stalks and sell them for fall decorations!

At Full Circle Organic Farm we'd pull basil plants in fall, dry the wood, and bundle it to sell for smoking wood to barbecue enthusiasts the following year. Orchardists might consider making small bundles of fruit wood for barbecues or wood-fired ovens in upscale restaurants. We also hung any herb bunches that didn't sell fresh and turned them into dried bunches.

Flowers are another option. Growing annuals and perennials can be a profitable niche. Well-arranged bouquets will enhance the appearance of your display and attract impulse shopping. Sunflowers have become so popular that seed catalogs have special sections dedicated just to them.

One grower cuts and sells the blossoms from onions that have bolted in the field. At Full Circle Farm we had a small planting of artichokes for our first market years. We let the smaller, later artichokes bloom, because the showy flowers sold for more than the smaller chokes would have.

Growing Organic

Organically grown produce is another market to consider. More than a niche, but not yet mainstream, it's a rapidly growing segment of agriculture and enjoys some price advantage.

Organic growing requires more than just a substitution of "approved inputs" for "restricted inputs." It's a major commitment to improving soil quality and fertility and working with the environment. If you're currently growing with conventional practices, it may be several years before you'll be able to use the "organic" label and your yields may be less during the transition years. If you're starting a farm on fallow ground and you can show a history, you may be able to work toward certification your first year. Consult with your local certification group and talk to other organic growers.

There is expense involved in being certified and you must consider it as you would any other farm expense. If you want to use the term "organic" after the National Organic Standards go into effect in Summer 2002, you will have to be certified by a third party that is accredited by the government. Growers with gross sales under $5,000 per year are exempt from the requirement of certification and submitting an organic systems plan.

For more information contact an organic certification organization. [See Resources, Chapter 2, "USDA Organics Program."]

Business Considerations

Beyond the potential of every new crop for the market lie the business considerations.

Does the crop grow well on your land and under your growing conditions? Forcing crops to grow in locations far from where they evolved or outside their normal season brings another set of problems. Stressed plants are more prone to insects and disease. Can you get enough of a mark-up to cover the cost of dealing with these challenges?

How much labor does the product entail? Having labor when and where it's needed is the perpetual problem in agriculture and especially so with non-commodity food crops. Berries, beans and peas spring to mind immediately. For each of these crops, every single fruit must be handled one at a time and it takes a lot of individual fruits to make a pound or a pint. Be sure you know that the labor you need will be available when you need it — and at what price — before you go into these crops.

Know the cost involved in growing, marketing and transporting for each particular crop you sell at the market. Start out by figuring what it costs you to grow the product. One way to do this is to grow a small test plot and track your costs. For some perennial crops, there may be enterprise budgets developed by your land grant college. Then you need to know your costs of marketing, going to town, taking it to marketplace — all your time and labor. Vendors who don't know their true costs often end up selling at a loss. [See Chapter 3]

Adding Value

"Adding value" to a product means doing some additional processing that increases the raw product's worth to the customer. This may include convenience-oriented processing such as pre-packaging or sorting

Leather Britches greasy beans are dried on strings and sold in an Asheville, NC, market.

for size as well as other forms of processing such as drying, canning, seasoning and flavoring, or incorporating the product into crafts.

Value-added items work well with farmers' markets. As one grower said: "You can bring fresh berries to the market on Wednesday and if they don't sell, you can come back and sell raspberry jam on Saturday."

Yet another grower said: "Farmers are finding they can make more money in the fall on corn shocks than on the corn. Consumers are willing to pay almost anything for something to decorate while they will quibble pennies over food."

Value-added products extend the season into winter months and provide customers with wonderful house and holiday gifts. Farmers' markets are a great place to test value-added products before launching them into bigger markets. Store buyers have been known to cruise farmers' markets looking for well-accepted locally produced jams, vinegars, oils and more.

Since the requirement for having a certified kitchen to prepare processed foods is often prohibitively expensive for an individual grower, consider going in on a cooperative basis with other growers to make it affordable. With perhaps the smallest farmers' market in California, Laytonville financed the opening of a community kitchen that people can rent for $15 per hour.

As we've said, farmers' markets are great as a test-market for new products, and especially so with value-added. As Doug Cross, Canter-Berry Farm, Auburn, WA, said: "Get customer feedback and find out what they want. We sold our blueberry jam, syrup and vinegar before we sold chutney, but people kept asking, 'Do you make a blueberry chutney?' and we looked it up in the dictionary, made a sample batch, sampled it out for six months, ('too sweet' or 'too sour' etc.) before we started selling it."

BUSINESS INCUBATOR

Thousands of farmers have started their businesses through farmers' markets. Countless thousands of others have survived as farmers thanks to the higher income resulting from farmers' market sales. In fact, market success has lead even substantial operators to enter some of the more successful farmers' markets, often grossing thousands of dollars per day.

"Farmers' market are a great place to incubate a small business: 'Where for $10 a day can you go and do your own market survey, meet customers, and get started selling?' Judy Dempsey, in Perth, Ontario, started in business by coming to the Perth farmers' market selling prepared foods, and her business grew so fast at the farmers' market she left to open her Feeding the Hungry Planet restaurant in Perth, which has been written up as one of the top 100 restaurants in Canada."

— Bob Chorney, Exec. Dir., Farmers' Markets Ontario

Of all the valuable things farmers' markets provide to the agricultural entrepreneur, one of the best may be the ability to try out adjunct businesses, such as developing value-added products, building a customer mailing list and pursuing agri-tourism ventures.

In their report about The Farmers' Markets and Rural Development Project, researchers Gail Feenstra and Chris Lewis said that about seven percent of vendors in each farmers' market were expanding their businesses each year. Managers reported that farmers' markets provide important contacts for other marketing venues such as restaurant or retail accounts and CSA start-ups. Farmers at farmers' markets are taking advantage of funding available through government food programs such as the Farmers' Market Nutrition Program and the National School Lunch Program to provide fresh produce to low-income families and children.

Adding Value To Your Crops

— Mark Wall, *CFM News,* Aug. 1992, Southland Farmers Market Association.

Examples of value-added products include: seasoned nuts, juice, peeled garlic, dried fruit, guacamole, jams, jellies, lettuce mixes, garlic braids, almond butter, pickled products, chocolate-covered nuts and raisins.

Adding value by processing your product can involve simply cutting the stems off of broccoli. It can also involve a number of steps, as in preparing and packaging jams. Before embarking on a processing project, consider these factors:

1) What are the possible ways to process your raw product? For example, if you grow stone fruit, some processed products might include jams, jellies or dried fruit.

2) What is the consumer demand for the processed products you can produce? One of the great assets of farmers' markets is that you can talk to customers about their preferences. Also, talk to market managers to see what products they think will sell.

3) What are the costs involved in processing? By developing a projected budget, you can get a good idea of what your costs will be. If you are considering making jams, some of your costs will be the additional ingredients (sugar, pectin), equipment, (pots, etc.), jars, labels, and labor. Don't forget to add in labor as a cost — including your own. It could make the difference between pursuing and not pursuing a project.

4) What is your estimated profit? Estimate conservatively how much money you anticipate making from the processed product. This includes developing a price for your product and projecting future sales.

5) Test market your product. Another benefit of selling at farmers' markets is that you can obtain feedback from customers about a possible product before making an investment. This allows you to tinker with the product until you get just what customers want.

Regulations AAAARGGHH!!!

Before you start work on a new project, ask your market manager or Extension Advisor whom to call to find out what regulations you will need to follow, whether the health department, the county, city or state ordinances.

Check with your local health department about what is considered a "processed product." The health department in Los Angeles, for example, defines processing as "changing the form, flavor or consistency" of a product. Once you cut a raw item, it is "processed" because its form has changed. If you are selling a processed product, you will need to prepare your product in a kitchen approved by the health department. Many growers rent space from restaurants or churches that have commercial kitchens. ✿

Karen Durham, manager with the Bellingham Farmers' Market, WA, points out that managers don't need to look at farmers having other marketing outlets as competition. "We participated with other local ag groups in the county working on a farm map so people can buy direct from the grower on the days when the market isn't open. We did this to build the farmer-customer relationship and to help the farmer make a living from the farm. In the long run, if farmers are making a living from the farm it will only help the market. The issue of competition between markets and CSAs or supermarkets or farmstands is often raised, but if each market does well then all the farmer sales benefit because consumers get used to buying local and want to buy local."

Here's how some growers use farmers' markets in conjunction with other marketing outlets:

Community Supported Agriculture

Several growers reported happy marriages between CSA and farmers' market sales. There are even some farmers' markets that have combined the products of several vendors to provide weekly boxes for market customers. For a report on the Market Basket Program, see:

http://www.oxy.edu/departments/pperc/publications/ index.htm ("Farmers Markets").

"Six of the farmers out of the 50 who regularly sell at our market every week also have CSAs. The amount of money attached to their CSA pick-ups is added to the total amount of sales for that day at the market. The market provides the CSA farmers a 7-8 hour pick-up site in the middle of the city one day a week during the growing season. This is a great benefit for the CSA grower. They can also sell additional produce to new customers and do outreach to new CSA subscribers at the FM. I surveyed the farmers at the end of the season to see what kinds of connections they were making at the market. Three of our vendors were selling at a high-end restaurant through connections they made at the market."

— Chris Curtis, Mgr., University District FM, Seattle, WA

"We do four different farmers' markets and also have a CSA, and we feel it goes hand in hand with selling at a farmers' market. All of our pickups are at the farmers' markets. When CSA clients come to the farmers' market they pick up their boxes at our stand and they often buy something additional."

— Bob and Pat Meyer, Stoney Plains Farm, Tenino, WA

"Most of our CSA customers have signed up as CSA customers from having heard about it at our farmers' market booths. Many of our regular customers had expressed concern about getting to our farmers' market booth and finding their favorite products gone. Signing up for the CSA ensures that their produce is held for them."

— Lisa Bloodnick, Bloodnick Family Farm, Apalachin, NY

Farm Stands

At some markets growers report roadside stand owners coming to the farmers' markets to buy for resale at their stands. The farmers' markets are a good central place for them to pick up the products that are picked fresh daily. The markets lead regular customers to local roadside stands.

"At the farmers' markets we hand out brochures about the farm and a lot of people come out to the farm after they've met us at the farmers' market or picked up a brochure," says Ronald Smolowitz, Coonamessett Farm, MA. "This gives us the selling opportunity to meet folks that don't come out to the farm. Since our farm is off the main highway, the markets help maintain our visibility."

Farm Stays and Agri-tourism

Invite customers to the farm. Offer on-farm visits, demonstrations and workshops. Let them know their purchases support local open space. Use the farmers' market to distribute brochures and talk with customers, encouraging visits to the farm. In the process, you build a more lasting commitment from your customers.

A survey conducted in New York and Iowa showed that about 30% of farmers' market vendors in those states have engaged in agri-tourism activities—more than double that in California. Recent passage of California Assembly Bill 1258, pertaining to agricultural home stays, increases the potential for California farmers to benefit from this type of agricultural entrepreneurship.

Mail Order

Al Courschesne of Frog Hollow Farm in Brentwood, California, www.froghollow.com, successfully uses farmers' markets to promote his mail order organic peaches.

"In addition to direct sales, tourists provide an opportunity for vendors to develop and expand mail order businesses. Consumers who purchased products from the farmers' market while traveling often later seek those same products through mail order

Pesto, Apple Sauce and Cookie Dough: Setting Up a Community Code Kitchen

— reprinted with permission from *A Case Study of the Laytonville Farmers' Market: A Rural Community Market,* Christopher J. Lewis.

Another project underway in Laytonville that has benefited from the networking provided by the farmers' market is the development of a community code kitchen. Progress on the code kitchen is well under way. When finished, it will serve as a place for vendors to add value to their produce through processing and for students to experience hands-on learning in cooking, nutrition and the food processing and service industry. Irene Engber, one of the founding vendors at the market, sits on the committee to develop the community code kitchen. "The community kitchen will really help this market grow," says Irene, who also feels "value-added is where it's at!"

Irene grows organic produce on one acre at Black Oak Ranch, five miles out of town. Irene, like many of the other vendors at the Laytonville market, wants to add value to her produce to increase her income from a small space. She had been making pesto for sale at farmers' markets in the code kitchen at Black Oak Ranch until about two years ago, but she found it too difficult to schedule since the kitchen was simultaneously being used by the summer camp. The community code kitchen should provide her with better access to the facilities she needs, plus the opportunity to expand her business significantly.

In addition to providing the space for vendors to add value to their produce, the Community Code Kitchen will support a mentorship program through which vendors will hire and train students from a local high school interested in pursuing careers in agriculture and food processing. ✿

to give as gifts or for their own consumption. Several vendors offer special packaging for gifts and provide brochures and order forms promoting this kind of trade. Furthermore, the market has a printed directory with a brief description of each vendor's products and services. The directory gives traveling consumers the opportunity to continue to patronize the vendors' businesses even after they have returned home."

— *A Case Study of the Laytonville Farmers' Market,* by Christopher J. Lewis

Restaurant Sales

"There are some 22 restaurants in L.A. that send chefs to shop in the market. Restaurants like Spago and Border Grill come to the market on a regular basis. They bring a pickup truck and about four helpers, and spend about four hours shopping the market. They sample everything, talk to the farmers, and establish relationships with farmers. L.A. chefs are very competitive and to try to stay one step ahead of each other. The farmers kept saying we've got to do something for the chefs, so we started Chef Appreciation Day. Chefs are very loyal and come every week even when it's raining. A grower might say, 'My whole trip was worthwhile because one restaurant bought $200 worth of stuff from me today.' We had a catered breakfast reception for the chefs and gave them each a little market memento — a little framed work of art they could put in the restaurant."

— Laura Avery, Mgr, Santa Monica FM, CA,

Retail Outlets

"We're often asked: 'Where can we get them during the week?' and we tell them the stores where they can buy them. It makes a great sales pitch in selling to the stores, to tell them we promote their store at the markets."

— Matt Megrath & Walter Ross, Farmhouse Tomatoes, Inc., Lake Worth, FL

Value-added Products

According to participants in the Farmers' Markets and Rural Development Project, the possibilities are many and the demand seems to be rising for value-added products. Fifty-two percent of the managers questioned said that they had seen an increase in value-added products at their market over the past three years.

> "Markets like the Crescent City Farmers' Market are an important retail outlet for folks who are not large enough or rich enough to get their products into grocery stores... which is increasingly hard to do without paying for shelf space. They're a place to start."
> — Economics Institute, *1999 Report to the Community,* Crescent City FM

 ## THE QUALITY HARVEST

The Pick of the Crop

For beginning farmers, we state the obvious — know when it's ripe. Know also what the market quality measures are for your crops. While most farmers' markets exempt produce sellers from standard pack and labeling regulations, they do require adherence to quality standards. Bringing only your finest quality product to the market is the best way to attract customers and sustain your price. This standard, of course, varies with the demographics of each community, but everyone wants good quality even if not all want to pay top price.

By taking over the middle steps, reducing the handling and transit distances, and keeping control of the product, the direct marketer gains the profit advantage of getting vine-or tree-ripe produce to the consumer in good shape. This simply isn't possible in conventional channels where fruits and vegetables travel an average of 1300 miles to their destination.

Quality starts in the field. It can be maintained or deteriorate from that point depending on how you handle the product, but no post-harvest measures, no matter how sophisticated, can improve quality.

Maturity vs. Ripeness

There's a difference between maturity and ripeness. By USDA standards, a mature fruit or vegetable is one that can continue to progress to ripeness. Ripeness has definitions of color and softness. Marketing standards address size, shape, blemishes, wounds, scars, color and spoilage. They don't address taste or nutrition. To give the standards their due, if something has a totally funky shape, is bruised, rotten or beat-up, it's probably a clue about the nutritional content and taste, anyway. It's good to remember that market standards are a baseline, not an optimal standard. Standards can be found on the internet at:

www.ams.usda.gov/standards

or through your local USDA office.

Sugars and complex acids only develop while the product is growing. Once it's harvested, the challenge is to maintain that sugar in the product. If your crop is picked too green, you may be able to get it to change color and soften but with a few exceptions the flavor probably won't improve beyond what it was when it was picked. The longer you can leave it in the field while preserving keeping qualities, the higher price you will be able to command.

There is such a thing as too ripe, not only in terms of the quality standards, but also in terms of consumer acceptance. Look for optimal ripeness — that blend of eating quality with keeping quality. Your produce is going from the field to the cooler, to the truck, to the farmers' market, to the customer's vehicle, and finally to the customer's kitchen. It's not good enough that produce looks great in the field and the market stall if it looks like compost fodder when it gets to the kitchen. Do your own quality control. Take some of your product from your market stall, bag it, take it home, and use it as your customer would.

Harvesting ripe produce takes finesse and a gentler touch than conventional picking allows. Packing as you pick is an art form requiring good spatial skills. Training helpers is important. Teach employees your quality standards and don't assume they know how to pick a tomato even if they've done it before.

With Full Circle, as I was setting up for market, I took a box of our Radiator Charlie's Mortgage Lifter tomatoes out of the van and put it on the table. As I removed the lid, I could see the imprint of five fingers in the flesh of each tomato. Because our helper had worked on two farms previously, I had foolishly assumed she could pick tomatoes without instruction, and I had not passed on what I'd learned several seasons before. You have to pick the heirloom, thin-skinned, tough-stemmed Charlies by supporting their shoulders or you will inevitably dent them trying to get them from the vine.

Get a Handle On It

Once it's out of the field, produce quality deteriorates with every handling. Each transfer provides an additional opportunity for bumps and bruises, the primary cause of post-harvest disease. Insofar as possible, pick and pack at the same time. Bring the display container you will use into the field. If you're packing for two different marketing venues, e.g., fancy quality for farmers' markets and baby vegetables for restaurants, take both boxes into the field and sort as you pick. Remember, "baby" veggies are more delicate than market size. Keep backup supplies of hand

Worker at Ron Mansfield's GoldBud Farm in Placerville, CA, field packs tree-ripened peaches into lugs lined with foam sheets to keep this lucious fruit from bruising on the way to market.

tools, bands and other picking items with you to avoid extra trips back to the shed.

For bunched root crops, i.e., carrots, radishes, beets, baby turnips, and green onions, bring banding materials into the field and bunch as you go. At Full Circle, we used rubberbands because they conformed to the tops and held well when wet. If you put a predetermined number on your wrist, you'll have an automatic count of the number of bunches dug. We piled bunches onto recycled nursery flats, unstacked the flats at the wash area, and hosed the dirt through the holes in the flat bottoms.

Some crops such as green beans, peas and summer squash require picking several times per week to maintain productivity and provide optimal product quality. If you make multiple pickings and don't have same-day market outlets, put the pick date in a prominent place on the container so you move the first picked first.

Pick as much as possible in the early morning. Whether you're large enough to have a flat-bed or trailer in the field or you are using a cart to move your harvest, provide shade for your product. Canopies work best for larger vehicles, but the most versatility is probably offered by Reflectix, a foil-sandwiched insulating product that comes in rolls in a variety of widths. Look at your local home center or:

http://www.jademountain.com/insul.html

This is the same reflective material used for Blockade windshield sunshades. These can be laid across individual boxes as you go and moved up as you stack. Sunshades can sometimes be purchased in closeout stores and, properly taken care of, will last several seasons. Take produce to the shed every hour; cooling within an hour of harvest significantly improves the quality of your produce.

Packing It In

Some crops simply don't lend themselves to field packing because of specific cooling requirements or the need for washing or grading. The goals of packing are to immobilize the product, to cushion impacts, to avoid compression, to minimize loss and to facilitate sale. Choose packing materials to help you meet these goals.

Set aside an area of a barn, pole shed or shade canopy with waist-high tables; packing supplies; non-slip surfaces under foot; and fresh, potable running water with good drainage. Consider work-flow when you set up this area. Bring the produce in on one side and take it to the cooler on the other. Have a dry place for boxes, labels, scissors, knives and the certified scale within easy reach and away from the washing station.

Washing stations can vary in size and complexity, as do farms. The simplest is probably wash basins or dedicated plastic muck buckets and a hose with a spray nozzle. Extra greenhouse-type benches work well for drip-drying. If you're doing volume, get some movable roller conveyors so you can reconfigure on the fly as different crops come in from the field. Be sure you have enough room to move about in your packing area. Between the sharp implements, the supplies and the water, the packing shed is a prime location for workers' compensation injuries.

Write a safety manual and train your employees. For California growers, this is a legal requirement for doing business. Train sanitation, too. Remind people to wash their hands after using the restroom, and it would be useful to provide disposable gloves; they're cheap insurance. Wash basins, buckets, reflective shields, knives, scissors, and work surfaces — everything used from week to week — needs to be thoroughly washed and sterilized. Chlorine bleach is the most cost effective way to do this. If you have objections to chlorine, good, old-fashioned sunlight for a couple of days after washing with soap and water, and before reuse, works pretty well.

Cool It!

While you may read advice to pick produce the morning of the market for freshness, we recommend you pick 12 to 24 hours ahead, then clean and cool your produce. Doing this will dramatically improve the keeping quality of your product.

Proper post-harvest handling is probably the biggest thing missed by small-acreage growers. Vegetables are living things and have a respiration rate after they're picked, i.e., they consume oxygen and give off carbon dioxide and heat. A good example is that baby lettuce or mesclun picked and bagged at dawn but not cooled will feel warm in the center of the pack within a couple of hours. This is metabolic heat. Another form of heat is "field heat." This is heat picked up by the produce from simply being in the field. Produce self-cools while it's attached to its roots. Once it's harvested, it no longer has that ability and starts gaining heat from the environment.

The keeping-quality of your produce depends on your ability to remove the field heat and slow down the metabolic rate. How you do this depends on which crop you're handling. Water, or its solid form, ice, are the most efficient removers of heat. Think of your body in a swimming pool. Water does pretty well at getting the dirt off, too. Crops that cool well using water as a heat remover are greens, brassicas, lettuces, salad mixes, some herbs, and root crops. The challenge when using water is to remove as much as possible before final packing. Sitting in dampness promotes decay.

For other more delicate crops like strawberries, fruit crops, peas, beans, and herbs with fuzzy leaves, cool air drawn across the produce works well. Several years ago the University of California at Davis put out plans for a table-top, forced air cooler that could cool one or two strawberry boxes at a time. It may be possible to create a similar cooler using a room air conditioner, a box, and a fan.

There's a trade-off between packing in the field and getting produce cooled quickly. Packaging provides a block to free coolant flow and creates a modification of the atmosphere surrounding the product.

The packaging you use needs to be compatible with the cooling method required by the crop. Waxed boxes for greens and brassicas provide containers that can be ice- or hydro-cooled without deterioration. Paperboard boxes with large holes facilitate forced air cooling. Most other methods simply use the transfer of heat from the produce to the cold room or refrigerator air. This works but takes considerably more time and provides less quality cushion.

If you are going to market within a day and you can do so, pack in your market display container. This will save set-up time and eliminate one more transfer point.

Cold Rooms, Walk-ins & Fridges

Once you've removed the heat and slowed the metabolic rate of your crop, you'll want to maintain that crop under optimum conditions, starting with temperature.

Jim Thompson, agricultural engineer with the Post-Harvest Outreach Program of U.C. Davis once said: "Don't try to control what you're unwilling to measure." Whether you have a commercial cold room, a farm-built walk-in box, or a recycled restaurant fridge, you will need an accurate thermometer to know when your temperature is right. Commercial cold rooms usually have a built-in thermometer with a face reading outside the door. You'll need to get some kind of thermometer for farm-builts and recycled. A good refrigerator thermometer will do. Place it at product height where it can be easily seen and read it every morning and evening. Adjust your thermostat accordingly. Optimum storage conditions, including temperatures, for a wide variety of produce items can be found on the Post-Harvest Outreach website at:

http://postharvest.ucdavis.edu/produce/storage/index.html

Other good resources are *Knott's Handbook for Vegetable Growers,* and ATTRA's publication on post-harvest handling.

Consider getting a walk-in cooler to help keep products fresh.

"You can convert an air-conditioner to make a decent walk-in cooler. Ours paid for itself in the first year by helping keeping quality at the market throughout the day. It also helps to bring ice if it's really hot. We bought an old ice machine for $50 from a restaurant equipment supply company."
— Cheryl Boden, West Union Gardens, Hillsboro, OR

How much cooling space you need depends on two things: the size of your operation in general and the number of times per week you'll empty the space. Most direct marketers turn space quickly. Between our farmers' markets, restaurant and co-op sales, and our CSA, Full Circle Organic Farm turned cooler space every other day. The longer you hold produce, the more complex your system becomes.

If the price of a new, commercial cold room doesn't fit into your farm budget, there are less costly alternatives. Publication 21449 from the University of California is a nine-page booklet called *Small-Scale Cold Rooms for Perishable Commodities* that covers several options like marine containers and refrigerator trucks, and includes plans for owner-built cold rooms. Used restaurant equipment dealers may have walk-in boxes and/or large refrigerators available.

Here's what we at Full Circle learned over the years about different types of refrigeration.

- ✧ Used walk-ins: Check to see what's included. Generally flooring isn't, as these units are designed to install over a concrete pad with a drain. They may or may not come with the actual cooling system, and the cooling system may be based on something you're not familiar with, like ammonia or an out-of-date chloro-florocarbon such as freon that's expensive and difficult to replace.

- ✧ Most walk-ins run off three-phase industrial electrical standard and require their own circuit, as conventional wiring is two-phase.

- ✧ Walk-ins are designed for indoor use, so they're not weathertight and need to be under shelter.

- ✧ Used refrigerators may have worn-out compressors and also use freon as a refrigerant. Watch for worn seals and latches.

None of this is meant to keep you from considering or using these alternatives; we have done so ourselves. Just know you'll probably need more than the original quote and allow some extra cash for repairs, pads, and/or wiring.

If you use a room air conditioner, realize it will run hard almost continuously in a hot climate, and you will need to supplement the humidity in your cold room. [See Resources, Chapter 2] Room air conditioners are meant to move temperature only a few degrees and not into the 30s or 40s. For the most part, they are also designed to remove humidity, which produce needs to stay fresh. They will get you through the growing pains, though, and are more efficient in moderate climates. With tomatoes, peppers, eggplants and other chill-sensitive crops that need to be held just above 50°F, a swamp cooler and a walk-in cooler built from straw bales may fill the bill.

Humidity

Humidity and temperature are a balancing act. The warmer the air is, the more water it can hold. Think of Miami. Water moves from a wetter environment to a drier one until both are equalized. Dry air will literally pull water from your product, but the colder the air, the less water it can hold. If you can't decrease temperature enough, increase humidity around your produce to hold down loss.

Water loss is cumulative — once you lose it, you never get it back, so prevention is the name of the game. Produce is 95% water — *that* is what you have to sell. Product water loss is lost profits.

Using plastic liners or bags in boxes after the initial cooling will help prevent water loss. Damp, not wet, bath towels placed over roots, tomatoes, peppers, eggplant, will work for small-scale farms. Misters, manual or automatic like you see in grocery stores, work on a larger scale. Again, complexity rises with the length of time you hold the product.

Other Storage Issues

If you're storing your produce more than 36 hours, other issues like ethylene compatible crops and geotropism come into play. Take a post-harvest class and get a good reference book that covers your crops.

Some crops like onions, potatoes, and winter squash need to sit and cure between harvest and distribution. These guys like a different environment than your cooler will provide. Keep some space reserved for them.

An excellent resource on the use of chlorine bleach as a post-harvest disinfectant in wash water and on produce is Publication 8003 from the University of California called *Postharvest Chlorination*. Written by

Soulard Market,
St. Louis, MO

Trevor Suslow, this eight-page pamphlet has recommended dilutions and produce-specific recommendations. It also talks about non-chlorine alternatives and gives timely web references.

To Market, To Market

Now that you have your quality product in your cooler, it's time to take it out again and get it to your customers. Whether you take your produce to the local farmers' market 15 minutes up the road or to the urban market 150 miles away, the challenge remains the same — getting it there in good shape.

Taking your produce to market is another transfer point with the potential to degrade quality. If your vehicle is older and has a stiff ride, consider using egg crate foam pads under your boxes as cushion against bumps along the way. Pack your load tightly to reduce movement and stop shifting. If your truck doesn't have them, make load locks to keep your boxes from moving around as you go to market. A piece of 1x1-inch wood and two vice-grips will work in a pinch.

Larger growers with longer travel times will want a refrigerated truck. Mid-size growers can retrofit a panel van with a roof-top air conditioner. Smaller growers can build boxes with hinged lids from rigid foamboard insulation and duct tape. This and frozen one gallon jugs of water will keep produce cool on the way to market and throughout the day.

When you set up your market transportation, find a way to put your tables, display fixtures and other market paraphernalia in the vehicle so you can set them up before you move the produce. This saves set-up time and moving your product, plus it allows you to unload produce into space sheltered from the heat. Roof racks or side racks are an option.

At Full Circle Organic Farm, in both our original truck and our market van, we built a false floor. The tables, umbrellas, stands, pipe frame for the scale and product bags, etc., all went under that floor. We could pull into our market stall, set up and drape the table, ready our product slant display, and put down our mats before we touched a box of produce.

Think ahead when you pack your vehicle for market. Arrange your boxes in such a way that you can fill and refill your display without rearranging your pack. Maybe that means a single row of tomato boxes double stacked by variety next to a row of eggplants topped by pepper boxes next to two facings of squash. Put more of your hot sellers toward the front so you don't have to dig to reach them as they get low.

If you're dropping crews at multiple markets, pack the reverse of this for each market and pack and label each market separately. This will allow you to get your crew in the stall with the display bones ready to fill without having to rearrange boxes or missing a product.

It's a good idea to keep a checklist of what products and quantities to bring to each market and have someone other than the truck packer check it off again before you leave.

Another tip: fuel the vehicle on the way home from market or your last trip out. Having to stop on the way to market, or worse yet, running out of gas on the way, is not an experience you need to have.

 PREPARING FOR MARKET

How Much to Bring

Especially in a market that's new to you, it's difficult to predict how much to bring. The first day isn't a good indicator because customers aren't yet familiar with you and your products. When you bring new products to market, you often hear, "Oh, I didn't know you had THAT. I just bought it at the grocery store. I'll buy it from you next week." You may have better quality than the vendor they usually buy from, but they bought out of habit before they saw yours.

Your market research can be of some help here. If you're one of only a couple of vendors with a given product or you have something that sells well for you in similar markets, bring a generous amount.

Try to bring enough produce to last throughout the day, so that there's enough left for your last few customers. Develop secondary uses or outlets for what's left over. If you sell out early, increase what you bring by small amounts, or look at your prices — maybe you're underpricing your product. The aim is not to sell out, but to keep repeat customers.

A good rule of thumb is: 5-10% of your load comes home. If you're bringing home more, you're either going to the wrong market, bringing too much, or not doing a good job of selling.

Don't get greedy. If you do well with 20 bushels of string beans the first year, you may not necessarily do better with 60. You may saturate the market and end up eating them.

Develop secondary outlets for what doesn't sell at the farmers' markets: preserved products like strawberry jam and sorbet, salsas and other processed vegetable products; donate to soup kitchens; or make compost!

Products: Lemons

"If it doesn't taste good and look good, leave it home."

"Don't bring fruit too early in season or unload overripe vegetables at season's end. If the product doesn't taste good, customers get a bad experience and it hurts future sales potential."

"Don't bring the same things everyone else does."

"Talking down the product! Saying: 'I'm sorry, these beans aren't as good as they were last week.' Always speak of your product with pride!"

"Farmers here are afraid of taking product home. They'd rather bring in a little, sell out, and go home rather than bring extra and have to take any home. We have more public than product!"

"Not taking advantage of value-added."

"Too little product on display!"

In any case, you need to bring enough to have an abundant looking display. If you have smaller amounts, use a smaller table and baskets to keep the look luscious.

After the first two or three markets, it's time to fine-tune your product mix. Keep records. Start bringing products proportionate to sell-through, i.e., more of your hot items if you have them and less of the others. If you're doing multiple markets, shift products according to what the hot sellers are in each.

Insurance: Even if a market doesn't require it, it's a good idea to have liability insurance. It's not expensive when you consider the possibility of a lawsuit brought by someone tripping over a water jug next to your truck or cracking a tooth on a piece of peach pit in your homemade jam. Check with your insurance agent about adequate coverage. Farmers' markets have insurance, but individual sellers are generally not covered. [See Appendix]

Be Prepared

To get ready for market, prepare a checklist of things you need in order to do business, such as scales, bags, change and so on.

"What we're really doing is taking a store out to a different parking lot 300 times a year. It's very important that we take everything we need. Some things are trivial like thumb tacks. But if you forget the thumbtacks, you can't put up the signs. Preparing for market also means stocking up on recipes and other printed pieces. Every item for sale has a sign identifying it, often by variety, and nearly everything has a half-sheet with recipes or cooking instructions. The informational material is the key to recruiting new customers. At any market, on any day, there's always somebody who is there for the first time."

— Chip and Susan Planck, Purcellville, PA (*Growing for Market,* Dec. 1995)

Over the years at Full Circle Organic Farm, we found that as the season wore on we became dumber, not smarter, so we started making checklists and using other memory devices to be sure everything we needed got to market. One useful tool was "the Big Blue Box." This was just a cheap plastic tote but it allowed consolidation of all small market aids that might otherwise get lost. Within it were other organizers — a plastic zippered bag for price signs, another for recipes, a bag of clothes pins, a box of push pins, a box of assorted pens and markers, rolls of produce bags, etc. We also kept our grower certification and our organic registration in plastic sheet protectors connected by a ring for easy hanging. The box stayed in the van, and the only things that left the box at home were the table cloths for washing.

Your checklist might include:

⟡ Shelter: Patio umbrellas or a canvas patio (open-sided tent) provide shelter for yourself and your produce and help make a colorful display.

⟡ Stall structure: tables, tablecloth.

⟡ Containers suitable for your produce, as well as customer take-home containers.

⟡ Cash and cash box.

⟡ Signs: booth and product/price signs.

⟡ Scale: If selling items by weight, you'll need a scale with valid seal from the Weights and Measures Department of your town.

⟡ Educational materials: recipes, pamphlets and flyers — especially helpful if you're selling anything new or unusual!

⟡ Display items: sign-making materials like chalk and an eraser; tags (paper, plastic or cardboard), markers, scissors, tape and pens, bags, price tags, pocket knife, duct tape, markers, stakes.

⟡ Business items: pencils, pens, calculator, a sales and tax record book, tax charts, and business cards. A pad of note paper for jotting down new marketing ideas or special order requests from customers.

⟡ Personal comfort items like a mid-morning snack and plenty of water.

Bring a chair for the inevitable lull time but put it away when the customers come. Buy rubber mats like the ones used in grocery store checkstands. They will make all the difference at the end of the market day.

If you use a pickup with a standard length bed, bring an old hoe or other item to snag goods from deep in the back. Your knees and back will thank you.

Bring fresh, potable water in a spray bottle or pump sprayer to keep products fresh. Find creative ways to deal with the inevitable environmental problems. A lot of markets prohibit side-draped shadecloth because it creates a visual block in the marketplace. We bought colorful Japanese paper umbrellas and re-positioned them as the sun moved to keep our greens in good shape. They attracted customer attention, too. Don't forget water to drink yourself.

At the beginning of the season, after the cropping was planned, we created 4x5-inch price signs for each variety using computer clip art for appeal, and leaving a large space for the price. These were laminated at the local copy shop so we could use dry erase markers to make pricing changes as necessary. No more making signs while trying to set up the stall!

Farm Identification

"Have your name and telephone number on your bags and labels so people can call you midweek, so they can come to the farm and pick up something extra. Over the years I've had several vendors stop coming to the market, because their customers started coming to the farm."

— Charlie Springer, Mgr., Richmond FM, IN

Bring business cards as well as brochures about your farm and what you offer there so you can use the market to increase on-farm sales for your CSA, pick-your-own or roadside stand. For example, customers may purchase small amounts of blueberries at the farmers' market but come to the farm to pick large amounts for freezing or canning, etc., if they know doing so is an option.

Bring yourself! Farmers' market customers want to meet the farmer!

A note about personal appearance. Take a shower and put on clean clothes for market. This is a daily job interview and performance review. You represent your farm and your product. Be the picture of health, cleanliness and vitality. A funky farmer will overshadow great fruit in short order. Clean your fingernails — trust us, it matters. You can go "in costume" if it's not too outrageous. Overalls and a straw hat are fine, if you're into it. Matching t-shirts and aprons give a unified and service-oriented feel to the stall.

Be ready for the opening bell! You'll lose a lot of sales if you're not. As much as one-third to one-half of your daily sales can be made during the first thirty minutes of the market day. Do as much bunching, bagging and pricing as you can beforehand to prepare for that initial rush of buyers. The more you do in advance, the smoother your day will be.❀

*R*UNNING YOUR FARMERS' MARKET BUSINESS

3

"Manage your business and don't let it manage you! Don't try to grow everything, just what you love to grow and what makes money."
— Don Rogers, First Pioneer Farm Credit

KEEPING RECORDS

"Keep good records. Because of this I know what each vegetable grosses in dollars per foot of space. This allows me to adjust my planting each year, and continually increase my income."
— Chris "Marketman" Labeots, Baraboo, WI

OK, let's face it. Keeping records falls right behind root canals on the popular-things-to-do list. If you look at it as a battle plan to get and keep the most dollars on your farm, however, you might see it in a whole new light.

Especially with a perishable product, meticulous recordkeeping is essential to controlling risk and waste. Good records enable you to place your crops in the markets where you'll get the highest return. This year's records become the basis for decisions about next year's cropping patterns and marketing outlets.

What Art Lange of Honey Crisp Farm in Reedley, CA, has accomplished by using multiple outlets and keeping records, not only of pricing but of quality considerations for each market outlet, is to reduce the risk that a major portion of his crop will go unsold. By selling into his best markets when demand is high and supply low, he maintains his best prices.

Lange relates, "Some of the restaurants also order from us at the farm for pickup at the market. They don't get a special price at the market if we're in low supply. The price depends on supply and demand and quality. For us, selling to both farmers' markets and restaurants is a balancing act. We've tried to sell to one or the other but it doesn't work. If the fruit is a little too ripe the customers love it, but if it's a little too green the wholesalers will accept it because they're used to a lot greener. So we can pick the fruit a little greener for the wholesalers. Let's say we have a bumper crop of Babcock peaches — a fantastic peach but which has such a short shelf-life you can't sell very much of it to the jobbers. The jobbers try to bring you down on your price, but if you're getting $2 a pound for the fruit at the farmers' markets, you don't have to sell it for $1 a pound to the wholesalers. Most of our fruit sells for about $2 a pound and up at the farmers' markets and about $1.75 to the jobbers."

Create a list for each market you attend and every other outlet you use — an extended copy of your load list works well for this. Keep records of how much you brought, how much you sold, what your unit price was, how much you brought home and notes about special circumstances affecting sales. Events going on at the market, like cooking demonstrations or tastings, or in the general area, such as a ball game or a fair, can impact sales in one direction or another. Make a note of holidays. Sales may greatly increase the week of a feast like Thanksgiving or be slow the week when folks traditionally travel or eat out, like Mother's Day. Looking back at previous years' records for the same market can be really helpful here.

How much to pack for an individual market is part recordkeeping and part intuition. Look to your records to determine previous sales at that market. Plan to bring about 10% above what sold last time, then adjust for weather and any special event going on at the market.

If you sell out well before the end of the market day, you probably didn't bring enough. Consider 'sell-out' to be having only a couple of any item left, because the last of anything always sells more slowly. It's better to have a small amount of leftovers at the day's end. If you bring in one truckload of produce and sell out within an hour, either you should have brought more or your price was too low. If loyal customers come to see you and you're gone, they may go to someone else!

When you do multiple markets, it's useful to look at the differences in what is selling at each market. This allows you to tailor your load to the local tastes and get the best return. It also allows you to see if you're selling enough at any given market to cover your costs of attending.

According to an article in a 1995 *Growing for Market* newsletter, Chip and Susan Planck of Wheatland Vegetable Farms in Purcellville, VA, are meticulous record keepers. With as many as 14 farmers' markets in the Washington, D.C., area each week, including four Saturday markets, the Plancks have developed a system to maximize their revenue.

They created a form that is used at every market, every market day. The form tracks how much of each item is taken to market, the unit price, the time it sold out, or the amount left at the end of the day. All these forms are kept in a big binder, organized by market, and consulted at the beginning of the week. This allows the Plancks to plan where to slot their produce each week, sending the most of any given crop to the market where it sells the best at the highest price.

There is considerable variation among the markets the Plancks frequent. For example, they can sell 100 bushels of cooking greens a day at the Washington, D.C., market, where 95% of the customers are African-American, but only 35 bushels at a market in a predominantly Anglo suburb. Even among the suburban markets, there are nuances in sales patterns caused by a combination of customer preference and competition. Chip says, "The significance of that is crucial. It means we can make the most of everything we send to market. It's worth the coordinating time."

To see if a market is paying for itself, you need to know what it costs you to attend. This goes beyond the daily stall charge to a little cost accounting. You need to consider all costs specifically associated with that market as well as a portion of the overhead costs to the farm. Pay yourself. Place a dollar value on your time spent not only in the market itself but in loading and unloading, picking, preparation of point-of-sale materials and packaging supplies. Also figure in association dues, fuel for the vehicle, maintenance, insurance (vehicle and liability) and payroll costs, if any. If a market isn't pulling its weight and a price adjustment is out of the question, you need to pull the plug and find a market that will.

Don Rogers, a farm business consultant with First Pioneer Farm Credit, suggests setting up a winner/loser sheet as a simpler alternative to traditional cost accounting for deciding which crops to grow and which to drop.

1. Rank the crops you grow by looking at things like:

   ◇ Customers' favorites and what you're known for. Calculate sales minus variable costs for each of the above, e.g., each time you spend money for something in strawberries, write it down in strawberry category costs such as labor and seed costs (based on inventory of products taken out of the field). Not only do you have to know how much you produced but how much of this was actually sold, i.e., what was the percent sell-through?

   ◇ Ease on timing of crop, i.e., is it a crop you're always late on? By the time you get it to the market are other vendors also selling it?

   ◇ Hand labor required in producing and harvesting the crop?

   ◇ Price you are getting for the product at the market?

2. After each season, adjust the acreage and mix of yours crops using this ranking.

3. Try something new each year to put on the list and stay ahead of the competition.

4. Check competitors to see how they've changed.

Recordkeeping can be a tedious task, but being willing to do it often means the difference between staying in business or failing. While a pencil and paper still work, using a computer can dramatically cut the time it takes to find and analyze critical differences.

There are several easy-to-use, small business accounting packages on the market; all have some cost accounting capability. Perhaps the best known of these is QuickBooks by Intuit. It even let's you run payroll, helpful if you have employees.

If you grow vegetables, melons, and the like, the book, *Market Farm Forms* [see "Marcie's page" at the back of this book], comes with a diskette of templates that work with a spreadsheet program to allow you to track your predicted vs. actual harvest and sales in several markets per week, and calculates the percent sell-through by item. It lets you compare markets or markets vs. other outlets.

If the "business" of business is new to you or you need to fine-tune your operation, your local Small Business Development Center offers classes for minimal fees.

 ## STAFFING THE BOOTH

"If you hire someone who is friendly, cordial and nice you're going to make more. We evaluated returns at the end of the summer and noticed a big difference in whom we had sent to the market."
— Dan Haakenson, *The Small Commercial Gardener*

What draws people to your booth at the farmers' market are your merchandising skills. What induces people to buy your produce are interest, quality and perceived value. What keeps people coming back is your customer service. There's a business rule-of-thumb that it takes five times as much effort and re-

sources to get a new customer as it does to retain one you already have, so customer service is critical to your bottom line.

Customer service means friendly, knowledgeable staff, a convenient layout and minimal wait time. It can get hectic when you have more than one customer. Make sure you have sufficient help to meet demands, especially when popular products such as strawberries, sweet corn, and tomatoes first come into the market.

A minimum of two people in the booth makes it easier to wait on customers and it allows one person to take a break. You need to be able to restock even as you're selling. With only one person at the booth, you'll be waiting on customers, so the displays get low. Low displays signal lack of choice to customers who then look elsewhere. This causes a lull and potential loss of sales! This lull might be prevented if two people are at the booth so that one person can be restocking.

Use the same selling crew at each market visit, if possible. Like your permanent sign, familiar faces will help build a "known quantity" comfort level for your customers.

Hiring & Training Market Employees

"Fifty-seven percent of farmers already selling at markets indicated that a shortage of labor has been problematic for them, although not enough to prevent them from participating in farmers' markets. In addition, 38% of respondents said concern about having enough help to grow produce for a farmers' market affected why they had never, or no longer, sold at farmers' markets."
— *Barriers & Opportunities,* Farmers' Market Trust

Finding, hiring and training the right employee is critical to the success of your business. Luckily, these skills can be learned. In most areas the local branch of the state employment office fosters employer associations. These groups offer free seminars and workshops during the year on such subjects as interviewing skills, writing employee manuals, safety training and the like. The local Small Business Development

Center works with entrepreneurs to help businesses grow and succeed. They, too, offer low-cost and no-cost training for business owners.

Stu Leonard, a successful Massachusetts retailer, has noted, "You can't train 'nice;' you have to hire 'nice.'" Other employers have been known to tell employees, "If you're not fired with enthusiasm, you will be fired, with enthusiasm." You can't have a bad day when you're selling — you're in show business.

Hire employees legally. Most of us remember a Presidential appointee or two caught in a "nannygate": they didn't confirm that a potential employee was legally able to work in this country, and/or they weren't paying social security and unemployment taxes properly. These folks not only lost the opportunity for a great position, they had to pay back taxes with fines and penalties. In some cases they lost the employee and had to pay stiff fines for not checking their paperwork. Again, your state employment office will have forms for you and your employee and will sit down with you and show you how to complete them. Office phone numbers can be found in the "Government" section of your phone book.

For those of you with web access, a link to all state employment offices can be found at:

http://workforcesecurity.doleta.gov/map.asp

and Small Business Development Center offices by state at:

www.sba.gov/regions/states.html.

Before you can look for an employee, you have to know what it is you want someone to do. Write down a list of tasks. "Sell at the farmers' market" is pretty general. Make it specific: "Meet truck at the market space at 6:30 a.m. Erect shade structure. Help set out produce. Place price signs and recipes next to appropriate product. Greet customers. Correctly weigh produce and make correct change for customers. Restock product as needed. Consolidate product to keep a full display during market. Other tasks as assigned."

This list of tasks is the basis for your job description. It also lets you think about the skills you need in an employee, and whether someone else could do some of these things. With two people in the booth, you could have someone good at display, stocking and working with customers, and another who's a good customer person with strong math skills who can weigh produce and make change quickly. If you're one of the people in the booth, think about what skills might complement your own.

"When hiring help for the farmers' markets, look for a good salesperson. This is number one, even over having an interest in the produce, because selling is their number one job. Look for salespeople who are friendly and who like people."
— Gretchen Hoyt, Alm Hill Gardens, Everson, WA

Take the time to train your employees in all aspects of selling and make training continuous with an ongoing staff training program. One market manager reported that the most common mistake vendors make is bringing "know-nothing employees" to the market.

Paying above minimum wage may also be advantageous. Often, farmers have found that offering a living wage allows them to find more mature and motivated employees. The payback they see in increased sales more than makes up for the higher wages.

Develop a manual on how to do sampling, handling cash, dealing with customers, security concerns, and on product information, such as what products are upcoming and ways to cook and store the products.

Hoyt encourages employees to take products home and try them so they can say something real like: "Oh, I just put this jam on my toast today and I sure do like it!" She shows employees what kind of experience she wants customers to have in the Alm Hill booth.

While a manual is a great reference and learning tool, it's no substitute for one-on-one training. Here are the four basic steps in any training process:

✧ Tell them how to do it. Verbally explain the task at hand, one step at a time.

✧ Show them how to do it. Physically do the task. Do this separately from step one.

◇ Watch them do it. Observe carefully the entire process without interrupting or coaching.

◇ Fine-tune the teaching. Praise what went right. Retell and re-show what didn't quite work.

SETTING PRICES

"We all lose at the farmers' markets by trying to compete on low price. Rather than lowering prices, look for ways to make your food look better by washing it or improving the way you grow it, or by getting it more quickly to market."
— Gretchen Hoyt, Alm Hill Gardens, Everson, WA

"Sell top quality consistently and customers will keep coming back. I've seen time and time again customers are extremely loyal if you bring only the best quality to market. People sell geraniums at several stalls at our market, but at one stall they have geraniums that last all summer and into the fall, and people line up at that booth to buy them."
— Teresa White, Mgr., Cedar Rapids, IA

Customers seek quality first — then price. Farmers' market customers want freshness, ripeness and flavor above all else. Many are willing to pay a premium price for fine quality. So offer only top quality produce. Accommodate your customers. Guarantee your product. THEN, get as high a price as the market will bear!

Gail Hayden, executive director of the Marin County Certified Farmers' Market, tells the story of how five peach growers brought peaches to the market, creating an oversupply. The growers were trying to sell their peaches for $1.00 a pound. "Although the growers wanted to lower prices, I advised them to raise prices," says Gail. She explained that farmers' market shoppers were looking for varieties of peaches they can't find in supermarkets. Some growers lowered their price to 80¢ a pound, and did not sell out; some raised the price to $1.20 a pound and sold out!

Hayden's point is well taken. Consumers often perceive diversity and choice at the market differently than farmers do. Farmers like the ones above tend to look at diversity in terms of individual crops, i.e., how many vendors are selling the same items they have — peaches, melons, tomatoes, lettuce. Consumers tend to look at diversity in terms of types of crops — white peaches, yellow peaches, cherry tomatoes, slicing tomatoes, sauce tomatoes; types of growing methods — organic, biodynamic, IPM; types of display and merchandising skills; and individual farmers'/sellers' personalities.

The sweet corn that Gary Pahl, of Pahl Farms in Apple Valley, MN, sells at the farmers' markets goes for about 40-50% over supermarket prices — a cost customers are willing to pay because the products are guaranteed fresh, not more than one day old, and often they are picked the same day. "You're selling freshness," Pahl states. "You pick on Saturday morning and sell it that day while chain store produce is usually at least four days old. As soon as corn is picked the sugar starts converting to starch and loses flavor. With some of the new varieties this is a slower process, but it still doesn't beat that same-day freshness."

Be honest about the value of what you are offering. Don't be afraid to charge more if your customers agree that it is of superior quality. If an item is selling very fast, and you will soon sell out, you may have priced it too low for that situation; learn to judge the market by how things are selling and adjust your prices accordingly. Rather than establish a lower price perception by lowering a sign price, make a SALE sign for the remainder of market. Note, however, that a day of slow sales usually indicates few customers at market and this can't be improved by lower prices.

No matter what your products are worth, some people will be glad to pay what you are asking and some will tell you the price is too high. There is a mix of these customer types in any location and you need to determine what the ratio for each product you are selling is in order to maximize your day's sales. Some customer grumbling is to be expected: "Your competitor is cheaper." If only one customer in twenty complains, so what? Smile, and repeat the classic line, "He knows the value of his produce; I know mine," and use the opportunity to educate — explain your growing methods, uniqueness, freshness and so on.

Charging What the Market Will Bear

This method allows you to make high profits in times of high demand and limited supplies. Unless the quality and uniqueness of your product/products justify your premium prices, however, customers will soon go elsewhere.

Going Rate

Know what's going on in the market! Get someone to watch your booth for half an hour and walk the market. See who's selling what. If you say you're selling the best tomatoes in the market, you'd better make sure you are. Do a taste comparison. Note: While it is good to know competitors' prices in order to see if your prices are out of line, you should not set your prices solely by what others are charging. Perhaps you're offering products and services that justify a higher price than your competitors.

See if your state department of agriculture publishes a price report or an ag report that gives farmers some idea of what farmers' markets, supermarkets and wholesalers are getting for produce. Other guides are local supermarket prices, and other sellers at market. On the internet, you can find USDA price reports for fruits, vegetables and herbs at:

www.ams.usda.gov/fv/mncs/terminal.htm.

USDA price reports for cut flowers are at:

www.ams.usda.gov/fv/mncs/ornterm.htm.

Be careful about the perception of price fixing. Walking the market to note what other members are charging and even asking them about their pricing is not price collusion, it is simply trading information. Getting together with other members to "set" prices, however, is illegal.

> "For the folks who believe broccoli is broccoli and don't see any difference in supermarket produce and ours, we feel it's not worth trying to compete with the supermarket. Our customers are those who can appreciate that our produce is thousands of miles fresher than supermarket produce."
> — Tom Roberts and Lois Labbe, Snakeroot Organic Farm, Pittsfield, ME

Break-Even & Even Make a Profit!

> "Unlike many growers who yo-yo prices up and down following the supermarkets' lead, we believe in keeping prices steady throughout the year. By figuring our cost to produce it and adding a profit, we are able to keep our lettuce at $1 a head through the season, while grocery store prices go from $.60 to $1.50. Last year, when prices of lettuce went up to $2.50 a head in the supermarkets, most vendors also raised their prices. There were angry letters in the paper about the high prices at the farmers' markets. We kept ours at a dollar a head because we knew what it cost us to produce it. Our consistent price policy has brought a loyal following, with 80% of sales from repeat customers. They know our prices are fair and they know the quality is there."
> — Bob Meyer, Stoney Plains Farm, Tenino, WA

In the report, *Barriers & Opportunities,* by Farmers' Market Trust, 67% of farmers surveyed indicated they needed daily sales between $500 and $1,200 in order to sell at a Philadelphia farmers' market. This sales level is achievable at existing markets in Philadelphia where the average first year sales reported by farmers at markets operated by the Farmers' Market Trust are approximately $500 per day. About 16% of respondents were looking for sales above $1,200, a level that can be attained at well-established markets such as the Greenmarkets in New York City. In terms of profits, *a surprising 70% of those now selling at farmers' markets did not know if profits were too low* (emphasis ours). However, 68% reported that sales met expectations and 17% stated sales exceeded their expectations.

What sales do you need to make any particular market worthwhile? Know your costs of production and sales, so you'll know what you need to charge to make a profit. Keep detailed records and calculate profits per acre per crop. To do this, you need to keep track of costs and income as best you can for each crop. Calculate your break-even point per volume (quart, etc.) of product, and then add a profit percentage.

Market Considerations

While setting prices at cost plus mark-up is useful in setting the least amount you can charge to cover costs and make a profit, other factors should also be taken into account when determining price point.

Quality and selection of produce. A premium price requires a quality product. Customers may be willing to pay a higher price for an item if they feel the difference justifies it.

Competition. Regardless of cost and desired mark-ups, prices must be competitive with other sellers for similar products.

Uniqueness of product. How many other products like yours are in the market? The more unique your product is, the more you can set your own price as long as the price is fair in the customer's eyes. The more common your product is, the less leeway you will have in setting prices.

Time of the year. The first fruit or vegetable of the season may be able to command a premium price while end-of-season products may have to be priced low in order to sell. For instance, the first summer squash in the market may command as much as double the "main season" price. In the fall, however, when the winter squash starts to come in, and most customers have eaten their fill of summer squash, the price to get sell-through may have to be 30-50% less. Obviously, this begs the decision of whether you can pick and bring end-season squash to market profitably — maybe it's time to turn it under.

Market clientele. You may price your product differently in each market. Look at the volume you can move at various prices based on the area demographics, whether lower or higher income.

Be a Price Leader!

"Do not undercharge. Farmers have hurt themselves by undercharging. Be proud of your livelihood and charge what you need to make your livelihood. Don't try to compete with the supermarkets. Offer something different and bring your finest produce. It hurts business to bring day-old products."
— Chris Burke, Burke Organic Farm, Boulder, CO

"Rather than lowering prices towards the end of the day, find secondary outlets such as soup kitchens or non-profit organizations like AIDS hospices, McDonald houses, or food kitchens to whom to donate produce that doesn't sell at the market. Talk to church people to find these secondary outlets. There's usually a kitchen that feeds underprivileged children in your area. Don't sell it cheap and don't throw it away. It gives you a real satisfied feeling to donate it to people who need it. I'm not able to donate a lot of money to these organizations, but donating food gives the feeling of contributing."
— Bonnie Dehn, President, Central Minnesota Vegetable Growers

Be a "price setter" and have a great crop to back it up! What is the maximum amount you can get for a product? Go off-season to a really good supermarket and see what they're getting. Try to get at least this price in-season and do not lower prices if you can help it. Farmers' markets are an alternative to cost-plus pricing, so get as high as the market will bear.

One of the biggest mistakes many vendors make is selling too cheap, competing with supermarket prices. Supermarkets, however, frequently sell things below cost as a loss-leader to get the customers in to spend money on other items. Don't get caught in the "I can do it cheaper" syndrome. As a small company, you don't have the means, volume or experience to market products more cheaply than the supermarkets. Homegrown and organic is worth more!

Under-selling is bad not only for you but for the market. Popular items that sell in great quantity, may be sold at a wide range of pricing. Keep good feelings in the market by not creating an over-supply of any item or undercutting competitors' prices on a regular basis.

You cannot win a war against the big guns, especially the box stores. We're seeking quality buyers, not quantity buyers. Here's a general rule: a five percent increase in price gives you even net sales with a 14% drop in customers while a five percent decrease in prices requires a 20% increase in sales to stay even.

Cutting prices often results in only marginally more sales since it generates in many buyers a distrust of the product being offered at 'fire sale' pricing. Being known as the cheapest or always having a sale attracts the bargain hunters — customers who will go down the aisle when they find someone selling for one cent cheaper — rather than the quality-conscious customer who will pay appropriate prices. Don't reduce your price just as the market ends to avoid taking product home. You "train" folks that, if they wait until the end of market, they'll get a bargain, and they'll be back every week looking for a discount.

You also can move excess produce by finding other ways to use it. If you have too many apples, don't drop price; make pies, cider, or cider vinegar instead. Seek secondary market outlets such as sales to restaurants, grocery stores or other roadside marketers who don't have enough of their own produce.

It's actually less costly to do better marketing and promotion than to cut prices! Train your sales force to be friendly, hand out recipe sheets to stimulate sales, spiff up the appearance of your booth, and change the style or location of your displays rather than cut prices.

 ## PRICING TECHNIQUES

"Decide your pricing strategy, and then stick to it throughout the season; don't waiver during the season. Your customers are coming to you to buy fresh fruits and vegetables, because you are providing a product that cannot be matched in quality from any other source. They expect to pay more for this quality than they would pay for chain store produce."
— Richard Ashley, Dept. of Plant Science, University of Conn.

Price for convenience. Hit even numbers in spite of psychological barriers. Your high quality will overcome it and this makes it faster and easier to move products. Today's consumer is sophisticated enough to see through the 99 cent ruse. If items are priced at $1, $2, $3, etc., no coins are necessary. If you're selling flowers and you want to pass sales tax onto the customer, have your prices include the tax so they come out on the even dollar as above.

Multiple pricing. "$1 per pound, 5 pounds for $4." Offering savings by marking a price for multiple purchases as well as a price for a single item encourages multiple or higher-volume purchases. Four for a dollar pushes larger purchases than 25 cents each.

Volume discounts. If you sell in an area where people still process their own produce, encourage large purchases by offering volume discounts. Marketers selling large volumes of produce for home canning and freezing may encourage the customer to buy in larger units such as flats of berries, boxes of tree fruits, or 20- and 25-pound units of vegetables, including carrots or oranges for juicing.

Appropriate unit of pricing. Give some thought to the appropriate quantity or unit of sale for each item. Selling sweet corn by the dozen may not be appropriate if most of your customers are couples or single-parent families who will not be able to consume this quantity for several days or a week. Encourage smaller purchases so the corn will still be fresh when they eat it. Then they will likely return for more.

Reward Loyalty. For repeat and faithful customers, give extra produce rather than lowering prices, e.g., give a free flower bouquet to loyal customers who make purchases of $10 or more.

A sale item each week. Selecting a different "special" keeps your booth looking like there's something new happening all the time.

Evaluating your prices

Your price is too low if: 1) you run out of product before the market day is over, or 2) you have no complaints.

If you have slow product movement, lots of customer complaints, low sales per customer, or a lot of "lookers," it may be that your price is too high. Before you lower prices, however, ask yourself if you can do more to build the value of your product in the customers' minds.

Quality Prices, Quality Products

Offer something special. The key to getting higher-than-supermarket prices is to offer something special — such as freshness, higher quality or uniqueness in variety — that customers can't buy in the supermarket, then communicate this quality difference to your customers!

Stress quality and uniqueness. Perhaps your sweet corn is raised without chemicals or spray, for example, or you grow unique varieties like "Wonderful," "Sweet Sue" or "Gold Cup." The fact that people are coming to the farmers' markets means that they're looking for a reason not to go to the supermarket, so give it to them!

Ribbon gives a touch of class to gourmet goat cheese, jams, a bag of nuts or many other potential year-round gift items.

"Best ideas for getting top prices at the market? Signs on tables that say 'FARM FRESH' or 'PICKED LAST NIGHT'… Folks are usually willing to pay a little more for fresh."
— Diane Green, Greentree Naturals Farm, Sandpoint, ID

"You just can't get cheaper than the supermarkets. You can't compete on prices, so consumer trust becomes all important. Consumers are looking for fewer pesticides, for example. It's expensive to get certified organic in New York, so the growers bring photos to market to show customers their growing methods."
— Jane Desotelle, Mgr., Adirondack FM Co-op, NY

Guarantee satisfaction. Guarantee that your crop is better than what customers will find in the supermarket: "I guarantee each melon I sell, and if you don't like it, you can bring it back!"

As Ronald Smolowitz, Coonamessett Farm, East Falmouth, MA, says: "If products are not top quality, toss it; take only your best to the market. I give my customers my best quality products, and those customers are there no matter what my prices are, and they bring their friends and relatives. They tell me: 'I know your berries are really good; I don't find any mold in them. So I keep buying from you even though I know your prices are higher.'"

Use small-unit pricing. For expensive specialty items, price in small units. Instead of $5 a pound, make it $3 a half-pound or even $2 a quarter pound! Smaller-unit pricing makes it easier for the customer to buy and try out a new or expensive product. Similarly, try selling expensive items like strawberries, blueberries and raspberries by the pint rather than the quart. Snow peas, for example, may be as high as $4 per pound. This will make customers reluctant to buy. It is better to offer such items in more manageable units, such as a quarter pound for $1. Customers will pay more for two individual pints than they will for one quart.

The strawberries Smolowitz sells at the markets are prepackaged in pints, not quarts, and raspberries likewise come in a one-half pint size rather than pints. "People tend to buy in smaller quantities," Smolowitz says. "We get a lot of retired couples or single households and people don't can as much as they used to."

Susan Planck tells her employees that when an item isn't selling well in bulk, they should repackage it into quart boxes. "The quart box is the most amazing phenomenon," Plancks exclaims. "Visually, it looks like a lot. Little tomatoes amidst a bunch of big tomatoes won't sell, but little tomatoes in a quart box sell well."

Sell smaller packages for more. Diane Green, Greentree Naturals Farm, explains this strategy, "If I ask $2.50 for a pint of raspberries, people think I'm nuts and refuse to buy at that price when they can buy them for a $1.00 at the next stand. I package them in 1/2 pint containers, and sell them for $1.25 and sell out EVERY TIME. I have no idea why a smaller package for more money will sell better, but it works!"

Price hard-to-find items above the market. Do this for unusual products or where competition is less intense, especially where there are quality differences. Even when yields are great, maintain your price. You will not stimulate additional purchases with a lower price. People will only buy what they need.

Give samples. Let customers taste your quality! Cut slices: "Here, try one!" Especially with a new or unusual product, give out educational literature or recipes to show how to use it.

"Showcase" your product with great merchandising. Why do you think expensive jewelry is backdropped by velvet or other fancy fabric? Make dynamic displays using attractive packaging. Market manager Dana Plummer of the Downtown Waterloo Farmers' Market says, "Consumers will pay twice as much if they're at a good-looking stall that's pleasing to the eye, where samples are provided, and where the vendors are customer-friendly."

Provide service. This is what customers don't get in the supermarkets or "big box" stores. Be friendly with customers; ask your market to provide carryout service for large purchases or for seniors; provide nutrition information and storage tips; and suggest ways to use the product (recipes, etc.) to increase demand.

Maintain your base pricing. Try not to lower your prices even when your competitors are dropping theirs. If competing farmers drop prices, keep your original price even late in season, but give something extra. As one grower said: "If special sales and lower prices are appropriate due to overabundance of supply or promotional activities, we find that retaining the base price and then adding extra value is much better than simply getting a lower price. For example, when corn is over-supplied and other farmers are down around $2.75 per dozen, we keep our base price of 35¢ an ear, 6 ears for $2.00, and $3.75 per dozen. To attract the customer we offer 6 for $2.00 and then get a 7th ear free, or buy a dozen at $3.75 and get 2 ears free. We find people often buy a dozen at $3.75 to get two free. We get 27¢ per ear and keep our base price for future marketing. Our competition gets 23¢ an ear and will have difficulty raising the price in the future should the corn supply change. Again, quality is critical."

Finally, if and when you do make upward price adjustments, make them as little as needed rather than all at once.

Bottom Line

Does it pay? Check the bottom line.

Some farmers go to farmers' markets for the pleasure of talking to customers and getting feedback on their products but they fail to keep tabs on costs. They may be losing money without knowing it. Keep track of how much you take to the farmers' market and your costs of producing, transporting and selling your products. Be sure to include labor costs (your own as well as hired labor) and your personal expenses for lodging and food. Subtract the value of unsold food at the end of the day.

Compare your costs with revenues to determine your net farmers' market income; compare this with what you might have made selling through other marketing outlets. Are the farmers' markets profitable for you? Don't forget to consider non-immediate returns, like the benefits of using the farmers' market as a test market for new crops or making contacts with customers who may come to your roadside market, etc. The bottom line: watch your bottom line! ✿

YOUR FARMERS' MARKET RETAIL STOREFRONT

4

"You're driving in with a truck and setting up a retail store. Think like a retailer because that's what you are."
— Eric Gibson, *Sell What You Sow*

Once you start setting up to sell at a farmers' market, you're no longer a farmer; you're a retailer, and you need to think like one. As a retailer, an entirely new set of questions and challenges arise: In a farmers' market stall, for example, you have about three seconds to grab the attention of a potential customer and hold it long enough for them to get interested in buying something.

 ## BUILDING THE STORE

If you take your show on the road to weekly markets you have about 1/2 - 1 hour to build your store, erect displays and merchandise them before the market opens. Whatever you use to create your storefront, you will need to be able to put it up and take it down easily and quickly. Even if your space is permanent, you still need to be able to clean and stock it quickly so your energy can be used to make sales.

Shelter

Shelter has three main functions: first, to protect product quality and incidentally customer comfort; second, to provide your farm with recognition; and third, in some cases to define your sales floor.

Some growers who live in a mild or even cold climate may feel little need for tents or canopies for protecting product quality. Also, some growers have the benefit of historic market buildings or shelter spaces and thus have no need to erect one of their own.

Consider where your market located. Is it under the trees or in the open parking lot? Since most farmers' markets are held outdoors rain or shine, investing in a tarp or cover may be essential to protect your products from hot sun or rain. Be sure your structure has a minimum height of seven feet to allow adequate head room.

If you do feel shelter is necessary or desirable, here are some things to consider.

✧ Produce and flowers are visual sells. It is necessary to balance the need for shelter with the need for light on the product. Weather permitting, it may be OK not to use a canopy all because more light brings out the color and natural light is best.

✧ Color contrast helps attract customers' attention. Choose the color of your awning carefully. Colors affect the appearance of food. A blue or green covering can make produce look green; a yellow shade, on the other hand, can make it pop. Darker colors attract heat. White reflects sun and doesn't change product colors, but shows dirt.

✧ For selling in the winter months, indoors or at an evening market, bring along extra lighting. Indoors, use halogen spotlights (or track lights) rather than incandescent lighting. Fluorescent is a "no-no", as it makes everything look dead. Outdoors, a marine battery and 12-volt spots can be hung in the stall.

◇ Tarp and pole structures or pop-up tents create a more intimate setting with the four vertical posts defining the space. Customers must come into your space to buy. Depending on the area of the country, the newness of the market or your presence there, and what other vendors are using, this may be an advantage or a hindrance. Decide whether you want to fit in with how other growers are setting up, or stand out.

◇ Umbrellas may be market- or patio-style but can be trouble in the wind. Market umbrellas are actually designed to mitigate this by having a separate vent piece on top to prevent the wind from making it a flying projectile. Umbrellas give a more open feeling to the stand than tents or canopies and allow more light to the product. They offer less protection from the elements, however.

Some growers who live in a mild climate may feel little need for tents or canopies. As this pepper seller at Ferry Plaza FM, San Francisco, illustrates, nothing puts your product in its best light as natural light!

◇ Whatever you use, think safety first. Ask yourself what would happen if a 50 m.p.h. wind lifts your canopy ten feet up in the air and then it comes back down, weights pulling sharp poles toward people's heads. As this is written, a California market manager is on leave after hospitalization from such a head injury.

◇ Use hanging weights to keep pop-ups and pole structures from moving in the wind. With stronger wind gusts possible, cement cans or even buckets may be necessary; use them for merchandising or hide them under tables to avoid a customer tripping hazard. You also might tie them down with bungie cords using the weight of your display table or your vehicle rather than cans filled with cement which may be a tripping hazard for you or your customers.

◇ Anchor umbrellas at two different points and use only the vented type. If your umbrella can tilt, be sure it is high enough to be well above eye-level at its lowest point.

◇ Keep any displays in front of the space at least waist high so they are visible and less likely to cause a customer to trip.

[See Resources, Chapter 4 for more information on shelters]

Bigger is not necessarily better: If you have little produce, take a smaller space so you can fill it easily. The look of abundance is more important than the size of the stall. When we first started Full Circle Organic Farm, we didn't grow enough to fill an entire market stall, so we sold off the back of our 1953 Chevy pickup truck. We built stake sides to fit into the side-rail holes. Internal rails allowed us to use tiers. We set L.A. lugs (wooden-ended, paper-wrapped containers used for shipping fruit) on end, slanted from one tier to another. We had two tiers, three boxes wide, then tailgate space. It looked full and fabulous!

If you have a choice, try to get a stall where your customers face away from the sun and utilize shade caps or hats or umbrellas to protect yourself and your product.

Many retailing terms are used interchangeably outside the retail environment. This can be somewhat confusing to the novice retailer. To make things easier to understand, here are the terms used in this section of the book and what they mean.

◇ Sales floor — the space accessed by the customer to view, select and purchase your product.

◇ Backroom — space you use to store extra product, display fixtures, signs, bags and other sales tools. If you're in a weekly market, this is generally the back of your truck.

◇ Display — the general layout and physical structures used to hold your product.

- ✧ Waterfall Display or Fall — a mass display that seems to flow from a case.

- ✧ Tie-In Promotion – a promotion in which two products are displayed together and one item is given away or sold at a lower price with the purchase of the other.

- ✧ Merchandising — the creative handling and presentation of products on the sales floor to maximize their sales appeal.

- ✧ Selling — the art of serving the customer and exchanging your products for their money.

- ✧ Suggestive Selling — a marketing technique in which retail employees recommend tie-in or complementary products, such as cake and coffee.

Two-tiered round fixture at the center of a U-shaped stall space entices shoppers to circle it and brings them into the stall of Gathering Together Farm, WA.

SALES FLOOR

"We've learned over the years that the better things are displayed, the better they sell. You've got to attract people to your booth."
— Judy Medicus, Cat's Paw Organic Farm, Union Bridge, MD

Sketch out your plan on paper first. This can save a lot of time when you are setting up your stall space. The drawing should show the layout of the sales area, the location of display fixtures or tables, a list of the fresh items you are going to display, and the location and amount of space allocated to each one.

Another idea is to do a dry run before your first market. Lay out rope or chalk the sales floor. Erect your shelter or umbrellas, put up your tables, and set empty boxes or baskets where you think they will go. Use some of your kids' colored construction paper for color blocks. Stand back and look at the space. What needs a pickup? Is it visually interesting? If you walked by it, would you be able to tell, literally at a glance, what was there? Is the entire sales floor visible from the front or does one display block another?

Become the customer. Walk around in the space. Turn around in the space. Do it again with one hand holding a full shopping bag. Are you comfortable? Did you run into tables, floor stacks, or displays?

Two thoughts on U-shaped arrangements:

"Have the produce displayed where people can see it. Get it out front as close as to the people as you can. An inverted U makes a pathway into your stand so people can get close to your produce."
— Charlie Springer, Mgr., Richmond FM, IN

"We need to move away from flat displays. Lots of growers try to create more space with a U-shape but we found that a lot of people are not comfortable walking into a display. They feel you've got them there and that they have to talk to you or buy something. The answer is to go vertical or U-Shape outwards."
— Randii MacNear, Mgr., Davis FM, CA

There are other choices, of course. At Full Circle Organic Farm, we used a V-shape. This created an indent to draw shoppers to the product, but not such a deep place they felt surrounded. Shallow U shapes with side tables or wings less deep than the main area is long would be another solution. Randii's solution keeps the display space for larger vendors without the "cave" feeling. Again, this is a regional influence.

Give Your Customer Plenty Of Room

Vendors often have a small area, 20-27 feet deep and 10 feet wide, a typical pull-in parking spot including their vehicle display. Stacking baskets in the front and trying to draw the customer in may not leave enough room for more than one customer to stand on the sales floor. Don't try to pack too much in. It looks great but the stall gets crowded very easily. If your space is too small, it might be best to park elsewhere — get there early and unload to create a more open space. If you have a pickup, use vertical space and bring vertical cement blocks and boards to construct an on-site structure.

There is a retail term — "the butt brush." Researchers watched customers in several department stores. They determined that when a female shopper was brushed from behind more than twice, she moved on to a different area even if she desired the product she was originally looking at! This strong sense of space among Americans flies in the face of the "pack more in" display design.

Give the customer a space on the stand to assemble their veggies. The bigger the space, the more they buy. The bigger the bag, the more they buy (within reason)!

Plan Traffic Flow

"Put as much product between the customers and the checkout as you can, so that they will have an additional opportunity to buy more on their way to the scales. We make people walk 30 feet past islands of produce. They're standing in line and looking at the display."

— Mark Phillips, vendor, NYC Greenmarket, in *Growing for Market*, May 1996

"One grower has plastic baskets you can pick up at the beginning of their booth, not to keep but to shop within the booth. It's a 30-foot booth, and at check-out at the back of their booth, you hand in the basket and they bag it and tell you what the price is. This is more convenient than having people put it all in bags and then have to carry a bunch of bags around, and it saves them money on bags, too!"

— Mary Lou Weiss, Mgr., Torrance FM, CA

Let the customer flow in your booth lead to the checkout. Try to prevent long lines — customers may just leave.

- ❖ If you anticipate considerable demand for a product, locate it in two or three places.

- ❖ Designate a "pay here" line to speed up process and minimize confusion.

- ❖ Get enough help so lines don't get too long.

- ❖ Have one person handling the cash box and one assisting customers, and forming a line, rather than having customers throng around to try to pay.

It's OK to have a small line, however. In fact, it's a big plus! It makes your stall look like something's happening! It's like a shopping mall — crowds attract crowds. The trick is to have a line, but not long enough to get customers discouraged. You can regulate the line length by talking to people a little longer or hustling them through. Also, have product literature or attractive signs about your farm in eyeshot to attract their attention while waiting. Explaining how to cook something or the best variety for a particular use is another diversion.

Use All Available Space

One way to make better use of the space is to utilize corners. Corners are vital eye-catchers as well as selling points. Yet too many growers leave their corners unused while supermarkets have long recognized the importance of corners.

Vance Corum

Chilies make use of a tree at one end of the Pasco, WA, market structure.

"A dozen buckets of flowers on the corner of a stand will attract customers like a magnet. Yellow is a real eye-catcher. Farmers use it on the corner of a display even if they have only a little bit."

— Tony Manetta, Greenmarket, New York, NY

As the markets get more crowded, growers are learning to do more with less space. Learn to use vertical space, or "cubic footage" instead of square footage, and display an area instead of "setting a table."

"I even saw an onion grower using the tops of the onions to hang them from his canopy. People could just reach up and take what they need. Of course, it smelled like onion everywhere, too, and that was great."

The "Back Room"

For all intents and purposes, your market vehicle is your back room. Or you may use the space underneath your tables or even set up additional tables in the back of your store, the sides covered with floor-length curtains. This is where your extra stock, display fixtures, bags and packaging supplies, sign making supplies, and cleaning equipment should be — easily accessible to you but out of the customer's view.

Trucks. Be careful about the appearance of trucks behind your stand. You want customers to notice your product first, not the truck. Unless you have a vintage vehicle outfitted to look like the classic "farm truck," get the focus away from your truck! Strategies can include placing a sign with the farm name in front of your vehicle to make a backdrop for your display.

Cleanliness/Neatness

Today's consumer is critically aware of food safety and anything involving the food they eat needs to project cleanliness. Make sure your booth is immaculate.

Keep things tidy throughout the market day. Restock and rearrange your product continuously to keep the stall looking attractive. Empty boxes should be stacked neatly out of your way; better yet, put them back into the truck. Haphazard, loose boxes are a safety hazard to you and your customers; many times growers have fallen over their own boxes!

An attractive fabric sign covers the back of a pickup at Angel's Garden in Santa Barbara, CA

Keep a trash basket out front for customers, even if only for samples from other farmers. Keep another trash box behind your booth to help you keep a clean and uncluttered stall.

 LOGISTICS

Cashier Space and Cash Drawer

Bring enough change to the market so that you don't run out! Most other sellers at market will be glad to help out if you run short of change and you should be happy to do the same for them, but don't become a pest by relying on your neighbors to bring enough change for your operation!

Don't run out when the first two customers each hand you a $20 bill. Remember, if YOU are the farmer breaking the big bills, it means shoppers are coming to your stand first! Sometimes a seller who is leaving the market early or the person who collects the stall fees are good sources of small bills in an emergency.

At Full Circle Organic Farm, we ran a $100 cash drawer, or till, broken this way: 17 dollar bills, 5 fives, 4 tens, a roll each of quarters, dimes, nickels and pennies plus 2 more quarters. About twice a season, we'd have a change problem when we got hit by a bunch of $20 bills at the beginning of market, but for the most part the $100 till worked for us. If you're in a tourist area and are selling value-added products, you may need more change or you may need a check-cashing policy. If you're in an area where you know the pay cycles of the dominant employer, you may need more change around pay day – say the 1st and 15th of the month. For a large grower you may want to start with $200-300 in the till.

Cash Handling and Drawer Etiquette

Set up your cashier area facing your sales floor. Turning your back to make change is impolite and leaves you vulnerable to shoplifting. Also, plan to merchandise smaller, higher-value items, such as fancy jams, herbs and spices, etc., at the checkout area.

While you must decide how you will handle your cash at market, having a cash box keeps everything centralized and facilitates making change. Keep the cash box on a table where you can see it at all times. To conceal the box, place it inside a fruit box sitting on its side. Or drill a hole through your table and cash box and bolt it down. Need we tell you how often cash boxes are lifted each year by fleet-footed individuals? If you're in a permanent space, you may get a cash register and scale combination with a cash drawer that opens only at the completion of a sale. Another alternative, one we used at Full Circle Organic Farm, is an old-fashioned maple cash drawer with a lock and a bell – ka-chinggg. We knew every time the drawer was opened, and it was too big and heavy to pick up and stuff under one arm. We locked it if we needed to move away to help a customer or restock. We'd lean a box or basket on the cash box to create an incline for display space.

Some sellers prefer a market or carpenter's apron with at least three deep pockets for holding bills and coins. If you keep change in apron pockets, keep bills larger than $10 in your jeans or a deep pocket or lock them in the glove box of your vehicle. If you're going to use an apron, consider changing your pricing scheme to accommodate even-change transactions, i.e., even dollar amounts or change in quarters. Anything else will leave you fumbling or potentially chasing errant bills in the wind. If you're particularly adept at it, a metal change dispenser that straps to the waist may be another way to go.

Train your cashiers to handle cash properly. If two or more employees are working in the stand at one time, designate only one as the cash handler. The more hands in the till, the more chance that the till won't balance or a customer won't get the correct change. The cash drawer should be set up as follows:

Bills should be face up with the top of the portrait's head to the right. This makes it easier to keep the bills straight so you won't accidentally put a $5 in the $1 slot and you make change faster. Try to find a cash drawer with clips to hold the bills down. They're slightly more expensive but will pay for themselves in saved time. When you make change, simply pull the bill you want from under the clip. If you can't get a box with clips, use a large paper clip or lead weight on each denomination to keep the till neat and easy to use.

Change

Take the customer's money politely and place it above the cash drawer or on the lid of the till while making change. This lets you see at a glance what money the customer gave you and prevents misunderstandings. State the item price or sale total and what amount the customer gave you ("$6.27 out of $10"); then count out the change. Count aloud the coins to the nearest dollar and then the bills from the smallest to the total amount given to you by the customer. "That's six twenty-seven, 28, 29, 30, 40, 50, 75, seven, eight, nine, ten dollars." Give the customer the change, with a thank you, and then put the money in your cash drawer. You can't imagine how many customers comment with pleasure that you know how to make change!

Bounty attracts bounty as a seller from Phillips Farms in the Vallejo, CA, FM hands back change to a customer.

Some farmers find it useful to write down every sale. A calculator can be a blessing when things get busy. Battery-operated printing calculators assure customers they're being charged correctly. If you can't do math in your head and you don't use an electronic scale, get a calculator and use it.

Keep pens and a paper pad around for quick calculations, notes, and recipes on the fly. Pens will also allow folks to write checks, sign up for the mailing list and counter-sign travelers' checks and WIC coupons.

Security

Farmers' markets by their nature are joyous, chaotic places, and in the huzzah, it can be easy to lose your focus. Keeping the cab of your truck locked and putting the till in when you're restocking can save the day's receipts. If you have two people working the stall, one can restock in front while the other tidies up the cashier area.

While you should be able to make change early in the market, be wary of people trying to break large bills for very small purchases, say a $100 bill for $1.50 worth of goods. This is one way unscrupulous people decide whether you're a good "mark" — by getting some idea of how much money you have in the till! Also, protect yourself by periodically pulling some of the larger bills from the till. Lock them in the glove

box or drop them into a "lockbox" attached to the chassis that can only be opened back at the farm. If you get so many ones, or any other denomination, that you can't pull them individually from under the clip, count off 20, put a rubberband around them, and lock them away. Your till should never look full to the casual glance. Stash it, don't flash it!

Taking checks is an individual decision. There is no law compelling you to do so, but make sure your policies are clear and uniform. Maybe you only take checks from locals or only with a picture ID. From the security standpoint, it's a good idea to take only checks pre-printed with the writer's name and address. Ask for the customer's phone number if it's not already on the check.

Travelers' checks are about as good as cash but only if they are counter-signed in front of you and the signatures match. Don't be afraid to ask for a picture ID. You're looking for the picture and description to match the person in front of you and the signature on the ID to match the one on the check. Honest people will appreciate your thoroughness.

Good customer service skills will go a long way toward preventing problems. Greet every customer coming into your booth and make eye contact. Theft is a crime of opportunity. Friendly merchants who recognize their customers are not an easy mark and potential thieves will find someone else who is.

Vance has watched as a fast-talking charlatan bamboozled a farmer into handing over a $20 bill along with the "purchased" item. The thief convinced the farmer he had wronged his "customer." When the true wrong was uncovered, the charlatan absconded. Be ready, especially into a long, hot market day, to think clearly and control the situation when someone suggests they gave you a large bill. Remember: There are people who practice the arts of heist and smooth talking and often leave the victim feeling positive or unaware of the wool pulled over their eyes. Placing the bill above the drawer and carefully making only one transaction at a time goes a long way toward protecting yourself from such thieves.

Certain markets have had problems with theft rings — groups of three or four individuals who hoist wallets from customers walking from stall to stall with their handbags open. The "mark" or "chicken" is easy prey for a professional who lifts the wallet, passing it to another team member and walking away innocuously. This scene is usually played out in a more crowded market where even undercover police have a nearly impossible job noticing the theft in progress. Farmers can help their customers by encouraging them to close their handbags and keep them close to the body.

One farmer sheepishly admitted he'd been taken by three well-dressed women. As he packed up the rear of his truck, they pressed close around and reached across him to inspect his fruit. Of course, they didn't buy anything. As he pulled into his farmyard three hours later, he reached for the money roll in his apron pocket. It was lighter by $1600.

If you are taken by a thief, don't let the learning experience stop with you. It will probably happen again and again until all farmers learn how to be more aware. Immediately share your story with other farmers and your market manager. Use your experience to help prevent another farmer from being victimized.

Market Crime Watch

— Reprinted with permission from *Renae's Rutabaga Newsletter,* Feb. 1996, Renae Best, Sacramento Certified FMs, Elk Grove, CA

On the whole our customers are very honest. There are, however, a few bad apples. We can all help out by keeping our eyes open and being smart.

Over the last twelve years there have only been a couple of instances of cash boxes being stolen. Odds are it won't happen to you but why take a chance? We recommend that cash boxes be used only for loose coins. Aprons are your safest bet for your bills. Even cash boxes that are nailed to the tables are at risk of being robbed. How often do you let customers shop from inside your stand? Even the most unlikely person can grab a handful of money in the blink of an eye. Keep shoppers out from behind your stand.

It might seem like small potatoes to steal fruit and vegetables, but everything adds up over time.

Again this is only a small problem involving a few shoplifters.

Last Thursday a vendor alerted me to a woman shopper. He thought he had seen her put some vegetables in her bag without paying. He pointed the woman out to me. She looked like anybody's grandmother, nicely dressed with a big designer shopping bag. So I watched her from a distance. She walked in front of another farmer's stand and kind of hesitated for a moment. At the time the sellers were all behind the stand, and the lady walked on. The farmer left his stand. His wife and her mom were busy with customers. The little old lady circled back. Quick as a wink she dropped a small orange juice in her bag and kept on walking! I couldn't believe it! I had to bust a grandma.

Shoplifters seem to work in many different ways. Sometimes they will quickly fill a bag, set it down on the ground, fill another bag for you to weigh and only pay for one. Other times they will fill a bag, put it behind their back, then an accomplice will walk by and take it away. More often a shoplifter will just walk away and you think someone else behind the stand waited on him or her. If in doubt, ask your partner: "Hey! Did you get that guy's money?"

Most shoplifting occurs during the busiest time of the morning. What can you do about it? Be aware. The more eyes on your side the better. When you are slow at your stand and someone across the way is real busy keep an eye open for him. Report anyone suspicious to the manager immediately. Hire one of your small children to keep an eye out for thieves. They can easily see under the table for the two bag trick.

Together we can keep these small problems from becoming big ones. ✿

Choosing Scales

For the items you sell by weight, a simple spring scale hung from a bracket will suffice. It needs to be certified by the County Sealer of Weights and Measures. There may be a small charge for this. Check with the market manager and town clerk's office to be sure you comply. A legal scale is helpful but not necessary, however, if you sell produce by the piece or volume to eliminate the time and hassle of weighing.

Some sellers feel that hanging spring scales, for both the seller and customer, add authenticity and "market appearance." If you use them, place the customer scales within easy reach. Make sure the checkout scale shows weight visible to both you and the customer. Double-faced hanging scales do this seamlessly. Electronic scales, likewise, have displays on both sides. If you use a single-faced hanging scale, come up with a configuration that will be visible to both parties.

Lane Co. FM, Eugene, OR

"A battery-operated scale saved us a lot of money this year. We don't have to figure prices in our heads and round figures off as with a hanging scale. If you're serious about selling at the farmers' markets, get an electronic scale."

— Edie Barker, grower, Portsmouth, NH

As your business grows, consider purchasing an electronic scale. Manufacturer's Suggested Retail Prices for battery-operated, price-computing scales are around $500, but the web prices run $100-$150 less. [see Resources, Chapter 4] A price-calculating scale's greater accuracy will pay for itself quickly if you do large volume. Sometimes you can purchase reconditioned electronic scales for the same price as spring scales. Battery-operated, electronic scales that beep out the prices really speed up customer sales and avoid the tendency to round-down price, common with hanging scales. Every bounce on a spring scale costs you money in time. If you have intense activity in your booth, it pays to invest in an electronic scale. ✿

DISPLAY

5

"Study what the supermarkets do. They spend a lot of money to research things like the distance the average customer will lean in to select an item, and so on."

— Lisa Bloodnick, Bloodnick Family Farm, Apalachin, NY

"One of the maxims of selling anything in a retail setting is that you have about three seconds to catch the customer's eye. At a farmers' market the window of opportunity may be even smaller with so much color, fragrance and activity calling out to shoppers from every direction. With so little time to make your sale, you need a display that will stop shoppers in their tracks and pull them to your market stand. And how do you do it? First, learn the tricks of the trade, merchandising strategies that work for supermarkets and that will work for you, too. Go to the supermarket and survey the produce section. Notice what catches your attention as you scan the displays and figure out why that particular display appeals to you."

— Tony Manetta, Director, Greenmarket, New York, NY, in *Growing for Market,* May 1996

Earlier we defined display as the general layout and fixtures used to hold your product. The term is also used broadly by many market managers to refer to your entire stall as in "your display." Think of display a bit like stage-craft, like dressing a set for a play. What you do needs to provide a backdrop for the action without detracting from the product itself. Display sets the tone and is still an integral part of the market experience for the consumer. Display also distinguishes your farm — and you — from the other farms and farmers in the market.

Once you've defined your sales floor, decide what to use as your central display fixture or fixtures. This is the backbone from which the rest of your display will be built. Tables, platforms, or even truck tail-

gates may be used to display produce. You can use boards on sawhorses or milk boxes — whatever keeps the food off the ground and moves it toward eye level.

The most important feature of whatever you chose as your central display fixture must be SAFETY. Your structure must be sturdy enough to support your product and be jostled by customers without collapsing.

"Elbow to eye level lets customers see and evaluate the produce. Keep all food off the ground. Use a focal point or centerpiece to bring the eye to your booth. A salad bowl, made with your produce, highlights your offerings."

— *How To Improve Your Sales,* Southland FM Assoc.

In baseball the strike zone is over the plate and between the knees and the middle of the chest. In display the buy zone is between the knees and the top of the head. Product placed below knee level or above the top of the head falls outside the normal visual field and goes unnoticed. Even the zone between the knees and the navel is less obvious to most people than that between the navel and the forehead. Retailers have studied this for years. A classic example is found in the cereal aisle. "Adult cereals" are at about the 5 foot level and above, the prime visual awareness zone for adults. Notice the height placement of cereals like CocoPuffs and Lucky Charms. It's much closer to your navel, pretty much the eye zone of a 4-year-old child.

What does this mean for your display? If you are building a display yourself, try to build your backbone at the 3 foot level and go up and down from there. Three feet, 36 inches, is the height of most kitchen counters, and pretty much the belt height of average American adults today. By way of contrast, your kitchen table, and most conference tables, are between 27 and 29 inches high, putting displays that fall below table height low in the field of visual awareness. The more available your product is to the consciousness of your customer, the better your chance for a sale.

> "Place high ticket or new items like an exotic product right by your work area, so when people look at you, they see the product. If you're selling flowers, hold some of them right next to your face. Something about holding a product personalizes it or makes people notice it more. The product you're holding is the one people will buy! If there's something you have only a small quantity of, such as basil or green beans, hold it up and ask 'Would you like some basil today?'"
>
> — Gretchen Hoyt, Alm Hill Gardens, Everson, WA

When you hold a product you also bring it more into the visual awareness of your customer, both because of the higher position and because of the movement of the product itself.

Once you have the backbone of your display in place, it's time to start working the vertical lines.

VERTICAL DISPLAYS

Create a vertical emphasis both to increase space and to improve the visual look of your display. Tiered display shelves are very inviting and help make all products visible. Many growers and managers also feel "going vertical" is a better solution than a U-shape.

> "Stack your produce to create an appearance of plenty and to make it more visible from a distance. Start stacking from a few feet above the ground (never put food on the ground) and make tiers that reach above your waist on the table. Every item should be tilted to give the customer a better view and make your supply look larger. On the table

top, don't settle for just one level of produce. Stack boxes at the ends and stretch a board across them to create a second tier for smaller items."
> — *Growing for Market*, May 1996

If you're attending weekly markets without a permanent space, you must build your display on the fly each time. Folding tables or plywood across sawhorses will realistically be your choice for the backbone of your display. Because tables have the top tied down, they are more stable (less likely to tip) when slanted displays are built on them. If you use sawhorses and plywood, keep in mind the need to balance the weight across the display. Too much weight may be a bad idea at almost any height. A customer in California once tried to pull a watermelon from the bottom of the pile and had an entire table come down on her ankle.

The simplest way to create a vertical display on your table is to put a line of boxes with their long sides along the back of your table then place your selling/display boxes at a 90-degree angle to the first line — one end sitting on the top of the other box. Another quick way to do this is to using cinder blocks and a board to create the riser.

To create a vertical from your table down, you'll need to use something to support a board in front of the table, then stand the product boxes resting between the board and the tabletop. At Full Circle Organic Farm we built wooden blocks for this, but those little, wooden, two-step ladders could be quite versatile here.

Go even higher. You can hang dried flowers, bunches of herbs, ristras, onion or garlic braids from your canopy using S-hooks made from coat hangers. Be careful not to put so much weight on one side you unbalance the canopy. If you don't use a canopy, consider making a pipe arch from which to hang product, your banner, your scale or other items. We used two ten-foot lengths of 1/2-inch, EZ-pull conduit bent at right angles with a pipe bender. We had varying lengths of straight conduit we could couple between them. Our scale hung from this as did various products throughout the season.

Going Vertical: How some growers are doing it

Vance Corum

Market vendor in Arequipa, Peru, uses the steps of a building to create a stair-step display for his heaped flours and dried beans. His flour sack bags provide a natural display element.

Vance Corum

Hilario and Soledad Alvarez of Mabton, WA, draw extra curiostiy for their extensive vegetable line with a hanging wall of chilis at the Yakima Farmers' Market.

Garth Veerkamp

Kay Miyamura uses a simple 2x4 prop to create a 15-degree slope for his peach boxes.

Vance Corum

A stair-step and a smile show these bonsai trees to best advantage in Santa Monica.

"Our table is hinged at the front so the back can be elevated. This creates an attractive, comfortable display. We copied the height, width and angle from the local supermarket chain tables."
— Lisa Bloodnick, Bloodnick Family Farm, Apalachin, NY

"Our display tables are built with a 15% slope, with all of the bagged items like potatoes, carrots and peas out on the front three-quarters of the table. On the back we prop up Styrofoam grape boxes for cucumbers, summer squash, zucchini, cabbage, onions, etc. By tipping the tables we've really made our display stand out. It's different than any other at the market."
— Jay Visser, J-N-A Produce, Manhattan, MT

If you have a more permanent location or are talented with a skill saw, consider doing what Lisa and Jay have done and build the slope into your display.

Any crop can benefit from a little height. For perennials and nursery stock, use an empty 2- or 3-gallon container upside down to raise the plants off the ground where customers can see them better.

 ## DISPLAY FIXTURES

For value-added products, consider purchasing some easily moved table-top fixtures. [see Resources, Chapter 5] Stair-stepped displays create an array of depth, color and texture, and work especially well with vinegar and bottled products stacked row on row, for example. The height difference makes the product label more visible to the customer as well as adding interest.

"To display our produce at the markets, we use apple boxes as well as grape lugs that we get from supermarkets. The grape lugs are cardboard but they have wooden edges. We repaint them and put handles on them."
— Tom & Lois Roberts, Snakeroot Organic Farm, Pittsfield, ME

Look for used crates, baskets, or grape lugs ("L.A. lugs") from your local supermarket, and wash them thoroughly before using. Again, prop boxes or baskets at a slant toward the customers for easy viewing. Organic caution: If you are growing organically, be aware that organic certification rules may forbid using crates and boxes with chemical fungicide residues from commercial packers. Check with your certifying organization.

"Baskets are 'in' as display containers, along with stacked produce wooden crates, placed at an angle, with pretty table clothes, and lots of flowers."
— Diane Green, Greentree Naturals, Sandpoint, ID

Baskets are beautiful, but they need to be full. Crumpled newspaper or an inverted berry basket in the bottom can raise the remaining produce to the top. Baskets can be purchased in bushel, half-bushel, peck and half-peck sizes. Unpainted wood stays wet and cool longer when watered than painted wood or plastic. [see Resources, Chapter 6] New baskets, while attractive, may be expensive. Stopping by garage sales on the way home from market, or the flea market in the off-season, is a good way to pick up inexpensive display items. Bring all sizes of baskets and containers to redistribute your product as you sell down — this helps keep your display looking full.

Display containers should blend well with and enhance the appearance of your produce, not steal attention from it. Browns, brick reds, dark greens, dark blues and natural wood colors will contrast well with the many different colors of produce in your display.

"Cut-flower bouquets in cut-off coke bottles, 12 inside wooden crates, then slightly tilted toward customer side, and kept full at all times, gives an effective visual splash of color."
— Anneli Johnson, Mgr., Copley Square FM, Boston, MA

Plastic bottles, cut off gallon water jugs, pitchers and other water- and ice-holding vessels can be concealed inside baskets and boxes, leaving a strong display while still preserving the product.

Wood is good

"People are looking for that natural feeling and wood brings home that message."
— *Growing for Market,* May 1996

Tone-on-tone color scheme of natural colored soaps in older wooden boxes provides a sophisticated look that supports the price of this value-added product.

Using wooden flats or crates to display vegetable and produce gives a more 'country' or 'earthy' feel instead of using plastic. Old-fashioned containers also give a farm atmosphere to your booth: try a kitchen cabinet drawer, wicker or bushel baskets to highlight fruit or vegetables. Or put burlap bags over cardboard.

Showtime! A display fixture for every need...

Vance Corum

Bob Sullivan with 45-degree wagon pepper display at the Olympia FM, WA, gets the product to customer eye-level.

Vance Corum

Drop your stakes-side & set up your display on your truck! One of the first organic strawberry growers in California markets, Jim Cochran used a quality Swanton Berry Farm sign and colorful, voluminous displays slanted on his truck to attract buyers.

Vance Corum

This German grower sells dried flower arrangements in Munich's Viktualienmarkt using 8-inch sections of pipe soldered on a 45-degree angle to free-standing metal posts. He also sells from boxes and baskets, large and small, as well as using a lattice.

Vance Corum

Denison Farm keeps product in bins to resupply sloped display wicker laundry baskets at the Beaverton FM.

Vance Corum

Kingfisher Farm of Nehalem, OR, makes effective use of baskets as display fixtures to create height.

Vance Corum

These custom metal frames fit the standard packing boxes used by Bob Sullivan, WA, and can be set at different angles to make great use of vertical space.

Light is important

Sometimes the product drives the fixture. Honey, for instance, looks most appealing when light is allowed to shine through to highlight its color. Plexiglas stair-step table-top fixtures may be the best way to display this product. The same may be true of some juices and jellies. It's possible to place "warmer" fixtures

Natural light adds a sparkle to this already-sweet product! Marshall Farm's honey bear display at the Ferry Plaza FM in San Francisco.

around a modern look like clear plastic: a woven bee skep or hive for the honey; a couple of pecks with fresh fruit next to the value-added product; and flowers for anything and everything, just to give a colorful look and prompt a smile.

Sometimes changing the orientation of a fixture can increase sales. One grower had dried fruit in clear plastic tubs with hinged tops. By tipping the table in back by 10% he increased sales 50%! This made the products more inviting & accessible.

Creating falls

Lyle Davis, owner of Pastures of Plenty near Longmont, CO, says: "My background in retailing helps a lot. We use a lot of tier-stepping and waterfalls that make customers feel like they're reveling in 'abudanza' (Italian for 'abundance') when they visit the booth. The waterfalls create high displays of flowers or produce that spill out." The waterfall structures are supported underneath with boxes and crates.

Falls or waterfalls as they are also called, give the feeling that the pile of produce is endlessly deep. This isn't a haphazard dumping of a lot of produce; it's a purposeful construction. The displays of apples, pears, and oranges in the supermarket are really only two fruit deep. (End caps, at the end of aisles, are some-

Farmers and employees create waterfall displays during set-up time at the Davis FM. Notice the display goes from knees to eye level.

times deeper.) They are built on platforms that create the height. You can do the same thing – just make the center platform box the same height as one to three times the average diameter of what you are displaying so it will hide behind the layer. For an even more dramatic look build an extension off the table and continue the fall onto that.

Make It Easy To Buy

"Have plenty of plastic bags handy and accessible. Customers are accustomed to that convenience. Have some in your pockets to offer customers. 'Would you like a bag?' As soon as they accept your offer, you have made a sale."
— Dan Haakenson, *The Small Commercial Gardener*

Everything you do for display is worth nothing if your customers are unable to reach your product. Make it easy for them. Keep your display no more than an arm's reach in depth, and between knee- or waist-level and eye-level in height. Studies show that 75% of products purchased are displayed between elbow and shoulder height. Leave a space at the edge of the table where customers can set their parcels while getting out their money or bagging their produce. If they feel awkward in your stall, they will go elsewhere.

Take-home containers

Take home containers can become part of your display, make the customers' purchases easier, and add value to your product. Common types of containers designed to be sold with the produce include kraft (brown) paper bags, colorful shopping bags, plastic bags, boxes with handles, pulp board trays, and plastic or wooden berry boxes. Wooden baskets, cardboard boxes, and mesh bags also can be used.

You can use "lunch" type bags to sell by the bagful, or berry boxes to sell by the pint or quart. If it's appropriate in your market, ask the customer if they need the berry basket. If they don't, you can move the produce from the berry box into a bag allowing you to re-use the more expensive berry box over and over. This may not be appropriate in every market. Don't look cheap over a basket. There are other strategies to deal with cost.

While paper bags may seem more environmentally friendly, plastic bags for moist items are a necessity. Use paper sacks for small, individual items, and have large grocery bags for customers who buy a substantial amount of products. There may be regional differences here, too. If your customers are accustomed to plastic produce bags in the grocery store, chances are they will feel more comfortable using the same thing at your stall. See-through mesh bags are good, too, letting customers see the quality of your product while allowing air circulation — great for hot days.

Barrel bags (paper grocery store bags) can be purchased at many of the larger "wholesale-type" stores. [see Resources, Chapters 4 & 6] Among paper bags, generally flat-bottomed ones are better for produce needs; they are usually made of stronger material than the "card store" type of bag. Seedling flats may be bagged two to a shopping bag but trays made from cardboard boxes are more efficient at transporting large numbers of seedlings. Pick up a bunch of cardboard soda boxes/flats at a local retailer. These are only about 2-inches high, so they can be used for trays.

Line selling containers with carry-out plastic bags so that when a customer selects an item it may be picked up immediately — no waiting for sacking.

THEMES

"Generally the types of special selling displays can be broken down into five areas: production equipment, printed materials, actual crop material, kitchen help, and 'bits of country.'"
— Mark Wall, *Certified FM News,* Southland FM Association, June 1992

Displays can be built around a theme or suggestive of the farm name. This narrows the type of fixtures used for display and focuses the message. Subthemes can revolve around seasonally appropriate displays — Spring/Easter, Summer/4th of July, Fall/Halloween/Thanksgiving, and Winter/Christmas/Hanukkah.

Production equipment can include something as simple and different as an orchard ladder (taller is better) or a cider press. Interesting handtools, power pruners, pumps, drip irrigation bits or a small tractor will all bring customers over to your table. Antique equipment always attracts attention.

Crop materials can be something as simple as a flowering or fruited branch of your crop, or unusually shaped fruits and vegetables. If you don't have the actual branch, enlarge a color photograph and hang it as a backdrop.

"Kitchen items such as appliances and/or utensils for cooking, ripening, preserving, juicing, and cutting can increase sales by planting ideas for more uses in customers' minds. Examples of commercial or home-made items can also spur sales, such as salsa ingredients (with an example of salsa), samples of your crop pickled, or any item that uses your products."
— Mark Wall, *Certified FM News,* Southland FM Assoc., June 1992

The country or farm look

The niche for Lyle Davis at the Boulder and Denver markets is very high quality flowers combined with specialty vegetables. With twenty years experience as a produce manager at an Alfalfa's Whole Foods Market, Davis constructs stunning farmers' market displays. Farm antiques like old picnic baskets and old toys like little red wagons or goat carts are used as props to help create the "country look." Such items can be found at flea markets or antique markets.

Make displays that look like they came from the farm by using actual farm items. Wooden crates or boxes work well. Bales of straw are a great substitute for a table, particularly with fall crops, and sometimes you can even sell the bales, too. Even an attractive, "country look" tablecloth can add to your sales.

Even items that are NOT directly connected to your specific crop can entice shoppers. A wasp's nest or your hat or tin sign collection are examples of items that – although perhaps not unusual for farmers – would stand out for your customers.

Country boutique

When you have an expensive product, you need to have an elegant-looking booth. A high-end olive-oil or herbal vinegar seller, for example, might sport the "country/European look" with a rustic apron and tablecloths. White painted kitchen tables or other wooden pieces and floral tablecloths and painted baskets can give a boutique look. This style lends itself to gift-giving as additional sales potential.

> "Display your products in similar basket-style containers with colorful cloth liners, and provide gift bags and tissue paper that customers can make an instant gift with."
> — Georgia Paulsen, Mgr., Topeka FM, KS

Farm name themes

Kicke the Bucket Farm is a diversified market farm built on a converted dairy by the Kicke family. They use old milk cans in their stall to support boards for a display shelf. Glass bottles hold single sunflowers for sale. Standing buckets hold a variety of potatoes, onions, and roots. Buckets laid on their side "spill" varieties of eggplant, peppers and tomatoes across a slant table. Plastic bags are pulled from rolls strung on the handle of an old hoe suspended above the display.

The cashier stand is set up on three haybales set on end.

Seasonal themes

Seasonal themes work well such as fall squash and yam displays or summertime berries, figs and soft fruits. Do a complete rearrangement of your stall when the produce seasons change. Do not imitate supermarkets by trying to provide out-of-season products such as tomatoes in January. Produce has its best flavor, holding qualities and overall value in season, when it is available at its greatest volume and lowest price.

Spruce up your stand with seasonal items such as corn stalks and pumpkins after Labor Day to get your customers in a Halloween mood. This will pay off as the holiday nears. Think of interesting ways to display pumpkins such as bringing a step ladder and putting them on each step of the ladder.

Mobile displays

Sometimes high-value or heavy products, especially those needing refrigeration, can justify the expense of a full trailer display. State and local health codes can push vendors in this direction. Bakers may be able to justify the cost of a trailer if sales are good. One California farm uses a flat trailer for pumpkins and squashes, avoiding lots of extra lifting.

Color in display materials

Keep color in mind also when you are selecting display materials. A bright, but not gaudy, cloth, for example, will dress up your display. Use simple but effective color and background behind a beautiful natural product. Green is great beneath fresh fruit, for instance, but not over it.

Go easy on bright plastics. Customers like the "natural" look of baskets and burlap which make a nice, neutral backdrop to the colorful produce. The neutral colors of natural materials help accentuate the bright colors of the produce. Baskets are a perfect display medium and even cardboard boxes can be wrapped in burlap sacks to look "warmer." ✿

MERCHANDISING

6

"A farmers' market is 'theater.' Display, layout, containers, signage, composition, color, contrast, structures and lighting, as well as the products and service you offer customers and how you talk to them, all come together to tell your story. What makes you unique?"

— Leon Sugarman, architect and urban designer, San Francisco, CA

"Whenever possible, try to appeal to as many senses as you can manage. Mixtures of colors and different sizes can be attractive. Fragrance is a powerful draw. Cut some strongly scented samples just for the aroma. Noise also can be attention getting, such as country music wafting from your pickup (not too loud). Give customers the opportunity to touch something with an unusual texture. All these things can bring them right up to your table."

— Mark Wall, *Certified FM News*, Southland FM Assoc. June 1992

If storefront layout is the foundation and display is the structure, then merchandising is the paint on the building, the icing on the cake, the clothes on the model, the... well, you get the idea.

Over and over we hear the feedback from both successful growers and managers that professional presentation is vital to successful sales. Americans have been trained to buy with their eyes first. Are your products displayed on nice tablecloths and your piles of fruit or vegetables kept full? As one manager said: "Growers are going to a more upscale, polished look. It's not just a few boards thrown across some crates anymore."

Earlier, we defined merchandising as the creative handling and presentation of products on the sales floor so as to maximize their sales appeal. Merchandising is a blatant appeal to the emotions and the senses. Think of yourself as an artist with several pal-

ettes of colors to choose from: visual palette — color, contrast, shapes, sizes, scale; scent palette — herbs, flowers, fruits, spices; and touch palette — soft, firm, crisp, rough, fuzzy, cold.

 ## APPEALING TO THE SENSES

Visual Palette — Color Me Sold!

"It's the attention to color and detail that makes people want to come over to your booth and see what's going on. Like making sure that your basil is displayed so that the scent wafts into the market. Or doing beautiful geometric shapes with items like corn and carrots and tomatoes, and beautiful lines of color like beets followed by radishes, followed by white radishes, followed by black radishes."

— Tony Manetta, Director, Greenmarket, New York, NY

Use color and texture to enhance eye appeal. In a big market, you have only a few seconds to get peoples' attention, so use strong color contrast.

Capitalize on the rich color palate of your fresh produce. People enjoy food with their senses, so displays must be eye- and sense-appealing. Bright, vibrant color contrasts within produce groupings also lead to tie-in sales. When considering what to plant, use color as one of your criteria.

A good deal of what we perceive is based on color. Color and movement, in fact, are the primary differentiators in the visual world. This may be a good time for a review of light and the color spectrum.

Sometime along about the sixth grade, you probably were introduced to the wonders of a prism. A prism bends light causing it to display the separate colors of the visible spectrum. The visible spectrum runs from red at one end to blue at the other end with all other colors in between. At the center of the spectrum is yellow. Red, blue and yellow are called primary colors. All other colors are a mix of the three primary colors and are called secondary colors — the most common being purple, orange, and green.

When you put the primary and secondary on a color wheel, they line up like this: red, orange, yellow, green, blue and purple. Colors next to each other on the color wheel are called complementary colors, meaning they sit pleasantly next to each other, possibly because the secondary color contains the primary color next to it. Red and purple are an example of this. Colors across the color wheel from each other are called contrasting colors, meaning they provide counterpoint to each other, possibly because the secondary color in this case contains none of the primary color opposite it. Red and green are a good example of this.

White is the presence of all colors of the visible spectrum and black is their absence. Colored objects reflect their own color and absorb all others. White reflects all colors and black absorbs all colors. Clear and translucent colored objects, like colored glass and plant cell walls, transmit their own color and reflect all others. In photography, you'd call these filters.

Why is this important? Knowing something about color allows you to select colors for your awnings and umbrellas, fixtures and labels that complement and highlight your products. It also helps you avoid combinations that may be perceived as irritating.

"One farmer has all white tables and tent, lavender boxes, and white signs with lavender writing."
— Nancy Caster, Mgr., Irvine Center FM, CA

The grower above probably had berries or greens rather than tomatoes, colored peppers, oranges or peaches. The lavender and white color scheme would complement boysenberries and contrast with oranges or tomatoes.

"A friend of mine, a K-Mart manager, explained that supermarkets use either green or yellow to accent the produce. So we changed our boxes to bright yellow boxes to show off the green and red vegetables, and made the stand mauve. It was great advice and the bright yellow boxes have become our trademark."
— Dan Haakenson, *The Small Commercial Gardener*

Both men here have discovered what many commercial merchandisers have known for years — the eye is drawn to the color yellow, in the middle of the spectrum, first. At Full Circle Organic Farm, I selected yellow aprons and a yellow background table covering. Simply by the force of color, we drew the attention of consumers as they walked through the marketplace. Because we wore yellow, we had the added benefit of movement as well. Yellow also complemented our mixed vegetable offering.

If you don't have a lot of variety in your produce, create a color mixture with packaging or by arranging cut-flowers among the produce. Additional color can be added with fresh plants or flowers or by using bright shade awnings or signs. Be careful, however, that the reflection from surrounding colors does not cast an unwanted hue on the natural color of your produce. Awnings act as a filter, transmitting the color of the awning itself onto the produce. Because your reds and yellows have only reflected light from outside your awning to reflect their colors, they look duller and less ripe.

A few examples of crowd-capturing, profit-making, creative merchandising ideas include a "waterfall" of potatoes created by an inclined board covered with spuds of all shapes and colors; wicker flower-gathering baskets used to display a colorful collection of peppers, eggplants and squash; or buckets of flowers lined up according to the colors of the spectrum, creating a rainbow effect from a distance.

Grouping Color vs. Mixing Color

"With colors the key is similar to landscaping where the trend is to have large, full blocks of contrasting color rather than scattered and patchy color blocks. We might have a huge tier display with 10 varieties of sunflowers of all similar colors, for example, and next to sunflowers are the beans — Romano and purple and yellow-waxed beans in huge lines of parallel spilling colors, green, purple and yellow. Like items are grouped together, like summer vegetables and scallions and all the beans grouped with peppers and eggplants, and all the bouquets together. Common, like items are grouped together using large blocks of contrasting color."

— Lyle Davis, Pastures of Plenty, Longmont, CO

You can use large blocks of color to create the image of bounty, then group produce of a contrasting color beside it. For example, red beets, golden beets, radishes and turnips might be contrasted next to green broccoli, spinach, mustard and kale, etc. This is a color block merchandising scheme. Try different schemes to see what works best in any given market.

"Make checkerboards of black and red raspberries or yellow and red tomatoes in quart boxes, tiered on red plastic crates."

— Mark Phillips, NYC Greenmarket vendor, *Growing for Market*, May 1996

This is a contrast or pattern merchandising scheme and can work best with smaller quantities of product to create interest.

Sometimes what you think will work isn't as effective as theory would indicate. I'm personally fond of color block merchandising, so I filled my wooden boxes with bell peppers in four different colors and placed them on a slant in nice color blocks. For some reason, they weren't moving as we thought they should. My husband took an immense flat basket, 4-feet across, from the van and dumped my beautiful, well-planned display into the basket, mixing the colors. The peppers started selling like hotcakes! The contrasting colors and overabundance called to consumers from across the market.

"Draw a map of your table on Friday night when you know what you've got to sell and color in with colored pencils to see how color arrangement will look."

— Cheryl Boden, West Union Gardens, Hillsboro, OR

If you have product of all one color or muted colors, try for a sophisticated look by going for tone-on-tone. Use all the same colors, i.e., signs, tablecloth, etc., in a shade lighter or darker than your product. A four-color, high-end label can help your product stand out in a crowd.

Tablecloths and Coverings

If your tables are not covered, consider tablecloths. They create an elegant look for a high-end product. Nice tablecloths make your stand look neater and more attractive. If they're long enough, they also hide back-stock and clutter under the table. Make sure your tablecloths are washable and keep them clean. Solid colors create a more uniform look, while a small pattern hides the dirt better. Be careful with large patterns, however, as they might compete with the product.

Table coverings of bright fabric with fruits and vegetables are eye catchers but may overly distract the customer's eye from your product. Checkered tablecloths, aprons, and crocks help create mood, the "country look." Don't confuse "old fashioned," however, with shabby! Replace worn banners and tablecloths.

"Growers are going to colorful table coverings; a shaded shopping area for customers to 'linger' around; products displayed in similar basket-style containers with colorful cloth liners; providing gift bags and tissue paper that customers can make an instant gift with; and having products carded with significant information about the product history, contents or growing and eating information."

— Georgia Paulsen, Mgr., Topeka FM, KS

"Astroturf is out! People find it dirty looking. It gets grimy. It's also the 80s supermarket look — it's just not right for the market. People are replacing it with tablecloths and clean white tables."

— Mark Sheridan, Gen. Mgr., Santa Barbara FM, CA

The Scent Palette: It Makes Scents

"Growers here are doing a better job of getting all the senses going. One of our basil growers keeps a little basil on the side to crush, so that people are smelling it the whole time! Another example is the tuberose, a Mexican variety of lily, which has a fantastic scent. When they come into the markets, the growers can't keep them in stock.

"Tomatoes are another example of catching customers by smell. Some growers are picking the tomatoes with a bit of the green stem and the calax left at the top. The tomato itself doesn't have a smell, it's the green stem that gives the tomato its aroma! So when people pick this up, it smells like a home-grown tomato. They come in with their eyes, and then you've got their nose, and then you've got a sale."

— Mark Sheridan, Gen. Mgr., Santa Barbara FM, CA

Scent is a powerful invoker of memory and can enhance mood. In recent years, department stores have started using scent to improve the moods of shoppers and increase sales. Think aroma therapy. Scent, or more correctly the sense of smell, is also a major component of taste. Sampling of new and seasonal items is a good sales technique. Consider planting something fragrant if your normal crops don't lend themselves to this sense.

Don't overlook the power of the sense of smell, especially when your customers are hungry. Squash a couple of strawberries on the hot pavement, and the smell will waft through the air! The fragrance of apples, ripe cantaloupes and strawberries, or the tangy aroma of a freshly sliced, sweet onion can stimulate sales.

Touch Palette — Oh What a Feeling!

Texture is perceived visually as well as physically. The pebbly skin of an avocado or the soft down of a peach are noticed visually well before they are touched. The play of light and shadow over the surface emphasizes the feel of that surface.

Dimension and form are also perceived by vision before touch. Consider the many varieties of summer squash — dark green, green striped, or yellow cylinders; flattened, scalloped pale green or bright yellow orbs; pale green teardrops; and bumpy, pastel yellow crooks.

Consider the variety of textures in lettuce and salad greens!

Merchandising for Interest & the Suggestive Sell

Using a combination of colors, textures and fragrances will create interest and excitement in your booth. These variations will keep the customer's eye moving throughout your booth. You can use these merchandising schemes to suggest the uses of different products you sell.

Place compatible products together like salad dressing with greens, popcorn with apple cider, and impulse items (jams, jellies, flowers, crafts and gifts) for convenient sale near the cash register.

Organize products in related groupings, perhaps from the beginning of the meal to the end — salad items, cooking vegetables, herbs, citrus, soft fruits, apples and pears, melons, tropical fruits, and luxury items such as flowers and decorations.

Merchandise exotic specialty crops together as a group. Displaying them side by side with ordinary varieties makes customers wonder why they should spend the additional money for them, while placing them in a separate section helps emphasize the products' premium or exotic quality and makes them look different and interesting.

Contrasting textures and sizes of produce is also an effective merchandising tool. Zucchini, gold cukes, cucumbers and other cylindrical veggies can be stocked in different directions if next to each other.

Arrange in terms of color and texture — a mountain of radishes carrots bracketing greens. For a fancy look with a small quantity of green beans, arrange them in a sunburst pattern shooting out from a single, central tomato.

Creative touches enliven a produce display, e.g., carrot wheels, fresh flower bouquets, edible flower arrangements, garden-like groupings of lettuce and greens, baskets within the displays, or hand-stacked potatoes and yams. Enliven your display and avoid monotony by using tilted tables, barrels, produce baskets, buckets, paper sacks, burlap, pallets and bulk bins.

> "We had a vendor that had such a beautiful arrangement of veggies, placed in and around and on top of apple crates that the most common comment from customers was, 'I can't buy anything — it would put a gap in the display.'"

Have fun and remember your display should not be so picture-perfect that it makes people afraid to touch or take items. Make your display inviting! Removing one or two packages from a full display may even help customers start buying.

ABUNDANCE

> "People are attracted to large displays. They like to think they have a choice. Get as much out in front of the customer as you can, even more than you expect to sell."
> — Tony Manetta, Director, Greenmarket, New York, NY in *Growing for Market*

> "We have found that the bigger the display the more you sell. Some farmers have a tendency to put a few baskets on display and leave the rest on the truck. This person will NOT sell as much of the product as the one that brings it all off the truck for a huge display, even though they both brought the same amount to market."
> — Butch Hollister, President, Connecticut Farmers Association for Retail Marketing (ConnFARM)

"Pile it high and kiss it good-bye!" Abundant displays attract attention. At a New York City Greenmarket one grower displayed green beans in a small bowl which she refilled from a basket in her truck. The effect was that few people saw her green beans. In contrast, another grower made a mountain of radishes and the splash of color drew people from across the street.

Keep the tables full, piled high with product. Full, well-stocked displays make customers want to come and get it! Customers don't like taking the last of something from a bare, picked-over display; they want the best. A cornucopia of produce conveys abundance, prosperity and quality. Look at your booth from the shopper's perspective. An overflowing crate (kept stocked) will often outsell five half-full crates. Don't put two flats of strawberries on the table, for example, with 50 flats sitting on the truck! Show people volume!

> "Sometimes it's the little things. Everyone's selling tomatoes this time of year, for example, and we sell tomatoes by the quart in plastic baskets. So we add a tomato or two to make it look overfull."
> — Judy Medicus, Cat's Paw Organic Farm, Union Bridge, MD

Creating the Bountiful Look

Display in full baskets. Large amounts of produce attract customers; small amounts in a big basket can look "picked over." If you're running out of a product, put the remainder in smaller containers and keep them full or when quantities diminish, reduce the size of your display so it still looks well stocked.

> "Even if you have only one kind of product such as berries, put it in several sizes of boxes and use up your whole area, even if it's for just one item!"
> — Gretchen Hoyt, Alm Hill Gardens, Everson, WA

Peter Jankay of the San Luis Obispo County Farmers' Market Association, CA, believes the merchandising of a display makes a huge difference. "A person can have a mountain of peaches in one display and it looks junky, while another grower's mound of peaches may look great. The other grower may have put it together a little more meticulously or put it in lugs or in baskets. Each individual fruit is high-quality, so people don't feel they have to go through the pile to find a good piece of fruit. It has not only to taste good; it has to look good, too."

Stock fully, but don't pile products so high that it makes a customer feel that if they pull an item out the whole thing will fall. For most products, avoid piling them higher than 6-8 inches as they may bruise or tumble. Avoid steep pyramid displays, for instance, where products often roll off the top.

"Even if you don't have large quantities of produce you can create an illusion of bounty by turning baskets on their sides with produce spilling out from them."
—Tony Manetta, Director, Greenmarket, New York, NY

Be careful not to overstock, however, to prevent the risk of crushing tender items on the bottom or (in an air-cooled case) of blocking proper airflow. Some quality-conscious growers stack fruit no more than two layers high.

Other excellent merchandising ideas:

✧ Intersperse product with leaves, herbs or flowers;

✧ String balloons or chili peppers around the canopy or entryway;

✧ Interweave garlic braids with roses;

✧ Hang dried flowers, peppers or braided garlic from the latticework above your stall;

✧ Create a mini-florist shop, with flowers on the edge of the stall, wreathes and swags hanging from the stall.

PACKAGING

"A lady at our market sells flavored vinegars. She hand-dips the top of every bottle of vinegar in wax to seal it, and ties a bow around each bottle. The products are tiered, so the back products are as visible as the front products and she always has a fresh bouquet of flowers on her table."
— Patty Brand, Exec. Director, Friends of the St. Paul FM, MN

Clear plastic cartons or plastic tubs work well for many value-added products (cobblers, etc.) Netting over berry containers allows air circulation but keeps berries in place. But remember, you can get too slick. Fancy packaging that works well in an air-conditioned store may not work in a farmers' market. People want to feel and smell the product. When packaging makes an item less visible to customers, display an open sample, e.g., if salad mix is packaged, display a salad in a bowl without packaging.

Get Rid of Rotten Stuff

"Always get those few rotten pieces of fruit out of sight. Nothing turns a shopper off more than a big moldy peach sitting in the middle of a box of perfectly good fruit."
— Renae Best, Certified FMs of Sacramento, CA

It is painful to throw out perfectly good, but slightly damaged produce. However, it is necessary. Many customers are bothered by damaged produce. They will remember where they bought it and will be reluctant to return.

Remove produce damaged by customers. Corn that has been stripped or tomatoes squeezed to mush have no appeal. If you have seconds or culls, don't put them out on the table; keep them on the truck for the food closet.

Bulk vs. Prepackaged

"We have tubs of beans for customers who want to pick them out individually, and we leave bags ready-made for customers who know what they want."
— Cheryl Boden, West Union Gardens, Hillsboro, OR

"We bag up the peaches into 2-pound bags at about $4 a bag. With pre-bagged, people tend to buy more. There are always some people who want to pick their own, so we have an area they can pick out their own. Close to 80% of the people just take a bag. After the first couple of weeks they get to know me and know there are no bad peaches at the bottom of the bag."
— John Ellis, Farmer John's, Boulder, CO

You Are Part of the Display!

A Market Tour with Randii MacNear,
Manager, Davis Farmers' Market

Abundance

Abundance is what brings people to the market. In our technological society, people-to-people abundance is vanishing. Most market managers and farmer/vendors know the "pile it high and kiss it goodbye" principle about product abundance in a booth, but the same applies to the people in the booth.

Think abundance! Can we make our markets and our booths welcoming and bountiful and one that customers will enjoy? Unless you enjoy being with people at the market you should find someone else to sell your products, because what you're selling is yourself. You are part of the display! Of course you grow the best products. It is you who are behind the stand that counts!

Walk around the marketplace and look at other displays. Ask yourself: What is it behind this display that I like? Most of the time, the person behind that booth is really happy and loves to be there. Have people take pictures of you — are you smiling and look happy to be there?

I can walk around the market and tell who's having a great day and who's having a terrible day. Here is a sweet pea grower. He is a joy to have at the market. He puts a sweet pea in everyone's hair and they also buy his sweet peas. Here is an organic nursery seller who does a tremendous amount of one-on-one with customers. He also does well week after week.

Here are some organic farmers who have a warm and fuzzy feeling to their booth. Bring kids to the market — it adds vibrancy. Look at her big smile! Her farm is mortgaged to the max but you'd never know it from her smile!

This is crucial: Don't let anyone or anything take those four hours at the market away from you. Don't let any problems with other sellers, or any problems with your children or your spouse, interfere with your hours at the market. Commit yourself to that market for four hours. On the way to the market take a deep breath and clear your consciousness.

Booth

If a vendor asks the manager, "What's wrong with the market?" Ask them, "What's wrong with your stand?"

Make sure your booth is immaculately clean. People are thinking about food safety nowadays and anything involving the food they eat needs to be immaculately clean.

When you have an expensive product, you need to have an elegant looking booth. We have an olive oil seller who has the country European look with a rustic apron. Market umbrellas are a nice way to make your booth look nice, especially in green and white and maroon.

Improving displays

We work with our sellers with suggestions about color, height and so on, and we invite experts such as people from the landscape or architect design department at the local college or students in these classes. Also look at other stands or in retail stores to find people selling similar products to what you are selling and see what they're doing with their products.

We take slides of our sellers' displays and we ask design experts to come to our annual meetings to critique them. It is a courageous act on the part of the vendors to have their displays critiqued publicly. However, there is no shame, no blame — it's only a question of finding how we can do it better. There are no mistakes, only lessons. How can we improve our display and our stands?

Pretty soon the whole market buys into the idea of improving their stands, and the vendors even start coaching each other. The key in dealing with vendors is to coach, not criticize. ✿

The decision to display and sell your produce in bulk or prepackaged depends largely on your clientele, the produce item, and where you are selling. If your customers are commuters who want in-and-out convenience, selling by the count or by prepackaged units makes sense. Ready-to-use items such as fresh herbs or salad mix might sell well prepackaged. Home canners, or ethnic groups accustomed to open-air markets where they can pick out their own produce, may prefer buying in bulk.

> "People's experience at the supermarket is that there may be some bruised product in the bag, so many vendors let the customers bag products themselves."
> — Randii MacNear, Mgr., Davis FM, CA.

The customer's perception of choice is everything. Some consumers will like the convenience and quick checkout offered by pre-packaged goods. For others a large part of shopping in the farmers' market setting is being able to select their own fresh produce from the farm. Consider a scheme that allows the maximum choice for your clientele.

Be aware that where you sell can be an important factor in whether or not you choose to prepackage. California law requires that all fresh fruits, nuts and vegetables sold in closed, consumer containers shall be labeled with the name, address, and ZIP code of the producer and the identity and net quantity of the commodity in the package. Some growers avoid these "closed" container requirements by putting a tie on the bag after the sale is made. This means either pre-printed or hand written labels on each package — a requirement that may mitigate the speed of the sale picked up by prepackaging. Research the requirements in your area before making this decision.

Selling in bulk, by weight, is still popular because people are used to buying by the pound and feel they are getting full value for the price. It also avoids the controversy in pick-your-own sales of over-filling the containers. Selling by weight requires the use of accurate scales. In most jurisdictions scales must be "legal for trade" and certified by a county authority before they can be used in a market setting.

Here are some comparisons:

Packaging advantages

✧ Helps maintain freshness;

✧ Can enhance product and market appearance;

✧ Provides customer convenience — eliminates bagging and weighing;

✧ Provides seller convenience — easier to move items around, less work at checkout;

✧ Gives a way to list price, seller's name and address, recipes and other information; and

✧ Protects product from damage.

Bulk advantages

✧ Consumer can choose quantity;

✧ May appear fresher to consumer;

✧ Consumers tend to buy more of certain items (e.g., nuts and dried fruits);

✧ Enhances market's "home-grown image";

✧ Less refrigeration needed for bulk produce;

✧ Reduced labor involved with packing, weighing and labeling;

✧ Reduced cost for packaging supplies; and

✧ Appeal for ethnic groups who may be used to buying bulk.

Which way you go may vary by the time of year or point in the season. Do your homework first to make sure you get what you need to stay in business. [See Pricing, Chapter 3] Tom Roberts and Lois Labbe of Snakeroot Organic Farm in Pittsfield, ME, change their units of sale depending on where they are in the season. Some items such as carrots and beets sell by the bunch early in the season when they first come in and are smaller; later when they become larger, the tops are cut off and the roots sell by the pound or are packaged in three-pound bags. Carrots, for example, sell for $2.50 in a 3-pound bag. Roberts explains, "We usually do better putting them in 3-pound poly bags. It's so convenient for customers to just pick up a bag. Sold by the pound, people may just pick up a few for that evening's meal. Very few people buy very much (quantity) by the pound, yet they don't seem to hesitate to pick up a several-pound bag."

The chief advantage to prepackaging is convenience — easy sales at the market and fast checkout. If you prepackage, however, you will spend time weighing, packaging, labeling, and packing the packages for market. This incurs costs for labor and packaging. Certified scales must be used in establishing the weight of the pre-pack. Leftovers must be dealt with. Are you giving them to a soup kitchen or other hunger program? If you compost your leftovers, you must spend additional time to unbag them, then recycle the bags — a cost probably not accurately assessed or passed on to customers.

Unit Pricing

Selling by volume, piece, or unit rather than by weight generally saves time on the sales floor, both for the customer and salesperson. Unit pricing makes the checkout move more quickly and allows the vendor more time to talk to customers.

"Most of our produce is sold pre-bagged at the market except for the large items like zucchini, summer squash, cucumbers and cabbage. It takes a lot of time to weigh the products. Also people pick through products and we end up with a lot of damaged product. Weighing with a scale takes time and tends to form lines. People also tend to buy more with a pre-bagged product, where they have to take at least a bag. The farm's potatoes are sold in three different size bags, a 2-pound, a 5-pound and a 10-pound, and are graded with the smallest baby reds in the 2-pound."
— Jay Visser, J-N-A Produce, Manhattan, MT

"Everything is pre-packaged at my stand. I weigh it in one-pound bags. Other vendors have scales and let the customer weigh it, but you have to give up space for them to do this. I also price to include tax for minimal money handling. We have a 5% tax, so I sell an item for 95 cents — $1.00 with tax. It moves faster this way."
— Diane Green, Greentree Naturals Farm, Sandpoint, ID

Products sold by the unit, such as pumpkins, larger winter squash, melons or watermelons, work best grouped by size and priced accordingly. The customer readily sees the correlation between price and size. Price in $1 or 25 cent increments for easy-move pricing or sell by the bunch or bag. Not having to weigh things means faster transactions. Lining display containers with carry-out plastic bags enables the customer to select items with no wait for bagging.

For units containing more than one item, e.g., "Sweet, white corn 5 for $1," the layout can allow for some pre-bagged and some bulk so customer preference is accommodated. Other examples of unit pricing are berries sold by volume, i.e., quart or pint, or fruit sold in peck, 1/2 peck or 1/4 peck baskets.

Packaging for Today's Consumer

In the summer of 2000, the Farmers' Market Federation of New York ran several surveys and focus groups to get a better idea of what consumers' wants and needs were within the context of farmers' markets. One panelist in a two-person household on a fixed income craves the fresh fruits and vegetables he gets at farmers' markets and appreciates vendors who sell

Clear plastic packaging preserves the freshness of Mrs. B's baked goods in Yakima, WA, while allowing the shopper to see the product. This strategy also works well with fresh product like berries and cherry tomatoes. Also note the slant-shelved baker's rack with her business name on top. Again, slope shows more of the product to the customer, making it visible from 20-30 feet away.

small quantities and various quality grades at reduced prices. As boomers become empty-nesters, smaller households and today's rapid-paced lifestyle dictate a different type of packaging than was done previously.

> "We're finding that people don't cook. Ten years ago people would stop at our roadstand and take a dozen ears of corn and not even blink an eye. We have people stop today and take two ears of corn… 'Oh, can I take 2 ears of corn for my microwave?'"
> — *Barriers & Opportunities,* Farmers' Market Trust

> "Grocery stores have switched over in the last several years to take-home, throw-it-in-the-microwave, put-it-on-the-table items like vegetable trays or salad mixes. We're living in a two-worker family society. People don't spend a lot of time cooking and they typically purchase for one or two meals. Instead of 20 pounds of garden peas, they'll take a 2-pound bag or they'll take six ears of corn. So we display in pre-packed and smaller quantities as much as we can, in addition to offering our bulk pack."
> — Allen Shoemaker, Shoemaker's Home Place, Blackfoot, ID

 ## SAY IT WITH SIGNS

Signage is a merchandising feature often overlooked in the planning process. Well thought signs can add color to your stand, provide information to support a sale and create "brand" for your farm. Signs can be divided into three basic categories: price signs, information signs, and brand signs.

Price Signs

Generally, prices should be clearly marked on or near the products. Consumers are used to shopping retail stores where they don't have to ask about prices. If people have to stop and ask, they'll assume it's too expensive. A large, attractive chalkboard or white board rather than individual price tags for each container of produce can work if you have just a few items. If you have a long list of items, put the price on or near each item and a reader board or chalkboard to highlight what you are offering. Be careful how you write prices: "$.10" can look like "$10" at a glance — better to use "10 cents" or the cents (¢) sign.

For sales of higher value crops it's better to show the pricing of quantities normally bought and consumed within the week. An example of this might be snow peas, which are most commonly used in Asian dishes in combination with other ingredients. They are usually purchased at market in 1/4 to 1/2 pound quantities. This is a high value crop, in part because the picking is so labor intensive. Around California, snow peas sell for $4 to $6 per pound. Consider pricing yours in 1/2 pound increments instead. Your sign now reads "Snow Peas $2.50 / half pound" — a perceptible difference.

Some markets have rules that individual items must have prices posted with them rather than on a board. Check your market's rules before deciding how to display your prices.

> "We hired an artist to make signs with borders. The basic sign can be used over and over. Felt tip markers are used to put the prices on the signs and the signs are laminated so that we can use fingernail polish remover to change prices. The signs are placed next to or on top of the produce. Plastic sticks purchased from a garden or floral supply store with three prongs hold the signs in place. They can also be stuck into a potato or a flower vase. An alternative is to put prices on a chalkboard off to the side or in the back."
> — Gretchen Hoyt, Alm Hill Gardens, Everson, WA

> "We use 5x7 inch cards with each type of product, laminated so they can withstand the weather. To change prices, computer print labels are pasted on the cards, which can be tricky in wet weather. In addition to prices, the cards carry the name and description of the product."
> — Rudd Douglass, Blueberry Ledge Farm, Gardiner, ME

> "Some growers paint the name of the item on wood, and write the price on a card that can be attached, to give them flexibility to change prices. One farmer uses small chalkboards from a toy store and tucks them into the baskets behind the produce."
> — *Growing for Market,* May 1996

A Business Without a Sign is a Sign of "No Business!"

— Fresh New Ideas, marketing column written by Cappy Tosetti (ctosetti@wcn.net) for the *Capital Press Agriculture Weekly,* Salem, OR.

Think about it. Everyone from the lumber yard to the laundromat has a sign in the front window that lets people know about his or her products and services. It would be pretty foolish to go to the trouble of setting up shop without one.

Perhaps you're saying, "Yeah, that's crucial for a retail storefront, but we're just a small farm selling berries and vegetables at a Saturday market. Why hang a sign when folks walking by can easily see what we have to offer by looking at our table or the back end of the pickup? It's an added expense that's not really necessary."

Erik and Kay Dee Cole of Cole Garden Farms in Corvallis, OR, have a different outlook on the subject.

"People seemed to gravitate to our booth after we had a sign made," Kay Dee said. "I think they see us as a real business and that we're serious about what we do.

"We'd been selling herb plants and annuals for three years and just recently decided a sign would help make our booth look more professional. At first we thought it would be expensive, but the fellows at Van Dykes Signs in Tangent, OR, designed and created just what we wanted for only $30.

"We wanted something that looked fresh, green and living with just our farm name and location on it. Since we sell a variety of plants, it had to be fairly generic. Their artist drew up a few examples for us to look at, and we fell in love with the one with an ivy border. It's perfect. I just wish we had done this sooner."

Signage does more than send people in your direction — it gives you credibility and name recognition. It completes the package like the ribbon on a birthday gift and the icing on the cake.

It's a snap to get just what you want nowadays because modern technology has developed snazzy computers that churn out a wide variety of type styles and colors in vinyl that adhere to canvas and other materials.

Katherine Ankeny and Kellie Green from Out of the Blue Organics in Sweet Home have also gone the extra mile by creating their own artwork on their canvas sign.

"We wanted something whimsical, inviting and fun, so we plunged right in and designed it ourselves," Ankeny said. "Neither of us is an artist, but we gathered ideas and came up with a plan using bright, clean colors such as blue, white and yellow along with a farm scene painted in the corner."

These two women, new vendors at the Corvallis Saturday Farmers' Market, have already made a name for themselves in just a few weeks

This booth sign above their canopy attracts hungry customers from afar to Beckmann's Bakery at the Jack London Square FM in Oakland, CA.

selling fresh salad greens and vegetables. Folks flocked to their charming booth filled with bouquets of purple lilacs tucked between baskets of produce lined up on sturdy cedar-slatted tables. Everything was snapped up in record time along with their "recipe of the week" cards featuring a zesty salad dressing. "People kept asking us what we'd be bringing the following week, and many asked for more salad dressing ideas. They said they'd look for our farm sign."

So, next time you're at Saturday Market in Corvallis, check out Cole Garden Farms and Out of the Blue Organics. You can't miss them — just look for the signs! ✿

Signs of Success

If you could generate 25 cents more with each customer, how much would that mean in sales? Signage is an effort that guarantees results!

Focus on features and benefits. There are three questions that most customers have: What is it? (Features). What is it good for? (Benefits). How much does it cost? (Price).

Let people know what the product is good for and how it's used. This is a service that the employees at Wal-Mart or Safeway often don't match.

Focus on the sizzle! Sell the romance, the story, the benefits. What is it about this product that will make the customer want it? Do creative listening with your customers to find what it is about this product that makes it special and unique. Is it a hard-to-find variety? Make it special, but still fact, not fiction.

Be truthful. Don't overwork superlatives such as "new" or "fresh". Instead of saying "fresh," say "fresh-picked this morning" (if it's true).

Vicki and Charlie Hertel, Vicki's Flowers and Produce, Cornelius, OR, are known for good corn. Their son promotes it at this Portland area market with a sign that proclaims, "Picked fresh this morning!"

What should your signs say to clinch the sale? Look for a benefit such as superlative taste (and give samples to prove it), or a savings in time, money, or stress. ✿

Making price signs ahead of time, in a way that allows you the flexibility to change price as market conditions change, will save you time and make you money.

Laminate your product signs, so they can be re-used. Use dry markers, grease pens or dry erase markers so prices and other information can be updated easily.

A green chalkboard along with several colors of chalk works well for posting a price list. Poster board and felt tip pens (green, red and blue are good colors) are also convenient. Print as neatly as possible.

Department store metal sign-holders with slots allow you to replace the signs as needed for product or price changes.

There are two schools of thought on the merchandising impact of pricing signs. One is to use consistent labeling in your display so it doesn't overpower the product. This can also help with branding. Signs are the same size, background color and style. They may include the farm name on the sign.

The other school of thought is to use card stock that contrasts pleasantly with the product, such as yellow for blueberries, or buff for other products. Use red or orange markers to do the lettering. Avoid stark black on white; white card stock shows dirt, and is glaring in bright sunlight. Use lots of signs! Blue, green or red markers are preferable to black. Color-code your signs, i.e., use neon red for tangelos, green for avocados, etc.

Product Information Signs

"Product signs at the booths are giving more information. There are more signs saying 'Organic' or 'No Chemicals' than there used to be. The signs are also including cooking and storage tips, and there's more identification than just a price tag. People are asking more questions than they used to ask. The population is getting more generations removed from the farm now and they're not as familiar with what things are at the market in their raw state. Market customers don't know how to prepare products so we're getting a lot of questions like: 'What is it?' and 'What can I do with it?'"

— Diane Eggert, Exec. Dir., FM Fed. of New York

Label everything. Research shows that market customers want to know where their food comes from. Post significant information about the product history, contents or growing/eating information. The more information your signs can convey, the better: Can this be eaten raw? How do you cook it? Is it a nutriceutical? What can they compare it to?

Information labels add value to your product and differentiate you from your neighbor. Again, you can create a uniform look by using the same color and style for these signs. It's possible to combine these signs with price signs by leaving a space in which to write price. As you do this, remember people read from left to right and top to bottom. By putting your price in the bottom right corner of an information sign, you have a better chance your customer will actually read the sign.

> "Right now we have a lot of Aconcogua peppers coming on, which is a very unusual variety, and we're making a sign saying they're very sweet and don't have bitter taste. The sign is a foot and a half tall, and we place it behind the display of vegetables with tear-off recipe sheets at the bottom of the sign. This works great with unusual vegetables. You need to let customers know how to use anything new."
> — Judy Medicus, Cat's Paw Organic Farm, Union Bridge, MD

If you are offering a new or unusual variety, label it and consider having a handout on how to prepare or store it. Especially label specialty items not readily identifiable: "Arugula adds zest to your salad!"

Be creative in your product signs. "Sweet, Ripe Kiwis," "Savoy Cabbage, Crisp & Crunchy," "Walnuts: Crack 'Em Yourself," etc.

Little, erasable, slate boards placed in baskets make attractive, point-of-sale signs.

> "Labels are easily made using stick-on labels designed for putting on computer disks. These are available at business supply stores along with a computer program to design the labels. Several hundred labels and (computer) program sell for under $10."
> — Robert I. (Bob) Neier, Extension agent, Wichita, KS

Here are more tips on what to say on signs:

✧ Product description: Let people know that your product is crunchy, tangy, tart or sweet. Use colorful language to describe your crop: "Slender and Tender Green Beans," "Crisp cabbage straight from the field," etc.

✧ Provide useful information: "Good for soups" or "2 lbs. of these apples make an 8-inch pie," etc.

✧ Guarantee product: "100% Happiness Guaranteed! Tell us next week what you think."

✧ Highlight what you are offering that day. Give USDA nutritional information with vitamin and mineral content.

✧ Give a brief history of the product, i.e., where it originated, how it came to this country, what traditional dishes use it.

The pamphlet, *Helpful Hints to Be Successful at the Kitchener Farmers' Market!* (Kitchener, Ontario) puts it this way, "Promote your positives! Make sure your signs promote the positive things about your product: home-grown, organic, hand-crafted, Grade 'A', additive-free, MSG free… Let people know if your product was picked fresh this morning by the headlights of your truck! It makes your product much more desirable than what's available in stores!"

One note of caution: Read your market rules before you work on your signs. Some markets discourage or outright ban certain phrases they feel are misleading to the customer.

One grower lists the transplants he sells each spring on a sheet of paper with color, size, name and days to produce. This way customers don't have to ask what it is. It frees him up to check out what they want and collect money. The sheet changes from week to week as one variety sells through and another becomes available. Because it's done on the computer, the changes are easy.

> "Variety names cause commotion. People like to know what they are buying. Some farms use computer labels with their signs and bright pictures. These are real eye catchers!"
> — Renae Best, Certified FMs of Sacramento, CA

"Since other vendors at the markets may be selling out-of-state products," explains Jim Beulke of Beulke Farms in Wanamingo, MN, "we are careful to have 'Locally Grown' or 'Minneapolis Grown' signs prominently displayed. Locally-grown is definitely a big pull at our markets."

Doug Cross of Canter-Berry Farm in Auburn, WA, uses signs to educate his customers. "What can you do with blueberry vinegar?" one sign reads and then gives the answer. "People will still ask," says Cross, "so you need to speak to them as well. Talking is just another way to get it across to them."

These ideas are really about one thing — differentiation. What makes your product different from the other products in the market? What makes your farm different from the other farms in the market? Why should the customer buy from you?

Directive signs. Don't be afraid to put out signs like: "Please do not squeeze the peaches." People respect this. You don't want to offend anyone but you do want to keep the produce looking good. Signs that educate as well as caution can be used: "We pick 'em ripe so you don't have to squeeze to find a good one," or "Unlike supermarket tomatoes, these are picked ripe and bruise easily. Please don't squeeze" or use a cartoon of the fruit or veggie with a face and legs and a speech balloon that says, "Please don't squeeze me, I bruise easily."

"Tree-ripe tastes so much better than brown bag-ripened fruit. Customers come back again and again! They really like it soft but not too soft — it's a challenge! Since some customers poke something and take the one next to it, however, our booth has signs: 'Very ripe, soft fruit,' 'Do not squeeze fruit!' or 'Squeeze my fruit and you get no fruit!'"
— Art Lange, Honey Crisp Farm, Reedley, CA

Farm Name or Brand Signs

Vance Corum

Branding is the art of connecting your name, farm name or product name with a value held by your customer base. For fresh product it's freshness, health, wholesomeness and possibly the "farm."

Jeff and Annie Main of Good Humus Produce, Capay Valley, CA, emphasize the personal nature of their connection with customers by using first names on a laminated, hand-colored sign hanging on the front of a display basket.

For value-added products it can be taste, comfort, gourmet treat or many other things. You want folks to think of these values when they think of you and to think of you when these values spring to mind — this takes repetition of your name many times over.

"Develop name recognition. A customer arrives at the farmers' market for the first time. What are they looking for? Something familiar! If they have seen or heard your sign or name before, they are more likely to visit your stand first. Use a large sign to identify yourself. We purchased a custom-made sign that mounts on the back of the pickup. As customers approach our stand, they can see our name in large letters behind the stand."
— Dan Haakenson, *The Small Commercial Gardener*

Merchandising Lemons

"Not posting item prices. Vendors often think they need to hide this information from other competitive vendors. You're not selling to competitors; you're selling to customers who are used to seeing prices posted in supermarkets."

"No signage!"

"Not posting farm name; people want to know who you are."

"Not taking enough change to the market."

"Not replacing an item if a consumer complains about the product quality!"

Display your farm name prominently so customers can find you and remember you easily. An attractive wooden sign with your farm name and logo painted on it, or a booth banner showing farm name and farm location, helps your customers come back to you week after week and makes it easier for them to refer friends to you. You can also utilize booth flags with symbols showing pictures or symbols of products offered at your booth.

For the same reason insist on setting up in the same location throughout the year. Make sure your farm sign is well above your display so customers can see it above a crowded booth.

Bags. Having your farm name and logo printed on bags is an excellent low-cost way to keep your image in the customers' eyes. Your state department of agriculture or farmers' market association may have a program for cooperative purchases of printed shopping bags.

Printed materials. Nutritional information, books on production, marketing order pamphlets, recipes and clipped articles (you might want to copy them for interested customers) all make your customers value your participation in the market.

Mailing lists. Building a customer mailing list provides vendors with an additional market for suitable products, particularly for those products with added value. Marketing through the mail provides an opportunity to capitalize on tourist traffic and infrequent or seasonal customers. Building a customer mailing list or data base is also an important step towards developing an internet marketing venue. Internet commerce is a relatively new form of direct marketing already being used by a small number of producers, especially those with non-perishable or preserved products.

With a gift pack on your table, you are more likely to spark people's interest in your mailing list. Have a clipboard sign-up sheet or provide slips of paper with lines for name, address, city, zip, phone and e-mail. Hold a drawing periodically for a small gift if you want to build a list quickly. Valicoff Fruit Company of Wapato, WA, signs up customers on their computer at the Pike Place Market and allows them to select gift packs to be sent on a specific date. They hand out free apples to "buy" customer time so that they can describe their website,

www.applesonline.com

to a good number of the market's nine million annual visitors.

Pulling It All Together

Encourage customers to remember you by having something unique in your stand! Make sure your stall has its own personality which will make it easier for shoppers to remember you and buy from you again next week!

Get out in front of your display and look at it critically from a customer's point-of-view. Everything should be clearly visible, alive and enticing. If it doesn't command attention, change it. Then come in and review your display close-up. Sort through each box and throw out the ugliest products that detract from the in-close visual impact.

Develop a focus

If your focus is herbs fill up your space with fresh herbs, dried herbs, herb plants in various size containers, potpourri and sachets.

From the lady bugs on the canopy to his backdrop, T-shirt & hat, YES! brand ladybugs prove that with a consistent, positive image you can even sell ladybugs to gardeners at the Beverly Hills FM, CA.

"One of the biggest draws to any one stand at a farmers' market is YOU! Those of you who come to the market neatly dressed with smiles and ready to greet your customers with helpfulness are going to have a great day! Others who won't make the effort to shave or comb their hair or even get up off the tailgate of their truck when a customer approaches are going to have a lousy day! The choice is yours. Remember the way you look and your attitude should add to the beauty of your stand!"

— Renae Best, Certified FMs of Sacramento, CA

Attire

"It's important to have not only the farm name, but your personal name displayed on your apron. People I don't even know come up to me in the markets and say 'Hi Donna!' They like to feel they're not buying from a stranger."

— Donna Sherrill, Sherrill Orchard, Arvin, CA

Incorporate yourself into your display. Customers are coming to see you, too — you are part of the show! Wear a colorful apron or farm-type hat, and put your farm name on your apron or cap. Wear a costume (overalls, funny hat, bright shirt, etc.) and wear a nametag, so people can walk up to you and say, "Hello, Joe!"

Dress to reflect your stand and model what you're selling. You might want to get a colorful tablecloth and matching aprons or t-shirts for your staff to wear. Everyone with Peacock Farms in Dinuba, CA, wears a blue T-shirt with a gold peacock emblem. Many personal items can reinforce your products, from cherry aprons to apple or pumpkin earrings.

Personalize with photos and bulletin boards

Garth Veerkamp

Display a picture album or a display board on a tripod with photos of your farm and family, the gardens and greenhouses, or even a bird's eye farm view to help personalize your business. Customers love to see where the products you sell come from. Have albums of your farm and products as well as

Poster board at Wilson Farms shows the printed paper bag, brochure and one-page handouts plus picture of the entire farm crew and a miniature farm stand made from popsicle sticks.

any articles that have been written about you and your product for customers to look though. While customers wait in line at your booth, you can talk with them about your farm and farming practices. This helps customers feel part of your operation!

And Smile! ✿

Sales & Promotion   7

*"These markets I go to, people just love you. It is a very gratifying experience. You're making
money, performing a good service, and they love you for it."*
— Greenmarket vendor, New York City

A lot of folks recoil at the concept of "selling."
We've been trained as a culture to view sales as
an arm-twisting, high-pressure, slick, less-than-truth-
ful occupation, whose practitioners get you to purchase things you neither need nor want — think selling iceboxes to Eskimos. No wonder we often hear,
"I want to be a farmer, not a salesman!" Most farmers
would rather do anything but something called sales.

Actually, sales is none of the above. Certainly
today's consumers are far too sophisticated and,
frankly, far too tired of sales pitches to have any of
this stuff "work" on them. In its simplest form, retail
selling is the art of serving the customer and exchanging your product for their money.

IT'S A PEOPLE BUSINESS

*"The most important tip I would give a farmer is
to treat your customers as if they were the most
important people on earth."*
— Butch Hollister, President, Connecticut Farmers'
Association for Retail Marketing

Butch says it all. Your customers ARE the most
important people on earth when you're in front of
them. You can grow the best product in the world or
have the best chutney recipe, but if no one buys them,
you're out of business. Your farm and business exist
only because of your customers.

The friendly interchange between farmer and customer is the heart and soul of a farmers' market. People
come to farmers' markets seeking a more personal
shopping experience than grocery stores offer, part of
which is getting to know the farmer who grows the
food. That relationship is what will bring them back
again and again.

*"People today are looking for a connection, not just
a quick change-maker. Have a nice comment for
everyone. You don't have to be a used-car salesperson, just be real. People are looking for a 'real' experience at the farmers' market; they're not looking for another cashier at the grocery store."*
— Gretchen Hoyt, Alm Hill Gardens, Everson, WA

The most popular growers are those who provide
entertaining conversation, a bit of education about
their produce and some indication of interest in their
customers, without getting too familiar. "You have to
like selling to people," explains former Greenmarket
director Barry Benepe. "You have to like to chat. You
can't be a wallflower."

Greet customers. Say, "Good morning or hello."
If someone is looking at your beets, say: "I just packed
those this morning. If you have any questions, let me
know." Don't be a pest but let them know you're there
and ready to help them. Each customer is an individual — some customers appreciate additional information, while others consider suggestions too
"sales-y" and just want to shop.

Project an image of wanting the customer's business. Eye-contact is also important. Don't wear sun-
glasses unless you absolutely have to. It helps to re-

member you're not just providing a head of lettuce; you're providing the farmers' market experience and yourself, a real life farmer.

"Don't just do farmers' markets 'for a living.' If you don't enjoy it, and you're tired, it'll show and customers will walk away."
— Cheryl Boden, West Union Gardens, Hillsboro, OR

Farmers who are not "people persons" may find they are not good in the market. The solution for many direct-marketing farm families is to assign the job of working with customers to the most outgoing family members. One farmer says, "I always take my mom — she's friendly and she loves to chat with customers."

Don't let shyness prevent you from becoming a topnotch customer service person. Simple human warmth, and the sincere desire to serve the customer are more valuable selling traits than having an extroverted personality. According to Vallejo, CA, market manager Brooks Kleim, "Two growers can have markedly different styles, yet be equally effective. The desire to serve the public seems most important."

"We have one farmer who sells hard-neck garlic, which doesn't have a lot of shelf life but has a great taste and comes off the stalk easily. He's convinced customers that it's a great product. He's a good sales person, engages every customer, and speaks to each customer as they come in: 'Hi I'm farmer so-and-so and I want you to taste my product.' Then he'll give them a fact sheet about his product. These are not new things but not everybody does them. If he's not in the market I'll have people asking where he is."
— Karen Durham, Mgr., Bellingham FM, WA

Putting on a Show vs. Hawking

"The secret to promoting the farmers' markets is to promote the market as an event, not just a place to buy food. Most customers are there not just for the vegetables but for the atmosphere and entertainment. When I sell pumpkins I dress up as a scarecrow and we call it the 'Kodak moment.' People climb up on the giant pumpkin and have their picture taken with me as the scarecrow. I started this picture taking 21 years ago and now the children of the children are coming, so now it's a tradition. I'm not out to sell pumpkins, but to entertain, so the children and their parents will have a favorable experience and want to come back to the farmers' markets."
— Bonnie Dehn, President, Central Minnesota Vegetable Growers

---

A Recipe for Selling at Farmers' Markets

—Reprinted with permission from *Growing For Market,* July 1993

Mark Cain of Dripping Springs Garden in Huntsville, AR, has found a simple way to dramatically increase flower sales at farmers markets: He makes bouquets on the spot, turning the sale into a sort of theater.

"It's something people love," he says. "We have people flocked around us all the time. People will stand there hour after hour and watch us make bouquets."

The flower business, part of a larger market garden, has sales of $300 to $500 a week from mid-May to the end of September, Mark says. He and his two partners make up a few buckets of bouquets before the market and those sell to people in a hurry. Most of the flowers are carried to market in separate buckets, to be assembled according to the customer's wishes.

A sign advertises custom-made bouquets for $2.50, $5 "and up." The size is not set by stem, but by feel. Mark knows what a $5 bouquet looks like, and its exact size varies by the relative value of the flowers he has to offer that day. "If somebody says they want a $5 or $10 bouquet, we'll add some of these dramatic flowers like Dutch iris or gladiolus," he says.

And when a customer orders a $10 bouquet, Mark will make it pretty spectacular. "Five people standing in line behind them will say 'I want one just like that,'" he says. ✿

In a Greenmarket a sprout seller says, "What would you like? One-half alfalfa, one-quarter sunflower, one-quarter clover," and he scoops it up, boom! boom! boom! and puts a lid on the container. He's a great showman! Put theater in your farmers' market!

Yet whether to "hawk" or not is a delicate question. It depends on how you do it. Shouts of: "Delicious and nutritious!" "Come and get your kohlrabi!" "Give peas a chance!" or (in the case of a farmer selling honey) "Pure and sweet, just like the ladies!"— at best, lend a festive, joyous mood to the market. At its worst, hawking creates a low-vibe, carnival atmosphere and makes customers feel uncomfortable. It can be especially irritating to vendors if loud and continuous all day. Use discretion if hawking is permitted at your market.

Serving a Crowd

"Quick service is a fine art. Customers are usually in a hurry and appreciate fast service, but you don't want to be too quick as to be rude. You could also lose add-on sales if you don't give the customers enough time."
— Chris "Marketman" Labeots, Baraboo, WI

Serve your customers quickly and give them your undivided attention. Try to develop a system for serving customers in the order they arrive. If you show your eagerness to serve the customer, they will forgive having to wait for a good product because they feel you're doing your best to serve them. Make eye contact with the next person in line to let them know you see them there.

If a line does build up, talk to the people, offer samples as well as pamphlets about your farm and products while they are waiting. Thank customers for waiting (acknowledge their wait). If long lines are chronic, hire more help during peak hours and consider other ways to speed up the checkout process.

"Be prepared for the rush. Sales during our first hour are often 1/2 -2/3 of the total sales for the day. We use up to six people, three cash boxes and three scales to keep customers flowing smoothly through our stand. Four people are selling while the other two are refilling boxes and providing customers with plastic bags."
— Dan Haakenson, *The Small Commercial Gardener*

Have enough courteous personnel to get the customers served as quickly as possible. People are especially harried if they're on their lunch hour. If you're doing a mid-day market, consider expediting sales by pre-packaging your products. This eliminates the need to weigh every item, thus saving time.

Keep busy

"Stay busy! Even if your stand is perfect, fiddle with something. Make customers feel like you're not waiting to pounce on them. Keeping busy also conveys prosperity and abundance and makes customers feel comfortable."
— Gretchen Hoyt, Alm Hill Gardens, Everson, WA

Don't just sit behind your booth and wait for people to come to you. Polish your apples, offer samples, freshen up the display, and replenish the supply. If you appear disinterested in your customers, they will be disinterested in you. When things slow down, use the time to restock the display, bag more produce, clean up around the table, and move excess cash from your apron or cashbox.

 ## IMPROVING YOUR SERVICE

"The best 'advertising' for the market is the simple, age-old, farmer-customer, one-to-one contact. The customers ask the farmers questions like: 'I'm growing such and such potatoes and having trouble with scab. What should I do for it?' And the grower might answer: 'We're organic and we do this and this and this,' and the person may walk away satisfied, even though there may not be an immediate sale. They'll be back to the market and probably to that individual vendor."
— Mary Carpenter, former Mgr., Dane County FM, Madison, WI

Learn to listen to your customers. If a customer is looking at the cabbage, you might ask, "Do you use sugar when you put up sauerkraut?" After the ensu-

Selling What the Customers Want

Jerry Rutiz, a grower of mixed vegetables near Arroyo Grande, CA, became one of the top salesmen at the Santa Monica Certified Farmers' Market by following the oldest principle known to marketers: giving the customers what they want. "If a customer is looking at my basil," says Rutiz, "I ask, 'Is there a variety you'd rather have?'... and they might answer, 'Yes, cinnamon basil,' or 'Yes, purple basil.'"

Rutiz looks for specialized varieties that the supermarkets don't carry, such as Chantnay carrots ("a sweeter, crispier carrot than you get in the grocery stores"), and Blue Lake greenbeans ("better tasting, more tender").

"I try to find out what the customers want and no one else in the market is growing," Rutiz continues. "I also ask the manager what is lacking in the market. Once she told me no one was growing brussels sprouts, so I grew that. This usually works for a few years, until other growers catch on and start growing it — then I try something else."

At least a third of Rutiz' prod-ucts are unusual crops, for which little growing literature is available. "Experimentation gives me a challenge. If I planted lettuce year after year, I'd get bored. I'm trying new things all the time and it keeps me interested.

"Most of my varieties are not available in the supermarkets, so I don't have to follow their prices," adds Rutiz. "I figure what it costs me to grow and market a product, and then I set my price. If I can't get the price it takes to make a profit, I stop growing it." ✿

---

ing discussion about canning, the customer may go home with 20 pounds of cabbage to make canned sauerkraut.

Take impromptu customer service polls. Ask questions like: "How can we serve you better?" "What else would you like to find at our booth? (new varieties)" Find out what customers like about you, what isn't working for them, and what else they wish you would offer. The customers' wish list is your key to new income opportunities.

Listen to yourself. Consider buying a tape recorder; turn it on during a busy hour to record your conversations with customers and play it back. Is your presentation repetitive? If so, vary it; look for other ways to communicate the same idea. Are you pleasant with customers? Are you honest and sincere? Listening to your conversations with customers helps you improve these things. Listen to other vendors and visit other booths in your market and also visit other markets.

Try to remember what each customer has purchased previously and ask them how they liked the product. You might even point customers to other vendors if you cannot provide a service for them.

Satisfy special requests if you have time. Carry large purchases out to the customer's car, especially for elderly customers.

To encourage large sales at your booth, let customers know that you will hold their purchases for them at your booth if they pay now. They can come back later to pick them up.

> "Always try to get a bag in the customer's hands. If they have a bag they will buy something."
> — Chris "Marketman" Labeots, Baraboo, WI.

Be Reliable

"One of our most successful growers is certified organic, which is a big draw for him and establishes a niche. He's been a long-time grower with the market and is very knowledgeable. He tells his customers all kinds of information about his products, how to use it, cook it, and his farming methods. He shares all this with the customers and they really like this — they like to know what they're getting. Another of our most successful growers has massive amounts and a great variety of fruits and vegetables throughout the season. He rents two spaces and sets up in an L-shape with two canopies with row after row of fruits and vegetables. He sells it by the bunch and by weight depending on what it is. Both of these growers are very picky about what they bring to market. The customers know the carrots will be sweet and that they'll always get great quality produce from them. The customers know they can trust them. In the six years I've been here, they've never missed a Saturday — customers rely on them."

— Barb Klimstra, Mgr., Redmond FM, WA

Selling your produce yourself is ideal — no one sells it like the farmer who grew it. But if you'd rather grow than sell, hire enthusiastic employees and have the same people represent you at the market. Be consistent and dependable.

Keep regular hours at the market. Bring enough product to stay the entire market. If people come to find you and you're not there, they go home disappointed. Part of keeping good relations with customers, as well as other vendors and market management, is not leaving the market before the posted time.

Guarantee Products

"Guarantee your produce. We bag all of our produce and include a written money-back guarantee. If a customer is dissatisfied in any way, they do not need to return the merchandise; they just mention what was wrong, and we replace it with fresh vegetables or return their money."

— Dan Haakenson, *The Small Commercial Gardener*

Have a "Satisfaction Guaranteed" policy for everything you sell. If there is a complaint, simply return the money or replace the purchase. Arguing will only lose you additional sales. It's a matter of establishing trust with the customers. If they know your product is quality they'll return week after week

Keep Customers Coming Back

"Find out what the customer wants and give it to them. Customers want different things. Some want mild onions, some strong. Some want low prices, others want to make a purchase as quickly as possible, regardless of price. We do our best to get to know our customers and cater to their individual needs. This policy goes beyond friendliness and courtesy. If a customer comes to our stand with vegetables from other vendors, we offer them a large bag with handles to carry it all to their car. We try to give them a reason to come back."

— Dan Haakenson, *The Small Commercial Gardener*

Better customer service is the key to repeat business. Serving your customer is always number one and comes ahead of everything else. Straightening the displays, talking on the telephone, or socializing with other farmers must take a back seat to serving customers.

It takes five times more energy and resources to get a first time customer than to keep one you already have. Your main goal is keeping customers returning to your stall week after week. Try to remember customers' names or at least something about them if you can. Be nice — give something extra, especially your long time customers. In any market five other sellers may be selling what you're selling and you need to give customers a reason to return to you.

"I'm a stickler on customer service — even if a person is walking by my booth, I teach my kids to say, 'Good morning! How are you today? Are you looking for anything special?'"

— Sue Goetz, Goetz Farms, Idaho Falls, ID

Helping the Customer Buy

"Every salesperson hears a prospect say, 'Your price is too high.' What the prospect is really saying is that their desire is too low. The key is to increase the prospect's desire rather than arguing about price. Establish the benefits, create more desire for them, and minimize the price compared to the benefits."

— Adapted from the *Master Salesmanship Newsletter*

Educate your customers about your products. The more the customers know about your product, how it is used, and what goes into producing it, the more they are willing to pay a premium for top quality. Look for the benefits in your product. Produce fresh from the field has a higher nutritional value. It keeps in the customers' homes longer. They know who grows it — you! They know how it's grown and they can ask you questions. Maybe you don't use preservatives in your product. Maybe your cider is fresh pressed yesterday and ozone preserved, rather than flash pasteurized.

Providing Product Information

Add value and service by helping customers choose the best produce for their needs. Suggest good ways of using produce and keeping it fresh. Give out simple recipes. Put together a mesh bag of all the ingredients customers need for a great salsa, with a recipe sheet enclosed. Encourage feedback from customers.

People are busy and not used to cooking and prepping food, so offer tips on what you grow. Answers questions concerning varieties, growing methods, storage, cooking, serving and nutrition to help sell your produce. The personal touch at farmers' markets is one of the crucial "edges" over the supermarkets.

Prepare to answer questions about your products such as when peak supplies are available or what quantities to buy for canning and freezing. Make sure your employees and family members are also well-informed.

Convey your enthusiasm about your products to your customers — it's catching. Instead of saying, "Lettuce, $1/head," you need to get into the ambiance of the product, giving the varietal name, like, "Winter Red Romaine," and describing how it's fresh that day and why it's premium quality.

Storing produce at home

"Customers' changing eating and shopping habits are a constant challenge for farmers' market sellers. People under 35 don't can (put food up for later) so much — very little — and they aren't familiar with a lot of our products. We hand out flyers and recipes so they know how to prepare our products. Garden beets or rhubarb, for example, are items they don't see in the store, so we have to educate them how to make a rhubarb pie and how to prepare and store it."
— Allen Shoemaker, Shoemaker's Home Place, Blackfoot, ID

GMOs & Farmers' Markets

— by Jeff Cole, Executive Director, Massachusetts Federation of Farmers' Markets

We see an increasing demand for organic produce in our state. More customers are willing to spend extra for pesticide-free fruits and vegetables. We're hearing more questions and concerns from customers regarding genetically-engineered crops ("genetically-modified organisms," or "GMOs"). Customers want to discuss the situation regarding GMOs, and they are asking the growers if the crops they grow have been genetically modified. Consumers' main concern with GMOs is: "What is it all about?" and

"Does it pose any danger to me?" Most growers are saying truthfully, "I don't know." Customers are often disappointed that the growers can't provide the information they want. Growers need to pay a lot more attention to this issue.

How can farmers educate themselves about GMOs? Probably the internet is the best place. Genetic engineering is such a quickly evolving, controversial subject that it takes an electronic media like the internet to keep up with it. The globalization of agriculture and increased food imports have affected farmers' markets, as well as all local direct agricultural marketing, as a double-edged sword. The farm-

ers' markets attract those individuals who have determined that they do not want to buy products from out of the country — they may feel there's a pesticide residue issue or they may look at it as support for local American agriculture. These people don't know where the products are coming from in the supermarkets, or what's been used in producing them, and they have difficulty getting answers to those questions in supermarkets. At the farmers' markets they're dealing directly with the producer and they can get answers to their questions and see the face of the person who grew it. ✿

Talk to customers about storage tips as you serve them: "Now put these peaches in a brown paper bag and they'll ready to eat in a few days." People waiting in line will also appreciate the information. Give suggestions: "Use this in two days; this will last all week; don't wash until ready to eat; place in water vertically in refrigerator." If you don't know, call your Cooperative Extension office and find out. They may even have handouts you can use.

"One night in a paper bag will help the peaches reach their peak flavor." Sign tells consumers how to further ripen stone fruit.

"Canning and freezing is quickly becoming a lost art. Because of the availability of fresh, frozen, and canned vegetables, young families have quit storing produce for themselves. Some of that is due to the hectic lifestyles we live, where canning might be too complicated or time consuming. However, much of the lack of interest is because of ignorance on exactly how to get the job done. If we take the time to educate our customers we will have the opportunity to provide the produce to them. We would recommend starting with salsa because of increased interest in this product."

— Dan Haakenson, *The Small Commercial Gardener*

Nutrition information

Know vitamin content and each product's health benefits. Carrots and winter squash are excellent sources of beta-carotene, the precursor of Vitamin A. Potatoes are an excellent source of potassium. [See Resources, Chapter 7]

Nutritional knowledge is basic to produce retail selling. You should be able to answer many customer questions concerning food or at least direct them to appropriate resources. Again, your Cooperative Extension office may have handouts you can use. Encourage your market manager to ask for Master Gardeners and Master Food Preservers to staff a booth at your market on a regular schedule.

Gardening information

Some of the most successful farmers we know are willing to share their "secrets" with their customers. This helps establish a relationship with customers. Let's face

it: Someone who has tried to grow any food crop at all is more appreciative of the time and effort it takes to bring food from the soil. These folks will no doubt be your most loyal and supportive customers.

"The idea is to get people to think about what they're buying in food. They can go to Wal-Mart and get a 6-pack of tomatoes and have no idea what they're getting. That tomato might do well in Indiana but can't grow in Maine. We sell seedlings at the market and we sell the customer a variety that will work for them locally, because those are the varieties we grow ourselves.

"We ask them what they want. If they want a tomato for canning, we sell them a heavy producer rather than an early-season variety. By asking them very specific questions about what they want in a tomato, we are providing a service the big supermarkets can't provide. They might want an oddball tomato like a red pear-shaped cherry tomato.

"We also answer their gardening questions like, 'My cucumber plants died — why?' I'll query them about their growing conditions and tell them why, so I'm their plant doctor. This kind of consumer education has to be done on a one-to-one basis with a local producer rather than mass-marketing, and when the whole farmers' market has this attitude, it makes a great impact on the customers so they want to keep coming back."

— Tom Roberts, Snakeroot Organic Farm, Pittsfield, ME

Recipes

"To promote new or unusual varieties, we hand out recipes at the market. The ones that work usually have only a few ingredients. No more than five or six ingredients max. Concentrate mostly on the few items you're trying to push that day, whatever you're trying to move — don't clutter the stand. And it's also best if all the ingredients are available at the market. People shopping at the market are looking for something they can fix that night. With our pesto recipe mix, if we put out a pesto recipe with our basil plants, I will triple sales. We put a pile on the table, and they read it right there on the spot and pick up some basil. It's so simple they can read it right there."

— Lisa Bloodnick, Bloodnick Family Farm, Apalachin, NY

One of the most productive ways to educate buyers and promote your products is with recipes. Especially for oversupply, in-season crops, print recipes. You can use recipes to teach inexperienced cooks how to use farm-fresh fruits and vegetables. Shoppers especially need suggestions on what to do with new or unusual items. Use fairly simple but unique recipes that use at least one or two of your products. Offer a variety of recipes and include your farm name and phone number on each one.

Format and print your recipes in the off-season so they'll be ready when the crop is. Consider having the printer pad up the recipes so that you can put them on a special display and customers can help themselves. Use the reverse side of the recipes for promotional information about your farm.

"Make sure recipes are available when there is something new. With pickling cucumbers, for example, which the farm generally sells three tons a week over a three week period, we give out our own recipes and get others from Extension Service. The internet is another source for recipes. We found over 2000 recipes for fava beans by searching the web."

— Bob & Pat Meyer, Stoney Plains Farm, Tenino, WA

Everyone becomes stagnant with meal repetition and new ideas are exciting. If customers don't know how to use spaghetti squash, give them recipes and they're hooked. They may not necessarily buy this week, but if they go home with a recipe, they probably will buy next week.

Looking for innovative ways to use your product in recipes? Have recipe contests from the customers. Or work with a chef to develop new uses for your products and to find out what other products the chefs or consumers can use. The mesclun mix craze got started because Warren Weber, a California Bay Area farmer, worked with local chefs to find innovative ways to use the new salad greens available.

Consider the time of the year. Concentrate on quick and easy recipes — nothing too complex that keeps customers in hot kitchens in July. Better yet, use recipes that call for grilling the vegetables or roasting over coals.

Sampling

"I consider sampling to be the most effective marketing method available."

— Jay Conrad Levinson, *Guerrilla Marketing*

If your produce is suitable, offer samples. A taste is worth a thousand words, and many of those who try will buy.

"People tend to graze through the market before they buy and they make decisions based on what tastes good. Farmers are selling themselves short if they don't give out samples."

— Mary Lou Weiss, Mgr., Torrance FM, CA

Product sampling is especially important for introducing new products or varieties, especially ones that taste great but are sometimes hard to sell. People don't often buy unfamiliar products. Over sugar snap peas, one grower had a sign that read: "Free sample — taste one. Edible pods — crisp, sweet. Eat the whole pea!" People expected them to be tough, because they're big like green beans. But after sampling them, the customers were surprised to find they're tender and stringless.

Sampling is not only the best advertising you can do; it's also inexpensive. Hand a customer a small paper cup of cider, and they'll probably want to purchase a gallon — that's cheap advertising! Lots of growers hesitate to give away free products, but if giving away $50 in samples makes the difference between a $300 day and a $900 day, it's worth it.

Over a display of apples with nine different varieties, for example, you might set out a sign, "Please Sample." This makes it easy for customers to find out which one they want.

Continued on page 86...

Selling to Ethnic Groups

An interview with Steve Salts, truck farmer and author of *Around the World at Farmers' Market: A Handbook for Small-scale Grower-Marketers of Ethnic and Heirloom Vegetables, Fruits, and Herbs.* [See Resources, Chapter 2]

Q: Aren't ethnic groups generally a lower-priced market compared to the Anglo-American customer? Aren't they used to buying at open-air markets at comparatively low prices?

Salts: Yes and no. It's certainly not a top dollar market like selling to trendy yuppies, but it's definitely not bottom either. You've just got to be prepared to haggle. Most American farmers don't like haggling — it runs against most Americans' grain. Yet most ethnic groups just don't like having a set price. I usually set a price at high-middle, and I'm willing to dicker down to middle or low-middle.

I tried an experiment at a farmers' market once. I set a price ridiculously low on some cucumbers and yard-long beans, almost giving them away. Some ethnic customers still wouldn't buy it, because I wouldn't dicker! The next week I set the price high, and they dickered down and ended up paying twice what they would have gotten it for the week before! It's not so much the price they get it for, it just runs against their cultural grain to pay the asking price.

Q: What are some of the advantages of selling to ethnic customers?

Salts: Customer loyalty, volume, and consistency. Once ethnic customers find that you've got what they want, and that you are nice to them and cater to their culture, they will come back week after week, and year after year. Selling to ethnic folks may not be for everyone. You have to enjoy dealing with peoples from other cultures.

I've found ethnic groups to be a great niche market for me because there's very little competition. I may not be getting the price that some other sellers are getting selling to the yuppies, but my ethnic customers are a lot more stable. Yuppies can be very trendy, but the Chinese, the Indians, the Arabs and the Vietnamese have been buying the same vegetables for thousands of years. Ethnic customers aren't so much into food preservation, like canning — but many do make preserves such as kimchee or pesto or chutneys or pickles that take large quantities of produce and herbs. They also eat a lot more fruits and vegetables and they're a lot more accustomed to cooking from scratch. Even college students from other countries cook from scratch, believe it or not — it's not all phoned-in pizza. And then there are traditional banquets for holidays and weddings and the like that take LOTS of traditional veggies.

The tradition in their countries is shopping at open-air markets. They don't want their produce all wrapped up in plastic.

Q: What's most important in selling to ethnic groups?

Salts: You not only need to grow the crops the peoples are used to, but to cater to their cultures. The social part is VERY important. You're selling a service and experience — not just veggies. It's the ultimate relationship marketing. We try to offer a social experience to our ethnic customers — greeting them in their native languages, asking their advice on ethnic cuisine, learning something of the geography and customs of their homelands, etc. I try to find out what their holidays are and have special items in stock when their holidays are coming.

Basically, just talk with them: "Are you from India? What part of India?" They're usually surprised anyone is asking them such a question, but they might say, "Andhra Pradesh." And I say, "Hyderabad?" And they just about fall on the ground: "Oh, you used to live in India?" Well no … but it all boils down to showing an interest in their culture.

A supermarket COULD try to compete with us on the product front — but can you see them doing it better on the social front? We have such an advantage! Small market grower-marketers can stop griping about unfair competition from factory farms. We just have to connect with customers who want to buy the "goods" in which we have a great comparative advantage. And those goods are not only great products but service and relationships.

Q: Yuppies are getting to be a difficult market to sell to. They purchase small amounts, and they want everything prepared. I've heard that ethnic peoples are the future of farmers' markets.

Salts: Well, we do sell to so-called yuppies also, and value their patronage, though it's true that they rarely buy much quantity. They like exotic produce but usually buy one of this and can you give me just a pinch of that. We find that so-called ethnic customers buy and use fresh veggies greatly in excess of their percentage of the total farmers' market customers — and patronize farmers' markets more than do Anglo-Americans. Perhaps 50-60% of our current farmers' market customers are ethnic, and the proportion of ethnics in the population is growing rapidly. If present trends continue, the Census Bureau projects that non-Hispanic European Americans will be a minority by the year 2050, with the nation 25% Hispanic, 10-12% Asian-Pacific Islander and 16% black.

Q: So your book gets into some of the basic ethnic languages a farmers' market seller might learn?

Salts: Yes. I will have a glossary in about 20 languages for elementary farmers' market terms such as greetings, "yes," "no," numbers,

Customers are 80% Asian and 10% Indian in Milpitas, CA.

etc. It doesn't include all 2500 languages of the world, but some of the basic ones like Arabic, Spanish, Portuguese, Korean, Chinese and Vietnamese.

Q: Could you tell us a little about your own market mix?

Salts: Our marketing is approximately 50-60% farmers' markets, 20-25% ethnic and vegetarian restaurants, 15-20% CSA, 5-10% on-farm sales, booths at festivals, etc. Our product mix is perhaps 25-30% "standard" veggies (even Chinese like sweet corn); 25-35% "heirloom" old-fashioned varieties (tomatoes, sweet sorghum, wild blackberries, etc.), and 50% ethnic veggies, mostly Oriental but with generous and increasing dashes of Middle Eastern, Italian, East European, Asian Indian, Southeast Asian, Mexican, etc.

We try to offer both products and services that the Super Megamarkets and Fast Food International can't. We offer very fresh, carefully harvested, great-tasting, old-fashioned or ethnic produce,

often with "weird" appearance or short shelf lives, served up with a generous side-dish of advice, multicultural socializing, and just plain old personal friendship.

Our heirloom veggies tend to draw a lot of vegetarians, gourmet hobby cooks, older people ("Why my grandma used to grow that in her garden! I haven't seen that in years!"), and curious passers-by ("What IS that!?"). Actually, heirloom veggies could be considered just another sort of "ethnic" veggies — the veggies of our own fast-vanishing traditional American culture.

People are often loathe to buy "weird" veggies at first, so we give away a lot of free samples, plus recipes or suggestions for use. We are building a steadily growing clientele of "addicts." "Why you WERE right! That crazy fuzzy tomato / red okra / guinea bean / (or whatever!) tasted great! Can I get three pounds this week?" ✿

Continued from page 83

One farmer in Vermont who sells many melons has samples of each variety and explains the differences, soil conditions, etc., and how hard it is to get sweet melons to ripen. He sells around $1000 worth of melons in the three weeks of the season.

Donna Sherrill provides easy self-serve juice samples in Studio City FM, CA.

Cooperative Extension and the Auburn FM, CA, sponsored this potato tasting.

In traditional food merchandising there is an adage that for every 10% of oversupply, prices need to be lowered 30% to move the product. So rather than creating an oversupply in the market, give some excess produce away as free samples.

> "We slice up tomatoes and put out tasters, and start hawking our slogans: 'When was the last time you had a really great tomato?,' 'Taste the Farmhouse difference,' and so on. We put on a show!"
> — Walter Ross, Farmhouse Tomatoes, Inc., Lake Worth, FL

Sampling slows shoppers down, giving you time to talk with them, which usually results in a sale.

Sampling to sustain a price

> "A lot of fruit looks alike and most people can't tell how it tastes just by looking at it. Most customers don't want to pay $2 or $3 a pound for tree-ripe fruit, but once they taste it they can't resist."
> — Art Lange, Honey Crisp Farm, Reedley, CA

> "Sampling is critical, not just for new items, but for items which taste great but are expensive or may not look good. Let's say you've got really sweet carrots, for instance, that you have to charge a high price for because they have less yield, expensive seeds or they're harder to grow. Without sampling these great carrots, the customers won't know it's worth paying the extra money. Some of the really ugly products can taste delicious. Calico corn, for example, has a white and yellow appearance and it looks like there's something wrong with it, yet it's the most delicious corn."
> — Donna Sherrill, Sherrill Farms, Arvina, CA

At Full Circle Organic Farm, we were one of the first to bring heirloom tomatoes to market. Radiator Charlie's Mortgage Lifter was one of our signature tomatoes. Charlie's are a huge, pink-red slicer, but they aren't perfectly round, and they have a tendency to shoulder crack. It's a funny-looking tomato to a public used to perfectly round, red orbs designed for long-distance shipping. We sampled the Charlie's for the first couple of months the first year we brought them to market and sold out from then on. We even sponsored and set up a tomato tasting of all our heirloom varieties for the entire market. Everyone's tomato sales went up. We regularly sold our heirloom tomatoes for $1.25-$1.50 per pound when conventional tomato prices had dropped to 69 cents per pound.

Sampling how-to

Provide sliced vegetables, melons, or fresh berries in clean, covered dishes and provide toothpicks, napkins and spoons or wooden ice cream sticks. Have a trash can available. Don't cut up too much fruit or vegetables at one time so as to keep them fresh. If you are cutting samples in the market, keep a bucket of sanitizing water to rinse your knife in and to wipe fruit with before you cut it.

Invite customers to sample; people are far more inclined to try it if it is offered to them. If you are going to sell a lot of one product, you'll need some extra helpers. Get them out in the crowds to hand out samples; that will really bring them in: "Taste this!"

Check with the market manager and/or your county health department for health regulations concerning sampling. The most common regulations are that samples be prepared in a health department certified kitchen, that they remain covered, and that perishables be kept iced. You are usually required, for example, to give samples on a disposable utensil without anyone's hands touching the sample, and you may be required to wear food service gloves and cover your hair. All this may seem like extra trouble but samples make sales!

Up the Sale

Have tie-in merchandise next to your produce. If someone buys salad mix or lettuce, ask if there's a dressing they'd like with it. Ask what they are serving for the meal and suggest a dressing.

Have introductory offers for new products: "Free arugula with purchase of zucchini."

Joe Smith, a farmer in Denton, MD, has a great idea. When looking to see what will be ripe for market the next day, he might find just one pea that's ready, but he'll pick that one pea and take it. He'll post it prominently in his booth with a sign: "Ready Next Week!" This tantalizes customers and they come flocking to his booth next week to purchase the fresh-picked peas.

Write down addresses from the checks you take or invite guests to sign a guest book for a mailing list. Send flyers before next season to remind faithful customers when and where you'll be next season.

Plan ahead and help your customers do likewise. Let them know what items are coming, and which varieties are best for home canning or freezing. Post a harvest schedule in your stall.

Finally, as customers leave, express your sincere thanks.

Handling Complaints

"Take breaks during the day. This is necessary to keep you cheerful and fresh with customers. One woman was furious; the market manager had told her I had berries but I had run out. She was yelling and very upset. I said, 'Oh, you must feel bad having come all this way,' and she smoothed right out. I turned her onto a neighboring vendor who had berries and she's been my customer ever since."
— Gretchen Hoyt, Alm Hill Gardens, Everson, WA

Don't argue with customers. Your object at the market is to sell, not to win debates. If a customer complains about bad produce, offer to give their money back or a replacement. It pays off in the long run by developing loyal, long-time customers.

Listen to customers carefully. Allow them to blow off steam. Show empathy and concern; show that you value their business. Ask questions to obtain details and solicit solutions. The fault may be the customer's; perhaps the customer neglected to cool the produce properly. Give them another dozen ears of corn anyway, saying, "Try to get it into the refrigerator right away, and if you eat it within a day, I think you'll be more satisfied."

Customer Service Lemons

"A passive, 'take-it-or-leave-it' attitude. When I see a vendor reading the paper, it is never a surprise that he/she does not make many sales. I wonder why they bother coming to market at all."

"Complaining about others' successful businesses, while ignoring their own. Be a pro! Don't berate or belittle the competition. If you can't sell your produce on its own merits, you probably don't have quality products. Customers pick up on this and go to your competition."

"Assuming customers know how to care for and cook with fresh foods."

"Taking personal or business problems to the market. You've always got to put on a smile for the customer and make them feel you're glad to see them." ✿

PROMOTION

Product Literature

"We give customers a handout sheet with every bunch of flowers we sell that includes tips for handling and care of the flowers. Our flowers are fresh, carefully wrapped and guaranteed to last a week — a rose from the florist can be eight days old."

— Chet Anderson, The Fresh Herb Company, Longmont, CO

Learn to use desktop publishing software and techniques. In the slow season you can make up educational brochures and flyers on your computer. Contents for such hand-outs might include:

✧ An explanation of product history and nutritional values of assorted produce;

✧ Special recipes for low salt, low fat, low sugar, low cholesterol, or high fiber foods;

✧ Your farm story to get the consumer more in touch with what you and your farm are "all about;"

✧ Advantages of buying locally-produced food; and

✧ A "position paper" if you're using special farm practices you want to advertise. Such an information sheet could save your vocal chords, considering the oft-repeated refrain of "Is this sprayed?" heard at a typical urban market.

"The farmers' markets hold great potential for people to learn about farming," Gretchen Hoyt says, "The only thing most people know about pesticides is 60 Minutes and the Alar scare, and you can tell the consumer exactly what you're doing with your product. We at the farmers' markets are the only farmers they might meet, so we are the representatives for agriculture. The farmers' markets give us a chance to talk face-to-face with customers and let them know the issues we're dealing with. Let them know we provide 40 jobs for every person on the farm, we keep the land open for future generations, and that we produce good, healthy, high-quality food. Family farms are in trouble, and we need to show the people that agriculture is not the bad guy, that without agriculture around the cities we will lose all the beautiful scenery. Get involved in your market politically. In many markets we're finding that spaces formerly reserved for farmers have been given to dumpsters or produce broker coolers."

Newsletters

Publish a weekly one-page newsletter to let customers know what's in season, recipe contests, and other events. Perhaps quarterly you can do a more substantial one with pieces on the farm, growing conditions, kids' games, etc.

Brochures

— Dan Haakenson, *The Small Commercial Gardener*

Brochures can accomplish many things for you. We recommend the following guidelines:

✧ Differentiate yourself and your operation. Capitalize on who you are, because customers like to know something about the farmer that grows their food. Many have lost contact with rural life and this is one small way to bring it back. Explain any special things you do to enhance the quality of your operation, how you are different from other growers.

✧ Personalize your operation. Include a picture of your family and a short biographical sketch.

✧ Provide your market schedule. We have a rather complicated schedule, so we include it in the brochure for permanent reference.

✧ Introduce prices. If your pricing will be fairly stable, include base prices for all major vegetables with a short discussion on pricing policies.

✧ Establish a guarantee with a strongly worded promise to replace any produce your customers find unacceptable. ✿

THE NEW FARMERS' MARKET

"Newsletters provide a different service to your customer, providing current information and ideas. Write the majority of the copy prior to the beginning of the season. Then, during "crazy season," supplement the prepared material with current information. Each season is unique and brings new challenges. A timely article will help bring credibility to your newsletter. Keep the copy light. Try to entertain as well as inform your customers."

— Dan Haakenson, *The Small Commercial Gardener*

Local Media

Newspapers. Submit educational articles to your local newspaper food editor. A well-written, factual article is frequently welcomed by short-staffed local papers, and may be picked up from there by larger regional papers.

Public speaking. Present educational slide shows at local service and garden clubs. As an expert in your field, you will be consulted by all kinds of people — and perhaps even be invited to speak at the local junior college on your chosen topic. These contacts will bring some of your best customers.

Television. Many local morning and noon news shows are looking for local color to highlight the seasons. Let them know you are available to demonstrate a recipe on television or answer questions about fruits and vegetables. Local-access cable channels are another video venue.

Paid advertising. While most promotion can be done better with effort than dollars, it may be worthwhile to place paid advertising in a popular, local publication.

"A change that has been very effective for us is the format of our ad in our weekly Pennysaver. Instead of laying out an ad, I write a letter addressing it 'Dear Friends.' We have never had as good a response to a written ad as we have this type."

— Peggy Frederick, Strawberry Valley Farm, Whitney Point, NY

This laminated newspaper article hanging in the stall of Rossi Farms, Portland, OR, lets passersby know their farm is newsworthy.

E-mail

Put your e-mail address on your business cards, flyers, recipes, and newsletters. E-mail is great for answering customers' questions and handling correspondence. Typical e-mail communications might be to ask you if you will be at the market next week, what you will be bringing to market, or to request a specific item or quantity like a bushel of pickles for canning. E-mail is an inexpensive and easy alternative to the telephone. If your market also has a website, make sure your e-mail address is listed on their list of vendors, so customers can contact you.

Encourage customers to e-mail orders before coming to the market. You can pre-bag their orders so they don't have to worry about getting to the market early to find products they want. This also works when customers need larger quantities for special occasions. Services like this help create loyal customers and enhance sales.

Electronic commerce is a tool for selling to chefs or wholesalers, who might welcome the ability to order large quantities using e-mail.

Tell Your Story

"What's the story you want to tell? If you stand for something, relate that to the customer. Write down in 25 words and positive terms how your stall or farm is different from your competitors.

"Make some flyers describing your farm and produce to put on windshields and in store windows a day or so before the market opens. This will spread your name around and encourage customers to come to your booth. Develop weekly flyers to put in each bag of produce with recipes and news about your upcoming crops.

"Put the days and hours of your market on your business card and get in the habit of handing it out, 'Here take a card.'

Eatwell Farm: Going Online to Promote Booth Sales

Located on 17 leased acres between Davis and Winters, CA, Eatwell Farms produces 12 acres of over 50 kinds of market vegetables, five acres of small fruit, and the farm's specialty, 20-30 heirloom tomato varieties, sparking the farm's nickname of "tomato wonderland."

According to co-owner Nigel Walker, about half of the farm's produce is marketed through a 2 1/2-year-old community supported agriculture (CSA) project; about 40 percent through the San Francisco Ferry Plaza Farmers' Market (a two hour drive from the farm); and about 10 percent through independent grocery stores and natural food stores in San Francisco.

Like many other growers, Walker used a computer for basic business purposes of accounting, making price signs, and a spread sheet for harvest records until a few years ago. In 1995 Walker set up a simple website for the farm. The site carried information about the farm and the varieties of produce grown. They posted the farm website address at the Ferry Plaza Farmers' Market, where it created an immediate stir amongst customers and led to several newspaper articles and a spot on CNN. "Back in '95 very few farmers had websites," Walker explains. "They found an angle in us as the little podunk farmers who had a website."

Beyond the immediate publicity value, however, Walker found an ongoing practical use of the internet in the fact that a high percentage of his Bay Area farmers' market customers had internet e-mail, and he saw this as an inexpensive way to keep in regular contact with his customers.

Occasionally, regular customers send weekly e-mail orders to the farm and then find it pre-bagged and waiting for them at the market — this saves them from having to come early to purchase items that usually sell out. "In addition, customers can e-mail special requests like: 'I'm having a get-together next week for some friends, could you please bring me four bunches of lavender and six boxes of tomatoes,'" says Walker. ✿

"Make your product available to customers on off-market days as well. Provide customers with a phone number and address so they can contact you and arrange for pick up at your farm or business on days the market is not open."

— *FM Forum,* FM Federation of New York, Summer 2000

Finally, if your best efforts at selling are being scuttled by poor market management, i.e., if your manager is not presenting or displaying the market in the best possible way, talk to him or her. If things don't change, find a new market. ✿

PORTRAIT OF A MARKET

8

"Market is community. People get to know you and you get to be trusted."
— Ali Edwards, Fan Tan Farm, Santa Cruz

— *A Case Study of The Davis Farmers' Market: Connecting Farms and Community,* by Heather Podoll. UC Sustainable Agriculture Research and Education Program. Part of a *Study on Retail Farmers' Markets and Rural Development* in conjunction with researchers at Cornell University and Iowa State University; funded by the Fund for Rural America, USDA.

The Davis Farmers' Market is one of the most well-known and successful farmers' markets in the state of California. The involvement of numerous community organizations, businesses, and individuals has established the Davis Farmers' Market (DFM) as a center of local community life and culture. The ambiance of this market attracts large numbers of local families and students, as well as visitors from all around California, the U.S., and abroad. The market serves as a community gathering place, tourist destination, and source for a wide range of direct-marketed fresh vegetables, fruits, flowers, prepared foods and crafts. As such, the DFM provides a unique forum that has fostered the development of many small businesses and has played an important role in the larger business community of Davis.

The city of Davis is a university community known for its strong commitment to progressive and innovative ideas, as well as a dynamic, involved citizenship. The University of California at Davis (UCD), with more than 25,000 students, plays a prominent role in this city of 56,000 people. In addition to contributing a diverse population of students, faculty and staff from around the world, UCD also hosts a wide range of educational and research programs, university organizations, and outreach programs. The wealth of resources within the city of Davis and the university community have been important in the development of the Davis Farmers' Market.

HISTORY OF THE MARKET

The Davis Farmers' Market was started in 1975 by a small group of local organic farmers and community members. During its first year of operation, the market hosted about ten local growers. The DFM was created with the objective to support local farmers while providing consumers with fresh, locally grown produce. By facilitating direct sales from grower to consumer, DFM founders saw an opportunity to support small and beginning growers, who were often unable to compete in conventional marketing arenas. The fee scale for DFM vendors was set as a percentage of gross sales, reflecting the original intention that small growers would not be prohibited from participating in the market.

The creation of the DFM was closely connected with the establishment of the Davis Food Co-op, an early alliance that provided stability to the new market. For about six months after the farmers' market first opened, DFM organizers, who were also operating the Davis Food Co-Op, offered to buy all remaining produce from farmers' market vendors after the market closed. Ann Evans, one of the DFM founders who later served as mayor of Davis, explains that through this "insurance program," market organizers "were able to entice farmers to come to the market while the clientele was building." This was important for helping to create a consistent market for vendors and customers during the critical time when community awareness of the market was first developing.

Jeff and Annie Main are two of the original market founders who still sell at the DFM today. When they started their organic farming business on three-quarters of an acre in 1975, they quickly found that wholesale markets were virtually inaccessible to small farmers like themselves. However, the Davis Farmers' Market offered them a consistent marketplace where they could sell their produce at retail prices. In the beginning, they often had to deal with low volumes and variable product availability — typical challenges for small, beginning farmers. Unlike other marketing outlets, the DFM could easily tolerate fluctuations in quantity and variety as Jeff and Annie "grew their business" from the bottom up, and learned the skills they needed along the way. Being part of the DFM also helped them to develop the network of support they needed to survive in a young industry (organic

farming) with little agricultural experience. Jeff and Annie's original vision of connecting local agriculture with local consumers still guides their farming goals and strategies. Today, their farming business, Good Humus Produce, remains one of the mainstays of the DFM.

The Market Today

A young farmer starting out would find a very different setting at the DFM today than the market's environment of 25 years ago. The DFM is now among the largest farmers' markets in California, with an average of 85 vendors every Saturday. Over the course of the year, 180 different vendors attend the market. While many of the vendors are still local, others come from all across Northern California, and even as far away as Oxnard and Santa Maria in southern California. Operating year-round, the Saturday market attracts 5,000 to 7,000 people each week, and up to 10,000 during special events. Annual gross sales exceed $1.5 million. The market is governed by the Davis Farmers' Market Association, a non-profit organization, through an 11-member board of directors consisting of eight farmer-vendors, one non-agricultural vendor, and two community representatives.

The DFM still operates in its original Central Park location, but many improvements have been made to the park, enhancing the environment of the market. In 1993, a covered structure was built by the City of Davis to house a large portion of the market's vendors, and make year-round operation more viable. The city's master plan for the park guided the construction of a large deck adjacent to the structure, which was funded by the Davis Farmers' Market Association.

Structure built by the City of Davis alongside Central Park.

Randii MacNear

BECOMING A CORNERSTONE OF THE COMMUNITY

Randii MacNear, manager of the Davis Farmers' Market, was hired in 1978. Over the years her role as manager has been shaped by the market's board of directors to facilitate a central objective of the DFM: creating a network of community support and participation in the farmers' market. In the beginning, Randii saw that the DFM was perceived by the local business community as a vehicle to primarily benefit farmers living outside the city, without providing direct benefits to the city itself. To overcome this perception and to cultivate a broad level of local support for the market, she and the market's board set out to develop relationships that would establish the market as a vital part of the community. This has been the central theme around which the DFM has developed. In fact, the DFM has become such an important part of the Davis community that today it is difficult for many people to imagine the community without the market. Randii explains, "Early on, I got involved with promoting the community through the farmers' market. Now, the farmers' market has really become a showcase of the community — the shining star of Davis; it exemplifies what the community really is."

Randii's dedicated effort to connect the DFM to community activities and organizations in every possible capacity has involved participation in numerous civic and educational organizations. Randii has served as president of the Davis Chamber of Commerce, and she has been deeply involved with the Downtown Davis Business Association, various UCD activities, the community's International House, the Davis Joint Unified School District, the California Department of Health Services, the Children's Fruit and Vegetable Five-a-Day Campaign, and many others. She has also played a leadership role in the statewide California Federation of Certified Farmers' Markets, and she regularly gives presentations at conferences and meetings throughout the state. In all of these activities, Randii has established relationships between a wide range of organizations and the DFM, gathering ideas and opportunities for promoting the DFM locally, regionally, and statewide.

Building a sense of local community ownership of the DFM has also been an important goal. An area of the market open to community groups and political organizations and candidates has given a strong voice to local politics and community issues. Over 500 non-profit organizations do outreach at the market each year, helping to raise an estimated $1 million that goes back into the community. School and community group performances are often the entertainment at the market during special events. Monthly market events, typically co-hosted with community and business organizations, the City of Davis and groups from UCD, bring together local non-profits, county-wide agricultural groups, local schools, farmers and citizens. Randii explains that the 1999 Fall Festival, one of the market's largest events, involved participation by at least 25 different community groups. Activities included the Soroptimists running a pumpkin patch for children, 4-H groups showing their animals, the Davis High School Key Club selling pies, the UCD Chemistry Club giving demonstrations, the UCD Raptor Center displaying owls, the Davis Science Center presenting hands-on exhibits, and many more. Through these events, the market serves as a showcase where community organizations can promote themselves, conduct fundraising, and connect with the larger community.

Weekly events at the market, such as cooking demonstrations with food tasting and free recipes, provide education for the community about nutrition, diet, health and agriculture. Institutions in the area related to these issues are brought together to promote these events. Randii also promotes the DFM through local schools by conducting workshops on nutrition and agriculture in high school home economics classes and elementary science classes. Student interns from the California State University Sacramento Nutrition Program help with demonstrations at the market and with nutrition programs in schools.

Another way the market gives back to the community directly is through donations of food by the farmers to emergency assistance programs. Randii estimates that 95% of the fresh fruits and vegetables served at community meals and sent to the Yolo County Short Term Emergency Aid Closet come from DFM farmers.

Tourism and Impacts on Davis Businesses

In addition to serving local residents, the Davis Farmers' Market is an important tourist attraction, bringing visitors into Davis from other parts of the state and beyond. The DFM has worked hard to establish itself as the biggest "event" in Davis, a defining institution of the community which is recognized throughout the region. With this distinction, the DFM promotes itself as a destination for the many visitors who come to Davis, particularly those connected to the university. Through conferences, symposia, and other events on campus, UCD plays a particularly important role in drawing out-of-state and international visitors to the city. These visitors represent an important market that the market association targets through relationships with various UCD programs and planning committees. The attraction of the DFM helps to provide a "bridge" for these visitors into downtown Davis.

Promoting the DFM as a tourist destination has become a priority of the market association, and has begun to play a role in shaping the marketing goals and strategies of some market vendors. Through her work with the Davis Chamber of Commerce, the Downtown Davis Business Association, and UCD, Randii is involved with several committees that aim to promote tourism and attract visitors to Davis. She works with these organizations to host events and prepare marketing and tourism brochures that promote the DFM, among other aspects of the Davis business community.

Other Davis businesses reap the benefits of increased visitor traffic through the city, as well as the positive image the DFM reflects on all of Davis. DFM has tried to be very sensitive to the needs and concerns of the downtown businesses. As an active member of the Downtown Davis Business Association, the DFM promotes downtown businesses throughout the year and especially at certain market events. For example, one market day in June is dedicated to "Chamber Day," in which the Davis Chamber of Commerce sets up a large business fair in Central Park with over 100 displays by local businesses and chamber organizations.

Contribution to Growth of Vendors' Businesses

Aside from the contributions that are made to community development, attracting a large number of people each week to the farmers' market has a fundamentally pragmatic purpose: providing a customer base for market vendors. Certainly, one of the most important functions of the Davis Farmers' Market is to support the success and development of the agricultural, craft and food businesses that sell at the market. The DFM fosters the development and expansion of vendors' businesses in a number of ways.

Beyond the level of individual sales to tourists and community members, Randii tries to help agricultural vendors make connections with local restaurants and grocery stores which are interested in buying fruits and vegetables directly from farmers. She frequently invites chefs from local restaurants to participate in cooking demonstrations at the market, giving them an opportunity to test produce from the market in their recipes while promoting their restaurants to the market customers.

Even within the market, business relationships are formed between vendors. For instance, some of the restaurants and prepared food businesses that sell at the market purchase ingredients from other market vendors.

Panna Putnam often buys vegetables and herbs from farmers at the market to use in the samosas and other Indian food that she sells. Panna started her business, Samosas to Go, at the DFM. Inspired by the idea of marketing Indian food to American tastes, she felt the Davis Farmers' Market would be the perfect setting for her new business. Building on the infrastructure already in place at the farmers' market, she was able to start out with a relatively small investment in a food cart and equipment. Her business has grown as she has built up a steady clientele. Contacts made through the DFM often lead to catering jobs for parties and festivals. Panna has developed several products from her experience selling at the market that she now sells wholesale to grocery stores. While she expects that the future expansion of her business will primarily come through more wholesale sales, Panna explains that the DFM will always be important for her business as a low-overhead storefront and an incubator for developing new products. "We will only introduce a product at the wholesale level when it has been tested through the farmers' market. Then we can approach stores, knowing that it is a good product and it will sell." In this way, she does not have to invest in costly labels, packaging and nutritional analyses before she is sure that a new product will be successful.

Vendors at the DFM have frequently used their experience at the farmers' market to help them enter other marketing channels. The large number of tourists at the DFM, for example, makes it a good place to begin developing a mail order business.

Les Portello sells almonds at the DFM in various forms — plain, salted, flavored, and made into almond butter. He is a former senior agricultural economist at the California Department of Food and Agriculture. Les sees farmers' markets as a very important way to tap into the tourist market and promote "California grown" products. He has mail order customers from outside of the local area, and even out-of-state, who have bought his products while visiting a farmers' market. Les is interested in developing a statewide effort to promote farmers' markets to tourists. He explains that the unique atmosphere of farmers' markets offers a marketable experience for tourists. "This is the reason

The Davis market served as the startup for Panna Putnam's business, Samosas to Go.

people go to wineries [to buy wine]; they are looking for a good experience." In the same way that the wine industry and certain agricultural areas in California like Apple Hill have built a strong tourism industry, he feels that farmers' markets have the potential to generate significant growth for agricultural businesses through tourism.

Even as vendors businesses expand into new markets, the farmers' market usually remains an important component of the overall marketing strategy, and can complement other marketing outlets. Paul Abramovitz of Affi's Marin Gourmet has been selling vegetable spreads and fruit dipping sauces at the DFM since 1994. Their products are now sold in several grocery stores in Davis. Paul says that the farmers' market is a great place to promote his products, even if customers end up buying them in the stores. He offers generous samples of his spreads on crackers to everyone who passes by his stall. He explains that farmers' markets provide instant retail cash, while his wholesale accounts with stores have delayed payments. Because of this, farmers' markets play an important role in maintaining the necessary cash flow for the business.

Annie and Jeff Main have directed an increasing amount of their sales into their CSA over the past several years. The CSA offers certain advantages, such as being able to pick exactly the amount of produce they know they will need, and providing money up front from subscribers to pay for farming expenses. However, the Mains feel that maintaining a strong presence at the farmers' market is important for ensuring the stability of their farming business. Because the CSA requires a quarterly payment in advance by the subscribers, sales through this channel may be more likely to decline in times of economic hardship. They explain that being part of the farmers' market is likely to provide more stability in their marketing opportunities over the long term. Annie also notes that the relationships they have established with customers through the farmers' market have given them a longstanding presence and base of support in the community.

Another benefit that the DFM offers to its vendors is assistance in developing better marketing and presentation skills. In the many years that Randii has been managing the DFM, she has watched many vendor businesses develop, expand and struggle. She tracks weekly sales of all the vendors, and tries to work with vendors to improve their marketing approach when she sees sales slipping. DFM newsletters for the vendors also offer marketing ideas. In addition, the market association hires consultants for workshops at their annual meetings to analyze stall displays and provide suggestions for better design. In order to reach out to the large number of vendors who don't attend the annual meeting, and those who are reluctant to have their display critiqued in front of a group, the market board has arranged to offer individual consulting sessions to all the market vendors during the coming year. Randii explains that while relatively few of the vendors have taken advantage of these opportunities, those that do have benefitted.

CHALLENGES & OPPORTUNITIES

Although the DFM was founded with the intent of fostering the survival of small and beginning farmers, the market today is full, thus preventing most new farmers and start-up businesses from participating. In fact, there has been a waiting list for the Saturday market for the last 15 years. Randii says that currently the only new vendors she will admit to the Saturday market are those who offer a product that she doesn't already have represented at a certain time of year, or an organic product that is not offered by the other vendors. One suggestion was for the DFM to create a designated section of the market for "start-up businesses," but difficult issues with seniority have raised objections for such a plan. Some of the vendors feel that there are already too many vendors at the market, causing sales to be spread thin among those offering the same products. Providing opportunities for new businesses without sacrificing the success of current vendors can be a difficult balance to achieve.

Competition has become an increasingly important factor for farmers' market vendors in recent years, as vendors at the DFM are quick to point out. Owing to the growth and success of farmers' markets, grocery stores have improved their produce selections and displays, often trying to mimic the look of a farmers' market display. Grocery stores throughout California have also begun carrying more organic and locally grown produce. Although grocery stores will never be able to provide all of the services of a farmers' market, such as same-day freshness and direct sales from the grower, they have taken significant strides into areas once considered the domain of farmers' markets. In this larger climate of supermarket trends, it is important for farmers' markets to promote the unique services and experience they can provide.

Competition among vendors at the markets has grown significantly in the past ten years. The increasingly competitive environment has changed the outlook and goals of some vendors who have historically sold at farmers' markets. Dave Phillips is a fifth generation farmer whose family sells fruits and vegetables grown on 150 acres near Lodi at the DFM. They also grow wine grapes on 350 acres. Phillips Farms has been selling at farmers' markets in Northern California since 1979. Dave explains that increased competition has had important impacts on his family's business. Regarding farmers' market sales, he remarks, "over the last five years, the growth in it for us has stopped. I think the market is more or less saturated now." As a result of decreasing profit margins from farmers' market sales, they have decided to cut back on their product line for farmers' markets and expand more into wine grape production, where profit margins are much higher.

Many vendors have responded to growing competition by diversifying the products they offer, and expanding into more value-added items. Annie Main expanded her offering of jams, jellies and dried vegetables at their market stand after watching how people at the market spend much more money on value-added items than on fresh produce. Finding a certified kitchen where she could make her jams initially posed a challenge for Annie. She has used the kitchens in several local restaurants, but the hours when the kitchens are available have not always been convenient. Annie would like to do more with value-added products from her farm, but she is limited by restrictions on the types of products an agricultural vendor is allowed to sell. For example, she would not be able to sell zucchini bread made with the zucchinis from their farm because that would be considered a baked good, which can only be sold in the "auxiliary area" adjacent to the certified farmers' market.

Randii points out that as more and more vendors diversify the products they are selling, this continues to fuel the competitive environment in the market. She cautions that vendors need to consider carefully the impact that diversification will have on their business as a whole. She has seen instances where the pressure to become diversified has caused a vendor to take on more than they could handle, resulting in a lower quality product. Randii explains that as a manager, she is constantly trying to help her vendors examine themselves critically, in terms of their display, quality and abundance of products. She feels it is important that vendors are able to identify the strengths and weaknesses of their business, especially if they are attempting to make significant changes in their business or marketing strategy.

The development of a large, successful market like the DFM can have trade-offs in a loss of the intimacy that a smaller market offers. Close relationships between growers and consumers, and among the market vendors, are not as easily formed amid large crowds and the busy pace of a bustling market. As vendors expand their businesses to attend several farmers' markets each week, they often turn their stalls over to employees who interact with customers directly.

Some vendors have suggested that promoting more networking among vendors would be beneficial for strengthening relationships within the market. Panna Putnam suggested profiling a different vendor in each DFM newsletter, including a photo. By helping vendors learn about each other, this could encourage more collaboration on marketing strategies, in addition to strengthening the sense of community in such a large market. For example, Les Portello has thought about trying to coordinate with a hot food vendor who would be interested in serving roasted almonds from his stand as a condiment. Cross-promotional activities like this could benefit several vendors while introducing consumers to new ways of using their farmers' market purchases.

For some vendors, the expansion of the DFM and the growing competition from grocery stores has prompted them to put more attention on education for their customers. A few vendors provide recipes and nutritional information about their own products, while making an effort to talk with customers about the unique benefits that a farmers' market offers. Several vendors at the DFM mentioned that there is already a high level of awareness among many customers at the DFM about the opportunities a farmers' market provides for supporting smaller and local growers, building a sense of community through food and agriculture, as well as having a selection of high quality produce, including organic food products. This awareness among the Davis community is noted as a particular strength of the Davis Farmers' Market. Efforts to increase awareness of farmers' market unique benefits among the general public, through education by vendors and farmers' market associations, are likely to be very important for maintaining the strength and growth of farmers' markets throughout California in coming years. ✿

STARTING A MARKET 9

"The market serves as the 'front porch of Hollywood,' where people can relax and visit with neighbors."

— Customer, Hollywood Certified Farmers' Market, California

Many experienced farmers' market organizers would agree that their job is to coordinate a set of events resulting in a certain degree of planned chaos. Certainly, they recognize that they are only managers involved in the complex craft of designing an intricate web of people who are really the heart and soul of the market.

"The success of the Crescent City FM (New Orleans) owes much to excellent behind-the-scenes organization without which other markets have failed. As Manager Richard McCarthy noted, 'It's not as simple as finding a parking lot and notifying farmers.' In addition to securing a space, a successful market requires: staffing and security; parking; week-in, week-out continuity (rain or shine); garbage collection; safe food handling guidelines; knowledge of and compliance with local regulations; a name, logo, signage, phone number, and other elements that identify the market as a professional, stable retail operation; a governing board for resolving problems and complaints, accepting new vendors, and enforcing the market's own rules."

— Economics Institute, *Report to the Community*

Who Are You?

Let's define "you" here. You may be an individual. You may be a business organization — a chamber of commerce, a downtown redevelopment committee, a Main Street program. You may be a religious, social, educational or philanthropic organization — a church or ministerial association, a Lions or Optimist Club, a school or an American Association of University Women chapter, or a gathering of interested people who believe the time for a farmers' market is ripe in your community.

Some of the best markets have been organized by a single individual. Usually that individual is an organizer. That means he/she is able to get others involved in helping make this organizing effort a true community project. More people mean more challenges, and usually as you compound the challenges you get larger results, if you stay focused on the goal. Thus, even when "you" is an individual, it usually results in a collective "you."

WHY START A FARMERS' MARKET?

Do you want a farmers' market to build community cohesion? Do you want to do something pro-active to help local farmers? Do your downtown businesses need a promotional shot in the arm? Are your inner city residents faced with little or no shopping choices? Are you seeing farmland disappear and wondering how remaining farms can become sustainable?

Create an organizing committee that clearly establishes a primary goal of providing a viable marketplace for farmers and consumers. A secondary goal may be to improve downtown, but do not let revitalization become the primary focus or you will lose your reason for being a farmers' market organization. You must make the market work on its own; if you let development issues run the market, they will run it out of business. You have enough of a challenge sustaining a farmers' market with a side concern of sensitivity for attempts by other parallel organizations to do revitalization.

Certain markets have been organized specifically to provide access to fresh produce for low-income

West Richland FM, West Richland, WA

What's In A Name?

The Original Farmers' Market in Anderson, IN, is in the UAW Local 662 parking lot, not to be confused with The Original Farmers' Market in South Fayette, PA, or another by the same name in DuBois, PA. If four states can have a Springfield Farmers' Market – Illinois, Massachusetts, Minnesota and Vermont – certainly three states can have an Original Farmers' Market.

Let's think about names, not simply those like Bird-in-the-Hand Farmers' Market or Oil City Curb Market. As intriguing as they sound, they merely reflect the name of their city as thousands of other markets do. There's nothing wrong with that, but can you do more?

Choosing a name seems to have been fun for the organizers of the Duck Soup Co-op Farmers' Market in DeKalb, IL, and the Green Dragon Farmers' Market in Ephrata, PA (well worth the visit). The city of Chicago got creative with Back of the Yard Farmers' Market and there's the Old Farm Farmers' Market in Champaign, IL.

Place is usually the most common descriptor in a name aside from the event. You don't have to ask where the Mouse River Park Farmers' Market is located in Tolley, ND. Yet down in Dickinson they were more inventive with the Roughrider Home Growers' Market. Folks got downright inventive with the Pittston Tomato Festival Farmers' Market, PA. Groton's Happy Tourist Farmers' Market, VT, tells us clearly that the local population isn't enough.

Your goal may be to convey what, where or when as did the Hillsboro Tuesday Marketplace and the Astoria Sunday Market, both in Oregon. By choice, they lost out on the affinity the public has for "farmers' market," much as Mercado Alvarado did by choosing to reinforce a welcoming attitude toward the majority Latino population in Los Angeles.

The term "farmers' market" is now highly recognized and has a fairly positive association in people's minds, so you will gain immediate recognition using the term in your market name. People will remember it easier. There's no point having to spend extra time and money trying to teach people a name. You might be even more specific as with the Cave Spring's Organic Farmers' Market in Missouri. There are occasions where you may want to disassociate from the term if it reminds people of a past failure. In other cases you may simply want to clearly distinguish yourselves from another local market as the new Friday evening Napa Chef's Market did opening years after the Tuesday success of the Napa Farmers' Market.

Do a brainstorming session to list all the possible words that relate in some way to your planned market: community, downtown, park, square, plaza, fairgrounds, courthouse, open air, village, harvest, plentiful, produce, fruit, farmers, growers, fresh, quality, curb market, country, cooperative, township, outdoor, night, county name, Thursday, green, old town… If they don't make it into your name, they may be helpful in your advertising or press releases.

If your name is longer than three or four words, people are likely to shorten it for you. Of course, there are exceptions. The American Friends Service Committee developed San Francisco's Heart of the City Farmers' Market in front of City Hall. With a big heart logo in all its advertisements, the name is truly descriptive and effective, which helps people remember the name. Hopefully, the Healthy Powderhorn Farmers' Market in Minneapolis does the same! ✿

A Hmong crafts vendor adds to market culture and customer selection. Farmers' markets are a key entry point into the economy for small and new farmers and immigrants. Determine what vendors are desired and available before setting your vendor limitations and product mix.

residents in urban areas where supermarkets have fled. While this represents an opportunity to change the produce picture for many people, there may be a different set of issues to take into account. Frequently, the ethnic make-up is different from the city at large, which allows you to bring in minority farmers to meet minority consumers' needs. In some markets this has resulted in taking on the predominant characteristics of the people's home country, as in an eastside Vietnamese neighborhood of New Orleans. Similarly, in an Oakland market it resulted in an incredibly rich mix of ethnicity reflecting the colorful reality of Oakland neighborhoods — African American, Asian, Caucasian and Hispanic.

Many markets are developed with the goal of providing a community meeting place to celebrate the diversity of local produce and educate people about better nutrition. There seems to be ever increasing awareness of the difficulties facing farmers in the global marketplace. Communities are looking for a way to make a difference and starting with a local market seems the best place to take action — and it is!

Some communities want to generate more pedestrian traffic or promote evening events in the downtown or at a park. This may lead to more of an entertainment focus than a produce focus. Yet, that may be the best way to get people together in numbers to sustain the market.

You may decide that your goal is multi-faceted because the organizing committee represents various community interests. Some markets state that their goals are to provide a marketing alternative for farmers, a vehicle for downtown revitalization, support for local businesspeople and a friendly, community-oriented marketplace. Try to form a cohesive image of what you want to create and then the various elements that support that vision.

Feasibility

Whatever your key reason(s), first analyze whether your goal is desired and achievable. That may mean going to the business community to ask whether they will support the project or surveying residents to determine their enthusiasm.

Certainly you need to assess the local retail competition and determine whether a sufficient number of farmers are willing to participate. If farmers cannot compete on price with imported produce, is a more quality-focused market feasible?

Study the demographics for your community and perhaps several others surrounding yours. A survey in the newspaper — it never hurts to ask for free help — can lead to new observations about who your likely customers will be, or at least those who come as a result of newspaper advertising. Compare those characteristics with the general populace from statistics available at city hall. Figure out how you are going to reach every different segment of the population that you hope to entice, and consider whether you need to modify the message according to the population segment.

No matter who "you" are — an individual or a group — you need to ask many questions of feasibility as you develop a vision. Through a series of public meetings, allow plenty of time for the answers to evolve. If you have the money, a formal feasibility analysis may be valuable, but most markets choose to put limited financial resources into actual development. Nevertheless, do not avoid the challenging issues of who should benefit from the market, how that is possible and what roadblocks stand in the way.

Scope of the Market

Along with your general goals, you want to define who the market is for in terms of potential sellers. Is your market for producers only? Will you allow prepared foods, crafts and other non-agricultural items? These questions should spark a unique set of answers for you.

In California the scope was somewhat established by regulations promulgated by the California Department of Food and Agriculture in 1977 which were pushed into legislation effective in 2000. They clearly define "certified producers" as those who can sell exempt from standard pack in a "certified farmers' market." Both producers and markets are issued certificates by county agricultural commissioners. Naturally, market conditions being what they are, other types of producers (and non-producers) have wanted to get in on the act. This leads to market growth and the need for market rules and enforcement.

Certain markets have been established with more narrow guidelines, such as allowing only organic produce or producers only from within a given distance or specific counties. Many markets have more open standards, allowing "high-stallers" or peddlers, or defining an impact area of two or more states, especially in the case of markets near state lines. Not only are state lines rather arbitrary borders, but they may prohibit you from having the mix of products that you want. The onus is on the markets to create and implement a procedure to guarantee to their customers that the farmers are actually farming.

[See Managing the Market chapter for a more in-depth discussion of these as well as other issues your rules and bylaws might address.]

ATTRACTING FARMERS

Once you have your standard, set out on a path which has many branches. Don't depend on just one avenue for contacting farmers and other producers. Be ready for new outreach ideas to develop as you follow several of these steps:

✧ Visit established nearby farmers' markets, especially those on different days of the week.

✧ Drive country roads and make impromptu visits with farmers you see.

✧ Ask farmers for names of others with specific products you lack.

✧ Place ads in produce industry publications or local newspapers.

✧ Send press releases about your plans to encourage local newspaper stories. Any topic related to the market start-up can generate coverage.

✧ Write stories for rural publications including details about an informational meeting.

✧ Host a series of meetings around your state and make a slide presentation of how to display effectively at your market, plus packets outlining your plans.

✧ Place classified ads in local papers and ag trade bulletins.

✧ Ask crafts organizations (potters, weavers, general) for access to members through a newsletter article or their mailing list.

Direct Mail

Another method is a direct mailing to a large base of potential farmers and gardeners announcing the market opening and a meeting to outline your plans. It should include the time, place, speakers, topics to be covered, and an address and phone number for any interested grower who cannot attend. Your local Cooperative Extension Service office will likely help with the mailing and provide the meeting site. Many managers have found direct mail brings poor results; others use it effectively. Check the mail piece carefully for impact and follow up with a personal call or visit to those receiving your mailing.

Utilize resources where farmers are listed such as your state department of agriculture's Producer-to-Consumer directory, lists supplied by agricultural commodity groups, Farm Bureau, Extension Service, and state grower associations. Search for the list of participants at farm conferences.

Marin County: A Start-up Success Story

The Marin County Farmers' Market opened with 30 growers in July, 1983. Within two months more than 60 farmers were selling their produce there. According to the market's founder Lynn Bagley, the reason behind the market's start-up success was the work that went into the market prior to opening day.

"In our research into other markets, Bagley says, "I had heard of one market that managed to attract a lot of customers for opening day, but no farmers showed up. So I determined to get a strong commitment and then keep regular contact with the producers. We held pre-opening meetings, built a solid mailing list and kept everyone in touch."

"Everything goes into opening day. You've got to make it big and important so as to have patrons to support the farmers and vice versa. If you have two or three farmers there, how many people will keep coming? If you start out successful, it builds."

Bagley also did everything possible to let the public know about the event, such as holding a series of public meetings and organizing volunteers to call every other household in the zip code area. Volunteers put signs on major highways and two TV stations did features on the event. Front-page stories and features ran in the local papers as well as continuing stories throughout the season. This set the tone for the market's importance and on opening day most of the 30 farmers sold out within two hours.

After holding a re-opening fund-raising dinner for 250 people, the MCFM reopened the following season in May of 1984, hosting a School Day for 700 elementary school children. The Farm Bureau provided live animals; there were poster and essay contests for the kids, the Board of Supervisors competed in a milking contest, and farmers gave away produce prizes. The children loved it, and they went home and told their parents. Now known as Farm Day, the event attracts over 2000 school children each year.

Bagley says she chose the Marin Civic Center location "because it had a big parking lot. The location has also good visibility, a large sign on the freeway, and is a well-known Marin location." Conventional market wisdom, however, is to locate in a place that has already-existing traffic flow, something the Marin location did not have. Hard work and publicity overcame this. "There's no town in the world that doesn't want a market," Bagley claims, "and people will come if you do your publicity."

The key to fund-raising, Bagley feels, is to hold special events and turn them into fund-raisers at the same time. Through media attention, a special event draws more people to the market.

Some growers would like to eliminate competition by limiting the number of sellers. "I feel there is definitely a limit," says Bagley, "but the more farmers you have, the more significant the event becomes, and therefore more people come. Diversity is imperative — the more variety, the more patrons you can attract."

Bagley also advises making sure that the people selling are the real growers. Once you allow non-producers to sell, the quality drops, and it hurts the reputation of the whole market. People want to buy direct from the farmer. Be prepared also, "to do a lot of begging. That first year, I got tired of constantly asking for help."

Her commitment, focus on strong openings, and skillful execution of major events gave Lynn Bagley a keen reputation in California and beyond, providing the basis for other Bay area cities inviting her to develop markets in their communities. ✿

For the first mailing throw as wide a net as possible to be sure anyone interested will know about your efforts. You may be surprised by the distance producers will consider driving, especially if they come to your area for a market day immediately prior to or after yours. When you spread the word thoroughly, growers elsewhere will be talking about your market plans and help spread word to others.

Hold a Meeting

In Oklahoma City 140 producers attended a market informational meeting in 1988, the result of a mailing. They came from many counties, the farthest distance being 240 miles one way. One can never assume how much a farmer may be interested in your market. Depending on his contacts and the wholesale climate, he may be desperate to match his dream with yours.

One market in New York invited potential vendors to a dinner, introduced them to local businesses and showed them around downtown. A gathering or meeting is beneficial in answering questions and building confidence as growers see others that are committed.

At your organizational meeting determine the level of interest of growers along with their production volume and season on various products. Quantify the number of growers expected and clarify the reasoning behind the market location and organizational structure. You may want to sign them up immediately and collect their membership fee. Be ready to answer a challenging mix of questions candidly, especially about policies and costs.

Provide farmers with all your plans and solicit theirs. In seeking to match supply and demand, you will want to know how much volume of every different item you potentially have for the market. This will enable you later to write more compelling press releases and ad copy. It also may spark ideas for special events like a tomato or watermelon tasting.

Can they help find other farmers with additional variety to ensure a good product mix from early until late in the season? Have you covered your bases with specialty products including breads, pastries, processed nuts, pickled vegetables, pies, jams, mustards and vinegars? Have you talked to the best baker and most well-known organic farmers delivering to local restaurants?

Challenge yourself with a checklist of the foods that you eat. Then do the same with products that every eager friend wants to see at the market. To avoid heavy duplication of the same item, tell growers how much head-to-head competition they will have. Give farmers a sense of how many customers you expect, based on your planned promotional campaign. If you supply information so farmers can make good decisions, they will more likely help your market to succeed.

Market Size

When recruiting growers, consider the customer perspective. The rule of thumb is that one grower of a certain product is a monopoly, two amounts to collusion and three is competition. Customers expect variety and want choices. They will not have that without a good selection of vendors that provide for variety and competition.

You certainly need to consider the farmer perspective as well. They need to make money to continue. Therefore, be sensitive to their concerns about overly much competition. The challenge is to be sensitive to both groups, farmers and consumers, without letting either side demand too much. Some farmers want monopolies but customer numbers will suffer generally if you listen. At least two vendors selling the same item in numerous produce categories is a good idea to start. You need to distinguish your farmers' market from local supermarket competition.

"Findings consistently show successful urban markets have a strong integrated farmer component. Farmers benefit from clustering — the critical mass of producers with complementary products. A market with fewer than 12 growers will struggle — the more growers the more successful the market."
— *American Vegetable Grower*, "Community is Key to Market Success," 1995

Small communities may find 8-10 growers sufficient to meet expectations, but even a small market in a rural community may leave many potential customers less than enamored with the selection. Organizers need to take steps before opening to ensure that the best mix is possible because the average consumer is not as patient as a farmer in waiting for the market to grow.

Meeting customer desires and making the site seem full, you can sustain a market even at a small site without as much internal competition as you would hope.

The Santa Monica market now has nearly 100 vendors every Wednesday. Yet, it began in 1981 with only 23 farmers on its opening day. Customer response was strong due to an excellent publicity plan. Thus, the number of growers participating grew rapidly quite naturally. However, at that time there was only a handful of markets in the Los Angeles area, and this was the largest opening until that point.

Customer expectations have changed dramatically as the majority of the American populace now knows what a farmers' market is, not necessarily the case in the early 1980s. By the end of the century, it was not uncommon to have much stronger openings. Farmers often have realized that they have to risk along with the market organizers who have spent time and money to create a market. When Yakima, WA, opened in 1999, there were 53 booths filled and more than 4,000 customers. The balance was right and more vendors came the very next week. The right balance was achieved for a good start.

In metro areas where people may have become accustomed to 80-100 farmer markets, an opening with fewer than 30 may be difficult to sustain because people's expectations have been raised. Conversely, sustaining 30 may be difficult at first, especially if your population base is not substantial or you can't promise to get them all out on opening day.

You should be soliciting new farmers who want to join your early success. Acknowledge that the market isn't for everybody, but even when there is an apparent failure for a farmer, keep the door open for the future. Many farmers will try a market at a later date when it is more established; with a solid customer base, they succeed on the second attempt.

The "See-Saw"

Start as strong as possible. For every hour spent recruiting farmers and every dollar spent attracting customers, you will save at least double that later on. The most crucial element of development is strong recruitment of farmers. However, the concept of "build the market and they will come" should not be taken as an excuse to ride the coattails — or tailgates — of the farmers. An equally strong outreach should be planned to draw consumers because without them, farmers will drop away or bring less product in succeeding weeks. Thus, organizers need to have a keen sense that they are balancing the see-saw of supply and demand on the opening day of the market.

It usually takes about four weeks for the market to balance, that is, for the see-saw to find its right size. Your goal should be to build the biggest see-saw possible. Some farmers may fall away because the competition is too stiff, their product is not well accepted, they fail to give samples, the product quality is poor or any of a host of other reasons. Some customers will not return because it isn't convenient, they didn't find the right mix of products, parking was problematic, price or quality was problematic or any other reason. However, if you have done a good job building the see-saw, most of your customers and farmers are going to build relationships, have a good time, want to return and be willing to spread the word.

Captivate the Consumer

In the spirit of guerilla marketing, be aware that there is really no limit to the creative ideas that help announce your new market to the public. With everything you do there should be a consciousness about publicity. Every speaking engagement and every chance encounter at a restaurant provides an opportunity to publicize the market and get others joined in that fun process. Simultaneously, it gives you a chance to ask if anyone knows potential vendors.

In Hayward, California, Lynn Bagley organized a mini-tasting to which the public was invited via a newspaper article. Farmers came with their products to a community building downtown and gave people a taste of what was to come. Those attending became one more means of spreading the word.

Experienced market organizers know that a good market doesn't just happen. Vendors ultimately judge a market and their participation in it by the profits they take home. We can hope that they will appreciate the friendly atmosphere in our town, but if the customer count is low and profits insufficient, a farmer will go to a more profitable market. One by one, vendors will leave and customers with them. For a market to succeed, the organizer must supply enough enticements for both vendor and customer to view this farmers' market as the preferred alternative. This situation is particularly difficult for new markets because customers have built their expectations around produce departments in larger supermarkets, box

stores, specialty stores or even at other successful farmers' markets. A new market must offer comparable customer satisfaction around quality and price or replace it with a combination of friendly atmosphere, knowledgeable farmers and unique events.

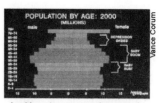

Looking at your area demographics, available from the city or a local library, will help you analyze who your customers will be and how to appeal to them. Continue analyzing since the market population is aging with the baby boomers.

The balancing act never ends. It may seem that everything is going along just fine, but if you lose two farmers in a 10-farmer market or eight of your 40 farmers, you may notice a drop-off of customers. Inevitably, some customers will have lost their favorite flower grower or organic tomatoes or specialty cheese. You can never be so comfortable as to think that you have the see-saw perfectly balanced. That's when you'll fall off and the community will suffer.

Farmers' Markets Through the Eyes of the Consumer

— *Farmers' Market Forum,* Farmers' Market Federation of New York, Summer 2000

Be customer-focused. Keep your business abreast of what the consumer wants, when they want it and how they want it.

During this past winter, the Federation held several regional workshops and conferences. Consumer panels gave presentations on what they are looking for at a farmers' market, and here is what they wanted, or wanted more of:

✧ Product diversity — as large a selection of produce and other farm products as possible, including more organic products;

✧ Homemade baked goods — many people are too busy to bake for themselves and enjoy the sweets they can get at market;

✧ Plants and nursery stock — many customers enjoy gardening and being able to get their garden plants at market is important;

✧ Dried beans, and a wide variety of hot peppers, both fresh and dried;

✧ Special events — they give the market a fun atmosphere and encourage community spirit among patrons.

Consumer panelists also wanted more children's activities like pet-

ting zoos, as well as fun ways to educate children about farming and nutrition, whether it's at the market or by making school visits. Individual vendors may want to plant a special flower or vegetable in a large pot at the beginning of the season. Bring it to market each week for the kids to follow the growth of the plant and the development of the vegetable and then give them a treat made from that particular vegetable at the end of the season. Talk to the children about the plant each week. Pique their interest and their curiosity so they look forward to seeing its growth and progress. ✿

LOCATION

A highly visible location with a landmark identity will make it more difficult for your market to fail. A hidden, poorly known location will make it more difficult for your market to succeed. Choose a central, landmark location in the community with easy access for customers, plenty of parking, visibility from main roads including freeways if possible, shade trees, public restrooms, and a telephone. Almost any site can work as long as you work.

The most critical factor that has limited markets' growth is a lack of parking. It can be overcome if the market has everything that people want, but inadequate parking will certainly dissuade many would-be shoppers, especially during inclement weather.

Look at population figures for a two-mile, five-mile and ten-mile radius from the site. Know where most of your customers will come from. Being on a heavily traveled road outside the main core of town may be better than a side street in the downtown.

Private Property

In the private sector, malls are among many businesses to see the benefits of hosting farmers' markets. Banks open their parking lots in St. Cloud, MN, in Oconomowoc, WI, and in Tilton, NH. Markets borrow the parking lots of doctors in Kennett, MO, an insurance company in Tacoma, WA, a bowling alley in Rushford, MN, the Ace Hardware in Columbia, IL, the Agway in Ballston Spa, NY, and a tea house in Salisbury, CT.

Train stations often create underutilized parking, perfect for markets from Newark, NJ, to Ypsilanti, MI, and on to Santa Fe, NM. While at times they are outside the immediate town core, the consequent advantage may be superior parking. The station building itself may lend old-world charm and landmark status to the market.

An architectural rendering helped in planning the visual impact and inspired vendor confidence in the Chef's Market situated in a winding, outdoor mall in downtown Napa, CA

Churches have opened their arms and parking lots from Delmar, NY to Gardena, CA and all over Tennessee (due in great part to the efforts of the late John Vlcek). Shopping centers from Minneapolis, MN, to Connellsville, PA, have welcomed the extra traffic. They are not likely to charge the market when it guarantees their mall merchants a regular supply of customers. In fact, various malls have paid thousands of dollars to attract a market. Malls in Sacramento, CA are competing with each other to have market manager and attorney Dan Best place a farmers' market on their property. They know the day will be decided according to farmer availability.

A major body of water yields a desirable atmosphere and vista, whether at the ferry terminal in Lewes, DE, or on Ferry Plaza in San Francisco, CA. In Stonington, CT, the market is at a fishing pier and in Ft. Pierce, FL, along a waterway, just as at Jack London Square in Oakland, CA.

Public Space

Many organizers prefer the philosophical and practical alignment with public sites, not malls. If our markets are each a collection of small farming businesses, it seems more appropriate to connect with and support other small, independent businesses rather than further the concentration of wealth in the few national and international corporations that dominate malls.

Public properties are appropriate for these public markets. They use the municipal lot in Kent, WA, the library complex in Worland, WY and the state park in Warwick, RI. Markets operate on Friday, Saturday and Sunday at several Pennsylvania Turnpike service plazas including Allentown and Valley Forge. In Washington state, markets also use Marina Park in Kingston, the park & ride lot in Gig Harbor, and the elementary school in Granite Falls. North Middle School in Menomonee Falls, WI, and Hope High School in Providence, RI, host markets as well.

Federal properties are also available, as with the Palo Alto Post Office. While USDA was promoting farmers' markets in the 1990s, it organized markets on property at twelve different federal agencies. It also published How to Establish a Farmers' Market on Federal Property, a brochure available at:

www.ams.usda.gov/directmarketing.

There is really no limit to where a market can be located. In Bourg-en-Bresse, France, it sets up in a large open plaza in the center of the city and winds its way into an abandoned gym where one wall was blasted out years ago. In Edmonton, Alberta, the outdoor market moved indoor one rainy day because the manager had the keys to the bus barn. Years later the city wrote a lease so that the market assumes responsibility for maintenance. Having an indoor home allows the market to run year-round and allows many more independent farmers and craftspeople to depend on the market for their livelihood.

Downtown

For many communities, downtown is the obvious choice. It is the center of all civic and business activities and the farmers' market is both civic and business. With business leaving so many downtowns, farmers' markets offer some hope of resuscitating the economic engine. The National Main Street Program has seen the impact and urged many downtown leaders to consider how to put farmers' markets at the core of community and business life, much as they have been historically.

Ruth Yanatta Goldway was such a leader as the new mayor of Santa Monica, CA, in 1981. She put her vision and commitment behind a farmers' market, blocking off a key street with 50,000 vehicles per day. Over the objection of some businesses like the copy shop that depended on easy parking, the city persisted in favor of numerous businesses that weren't getting desirable pedestrian traffic counts. Six years earlier a state attempt to inspire the market had failed miserably, but with new timing and an inspired leader the largest market in southern California was created. The market sparked a downtown renaissance and major economic development plan leading to many new businesses servicing the area.

"The market should be in a neighborhood business district which promotes the area as a cohesive whole. Area businesses and retail establishments surrounding the market play an important role in defining the market. This 'spirit of place' is an important part of successful markets."
— *American Vegetable Grower*, "Community is Key to Market Success," 1995

Any site is possible, so look for the characteristics you most desire and prepare to meet the property owner, which may be the city. Sell them on the market's community benefits before you address the specific location request.

In the Park

Parks have many advantages, especially aesthetically. Shade trees and grass increase produce longevity. People love a quiet park or even one with a youth area or exercise stations. These add to family-oriented and people-watching opportunities. Parks are known in many communities as a safe haven, a place to be refreshed, so a farmers' market fits well with this identity.

Some advantages can also be disadvantages. Lush grass can become a mudhole in bad weather. If you can move the market a few feet each week, the damaging impact of shuffling customers' feet may be minimized. Farmers need to watch out for irrigation heads if they are driving trucks across the grass.

Being next to the park may be sufficient. Having the nearby amenities of restrooms, a water feature, playground and grass to picnic on may be all you need. Keeping the farmers' trucks on the perimeter may be the perfect solution if the ground isn't solidly compacted. This is the answer in Vancouver, WA, where the market runs for two blocks along Esther Short Park, the oldest city park in the state. This new location as of 2000 followed the redevelopment of the park with a new playground that makes shopping with kids more enjoyable and a covered performing stage that brings events and big crowds to the market during good weather.

The market in Petaluma, CA, was also downtown until merchants complained and forced the market to move to a park. The market continued to grow while businesses suffered, realizing too late they had kicked the golden goose.

Pasadena's first market in 1980 was sited on a park known mainly to its nearby residents. With great publicity it succeeded in setting a safe, friendly tone for the neighborhood, at least on Tuesdays. However, while it has a reliable customer base, it is overshadowed by newer farmers' markets on more heavily traveled corridors, proving that high visibility and better parking can save many publicity dollars.

Ithaca, New York's market operated for several years around a downtown park. It built its customer base so that when it moved to a scenic but solitary location along the lake, its clientele followed. They had grown into a site where members contributed sweat equity to build a substantial open-air building with bermed parking for 300+ vehicles. Their transition succeeded because they had the vision to create a landmark location. That visioning process has continued with a project to draw customers down to the lakeside.

This is not to say that the Hancock, NH market behind the church in the horse sheds is not the perfect location for that community, but it may be harder for a visitor to find than the Goodwill lot in Dover or the Salvation Army down in Norwich, CT. Ultimately, we would hope that every location makes a community proud. At the least, location is a reflection even when it's the Wal-Mart lot in Green Bay, WI. When your market is at Market Square in Sturgeon Bay, WI, your landmark has a history and hopefully a more auspicious future.

Four multi-story parking garages with 1200 spaces surround this Arizona Avenue location in Santa Monica, CA. Initially selling to the sidewalks, the market later reconfigured to a more spacious, customer-friendly layout with farmers selling to the middle of the street.

Access

Thinking of our potential customer, what will attract him or her? We need to find a site which "feels" safe, convenient and accessible. Well-known, landmark locations generally fit the bill, but they may not be available to us. Whatever our ultimate choice, we need to describe the location so people can easily find it and then easily park.

No matter what the level of initial response to our market, we may feel we have done a great job because people are coming. However, a better reaction is to ask: "Why aren't others coming?" Through a phone survey of non-customers, we may realize that some people do not perceive our location to be accessible. Think of how to make the market easier to find. You may get a sign at a freeway ramp or a key turn, give a reference landmark such as a well-known restaurant, or add a key directional phrase to your promotional campaign.

Drivers must be able to safely pull off the highway and easily park, and signs must be located far enough ahead for people to plan their turn off the road. You may need parking attendants directing traffic off a highway to give an extra sense of safety and good organization, so people have confidence in the rest of your operation.

Parking

When researching a location, visibility and access are key factors influencing success. Parking may be overlooked. Of all location elements, parking is probably the key limiting factor in market growth.

If you struggle with holding onto 500 customers for 20 farmers, compare yourself to a supermarket. You have 20 checkout counters to their 10. All your checkers want to be busy. You probably need twice the parking space of the supermarket. They are open much longer hours for business; you want to squeeze customers into a tight timeframe to make farmers' marketing time valuable. If you aren't seeing the pedestrian counts you want and need, analyze your parking — a major issue for customers.

If you are comparable to a supermarket in the mind of most customers, you had better have parking every bit as convenient. If your market stands out head and shoulders from the competition — quality, competition, value, product diversity, exotic items, freshness, farmer friendliness — you may be able to get away with a less-than-stellar parking situation.

When you are confronted with parking challenges, find out how customers and ex-customers feel and experiment with solutions. You might try a pick-up zone staffed by Scouts who hand over the ticketed bag of produce when a customer drives up from a distant parking spot and receive a tip. You might pay the first 20 minutes of parking at a nearby lot where you have worked out a compromise price. Many cities have waived the meter fees on streets or in garages during market hours.

> "Market complaints are highest among small-town markets. The most common complaint, by far, is insufficient parking. The fact that small-town markets are younger and less well established in a particular location may explain why parking problems have not been resolved. Some solutions mentioned by managers included scheduling the market on off days, shuttle services and providing driveup tables for customers to pick up their purchases."
> — Farmers' Markets and Rural Development Project

According to Bellingham Farmers' Market, WA, manager Karen Durham, parking is the first word for downtown merchants. Their study showed people who come by car want to walk less than a block and a third, so they organized a deal with a local transit service to run a shuttle every 20 or 30 minutes from downtown. In California, Santa Barbara's attempt to improve market access with a shuttle from downtown parking structures proved futile — both expensive and used by only a handful of customers. The Davis market has struggled with parking, trying shuttles from various points in town and the UCD campus without success.

> "We purchased tokens from some community-owned parking lots nearby good for one hour of parking and distributed a few thousand free last year. This costs the market between $800-1000 per season."
> — Chris Curtis, University District FM, Seattle, WA

Think through the parking demands of your market. Consider average customer stay, sales per customer, market hours and farmer income needs in estimating necessary parking. If you plan to operate four hours, you will probably turn over each parking spot five to six times. If you want 2000 customers spending $10 each to provide 50 farmers an average of $400 daily sales, you will need about 350 parking spaces. Every market will vary. If you have limited selection, customer turnover may average 20-30 minutes. If you provide more selection and activities, such as entertainment or hot food concessions, that figure may approach an hour and will create extra strain on your parking. While that may be desirable in creating a community meeting place, you need to have a site with substantially more parking.

Safety

People in a buying mode should not have to watch out for bikes, skateboarders or an impromptu dog-fight! While it's nice to have dogs around, if someone is bitten or steps in an unauthorized deposit, you won't gain points in the customer service department. The health department also will respect you a little more if you separate animals and food by at least 20 feet. (In California, it's health law.) That goes for what's being sold as well. It's also a good idea to require farmers to keep food off the ground a minimum of six inches.

Avoid customers mixing with vendors as they unload and prepare for market. Insurance companies reward with lower rates your safety precautions such as keeping customers safely away from moving vehicles and canopy poles on the ground.

Restrooms and Other Amenities

The need for restrooms is not absolute, just practical. Many communities find them unnecessary, especially if the market has short hours. Elsewhere, whether required by law or not, restrooms are essential and have a determining impact on selection of the market location.

If a port-a-potty is the only solution, local companies frequently make a donation for the first season if you explain your financial need for community support to get your project off the ground. If you have to pay rent, you may want to look into full purchase of a unit as long as you estimate the cost of periodic cleaning and have a plan for transportation and storage. Hand-washing units also are a wise investment given the handling of fresh produce.

In other cases local retailers have gained sales for themselves by demonstrating an open-door restroom policy for market vendors and patrons. Parks, churches, malls, city hall, the fairgrounds and many other locations may have available restrooms along with other amenities including telephones and public seating.

Many other amenities may be included in one location, but not another. When researching various sites, list all the attributes of each location so that you can score them. Create a point system or rank the importance of ambiance, shade trees, public seating, drinking fountains, telephones, proximity to the river or lake, access to public transportation and other factors. Compare them to other major considerations like sufficient farmer space, quantity of parking, visibility from major thoroughfares and connection to downtown businesses.

 TIMING

Beginning a new market is like starting any other business — first impressions are critical. Hopefully, the media will spread a positive image of the opening. Certainly, your first customers will have tremendous influence on whether other residents come out to successive market days. So, you ought to prepare for your opening as if your business depends on it. You will get grassroots reviews comparable to a Broadway show opening. Indeed, market is theater, so make sure you have every aspect of the show wired. Do a talk-through dress rehearsal with your committee. Write a letter to your farmers to make sure they recognize the importance of getting off to a strong start. Then get ready for a bit of improvisation.

Seasonal or Year-round?

To set the stage, debate when you will make the most memorable impression that will lead to a strong word-of-mouth campaign within the local populace. Will it be in April with bedding plants and nursery stock or in July once your growers have a full variety of produce at good prices? At least for the first season, consider the later date. Your market will bring many more dollars to your growers in the long run if you start on the right foot. That long-term perspective honors all the selfless efforts of your committee and the hard work of your producers.

Similarly, you want to close the market season on a high note. Don't wait for four weeks of rain to dampen the enthusiasm of 70% of your customers. Hold a harvest festival and leave people with a sense of anticipation of the second season to come — a bit earlier next year.

If you intend to close at the end of October, or April if you are in a southern climate operating on a reverse schedule, you can always extend the season if you have sufficient commitment from farmers and customers. Market season is largely dependent upon growing season but considerably improved by hothouse vegetables, value-added products, crafts and other items you may include. Determine in advance what numbers you will need to avoid embarrassment as you publicly announce a season extension.

In this way you might plan to stay open all year-round. When we opened the Gardena Farmers' Market in 1979, we said it was seasonal. It was the first market in Los Angeles County, opening with five farmers and growing into the teens during the summer. As farmers met regularly at the end of market day in early fall, six of them committed to coming through an uncertain winter. With an extra outreach push for Groundhog Day in February, we grew to nine farmers and managed to survive. Serving the community year-round, the market reached the age of maturity — 21.

The length of your season, even up to year-round operation, may depend upon having a building. Even an open-air structure provides enough protection generally to extend a season by two or three months, possibly more if farmers have greenhouses on the farm and heaters in the market.

The year-round, five-day (or more) farmers' markets found in many southeastern states are more accurately wholesale produce markets operating with a farmers' market on the side. Their year-round operation is dependent upon wholesalers buying produce worldwide. The financial feasibility of an attached, year-round farmers' market may be dependent upon management of the larger wholesale market.

Day and Hours

What days and hours are best for the market? None are best absolutely. Yet selection of day and hours are critical in maximizing the customer flow into your market. What works in your community may be a function of other markets already in existence more than what your fifteen-person committee thinks is the best time. Saturday is the most popular day but large metropolitan areas have markets running every day of the week. Increasingly, this same planning is occurring in rural areas.

Analyze the habits and needs of your potential customers but take equal care in assessing the needs of potential farmers. If most of the farmers you want are going to a strong Saturday market, start by prioritizing the other six days of the week. How can you help farmers while serving customers simultaneously?

Starting in 1979, five markets were developed over a two-year period in the Los Angeles basin. Then in 1981, the mayor of Santa Monica was ready. Instead of competing with two Saturday markets, the city decided to start on a Wednesday, July 15. With 23 farmers and $11,000 in sales, the market was an instant success, the largest until that time. (Now 50 farmers at an opening is not uncommon.) The following two weeks farmer numbers increased and sales grew to $13,000, then $15,000. Nowadays, with around 100 farmers on average, Santa Monica's Wednesday mid-day market is still the highest grossing market in southern California.

Weekday markets often do well extending over the lunch hour. In a heavily trafficked, urban area, hours from 10 a.m. to 2 p.m. allow farmers to avoid rush hour in both directions, serve business people able to double-task during lunchtime, and provide seniors the chance to finish shopping early.

Saturday markets often run from 8 a.m. to 1 p.m., although it's not uncommon to open at 7 a.m. or earlier, especially where heat is a factor. Larger markets may stay open until 3 p.m. or later. Anything over seven hours makes a long day for farmers when time for packing, travel, set-up and break-down is added.

A Sunday market may be preferable for parking if your downtown gets heavy use on Saturday. In fact, because Sunday carries a more relaxed, family focus than Saturday, it may be the best market day. Some farmers may not participate on Sunday but this also can be true on Saturday when many farmers are already busy with other markets. Churches are frequently sensitive to the perceived competitive impact of Sunday markets, yet markets seem to open at 8 or 9 a.m. with little problem. Whether the market goes to noon or 2 p.m. depends upon the influx of church-goers to the market as each service lets out.

If you have an evening market in a business locale, work with retailers to encourage a regular change in their window displays and cross promotions with the market which will provide increased pedestrian traffic. The existence of each activity helps the other.

On the West Coast at least, the grandmother of all evening markets is San Luis Obispo. The event is known as "Thursday Night" and it attracts up to 10,000 people into the downtown core every Thursday from 6:30 to 9:00 p.m. Along with dozens of farmers and numerous crafts sellers, you may find local retailers and restaurants open for the occasion, a volleyball game, non-profits raising funds, a flatbed truck for campaigning politicians, a car show and who knows what else. Every Friday morning a group of committed leaders including the farmers' market manager meets to review the previous evening and deal with issues before they become problems.

Concentrated Selling Time

Hours need not be lengthy. If people can come within an eight-hour period, most can come within four or five hours. People generally will plan their day around a market visit so hours can be compact. Farmers want to be busy rather than waiting for occasional customers to straggle through. Customers also want to shop in an atmosphere of other eager customers, not feeling like every farmer needs to capture their attention.

Therefore, start with a shorter market timeframe unless you are appealing strongly to local artisans. If and when you need more time to serve a growing customer base and your farmers agree, announce that you are extending your hours by popular demand. To go the other direction, condensing hours, is to admit that your planning did not bring about the anticipated customer response.

In some communities two hours is plenty to serve most customers. To double the market to four hours would only bring marginal additional sales and waste farmers' time. You can never satisfy everyone with your hours, so make the best decision possible and revisit your decision when you have additional information.

Establish market hours with the buyers in mind — find out what day and times are busiest. Are Saturday mornings busy shopping days? If your market is located where businesses are located, then it's good to be open noons and especially when work lets out or shifts change. If the market is located on a commuting road, consider staying open till 6 or 6:30 p.m. to allow commuters to shop.

Staying open late may work if you know you can capture customers on their way home and farmers don't mind having an extra late evening. Generally it's a good idea to avoid opening and closing times that coincide with rush hour. A weekday 10-2 p.m. or 11-3 p.m. market will keep farmers from competing with the heaviest traffic.

Multi-day Potential

Many markets have experience going from one day of operation to two per week. Just because the community response is strong one day doesn't assure a second day success. In fact, it seems that the second day fails relatively more often than not. There seem to be several explanations. Markets don't do their homework to determine if existing or potential customer counts are sufficient; they don't invest the necessary resources; they assume if one is good, two is better; and they fail to calculate the total effort invested in their initial effort and duplicate it.

Even California's model market in Davis encountered problems when it decided to replicate its Saturday market. For years their Wednesday market has struggled along, getting about 10 percent of Saturday's sales volume. In spite of trying various hours, they continue to experience low sales half the year from 2 to 6 p.m. However, in 1993 they began Picnic in the Park, positioning the market as summer evening entertainment from 4:30 to 8:30 p.m. During picnic months they get sales nearly comparable to Saturday.

Similarly, when we developed a Tuesday market in Hillsboro, Oregon, we crafted a plan to market it to a dinner and entertainment crowd, knowing that Saturday was doing a fantastic job of selling produce. Instead of the Hillsboro Farmers' Market, it has a separate identity as the Hillsboro Tuesday Marketplace. Its start-up campaign involved a much larger group of community stakeholders.

In considering multiple days, clarify your goals. Are you trying to expand hours for your existing clientele or do you think you can double your sales with double the hours? Consider what's best for farmer sales, not just customer convenience. You may dilute the impact of your good market as farmer sales decrease on an average daily basis. It may be wiser to use limited farmer availability at different locales over several days of the week. Thus, each neighborhood or community has a special market day.

If you have a major site investment a multiple-day market may make sense. Some locations have weekend hours or more because they want to appeal to customers' desire for convenience.

However, farmers' markets shouldn't pretend to be all things to all people. We probably can't drop to a skeleton staff like a supermarket at 11 p.m. without losing the essence of what we are. Part of what makes farmers' markets special is limited hours, forcing people to come on farmer time and find a sense of community in the process. Most markets don't want to be open for the straggler who appears to shop in the middle of the night.

The Olympia Farmers' Market is a good, multiple-day model. It opens its spring season on Saturdays and once it is ready to declare summer, the market is open Thursday through Sunday from 9 a.m. to 3 p.m. The four-day operation enables it to pay off an $800,000 construction bond that the city issued in the early 1990s. The new structure is situated at a prominent location, a turn-around at the bottom of four lanes of traffic on Capitol Way.

"Start slow with Saturdays only and build into a regular three day per week market as produce becomes available and customer demand increases. Make sure your options for future days are outlined in your contract. Mornings are preferable due to the cooler weather which enhances the freshness and longevity of the produce, and six hours is ample time to remain in the marketplace."
— Sara Pollard, *Do's and Don'ts of a Successful Farmers' Market*

Experience in Torrance and Santa Monica, CA, has shown a better total result when opening first with a mid-week market. Initially Tuesday and Wednesday, respectively, each had a large population base to add a Saturday market years later. In other markets where a weekday has been the later addition, customers seem less likely to compare it favorably to the weekend market they're accustomed to.

A major part of the decision about multiple-day operation must be left to a full assessment of what your market farmers and customers want. Even San Francisco's premier Alemany Farmers' Market, a large open-air concrete set of shelters built in the early 1940s, had to keep cutting back from five days ultimately to one day, Saturday, as competition swelled. Now it has added a Sunday antique market which has had fabulous success meeting an untapped need.

Rain or Shine

Building loyal customers and farmers is dependent upon each knowing the other will come consistently rain or shine. Especially from a distance, farmers in sun may be unaware of rain across the hills. Conversely, a lengthy downpour may prevent farmers from harvesting while the market is sunny. With all but a very small market, it would be impossible to notify farmers and customers that a market day is canceled. Build customers' faith that farmers are depending on them to come and you'll probably have about two-thirds of your normal balance. Everyone will do okay and you will have kept the continuity.

ORGANIZER & MARKET MANAGER

"A good farmers' market has a good Market Master. You can count on it."
— Jeff Ishee, *Dynamic Farmers' Marketing*

In most instances there is one driving force behind the market, a person who is compelled to create a success. Sometimes it's a small group of people. Either way, this individual or group makes the outreach happen to form a larger committee and to supervise and carry out all the necessary activities. Someone has to make things happen, meeting deadlines on the timeline for start-up.

This innovator often becomes the founding market manager. He or she will oversee on-site operations during the market day, including assigning spaces to growers, enforcing market rules, and collecting fees.

If this person hasn't created the initial committee, find a dynamo through a press release, a job announcement and word-of-mouth within your circle of influence. More important than being knowledgeable about produce, the market manager needs to be creative, self-motivated, organized, flexible and a people person. A marketing background is helpful in working with publicity as well as with community leaders and customers.

As Randii MacNear, manager of the Davis Farmers' Market, says, "The best manager is someone who likes constant problem solving, is a good listener and enjoys the swarm — the people coming, sellers, hearing community desires and resolving issues. It's both the fun and the tough part. It's the magic."

Some staff are hired as contractors, but if the market is the majority source of income, he/she must be made an employee by law. Check with an attorney or certified public accountant. To avoid a conflict of interest, hire someone who will not be selling at the market. The manager must be above reproach in all vendor relations, including space assignments.

Manager Laura Avery, second from right, and assistant do weekly, live, public radio updates so listeners learn about the day's market picks in Santa Monica.

Dependent upon your budget, pay should be commensurate with ability and responsibility. Given many start-up budgets, that leaves a lot of latitude for the organizing committee or board to pay much less than the manager is worth. Since this manager is likely to age considerably in just a matter of months(!), you might establish a bonus related to several measures of success as defined by the board, not necessarily just getting more farmers involved.

The responsibilities of a market manager may encompass a full-time position with support staff in a large urban setting or it may be a relatively simple, informal relationship with a few vendors in a small community. There the manager may be a volunteer or a vendor who doesn't have to pay a stall fee. However, a paid position is recommended.

MARKET SPONSORSHIP

There are three basic models of the organizational structure. One of your early steps is to determine who will sponsor the market: the city, state or chamber; a grower association or co-op; or a community organization created to pull all the stakeholders together. Each type has its benefits. Under any structure you will need to identify the chain of command, give authority to the manager, define the separation of powers and clarify enforcement procedures. [Look at the

Dane County Farmers' Market story under "Managing the Market" chapter for a considered reflection on sponsorship, product limitations, space allotment and rule enforcement.]

City-run

A city may appoint a municipal staffperson to oversee the market and hire managers to tend to it on-site. Farmer space fees go into the market and the city's general fund. This structure works well in the City of Chicago markets as well as Ann Arbor, Michigan. The City of Santa Monica, California, established markets under its Economic Development Department and now has a total of four market days at three different locations. Laura Avery coordinates the program and manages the oldest market while three part-time staffers run the others.

This model gives decision-making responsibility to one key individual with oversight by city supervisors. Alternately, it might be the board of a chamber of commerce or a downtown business association making final decisions. Farmers are left to grow and market their products, knowing that an entity within the city is responsible for managing a substantial budget with many practical and political intricacies. The liability is that these boards may not have the time and background to make good decisions regarding market operation when they have their own separate organizational concerns. Success is often dependent upon a manager who gets input from farmers and makes recommendations that are largely approved by the supervising authority. Financial politics can sometimes get in the way.

Especially in the southeastern states, many markets are run by state officials after making a major investment in a wholesale-retail marketplace. Frequently, wholesale houses and a farmer shed co-exist on a property near a freeway intersection such as in Asheville, NC. In Georgia all nine farmers' markets are substantial, year-round, state-run operations. The state of Florida runs a handful of similar wholesale-retail markets, although many more farmers' markets are typical, seasonal, outdoor markets.

Grower-run

Growers often band together to form a co-op or association — or are organized into one by a founding dynamo organizer — and pay a nominal fee to join. The hired manager represents them in developing and managing the market. Many farmers believe that as producers, their board better understands what they need and how the market(s) should run. Certainly, they understand the farmer side better than a city staffer, but do they understand their urban customers, a necessary marketing strategy and the political scene as well as the city staffer?

> "I suggest that farmers' market startups go the co-op way instead of having one person in charge. I've heard of other markets where one person has the power to make all the decisions of when and where to set up. It's better to have a board to take everyone's point of view into consideration."
> — Jane Desotelle, Mgr., Adirondack Farmers' Market Cooperative, NY

The Adirondack co-op works for several upstate farmers' markets west of Lake Champlain. The F.A.R.M. (Farm Association for Retail Marketing) organizations created in the 1970s and 1980s throughout the southeastern states give farmers similar control over their marketing in numerous towns and cities.

If an association runs the market, the city will be more inclined to insist on good business practices leading to more professional managers. Good managers understand how to convey farmer concerns to city authorities without estranging them. Their greater challenge is incorporating customers' views when the farmer board may slant the view on many decisions. Having a couple of non-farmers on the board may compensate and lead to productive discussions.

Community-sponsored

The third model is a hybrid comprised of community representatives. The goal here is to establish a balanced steering committee or board of directors representing all stakeholders in the community. It generally has five to 15 people that represent farmers, artisans, business, chamber, visitors' bureau, city, Cooperative Extension, residents, media, faith community, civic and arts organizations, and others. Some individuals may prefer to serve on a non-voting advisory committee.

> "Growers alone cannot establish a farmers' market in a city. There must be a commitment and coordination between city officials and growers to get it done. A commitment on the part of the community is an essential partnership that must happen to make the place successful and sustainable."
> — *American Vegetable Grower,* "Community is Key to Market Success," 1995

While the community model may have a larger, time-consuming board, it often has a better read on the community's pulse and what new directions to take. The board diversity provokes discussion, confronts more issues that could become problems later and affords a greater number of connections to others in order to accomplish your goals.

The goal with any structure is to have a healthy balance of a strong manager and strong board (or supervisors). If either side is weak, the organization suffers. The major duties of the board include market rules and guidelines, problem resolution, goal setting, annual budget, executive director review, and advertising program approval.

The ultimate organizational structure may be influenced by location, geography and city size. While some believe it is essential for a market's day-to-day operation to be controlled by members rather than an outside entity, others recognize good management for what it is, regardless of whether it is under the control of members. The Pacific Coast Farmers' Market Association runs 19 markets in the Bay Area with a seven-person board of farmers and influential urban leaders, yet it is not a member organization.

No size fits all. We continue to imagine the best structures to fit our communities. At times the vendor base determines the organization and it isn't

Directional signs require minimal words for drivers needing quick information.

healthy. If that occurs, we can approach the community, ask what kind of market it wants and enlist the best people to help carry us to our goals.

Stakeholder Assistance

Who can help with the development and outreach for potential and fledgling markets? They will be stakeholders, whether formally on the board or not.

If you have enough volunteers involved, you may have a committee for every aspect of market development. Find an accountant and chamber member for the finance or budget committee, a farmer and Extension staff for farmer outreach, a good retailer and a newspaper staffer for publicity, city and business improvement association staff for location, an attorney and farmer for rules and bylaws, and a civic organization and city volunteer coordinator for special events.

Ask your city for specific resources even if they are not the sponsor. You may end up locating at a city street or park where bathrooms, barricades and storage are made available. Police and fire departments frequently want to sign off on safety questions. Economic development staff can connect you to key chamber of commerce contacts, refer you to helpful promoters, assist with street banner placement and encourage work with planning staff to locate the market where it can help local businesses. The mayor can cut the ribbon at your opening. Depending on the city's level of involvement and the likelihood of success, they may want to help attract major media attention.

Your state department of agriculture, Cooperative Extension, Farm Bureau, conservation commission and grower organizations can help with farm and political contacts, perhaps lining up a speaking tour in key agricultural areas. Ask for lists they may share or assistance with mailings.

A local farmers' market association may give you many forms of help including farm contacts, introductions, combined meetings, special event contacts

Producer-Based and Community-Driven: Another Perspective

In his roles as a public/farmers' market consultant as well as executive director with Farmers' Markets Ontario (www.fmo.reach.net), Bob Chorney has organized 80 markets, mostly in Ontario. Chorney's recipe for a successful farmers' market revolves around four elements: it must be community driven, supported by a community champion, producer based, and involve the right mix of vendors.

Community driven

"Farmers typically are great producers and all too often poor marketers," Chorney says, "and that's why most of the successful markets we've seen are community- rather than farmer-driven." Successful markets are community-based with a coalition of farmers, crafters, business people, politicians, extension people, and a "shopper" who visits a lot of markets and gets to know them.

Community champions

The term "community champions" refers to influential groups that are active and dedicated in their support of a market. They may be simply a core group of community-minded individuals, possibly including vendors, or they may belong to more formal groups such as business improvement associations, chambers of commerce, or service organizations. These people play a large part in establishing the groundwork for a market. The champion typically maintains an arm's length association with the market, but does not continue to direct the operation after it is up and running.*

Find a champion to get things rolling, with a steering committee of farmers, crafters, politicians, and business people. Groups can move mountains to get the market started. But often the farmers and crafters then feel they don't need those partnerships anymore and try to strike out on their own. Keep the partnerships strong!

Let people know what the farmers' market does for the social fabric of the community: it makes it a community gathering place. Let businesses know that the "ripple effect" is the best way to bring downtown sales. When the farmer comes to town the neighboring businesses also make money. What's the economic impact of these markets? It's important to tell that story!

Producer based

Surveys at Ontario farmers' markets show that 80-90 percent of customers come for the fresh produce. Consumers also say they want to deal directly with the primary producers. "Shoppers come to our markets for locally-grown fresh produce," Chorney says, "and we need to provide that for that them! When truckers and the peddlers find their way in, farmers' markets lose their producer base of farmers and crafters from the local area. We have to work hard to keep our markets producer-based."

Vendor mix

Fresh produce must be the focus of a market, since that's what consumers want. Chorney recommends a ratio of five or six "fresh food" food vendors for every craft vendor. His definition of "fresh produce," however, is quite broad, encompassing things like maple products, preserves, baked goods, flowers and bedding plants in addition to fruits and vegetables.*

Crafts can enhance the markets IF they are high quality, homemade items that reflect the spirit of the market. Markets should establish a jurying system for crafts to ensure that the quality and character of the merchandise fits into the farmers' market theme. The jury should be created as a body separate and distinct from the executive to avoid claims of favoritism or unwanted political influence.

"Flea markets and farmers do not mix," Chorney says. "A farmers' market shopper comes to the market for freshness and community interaction, meeting the producer, learning to prepare food for the table, and supporting the community. The flea market shopper comes to haggle prices and get the best price. It's a whole different mind set.

"What the farmers' markets are all about is that it's from the farmer to you. Keep telling the customers that! ✿

*"How to Build A Successful Farmers' Market," *Rural Delivery* (New Brunswick, Canada) March 1999.

and joint promotional campaigns. Alternately, they may be interested in a marriage of the old and the new, strengthening their organization and avoiding a duplication of efforts.

While your local business organization may not be ready to sponsor the market, they may be a major contributor through financial support, board members, insurance, publicity, printing, and numerous contacts for free or reduced-fee services. Most businesses recognize the benefits the market will bring through heavier pedestrian traffic so they are eager to distribute handbills and put posters in their windows.

Residents' associations, neighborhood centers, senior citizen organizations, development corporations, churches, social organizations and charities all have something to contribute to this community effort. The challenge is in taking the time to reach out to staffpeople and boards to see how they can help. The list is unlimited. Virtually everyone in your community has an interest in seeing the market established. Your goal is to help them see how their interest group will be served through the market.

Developing Community Support

The satisfaction achieved in creating a farmers' market may directly relate to the effort expended in building a cohesive community group that actualizes the market's goals. We can meet diverse needs by joining representatives from city government, local merchants, nonprofit organizations and farmers in the planning process, and allowing different nonprofit groups to set up informational tables at the market.

Reach out to all elements of the population. Include farmers who cater to a mix of ethnic groups, income levels and lifestyles. Each of these groups has different buying habits. Unusual vegetables and "seconds," labeled as such, create a more diverse buying group and make the market more intriguing.

Crossing the Columbia River from Oregon into Washington, these three arches hold Vancouver's permanent sign visible from Interstate 5, even though in 2000 the market moved several blocks to the state's oldest park.

Businesses unfamiliar with the benefits [see Appendix] may be reluctant to bring in a farmers' market because they fear it will be a distraction or exacerbate limited parking. Statistics and anecdotal evidence show farmers' markets are a boon to adjacent businesses.

Educate townsfolk about the benefit of nutritious, lower-priced fresh produce being more readily available, especially important in low-income areas where families often skimp on purchases of life-sustaining fresh fruits and vegetables. Set up a booth to give free samples and nutrient information on various products and general information about healthy eating habits. Contact your state agriculture or health department to see if your market can be approved to accept food coupons under the Women, Infants and Children (WIC) Farmers' Market Nutrition Program. Obtain promotional material and recipes from various commodity groups as well as the 5-A-Day campaign. [See Resources, Chapter 7 and General]

"Know your elected officials! What they do affects your market! Know who your planners are, your mayor and city council. Space is critical with city planning. Otherwise you get shlepped all over the place and each time you move it costs you a lot of customers. Bring the mayor to the market for a Cabbage Toss to open the market season. Each time the city council does something good for the market, invite them to the market and do a photofest. We have a photographer who is a volunteer at the market."
— Karen Durham, Mgr., Bellingham Farmers' Market, WA

Market Rules and Regulations

Rules generally define the type of market, governance, who may sell, permitted products, seller guidelines, standards of conduct, reservation and cancellation policy, and penalties for non-compliance. Every vendor should sign a copy of the rules so they acknowledge their responsibilities. The manager should maintain those copies in case any legal question arises.

Probably the issue most central to your market identity relates to integrity around the question of who can sell what. Neil Hamilton points out in *The Legal Guide for Direct Farm Marketing* that few states control the use of the term "farmers' market" by law. Maine is one that specifically establishes it as a place where two or more farmers offer for sale farm and food products at least 75% of which they produce.

The pure form of a farmers' market is one where all farmers may sell only what they produce. The huge success of the Dane County Farmers' Market in Madison, WI, reflects public support for this model where customers can get answers to any question directly from the farmer. The discussion of integrity and enforcement will be an important part of the creation of your rules.

Interestingly, Hamilton points out that the only recent court case regarding a farmers' market rule was Bowen v. Dane County Farmers' Market in 1996. The vendor had been suspended for not producing what he was selling according to market rules. The Wisconsin Court of Appeals upheld the district court's summary judgment for the market and fees related to their defense against a frivolous lawsuit. Hamilton notes what we can learn:

"First, courts will probably enforce the markets' rules as long as they are clear and are applied in a fair manner. Second, a market may need to be prepared to expend time and money to defend its actions in court. Third, while the case is unusual, because findings of frivolous lawsuits are not that common, it shows that a producer who sues a market when the facts are clear, may risk having to pay the market's court costs and attorneys fees."
— Neil Hamilton, *The Legal Guide for Direct Farm Marketing*

Assure safety and high standards by requiring members to obtain any applicable city, county, state or federal licenses. Food processors should have a certified kitchen; if organic they must use certified organic products. Rules may also cover stall appearance

and safety requirements. You don't need to reinvent the wheel — get copies of other markets' rules and decide what works best for you. Change your rules if needed.

It is not uncommon for localities and the state to waive registration or tax requirements for small producers. For instance, when nursery product offered for sale during the course of the year does not exceed $5,000 value, one may not be required to have a nursery license; check your state's code with your state agriculture department. Similarly, small producers may have a business license waiver below a certain volume; check with your municipality.

Develop a policy to discourage dumping of large quantities of produce at low prices. You might require farmers to stay within 10% of local retail prices, or to not go below wholesale prices, and to keep the quality and uniqueness of their products in mind when determining prices. Such guidelines prevent price wars within your market and prevent undercutting by hobbyists unconcerned with making a profit.

Get legal counsel to review all your written rules and procedures, especially around quality and minimum pricing standards. A legal marketing cooperative allows you to establish an acceptable range of prices. Members of the market sign an agreement to abide by the pricing policies. These policies might only apply until a certain time in each market day and until a fixed point in the season.

Establish standards for produce quality, cleanliness, display and marketing procedures. Do not allow dirty or distressed produce, unless you want to have a processing grade for home canners. If inferior produce is offered at a reduced price, the customer should be alerted. A "replace-or-refund" guarantee will reinforce customer loyalty and serve as your best form of advertisement.

"The fewer the rules, the better. Too many rules bog down progress and discourage participation. Second, rules should be written to keep the customer happy. If there aren't too many rules, and they are written with a positive spin, and are aimed to make the customers' experience a happy one, then everyone wins. Goals for the market need to be established. Only after the goals are clearly defined should a set of rules be written. And then the rules should be used more as a guideline than as a strict enforcement tool. If a problem arises, use a market committee to handle them. Never reprimand a vendor in front of a customer. Instead, do it privately and in a way that will keep the vendor smiling through it!"

— *Farmers' Market Forum,* Farmers' Market Federation of New York

One market learned the hard way, via a lawsuit, that it could not restrict its selling to vendors from within state or political boundaries. It could, however, specify that growers be within a certain mileage radius. This evidently did not interfere with laws addressing interstate commerce.

Licenses

By contrast, California law requires that all farmers must have a certified producer certificate ensuring that they grow within the state. The market also must be certified by the county agricultural commissioner who will periodically inspect the market to assure compliance with legal statutes about who can sell. Markets in other states do not have this enforcement support.

Familiarize yourselves with city, county, state and federal guidelines, especially agricultural and health regulations. Raw produce is generally not a problem but concerns about sprouts, sampling and value-added processing will draw health inspectors. A county health permit may be required for the market. The department will usually require separate permits for any producers selling a product which should be processed in a health-approved facility, e.g. jams, chutneys, baked goods.

City staff are usually involved with site approval and conditional use permits. You may need to go before the planning commission and/or the city council, so be prepared to organize a group of market supporters who can reinforce all the community benefits of your project. The city may have the entire market operate under one umbrella business license; since it is one entity, every vendor should not be required to have their own.

In some localities any producer can sell their own agricultural product exempt from any business license requirement. Various states also have codified protections for farmers' right to sell their own products free of municipal license requirements, including Arizona, Florida, Pennsylvania and Washington.

Bylaws and Articles of Incorporation

Bylaws outline the name of the corporation, mission, membership, board number and terms, officer responsibilities, meeting times and conditions, committee structure, executive committee, insurance and indemnification, fiscal year term and amendment process.

Find an attorney, willing to serve on your board, who can help guide you to the proper federal tax status in setting up a for-profit or non-profit organization. You might consider getting a 501(c)(3) status for your market. This is a non-profit, tax-exempt designation assigned by the Internal Revenue Service to educational and charitable organizations. A 501(c)(3) status is essential for organizations that would like get donations or grants from the private sector or foundations. Having a 501(c)(3) status allows you to raise money for non-profit projects. However, the more common route is another 501(c) designation, still non-profit but not tax-exempt.

"Because of the space we provide master gardeners, master composters, P-Patch (a community garden program) and Seattle Tilth, we are providing the public education and advice on food production, organic methods of growing and composting. We also staff and maintain our own information table with local ag news and information. Our chef demos and produce tastings are also effective public education events. It's these events and outreach that are the education component of our 501(c)(3) status. Our charitable component is realized through our donations to local food banks."

— Chris Curtis, Mgr., University District FM, Seattle, WA

Establish your mission, your purpose for being. Nancy Ricketts lists the goals of the Oak Park Farmers' Market, located in a Chicago suburb: "to enhance the quality of life in Oak Park by providing fresh, high-quality produce, a community meeting place, and consumer education."

The mission of the Yakima Farmers' Market, WA, is "to engage in activity to support Yakima Valley and other small and family-run farms and other independent businesses, and to create a vibrant, educational marketplace for the community benefit."

Articles of incorporation are filed alongside the bylaws with your secretary of state. These articles establish your incorporation by defining the corporate name and type, duration (hopefully perpetual), registered office and agent, purposes, powers, membership or not, the names and addresses of founding board members and ex-officio directors, dissolution process, reference to establishment of bylaws, amendment process, consent of the registered agent, and signatures of three incorporators. Look over articles of another market with a volunteer attorney or CPA.

When you choose a "corporate" designation, you decide if the market will be a non-profit or for-profit entity. You might become a "non-profit, mutual benefit corporation." To ensure that your market addresses all essential legalities, it is wise to have an experienced consultant or attorney draft and file your paperwork. The cost generally runs between $500 and $2000, well worth it in the long run.

BUDGET

Your budget reflects many of your principles as a market organization. It demonstrates the importance of the organization vis-à-vis farmer income, whether management is deemed professional or volunteer, and what are the priorities for sustainability in your environment. Much depends on where your market(s) is located and whom it serves.

An urban market may be part of a multi-market association with millions of dollars in sales and a several hundred thousand dollar operational budget. It may have an executive director and several staff paid salaries that would seem exorbitant to another market yet which may be relatively low in relation to the cost of living.

A rural market may operate independently with twenty-five thousand dollars in annual sales and a budget of under $1,000. The manager is likely to be a volunteer, a market friend or a farmer with minimal compensation.

What these two markets — and just about every other one in between — have in common is the desire for growth to ensure a future and to have a meaningful impact on their communities. The major difference is a few zeros. Each may face severe competition or threats to their sustainability. Each may feel unsure as to how they can operate next year. Each may wonder how they can do the needed promotion without an infusion of money. What they may need is to reconsider their financial structure.

So how are markets funded? Many have been given start-up money through a state grant, the city, a chamber of commerce, the downtown business association, a mall, businesspeople, a charitable individual or fund raising. For example, soliciting business and community sponsors to be listed on 500 color posters can raise several thousand dollars. Hosting a dinner or art show can do the same. In every case where a market gets funded, it starts with a dream, a plan, a budget outlining the necessities and outreach to find the fi-

Oakland markets are full of ethnic diversity among farmers and shoppers, all three developed by associations that run multiple markets in the Bay area.

nancial assistance. The dynamic, founding individual or group must have a clear vision and the ability to communicate it to a funding source.

They may distinguish a start-up or development budget from a regular operating budget. The development budget can have substantial costs for personnel, phone, travel, logo development, printing, office supplies, insurance, permits, signs, advertising and promotion. All these development costs are necessary to get the market off and running on opening day.

The benefit of a separate operating budget is that it allows you to see the true annualized costs of running your market; in planning year two you can compare expenses and income with the first year, unhindered by all the start-up costs.

An operating budget is based primarily on vendor fees. List all your costs in operating the market and a projection of income from space fees, membership fees, fundraising and other sources.

Fundraising

Some markets have outside funds for up to several years to ensure their financial stability. Certain markets also receive support from businesses that want their name or logo on market promotional materials. Markets may gain additional revenue through the sale of drinks or food items. For instance, the Marin County Farmers' Market, CA, purchases baked goods from three bakeries and resells them as a fund raiser.

Every stakeholder is a resource representing a potential source of funding. Cities have community development or other funds to assist. States have economic development funds or other sources that may be granted through a competitive process or by staff discretion. The federal government has also been a source, through several USDA programs including transportation and forestry.

Markets may need to look for grants from a local foundation, contributions from growers, or even loans or grants from individuals or organizations. Tie your promotional efforts to fund raising. Every time you ask for any assistance, include financial support in your request. It's a great way to gain tangible project support and if they say no, they usually are more inclined to help in other ways.

You can raise start-up funds by creating a poster and listing businesses and organizations in your community who contribute at various sponsorship levels. Hold a pancake breakfast and pre-sell tickets. People can make a contribution and not have to come. You aren't just raising money; you're promoting community ownership.

Fee Structure

For most markets the great bulk of the burden for financing operational costs rests on the farming vendors. Thus, it's a fair idea to give them an an-

The first Pasco, WA, market shed on a city parking lot was so popular, a second one was built the following year, making the market experience more enjoyable for all.

nual accounting of how their money is spent, although not every market chooses to do so. There are many scenarios for gathering income. Here are some of the most common fee structures:

⋄ Annual fee: One fee for the entire season, either equal or proportional to size. Expenses are projected and growers assessed, often with a reduction if paid in advance. Half the fee may be paid mid-season to protect farmers from one early bill of $300; the second assessment also may be adjusted up or down if the situation calls for it.

⋄ Annual plus daily fee: A fee for seasonal membership plus a daily fee when they sell. This provides start-up money from funds that are equally assessed.

⋄ Daily fee: Fee is usually based on total amount of space or frontal footage, regardless of sales volume. Farmers may suffer on weak days with new competition or bad weather.

⋄ Percentage fee: Farmers pay 4-8% of their sales, generally on the honor system and with a minimum fee to ensure basic expenses are covered.

⋄ Base plus percentage fee: Fee starts with a basic space-use fee and a percentage or step fee is added based on sales, again on the honor system.

One key issue to resolve in establishing fees is fairness. Is it fair to charge the same $150 per season to two growers, one who will gross $800 and the other $20,000? Is it fair to charge the same $12 per day of a grower selling $60 and another selling $1200? The first is paying 20% and the later 1% of income. Some will say that it's fair because each is using the same amount of space, like rent in a mall. Others will claim it is unfair because the small farmer is just as important to overall market identity, probably gives more friendly attention to customers, and should not have to subsidize the larger farmer's true share of the operation. (Besides, malls usually charge a base plus percentage; they want a share of extra profit.)

"Why force farmers to cheat?" one will ask.

"The market doesn't make liars of truthful people," another responds.

"Doesn't a percentage fee penalize large farmers who sell more?"

"Doesn't a fixed fee penalize small growers that we most want to help?"

"Should farmers be forced to reveal their sales?"

"In any other marketing venue someone else knows the farmers' income. The manager will keep individual incomes confidential."

You can easily see this discussion is never-ending, but you do need to make a decision. Whatever it is will be difficult to change years later because the status quo is hard to shift and you will have gained a following of farmers who believe that fee structure is fair. Markets with a straight daily fee tend to see the benefits of simplicity and avoid the fact that they don't know their sales. A market across town may operate with a percentage fee and know exactly how each holiday or week of the month affects gross sales.

Set your fees high enough to provide for adequate advertising and other expenses. Don't be surprised if personnel comprises 50% of your budget, perhaps with 35% for promotion and advertising, and 15% for insurance and office expenses. With a small, rural

market and a volunteer manager, the percentages will differ drastically.

Your budget will change based on your hours and choice of vendors. A downtown evening market might have graduated fees according to vendor type: hot foods pay 9% or $40 minimum, artisans 8% or $30, value-added processors 7% or $25, and farmers 6% or $20. If you state the standards clearly in advance, you can avoid a cart vendor rolling up and taking advantage of your market. This also requires that you clearly delineate the physical area over which you have city authority.

Fees Essential to Planning

The goal is to fairly charge according to the benefit that each farmer derives from the market. We want to help small, independent, family farmers. When a farmer sells product through a shipper, broker, wholesaler, retailer or restaurant, there is a fee which relates in some way to volume. There may be discounts with greater volume but it still costs more to ship more, and many intermediaries work on a straight percentage. So, farmers are not shocked in dealing with fees that are based on their sales.

When markets charge a percentage or step fee, they become better at business. They learn the numbers. Knowing daily sales like any other retail business is essential for making good decisions with the space fee income.

With sales figures a manager can analyze whether a marketing campaign is effective. Trying advertising or promotional ideas with a cost is necessary, but if you can only rely on farmers' anecdotal responses about sales going up, it is difficult to determine whether your expenditure paid off. You don't want to be wasting farmers' money. With good farmer income figures a manager can compare sales growth resulting from radio ads versus newspaper ads or posters done in the past.

Daily sales also help a manager to track how each farmer is doing and how they are impacted by their competition. The manager may see that a farmer's sales are level when they should be growing with overall market growth. When a farmer complains that competition is killing him, the manager may note that other farmers with the same product are doing well and additional competition has led to increased demand and more satisfied customers. In other words, knowledge of the full sales picture gives a manager the ability to defuse an angry vendor. Without that knowledge the manager would be limited to an emotional rather than a rational response.

Membership

Membership at farmers' markets is used to build a sense of ownership, give privileges to a defined group, establish seniority, collect basic operational money and provide a base from which to elect leaders of the organization. Some markets require it as a condition for selling, others have no membership, and still others make it optional with non-members paying a higher fee to sell.

Well-run markets often use membership as a basis for building camaraderie among farmers. There may be an annual dinner, perhaps covered within the cost of membership to encourage attendance, at which board elections take place.

Membership fees vary much like space fees listed above. They may be a modest $5 or $10 a year to cover postage and low overhead for a small market. To maintain a full range of market association services in a large, urban market, fees may amount to several hundred dollars per year. In some markets selling privileges are part of the membership fees. More commonly, selling fees — daily, monthly or by the season — are separate from membership costs.

For instance, a farmers' market may charge a membership fee of $35 per season and then charge a $20 daily space fee or a 6% fee; a non-member might pay $25 or 7%. Thus, a short season farmer might choose not to join as a member while most farmers would see the financial benefit of becoming a member and having voting rights in the organization.

Some associations provide for a consumer membership, giving them a sense of market ownership as well and perhaps the right to elect board members.

Other markets have a separate 501 (c)(3), nonprofit, tax-exempt Friends of the Market organization to encourage active customer participation and raise additional financial support for educational campaigns. This allows the market to solicit tax-deductible donations while keeping them separate from the market's taxable activity.

Insurance

A market should have coverage year-round to protect itself for all functions in which the market is involved. If a person attends a winter meeting and falls on a slippery step, you could get sued. A skateboarder falls or injures a customer. A dogfight occurs. A customer cuts her leg on a wire basket carrying green beans. A man says he got food poisoning from a processed item. You need protection. In the case of a suit against one farmer, basic coverage will protect all others. Markets generally encourage or require their individual vendors to provide proof of their own insurance. Consider directors' liability insurance for board members along with your normal liability coverage.

While you want a comprehensive general liability policy, make sure it includes product liability. Your city may have insurance that covers a farmers' market on municipal property — but you may need additional coverage. You'll need insurance if you're on private property. Do your homework. Costs vary widely from under $100 well into the thousands per year based on market size and because private carriers aren't sure how to classify farmers' markets in their rate schedules.

Nationwide and State Farm have long served the agricultural industry, but this is the key arena where regional or statewide farmers' market associations have saved markets money. The state association obtains a policy as the lead insured and provides it to markets and vendors. Generally a policy covering up to a one million dollar claim is sufficient. Call your state farmers' market association or department of agriculture. [See also Appendix]

Managing Risk at your Market

— Condensed from *Farmers' Market Forum,* Farmers' Market Federation of New York, Summer 1998

The first step in "insuring" your market is to practice good risk management. Are your market aisles clear and unobstructed? Do boxes and baskets stick out into the aisle causing a trip hazard? Are produce and plants in vendor spaces kept up off the ground level? Is the floor clear of easy-to-slip-on garbage or produce trimmings?

Are the grounds properly maintained — pavement in good repair, and any crumbling curbing patched or painted? Is your electrical wiring in proper order? Do you have properly-charged fire extinguishers located throughout the market? You may also want to consider asking a fire marshal to walk through your market and offer safety suggestions. Keep cars from the market's selling area — cars and people walking and shopping are a dangerous mix.

Spread the risk. Require your sellers to provide the market with liability insurance so that if someone is hurt as a result of a vendor's negligence, the market is not left solely defending and possibly paying on a lawsuit. More and more insurance companies are looking to this as a means of controlling their risks. It's just a matter of time before this becomes mandatory. ✿

Customer Service

Although we go into "customer service" in the Promotion chapter, it is important to remember that the concept of service should be built into your market from the beginning. Don't wait until after you start to read that chapter. You need to practice customer service principles right now!

Wheelchair customers, for example, prefer hard-surfaced markets because maneuvering on grass is difficult. Curb cuts or ramps facilitate wheelchair accessibility. For many lower-income customers, proximity to a bus stop is essential. Special busing from senior housing centers may be necessary to serve that clientele. The senior center may pay for their own shuttle or you might share the expense.

On-going Support

It's probably occurred to you by now that starting a market is a lot of work! And once you start it, there's the job of running it! Don't try to do all this alone. Join internet web discussion groups, go to small farm conferences, call a consultant, get some technical assistance, etc.

Join a farmers' market association or start one. There are now numerous state and regional farmers' market associations developed by the industry, frequently with governmental assistance. Through conferences and friendships within those associations, you can chart a steep learning curve. They offer many group advantages including cost reduction programs such as insurance and cooperative bag purchasing; educational workshops and programs; cooperative market promotion; networking opportunities with other markets, managers and producers; and collective government representation.

In certain areas both urban and rural you may find an existing farmers' market association that wants to host an additional market. It makes sense to combine resources and not replicate all the work done by another organization. However, if you have different goals or want to do it yourself, go ahead! The greatest number of markets are run independently by a unique collection of people in that community. ✿

$\mathcal{M}$ANAGING THE MARKET 10

"The best manager is someone who likes constant problem solving, is a good listener and enjoys the swarm — the people coming, sellers, hearing community desires and resolving issues. It's both the fun and the tough part. It's the magic."
— Randii MacNear, Mgr., Davis FM, CA

$\mathcal{M}$anagement is not easy, especially with dozens of independent farmer personalities. Throw in a board of directors to whom one must be responsible and you have a real job. Managing a market is like juggling seven different fruits and vegetables while surfing on 20-foot Maui waves.

You probably know that by now, and that's what you love. As some see it, that's the magic of the job, dealing with lots of personalities and issues, and learning to resolve disputes while weaving a sense of joy through all you do. Let's look at the issues and practicalities.

 ## DAY-TO-DAY CONCERNS

All management issues are areas where managers can spend considerable time. There are some overriding practical questions that influence a manager's ability to perform well.

Market Day

Some managers could write a book about their activities on market day. We'll try to be more brief. The manager can become a whirling dervish, spinning from one situation to another as he/she seeks to:

✧ Place directional and parking signs;

✧ Set up blockades and signs at entrances;

✧ Assure restrooms are clean;

✧ Maintain an information center with canopy, sign, recipes, brochures, news and promotional items;

✧ Have improperly parked vehicles towed;

✧ Assign vendors to their stalls;

✧ Handle late vendors;

✧ Ensure quality control;

✧ Interpret and enforce rules;

✧ Settle any disputes;

✧ Maintain a clean, safe and attractive market;

✧ Solve emergency needs with First Aid or EMT training;

✧ Handle health department and other inspections;

✧ Direct special events;

✧ Hold raffles or draws;

✧ Handle consumer relations;

✧ Conduct surveys;

✧ Collect space fees (with receipts) and load lists for market reports;

✧ Oversee break-down and clean-up of market; and

✧ Store signs and pack up info center.

General Responsibilities

For smaller markets a big portion of the job is done on market day, but that's really just "show time." Back-

Vance Corum

Kid-friendly signs direct children to a barnyard and creative, play area at the Portland Farmers' Market in Oregon.

Busker sign-up in Edmonton, Alberta

stage, during the rest of the week, you're doing all the tasks that make your market day(s) run smoothly. The manager is accountable to the Board of Directors or a steering committee (or a supervisor), reporting regularly to the president. Throughout the course of the week and the season, the manager frequently will be responsible for:

◇ Overall market administration;

◇ Market promotion, advertising and public relations;

◇ Vendor recruitment and quantity/quality control;

◇ Rule Enforcement;

◇ Establish busker policy;

◇ All information and communication including letters and newsletter;

◇ Food store price tracking for vendor comparison;

◇ Statistical information for timely reports;

◇ Compliance with all pertinent laws, codes and regulations;

◇ Financial planning;

◇ Board meeting preparation; and

◇ Other tasks, as assigned.

Office & Paperwork

Managers can become overwhelmed by paperwork just like any office worker. A manager is hopefully a "people person" so being tied to office paper is about

as fun as getting caught in a haybaler.

In many areas managers are using their own home phone, don't have a fax machine, have a poor or non-existent computer, are not connected to the internet, and are working out of subpar office space or a cramped corner in their home. There is certainly value to being frugal; however, if the result is that a manager feels unsupported and ill-equipped to perform their job at maximum efficiency, frugality has turned to waste.

A supervisor or farmer board member might ask, "Would I want to do what the manager does under those conditions?" None of us wants to feel like we are mercilessly dragging our manager through years of unpleasantness, and generally we are not. Often, it seems the board is simply unaware of the conditions under which a manager is doing their job. So, what's needed here is a bit of communication.

You won't get what you need, generally, if you don't ask, specifically. So, start your wish list, then decide if it's really important enough to be a desire. Then commit to getting it and put some passion into the request. Ask your board for more appropriate office space with a window and storage for market equipment that overflows your garage. Perhaps it will be in a local church, upstairs above a downtown retailer, visible commercial space on street level (better for storage), in a community center, at city hall or in the Cooperative Extension office.

Go to your local computer store and ask whether they have an older model computer that doesn't have a home. Check also for used computers in your local newspapers as well as on the internet at:

www.classifieds2000.com.

If you need top-of-the-line efficiency, ask your local charity with a formal letter or contact one of the major computer companies at their corporate office.

Explain how you can streamline your office, gain productivity and thus save or make money. They realize that, just like the schools, once they have you hooked, you'll probably buy your next computer.

New, or near-new, computer bargains are to be found at:

www.ebay.com.

"We're buried in paper. Everybody wants more paper — the WIC program, the Ag Commissioner, the market association. So I'm trying to look at what we can do to reduce the paper. We bought another computer, and we're looking into scanners. We've developed an 'accounts receivable' for our members with monthly activity statements and updated communications so we can track our successes and identify when market trends change."
— Mark Sheridan, Santa Barbara FM Assoc., CA

Farm out the financial paperwork to an accountant, either a volunteer, board member or professional accountant. Many are willing to handle the market ledger for around $50 per month if it's not too confusing.

Pay & Benefits

Whether your market is a one-person operation or several people working out of one office running multiple markets in your region, you can easily feel overworked and underpaid.

Again, if you want a change, create a plan to make it happen. Develop it with the help of one or two trusted board members — or co-staff if you're in a government position — to make sure that your request for additional staff support or an increase in pay is reasonable and doable.

For farmers their pension is tied up in their land; when they retire, they often cash out. Managers usually don't have that luxury; they need the greater pay now so they can start a pension program or a SEP/IRA. Of course, as markets gain stability and longevity, market associations and cities are beginning to develop pension plans along with other benefits. This is a proper challenge that managers need to take to their boards as markets age into maturity.

"Our main problem is we're understaffed. I hear about a wine festival where they have 30 people to pull it off on a weekend. But we might be doing six events a week with a staff of four! We just did a market survey, and we found that our industry underpays its people. Unless a manager is a part of a market association with multiple markets and a large association, he or she is not paid very well. It really takes a lot of skills to work with the merchants, the customers and the farmers. Managing markets needs to be recognized as a more valuable position than it is."
— Mark Sheridan, Santa Barbara FM Assoc., CA

Manager burnout is, but need not be, a problem. Communicating with other managers and networking at conferences provides a relief valve for frustrations, a sharing of common experiences and a learning experience for new ideas to implement. Attend your state or regional farm conferences or the North American Farmers' Direct Marketing Conference.

Managers who become isolated should call another manager somewhere in their state, or even around the country, and gift themselves a 20-minute call once every week or two. The payback will be enormous. Another opportunity to connect is via a farmers' market internet discussion group. [See Resources]

Burnout & Turnover

Too frequently managers are leaving their positions for the right reasons. They are justified but it doesn't need to occur. When a market board does not deal with fair pay, benefits, a regular personnel review policy, office equipment and other issues, they are abdicating their responsibility to be good stewards and overall managers of their association.

As an industry, we need to grow up. We've gone through the first 21 years of our market lives, in many cases, and we need to collectively decide that if we want a strong market in our future, we have to pay for it. This may mean a review of space fees is required. Going from $8 to $10 will probably not put anyone out of business. If it does, what kind of a business was it? Certainly not one with any profit. But that minor change will give the market 25% more money to operate properly. It may mean you can raise the manager's salary or purchase equipment or create more publicity so that the market can grow and increase its income even more.

Market associations or cities may need to come to grips with this issue, whether on their own or with a cattle prod. If they do not, they will cost their associations much more in the long run through the loss of a manager with experience, contacts and goodwill in the community. If they want to see frequent manager turnover, it says much about their own level of confidence in their board role, which brings up another issue.

We didn't touch on everything, but managers know that either you are incredibly organized, your market is not too big, or you need an assistant. Managers are big on to-do lists and mental note storage. Keep some post-its in your pocket or carry a clipboard. Wear a hat and a distinguishing vest with a nametag. If you have the same blue vest or funny hat every week, you will be clearly identifiable and memorable so vendors won't have to remember what you are wearing to refer customers to you. And just so you inspire others, wear a smile! It may be the best tool you can use.

Board-Manager Balance

How boards and managers view the issue of in-house competition (discussed later in this chapter) — favoring a free market versus a protectionist approach — is one example of the dilemmas that an organization and its manager may encounter. If a manager is put in the position of enforcing what he/she feels is an unjust policy, it may lead to termination or resignation. The organizational challenge is to provide direction and oversight, yet allow a manager to be strong. In the long run, an organization is healthy when it has both a strong manager and a strong board. Weakness in either or both leads to problems.

A manager needs to know what the role of the board is vis-à-vis the manager. Usually the board or sponsor role is one of policy development. Even if it branches into a more active involvement in market set-up, promotion development, volunteer coordination or vendor outreach, it's a good idea to have the manager as overall coordinator of all activities. There needs to be one person keeping a grip on all the market minutiae; let them manage.

One critical area is finding good board members. If they are producers, they have a self-interest in preserving and improving the organization for benefit of all vendors. They must be ready to withdraw from any vote where there is a conflict of interest and they could benefit individually.

Farmers and other board members need to know their input is valued. Sponsoring agencies may squeeze out the farmer voice and there will be few farmers willing to serve in the future. Yet, farmers are a critical voice to be represented in the management of your farmers' market, even if yours is run by a chamber of commerce, a church, or a social or educational organization. Make sure the farmers' opinions are clearly heard or you may lose them.

Market Volunteers

For many farmers' markets, volunteers are the angels-from-heaven that keep the market alive. Treat them well!

> "The secret in keeping good volunteers is to give them interesting jobs, rather than just using them to do the jobs you don't want to do."
> — Rose Munoz, former Mgr., Torrance FM, CA

Here are a few jobs that volunteers might perform for you:

- ✧ Design a cable TV cooking show;
- ✧ Gather farmer and consumer recipes for a market cookbook;
- ✧ Coordinate musical entertainment;
- ✧ Solicit chefs for cooking demonstrations;
- ✧ Distribute posters and fliers;
- ✧ Sell promotional items;
- ✧ Direct traffic and parking;
- ✧ Provide answers at the information table;

- ◇ Coordinate special events;
- ◇ Give farmers restroom breaks; and
- ◇ Distribute coupons and collect items for prize drawings.

We may think that a task is above or below the dignity of a volunteer, but there are all types of people. Some people simply want to help, to be of use. Others have an idea that would challenge the most capable professional. Our management challenge is to be supportive and diplomatic about the importance of every task that needs to be done. It helps to follow up with a thank-you note, a gift basket or even a volunteer recognition dinner at the end of the season. Be sure to include your property owner, the firefighters who hang your banner and the retailer that allows use of their restroom. What goes around, comes around!

Keep a wide view as you conceive of your next volunteer. It may be an architect, a minister, an attorney, a homemaker, a senior or a Rotarian. Along with all the social contacts you make, try calling a volunteer service center, SCORE (Senior Corps of Retired Executives) and VISTA (Volunteers In Service To America) — the Peace Corps to America.

Red Tape & Politics

The larger the city, generally the higher the fees to sell. When a sponsor raises fees, they would do well to explain it to their farmers much as a farmer may explain a price increase to her customers. There's volume to be sold and there's a cost to making it all happen in a big way.

Markets that are not very successful in small towns (or anywhere) should consider why. If you are not charging any fee, you don't value the service that you provide farmers. Everyone is used to paying for products and services. It may be time to involve farmers in creating a marketing plan and figuring out how much each should pay toward the active management of that plan.

Lynchburg Community FM, VA, has a permanent structure.

Permanency

Finding a permanent location is a critical issue for any market. It's not good to be forever moving your location, although as the Portland, OR, Farmers' Market found out in 1998, getting a rent increase was actually a blessing in disguise. They moved to a downtown university location and the market took off. However, it's a good idea to get your city planners thinking about where you may be able to operate more long-term as happened with the Vancouver, WA, Farmers' Market move in 2000 to a city park.

"The main thing that market organizers could do to help us is to locate good sites, even possibly year-round farmer-oriented sites. It is getting more and more difficult to market at certain places with zoning regulations."
   —*Barriers & Opportunities,* Farmers' Market Trust

If you are organizing markets in numerous places, you undoubtedly know how important it is to have each market be unique. It is not a matter of stamping out cookie-cutter markets. When Santa Barbara began a new market in Solvang, it worked to find new members from that area.

"The bureaucracy is complex, with conditional use permits, licenses, coastal development permits, weights and measures, and health permits. Santa Barbara, Carpinteria and Solvang are independent municipalities with their own regulations. Then in Goleta we deal with the county, since it's an unincorporated city. The process is getting more and more complicated. Now we must get re-approved every five years. It just gets tougher, more regulated and harder to maintain. We set aside money for project planners and lawyers."

— Mark Sheridan, Santa Barbara FM Assoc., CA

After a number of years of community service, especially if you have substantial growth, you should have the attention of city officials in acquiring a permanent or semi-permanent site as the Davis market has experienced. They had enough credibility after fifteen years that they were the major determinant in the style of the multi-use facility the city built as part of Central Park renovations. Since these markets should be sustainable, find marketplaces that are viable in the long term. If you can't find more than a five-year contract for a site, consider planning to find a permanent site with city or county help.

Regulations

Working with regulations is part of any manager's duties. You need to build a good, working relationship with your health department and the city. You may have health permits, business licenses, and state code to interpret for the market and even farmers. As Jay Visser of J-N-A Produce in Manhattan, MT, explains, "The biggest problem we see is the regulations involved in all aspects of farming. The paper work has taken the fun out of it. They've passed a law in Montana stating that all products sold in polyethylene bays need to be classified as processed products. They haven't enforced the law yet, but they could at any time." A manager may get involved interfacing with a state agency on this issue much as various managers have been heavily involved over several years in the creation of the California Uniform Retail Food Facilities Law (CURFFL) and its update by the Department of Health Services. If law is going to affect you, become an advocate.

"A lot of vendors are wanting to come in to the markets with baked goods like zucchini bread and banana bread, for example, but the Boards of Health are cracking down on the issue of certified kitchens because of outbreak of salmonella and botu-

lism. This is hurting the markets, because part of the appeal of the farmers' markets is the chance for the customers to get their fresh vegetables, as well as their pie and cookies and bread for the weekend. If you don't have a certified kitchen you can't sell them at the market."

— Susie Silberhorn, Mgr., Belvidere Farm and Crafts Market, IL

"About 43% of market managers mentioned obstacles to entrepreneurial development. The most frequently cited obstacle was inconsistent health department regulations — in particular, regulations about sampling and selling prepared foods."

— Farmers' Markets and Rural Development Project

If local people do not have proper kitchen facilities, encourage a cooperative processing facility. Follow the example of tiny Laytonville, CA, where a group did some grant-writing to set up a community kitchen in the winter of 2001. Contact your local Small Business Development Center for assistance.

Food Stamps

Your market should be authorized to handle food stamps (and food coupons, if your state has a program). You can increase your farmer and market income considerably and help low-income people learn to shop at a healthy place, where they can purchase produce with cash as well. Make sure farmers display signs stating, "We Accept Food Stamps," and understand policies on returning change up to $1 or other coupons.

Become familiar with the program and get involved in the discussion about Electron Benefits Transfer (EBT). Several markets nationwide had pilot programs in 2000 to test a new hand-held device for farmers to accept food stamps electronically. Over the following several years food stamp recipients will be receiving debit cards instead of paper food stamps. It appears that the lack of a farmer-friendly EBT system is negatively impacting low-income people's access to fresh fruit and vegetables af farmers' markets. Unless farmers' markets can handle this electronic medium, they may be excluded from the benefits of handing food stamp customers.

For resources on Electronic Benefits Transfer see the web page:

http://www.welfareinfo.org/electronic.htm.

Environmental Standards

Work with farmers to create agricultural systems that are more environmentally friendly. If your farmers are committed to certain policies, you may gain greater consumer acceptance. Two dozen farmers in the Pacific Northwest have been approved by The Food Alliance, which has a rating system focused on protection of natural resources, reduced chemical use and care for the welfare of workers. As they build greater awareness of worker- and environmentally-friendly growing practices, including pheromone mating disruption and black lights to control codling moth, TFA joins with many markets in educating and improving the system that feeds us all.

Ask your farmers to provide specific, printed or visual information that will help educate consumers to the positive, environmental steps you are taking. It is one more example of ways that you increase public confidence and support for your market. A link to a local organization may be to your mutual self-interest.

 ## MANAGEMENT ISSUES

As if "day-to-day" management concerns aren't enough, there are several on-going, broader issues that farmers' markets face.

Farmer Grown

Since the 1970s a new wave of farmers' markets has hit the country. By definition, farmers' markets are producer markets, meaning that vendors are also farmers. Yet, because they are not under corporate control, each has evolved with differing rules based on the goals of their creators. In some states regulation or law has impacted the type of vendors who may sell.

One major function is to support local farmers. Another is to provision customers with produce. These two functions sometimes can erupt as conflicting goals, leading to a philosophical and practical split within the ranks of farmers, managers and boards.

Producer-only

Those who favor a "producer-only" market see it as a means of supporting farmers by ensuring a fair and level playing field. Regulations are used to prevent or limit the selling of produce not grown by the vendor. Since resellers (peddlers, hawkers or high-stallers) may provide non-local produce or undercut the price of locally grown produce, their presence puts farmers at a competitive disadvantage. This regulatory perspective holds the high moral ground for agriculture in that:

✧ Customers have greater faith in a producer-only marketplace;

✧ Everyone appreciates the market's integrity and wants to tell friends;

✧ Farmers analyze their own sales' techniques rather than blaming peddlers for low sales;

✧ New people see product niches to fill;

✧ Farmers educate the public about seasons and crop failures;

✧ Farm organizations are more likely to support a program for farmers, and

✧ There is a connection between farmers and consumers.

These people are likely to yell, "Peddlers!" in disgust or point out that when a market has too many non-farmers, others take control and the farmer gets squeezed.

> "The purpose of peddling is to increase the appeal to customers but it raises customers' expectations to unreasonable heights and creates a Safeway-like atmosphere where seasons and weather mean nothing."
>
> — Clem Clay, Mgr., Berkeley FM, CA

They correctly show that farmers will have a tough time competing with wholesalers or peddlers who buy from any source without having to "take the good with the bad, like having a freeze or getting hailed out," according to Chris Burke of Boulder. Farmers can't compete with someone who can buy wholesale goods from areas with longer growing seasons and lower labor costs. Those people do not gamble with the unpredictability inherent in agriculture.

Vance Corum

Jeff Main, the Davis FM, shows that the key to media success is focusing one-on-one with the customer.

Consumer focus

The other school of thought focuses on the primary function of farmers' markets as serving the customer with the greatest variety. Here, regulation that discourages resale is seen as protectionist, creating an artificial market that favors farmers and encourages high prices. Markets that favor deregulation believe it encourages free enterprise, allowing any type of vendor to respond with greater flexibility to customer desires and enabling the overall market to more effectively compete with other retailers. (This implies that a farmers-only market doesn't provide competition for the consumer's benefit.) The major arguments are that:

 ❖ Peddlers are necessary because of limited, local produce supplies;

 ❖ There is more variety when allowing re-sale;

 ❖ Small producers are encouraged to sell products through cooperative arrangements;

 ❖ Customers demand certain products not grown in the area; and

 ❖ The disappearance of farms makes it difficult to maintain a base of home producers.

Markets on the extreme of this position may give a bad name to "farmers' market" by being more of a flea market with all kinds of products and sellers. However, most farmers' markets are not inclined to allow a free-for-all. They tend to feel pushed into allowing peddlers because of local agricultural conditions.

"The present-day realities of farming such as production and labor costs, and crop failures, etc., are putting pressures on the farmer... There might be consumer demand for a crop that requires equipment that is too costly for the farmer to purchase, for example. Rather than buy equipment, the farmer might purchase the crop from a neighboring farmer or from the wholesale market. Farmers are doing whatever they need to do to meet consumer demand and stay in business. Some markets are catering to a diversified crowd and allowing farmers to supplement what they grow, but this can destroy the markets by attracting hucksters who stop farming and only buy from the wholesale market."
— Al Smith, Mgr., D.C. Open-air FM, Washington, D.C.

It's a slippery slope. You want to help farmers so you let them buy to supplement their production. Soon you have people selling who are more hucksters than farmers.

Contrasting visions

The difference in these models is one of long-term vision versus short-term survival. Since both models have evolved worldwide for several millennia, neither school will necessarily win the debate; both will continue to discuss whether customers know or care if they're buying from the real McCoy.

The producer-only model has succeeded in major cities and small towns where organizers commit to the hard work of outreach. The consumer-oriented model has its proponents where distance, large growers, a small populace or limited local variety is the basis of vendors being allowed to buy outside products. They would like to be producer-only but can't see a way to survive with those restrictions. So, they lose the authenticity that gives the farmers' market its particular atmosphere and identity.

Some organizers suggest starting markets with a loose standard and reforming later. However, one might say, "once tainted, always unpure." Allowing peddlers because of "customer demand" may backfire in several ways. The standard that you set becomes familiar to your clientele. Why set the bar lower than you ultimately want it to be? You may set yourself up for a lawsuit by allowing, and then disallowing, resale vendors. If you bite the bullet and work hard doing outreach with every tool available, you may be surprised by the number of people who come forth to help build a truly local marketplace with real farmers. You also will avoid the label of being just another flea market encouraging hucksters and low quality. Reflect on your goals and the standards. The process will become clear.

Ultimately, markets often allow resellers because it is easier. Resellers can get almost anything they or the manager wants them to get. The Olympia, WA, market has had great success with good producers from a several-county local area. Oddly enough, it allows only two resellers to purchase produce from eastern Washington. Who knows how many more producers would be involved if outreach were done east of the mountains to replace the resellers? And would those farmers fill the voids on a consistent basis compared to the two very successful, and thus dependable, resellers? This consumer-oriented model actually protects resellers and hinders free market competition just as some argue that the farmer model protects farmers from the vagaries of a true open market.

Solutions

"Market quality seems to evolve to the level demanded by the consumer with some markets very quality conscious and others not. All markets are not the same in both product preference and product price. The most pernicious counterproductive element to damage markets is the buyer/reseller of products."
— Ron Enomoto, California farmer

Competition need not force price and quality downward if consumers in a local trade area demand quality. Your clientele are largely based on the way you position your farmers' market with a targeted advertising strategy, reflecting your values on quality and price.

To allow buying and selling opens the doors for farmers to be beaten. Yet, there is a difference of degree in allowing a farmer to buy off the wholesale market versus buy from or sell some product from neighboring farmers. In small, rural communities three or four organic growers may work together to get their products to distant farmers' markets or to maintain their presence in a small local market.

"Cooperative partnerships strengthen the community. At the market vendors cooperate to strengthen their businesses by selling each other's produce from time-to-time under a second certificate… This lets small-scale producers continue to market their produce at a certified farmers' market even when their production is too low to warrant their own direct participation. It also helps keep product diversity at the market."
— Comment from Laytonville, reported to have California's smallest farmers' market

Another option is to allow a member to buy an item to fill a product void, as in Camden, Maine. The member must have approval, must label it as bought and must wait for any other actual grower of that item to sell out. Somewhat north in the university town of Orono, that solution was rejected in favor of a recruiting drive to fill the voids. Looking for farmers rather than re-sellers when you need a product makes sense to farmers. It encourages farmers to plan and expand their acreage or variety. It requires a manager who cares enough about the consumer to search out products in demand. It is not as easy as calling a re-seller or having a farmer buy product from afar. But it does lead to a local agriculture with greater crop diversity.

The farmer-grown model also makes it simpler to demand the same standard if you allow crafts. Conversely, if you allow peddling of produce, it is difficult to disallow peddled crafts from around the world. The market becomes an entity where the best seller wins, not the best farmer. If we want to stimulate a renaissance in all forms of local production, we need to give those artisans of the soil and other materials the opportunity to present their craftwork to the public on a level economic playing field.

Enforcement

There are markets with a variety of consumer-oriented regulations. Some markets allow one farmer to sell for another while others permit a farmer to purchase a certain percentage of what they sell from another source. Some require that only the vendor sell his/her own production and others allow produce from various states and countries. Ensure that any limitation imposed on the vendor is actually followed, so that everyone knows they are playing by the same rules. This can be a major management challenge requiring a different set of rules and procedures, including inspections.

It's possible, though not easy, to change horses in mid-stream. Even with a 75%-your-own standard, the Hillsboro Farmers' Market in Oregon admittedly had a problem with enforcement. After fifteen years they were afraid of a lawsuit threat from one or two "growers" who seemed to be buying almost all their produce. Fortunately, in 1998 they began the Hillsboro Tuesday Marketplace in conjunction with the chamber and downtown business association. We pushed to establish a "producers only" standard for farmers and artisans in the new market. As a result the Saturday market later upgraded its standard. The threat of lawsuits never materialized.

Other markets operate under limitations of state law. Maine law requires market vendors to grow at least 75% of what they offer for sale. Individual markets can require that all products sold are grown, baked, or processed by the seller. Similarly, California law permits one farmer to sell product of another producer, but each market can require a higher standard, like 100%.

> "The farmer-grown issue is the hottest topic in our part of the world. Texas growing conditions are tough, and farmers have a hard time producing here, period. It's hard to compete with farmers' markets that are not truly farmers' markets, where the growers are reselling from the produce terminals. They call themselves farmers' markets but they're not farmers' markets at all. They mislead the public, and our state organization, the Texas Certified Farmers' Market Association, is in the process of bringing this issue to the Texas Department of Agriculture and seeing what we can do about truth in labeling."
> — Elizabeth Massey, grower, Sunset, TX

In the final analysis, the question of "producer-only" is not simply about standards, but enforcement. If a market allows farmers to bring 25% of their volume from a farmer up to three miles away or from within the same county, that standard is fair for everyone. The problem occurs when a farmer is bringing 10% his own production and buying the other 90% and management does nothing to stop it. Even a market that has a 100% grow-your-own rule is not exempt; some people will cheat and buy tomatoes down the road or in the wholesale market. It's up to the association to have farmers sign an agreement saying they understand that they can lose their selling privilege, and then remove them when they break the rules. It's the only way to maintain farmer loyalty and consumer trust.

> "The producer-only image is a definite plus for the market. In Minneapolis I know there are some farmers' markets that include dealers, and we get lots of customers that drive over from Minneapolis to come to the St. Paul market because they tell us

they know that they are buying local here… One of the things managers really need to stay on top of is the rules and regulations of the market, and what the growers have signed up for in the spring that they will bring to the market, and what they're bringing to market now. We do field-checks, and people have to fill out an application every year and tell us what they're growing and how much, and when they expect to bring it to the market. So if there's any question about what they're bringing to the market, you can go and look at their application, and if it's not there, it had better be in the field. Because if you go out and check and it's not, there are major fines. The first infraction is $500, the second infraction is a year out of the market plus $500, and the third time you're gone."

— Patty Brand, Exec. Dir., Friends of the St. Paul FM, MN

Set up your rules so that violators pay for your inspection program. Listen to farmers when they complain about corn appearing at the market in May. Make some phone calls. Certain markets have hired other managers to save money on long-distance inspections. By caring you show respect for the vision of your governing body's standards.

Commitment follows vision. Consider your organization's purpose in promoting a regional agricultural system that serves local farms and the community. If you focus only on the consumer, you may be short-sighted and diminish your chances of truly influencing farmers' attempts at sustainability. We can all do our part to keep them on the land.

Local

Whole Foods Market has begun defining "local." It has mini-signs, attached by velcro to larger price signs, which proclaim that the product was grown within 150 miles, or that it was grown in a given state. They have color-coded signs indicating "organic" or "conventional" production techniques. Quite adroitly, they have recognized customers' desire for more information. They build trust in their response.

Esther Kovari, president of the New Mexico Farmers' Marketing Association, notes, "One advantage the markets can play up is to promote the locally grown issue, because the natural food stores aren't buying much local." As Whole Foods and Wild Oats, each with more than 100 stores, swallow their natural foods competitors, they take on the major food chain mentality of buying from larger producers.

Your market needs a significant selling edge over all supermarkets. Ask yourself how you can draw customers for whom the supermarket is an easier shopping experience. If your competition is open 24/7 and your farmers' market is open only four hours on one or two days each week, what advantages do you offer? Fresh produce can be brought in from Chile but you can promote "local" with a definition that will make shoppers into converts. Disallowing "imports" promotes local agriculture and aids the regional economy. A mileage limit on where any product can come from is even more specific for shoppers.

The Ithaca Farmers' Market limits sellers to a 35-mile radius. This guarantees "local" is queen of the market. When such measures are enacted and enforced, they can serve to:

✧ Promote value-added processing as farmers and others look to expand selection;

✧ Guard against long-distance competitors with unknown labor standards or subsidized production inputs;

✧ Invigorate creativity as entrepreneurs realize they can compete on a local level;

✧ Guarantee quality because of social pressures;

✧ Increase the likelihood of inspections of the farm or production facility;

✧ Assure consumers they are re-circulating dollars in a local economy; and

✧ Build stronger social ties among producers and between them and customers.

On the other hand, certain areas with a population base aren't necessarily perfect for diverse production. The Astoria Sunday Market, begun in 2000 at the mouth of the Columbia River, invited farmers and artisans from both Oregon and Washington.

While 70% of the producers were local, some growers came as far as 300 miles one-way from the Yakima Valley. The commitment to "producers only" brought out many local artisans and hopefully will contribute to increased production locally as farmers realize they have a transportation advantage.

If producers come from a wider area, the market may be buffered from localized weather disruptions. However, the manager will have a greater challenge doing enforcement. Hopefully, no matter what the geographical range, farmers' markets can use their "local" standard as a marketing tool to attract customers well aware of the downside of our global economy.

The reason some customers support natural food stores with standards is because they want to trust a marketplace. They don't have time to review every issue. They want to come to a place where they can buy confidently, where there is a clear set of values. Some farmers' markets know this kind of consumer is the segment of the market they're shooting for. Others believe that customers don't care where the product came from; they're focused on price. If that's your market perspective, that will be the kind of customer you will get. While every market is entitled to its own values, some enthusiasts wish there were tighter, legal, "local" standards, including limitations for those choosing to use the term "farmers' market."

Supermarket competition

"The dinosaur is turning its head around."

According to Tony Manetta, director of New York City's Greenmarket program, farmers' markets are going to have to hustle to stay on the leading edge of supermarket competition. "Twenty years ago a ripe tomato was exotic," Manetta says. "Now the supermarkets are carrying super-sweet corn and low-priced greenhouse tomatoes from Holland, Canada and Mexico, organic lettuce mixes from Dole, and mushrooms like shiitake and oyster, and our markets have a challenge to meet in staying special. Differentiating ourselves from supermarket competition has become a major issue."

It depends on the local market area. Along the central coast of California, farmers' market administrator Peter Jankay feels that, "the supermarket can't possibly provide all the unique varieties people find at the farmers' markets, and certainly not the quality. You might find lemon grass in little packets at the supermarket but you won't find the beautiful, foot-long leaves of lemon grass that this one grower brings to the market."

That comparison epitomizes the difference between a large city and a small town. Farmers' markets have more strenuous competition in the cities with sophisticated customers demanding new varieties and superb attention to detail no matter where they shop.

> "The supermarkets are getting more variety as well as produce that looks good and tastes like something, but unfortunately that has been done mostly through genetics rather than buying local. I've recently seen some very interesting things in the supermarkets like beta-caratene enhanced carrots out of Texas A&M. It's really beautiful — it's a maroon carrot that's gorgeous, and to see this at a supermarket before I see it at the farmers' market caused me to pause.
>
> "It's like the dinosaur got hit on its tail 20 years ago, and it's finally turned its head around. Some New York supermarkets are doing a superb job in changing the image of what supermarket produce is like. I see more good quality, more diversity, and the kind of attention to detail that I only used to see in farmers' markets."
>
> — Tony Manetta, Greenmarket, New York, NY

Marin County Farmers' Market founder Lynn Bagley, director of the Golden Gate Farmers' Market Association, sees a downward cycle:

> "The farmers are stressed. The more markets there are, the more the supermarkets copy the farmers' markets. More farmers in each market also leads to increased competition, so the farmers make less money and have to go to more markets. They can't seem to find the time to do the things that bring people to the farmers' markets in the first place, like being on the leading edge of product variety and quality.

"Stores have gotten quite competitive. They have a lot of variety and in some cases they are introducing varieties that are not even available to farmers' markets. New products almost always used to be introduced at the farmers' markets; now there is much more crossover. Products like the mesclun mixes and the fuji apples, and white varieties of nectarines and peaches... we had these five years in the markets before they hit the supermarkets.

"Even the flower vendors are not as creative as they used to be... You'll see unusual varieties at the supermarkets that are not even in the farmers' markets. I bought a very unusual mum at the supermarket the other day that I've never seen at the farmers' markets — a beautiful lavender mum with a yellow center — and things like that never used to happen. Excuse the pun but with flowers it's the status quo at the farmers' markets. Wreath-making should be more artistic, more interesting and more unusual at the farmers' markets than anything you could find anywhere, yet it seems that there is not the level of care with wreath-making that there used to be. When you lose that you lose everything."

   — Lynn Bagley, Dir., Golden Gate FM Assoc., Novato, CA

One way Bagley suggests to arrest the downward spiral of quality and competition is to work closely with restaurants. "There's a lot of creativity going on the in the food industry with the chefs and restaurateurs. The chefs are mixing foods from different ethnic groups and preparing food in a synergistic way from lots of different styles of cooking, such as back-to-the-country cuisine. All these styles of cooking are infusing creativity and the quality is very, very high. That's how the mesclun craze got started — with a farmer working with a restaurant."

"Over-expansion nearly always kills quality," Bagley continues. "The markets are too consumed with the money and they're losing the meaning and purpose of the markets... They're cutting corners and in the end it will also downgrade the economic viability of the markets, when customers no longer feel there's any difference between the markets and the supermarkets." Tony Manetta offers his solution:

"We've been telling growers that they have basically two cards left to play. The first is the heirloom varieties... It's the sheer novelty of what's coming into the markets that's keeping customers coming back. The supermarkets are starting to display some heirloom varieties, but the quality is often very poor — it's seems it's there strictly for show. The other aspect of the farmers' markets that the supermarkets will never have it is the farmers themselves. Farmers being on-site is a critical component of the market, yet as the markets grow, we're seeing more and more employees at the market rather than the farmers themselves. We feel there is an impact in not having the direct connection with the customer."

Manetta continues: "Some supermarkets are trying to get in on the locally-grown angle, and if they are really doing that, bless them... The reason they're doing this is because they understand business, and they know that this is what people are looking for. So the dinosaur has evolved; the supermarkets are responding quicker and evolving faster than they used to."

"It gets back to consumer education. Do we want local, fresh produce, or corporate-grown food heavily laden with chemicals that's been on a truck for three weeks?"

   — Lynn Bagley, Dir., Golden Gate FM Assoc., Novato, CA

"I hope to beat the supermarkets on customer service. Markets need to start going the extra mile and help people park and carry their bags out. And the farmers need be on the front line of service with courtesy and customer service. The supermarket can't have 30 people behind the tables waiting on you, smiling, and saying, 'Come back next week!'"
   — Mark Sheridan, Santa Barbara FM Assoc., CA

Not all supermarkets are competitors. Various smaller operators, usually family-owned, have allowed farmers' markets in their parking lots. Williams Brothers allowed one to operate in Morro Bay, CA, for 12 years. Customers bought strawberries at the farmers' market and their canned goods and milk in the supermarket. Then the supermarket decided to develop the property. Six months later, the store admitted that Saturday had been their busiest day and they wanted the farmers back.

> "There are some things that the supermarkets will never be able to compete with us on, such as product freshness. Then there's the pickup trucks at the markets and the whole ambiance of the farmers being there, and the opportunity to ask the growers: 'How did you to grow this?' and 'When did you plant it?' This is impossible to do at supermarkets. People come here to talk and to see friends and to visit and there's a whole social fabric that's developed."
> — Peter Jankay, Admin., San Luis Obispo County FM Assoc., CA

Competition within your market, and the resultant choices, may be your greatest advantage over supermarkets. While they offer only one or two varieties of tomatoes, you may have three or a dozen tomato sellers with 30 tomato varieties! Design your rules to encourage other farmers' market "advantages," such as premium quality, one-day fresh, and a friendly social experience.

Price may be another advantage which markets in certain areas should emphasize. The same corn that Charlie & Vicki Hertel sell 4-for-$1 in Portland, OR, sells at 8-for-$1 in their hometown Hillsboro market less than 30 miles west. When the cannery is paying only a penny an ear, even that hometown bargain price brings the Hertels a great profit by comparison.

All seem to agree on a few advantages where we can capitalize: market ambiance, unparalleled freshness, innovation through new varieties and unique processed goods, customer service, education and the farmers themselves. Most of our superior position relies on the degree to which farmers take pride in creating new products, providing knowledge unmatched by a stockboy, talking about their farms and giving people a direct connection to the land.

Competition Within the Market

When one farmer brings a small volume of peas or corn and sells out quickly, he may feel threatened by a competitor recruited by the manager. However, the manager needs to focus on pleasing customers so they tell their friends that the market is a reliable place for purchases. This competition factor is more powerful than many farmers, concerned about their own financial welfare, may be willing to admit. True free market competition is one of the reasons customers become loyal to farmers' markets versus the supermarket, which only has one option for most produce selections. A good manager ensures that competition exists and educates the farmer to the fact that overall market sales increase with a more competitive market. That makes for contented customers and leads to the continual development of new product opportunities in a constantly changing rather than stagnant market.

Do you limit the number of apple or tomato growers or do you let the market dictate? A laissez faire approach may be best. Like the manager of a wholesale produce market, you need not control product supply and demand. Let every grower have free and equal access and let the consumer enjoy the result of fair competition. In other words:

Manuel Lawrence knows how to sell $1.25/bunch organic Nantes carrots at the Grants Pass Growers' Market: "Pile 'em high and kiss 'em good-bye" with a humanized carrot figure at the top of his price sign and another large carrot reclining on an overhead sign.

Who's the Competition?

— *Renae's Rutabaga,* April 1999, Renae Best, Sacramento Certified FMs, CA

Focus on the bigger picture. See the forest, not just the trees. Together we are a market. We compete in a world of markets. Our main competition is with the major grocery store and discount food outlets, not with each other.

The primary competitive edge that we have over the grocery stores is that we have a number of different farmers and give a number of choices for the same product. Sure we talk about vine-ripened and tree-ripened quality, but the primary distinction we can make over our competition is that the customer has more than one choice.

Our success is built on the promotion that we are the "shopping mall of farmers," the one-stop shopping for locally grown produce. We are in competition with the grocery store for the type of customer who wants a choice.

Customers who don't care about more than one choice will always shop at the grocery store. Grocery stores are convenient and quick shopping. We are not. At our farmers' markets customers need cash, have to pay at each stand, walk around with multiple bags, take many trips to the car, shop during our time schedule, brave the weather, and on and on. The types of customers who come to our markets are not just after quick and convenient. These people are shoppers!

Again, we are a "shopping mall of farmers." A full market of farmers attracts and keeps more customers. If you have ever been to a shopping mall which is dying, you will see a couple of big stores and a lot of vacant little shops. Slowly the customer base falls down to the point that even the big stores leave. Where do they go? They move to successful malls which have no vacancies and all their little shops are full. Successful malls that are drawing the customer by providing them what they want. Many choices. A shopping experience.

We all have to promote the merits of the market for it to be successful. Let's keep the competition within the markets friendly and positive. Don't disparage each other — especially to, or within the ear shot of — the customers. We are a market of many good choices. Where else can the customer get so many good choices? Certainly not at a grocery store. ❀

"Don't look at farmers' markets like clubs. Make room for new growers."
— A farmers' market manager

Many other managers take a more protectionist tact, often due to farmer pressure. Especially when it is board member pressure or board policy, a manager is hard-pressed to stand for an open market.

Yet the market may suffer. If the consumer is finding less competition and fewer options of variety, quality and price, they may not be as enthusiastic in their word-of-mouth encouragement of other customers.

"Fair and healthy competition is what creates the market. The opportunity to choose between two or three tomato growers is what brings customers to the market. It's like a shopping mall — if you've got several stores selling dresses, you're going to have a lot of dress shoppers."

Rules and procedures help a manager determine who is admitted. Some require on-farm site visits. Markets establish waiting lists and prioritize those with new and different crops over those who have more of the same as existing growers. One goal is to avoid too much competition within any category. "Too much" depends on the eye of the beholder. When you let growers into the market without rhyme or reason, you are being disloyal to the farmers who are there; they may react by going to another market as soon as they can. On the other hand, if you don't allow for any additions or changes, you may not be responsive to customer desires and you may lose them. Finding the right path between these extremes of farmer protection versus consumer service is where a manager shows true management finesse.

In some markets the limitation on the physical range or geography of vendors is based on the desire to serve local farm interests and limit competition from afar. This is quite valid if codified in the organization's rules and bylaws. However, this cannot happen under California law that allows any California farmer to sell at any certified farmers' market. For example, Santa Barbara cannot stop a Butte County pistachio producer from coming 400 miles to compete with a home-county grower, even the board president.

Managers may limit participation, and thus competition, based on physical limitations of the market, a waiting list, seniority or any means that guarantees fair and equal treatment. Grower challenges to poor policies or implementation will continue pushing management to higher operational standards.

In the process managers realize they are the lubricant between farmer and consumer. They must strive to represent the interests of both groups, much as a Department of Food and Agriculture, by its name, indicates its concern for both consumers and farmers.

Market Proliferation

"Too many farmers' markets everywhere. Farmers are stretched too thin."
— Dale C. Whitney, Mgr., Harbor Area FMs, Long Beach, CA

The popularity of California's nearly 400 certified farmers' markets has brought problems. With more than 50 markets in Los Angeles County alone and almost 100 in the nine-county Bay Area, many farmers and managers have complained for years about the oversaturation of farmers' markets. The overabundance forces farmers to sell at more markets without substantially increasing their take-home income. And it isn't just in California.

"Every community wants a farmers' market, so anyone who opens within a 100 miles of us will be competing with us for farmers."
— Ginger Rapport, Mgr., Beaverton FM, OR

It is not surprising that competition between markets has developed in numerous areas. Yet we need to remember that we are working together to build a consciousness about buying at farmers' markets instead of other retailers. Here is what can happen:

✧ A neighborhood group starts a market two or three miles from an existing market to serve a specific ethnic or other population.

✧ A philosophical or practical break occurs within a market leading some vendors to start another market close-by. Experience shows that the new market usually has more hurdles than the established one, unless the new market has financial deep pockets.

✧ A shopping mall uses substantial resources to kick start a market and lure customers from their competitors.

✧ A downtown business association feels business slipping away to malls, with or without a market, and commits members' contributions to boost waning customer counts.

The variety of scenarios is limitless and it cannot be stopped. We need to more creatively market our markets to survive the inevitable development and winnowing of markets.

Markets in close proximity are problematic for farmers who feel forced to sell at more markets to gross the same volume as they did with fewer markets. The customer base is being split, but it is also growing. Vendor sales per market may drop, but who is to play God and determine which markets are allowed? Open-air markets have the competitive edge in flexibility; they can respond quickly to demographic shifts in a city. They may move to a new site, draw more minority vendors or otherwise reflect the new local character.

"Keep the markets worthwhile to the growers. Don't expand markets so fast and dilute them so much that the farmer has to go to seven markets a week to make a living selling at farmers' markets. Educate customers to build a customer base."

Most sectors of the economy are flexing in response to the competition with lightning speed. High tech firms are changing course weekly rather than annually. Farmers' markets aren't protected from these rapid changes. If there are too many markets in an area, the weakest will be sifted out as farmers become dissatisfied with low sales, or they will continue with a committed mix of farmers and customers who appreciate the charm and intimacy.

In 1989, there were claims that much of Los Angeles County had reached near saturation with two dozen markets. The number more than doubled over the next 10 years, with no end in sight. The volume of total sales also grew substantially. The industry may feel a certain squeeze play is on, but it is no different than that felt among the supermarkets and their competitors, the big box stores and specialty retailers.

We have not reached the end of our expansion phase, never mind the settling-out phase. This occurs among supermarkets as well. During 2000 seven new supermarkets were built in Clark County, WA, (coauthor Vance's home). Seven independents went under. With this "replacement" the largest supermarkets consolidated a greater share of the market, exacerbated by mergers. The result threatens midsize farmers and wholesalers, since produce contracts are primarily with larger farms.

By contrast, an ever increasing number of players easily enters the democratic world of farmers' markets and helps it expand, albeit with some negative consequences. We had better stop complaining about competition within the farmers' market world and begin squarely facing the challenge of finding and keeping customers that will otherwise be siphoned away by the huge retailers. We had also best realize that there will be a shaking down of our industry as we reach saturation yet find ourselves faced with still more new farmers' market development.

One in five California market managers says that finding new vendors is one of their greatest challenges. The good news is that four in five don't think it is so critical, so perhaps the issue is how many customers you have in your market. Somehow it seems that all the strong markets have a waiting list trying to get in. If you're weak, it may be a cop-out to put the blame on not enough farmers.

Yes, in certain areas farmer recruitment is a problem, but market after market has been able to encourage new entry farmers and other food producers because they created a demand. What producers need to see is a workable plan to increase supply and demand simultaneously.

There is no practical way to stop the creation of additional markets. Through city government or nonprofit organizations, the consumer clamor for easier access brings yet another market into existence. The farmers' market movement is still historically very young. No one really knows which markets are meant to be successful over the long haul. A new one may do a better job and cause an old market to improve or slip quietly out of existence. Certainly, if given areas are, indeed, oversaturated with farmers' markets, we must admit that this "problem" results from the success of our own movement. We can be sure that individual preferences and market forces — neither ever static — will bring about a balance which constantly changes over time. A greater balance point will come; our market world is young.

Farmer & Public Education

Organize a Friends of the Market nonprofit group. This is a great vehicle for educating everyone in the community about the real concern of maintaining ag land in your area or keeping farmers viable on it. Elevating the knowledge level of consumers, you will create goodwill, loyalty to the market and greater understanding of farmer issues.

When legislation or regulation is being considered — an urban growth boundary, a sale of an urban farm, run-off standards, spraying practices, right-to-farm, organic statutes, purchase of development rights

(PDRs), transfer of development rights (TDRs), the forced relocation of your market or any other issue — a Friends group can help raise awareness.

"With The Friends of the Farmers' Market program, we do educational programs to train and encourage farmers, as well as help raise public awareness about the importance of farming. The existence of farm land around our towns is very critical to the quality of life here."
— Esther Kovari, President, New Mexico Farmers' Marketing Assoc.

Farmers or market people can lead the way. Gerald Bentryn, a Bainbridge Island, WA, farmer, decided to help protect the remaining farmland on the island and printed bumper stickers to advocate purchases of Puget Sound Fresh produce. Down in Goleta, CA, Michael Ableman created a nonprofit to purchase an urban farm, largely through educational and financial outreach efforts. A Friends group can do much the same, helping preserve urban farmland or assisting farmers in maintaining their way of life in the face of land or regulatory pressures.

Large-Scale Farmers

Admitting large-scale farmers is a volatile, underlying issue in various markets. Farmers and organizers feel that the main purpose of farmers' markets is to help keep small farms viable. On the other hand, if the market doesn't have a steady enough supply of products from small farmers, the market may be wise to include larger producers for the market's own survival. It is the same sustainability issue, for vendors and markets, which we face with the question of including peddlers. The challenge is to organize and involve enough small-scale producers to make your market viable for the consumer.

"We feel the market needs a mix of smaller and larger growers. It's like in a mall, you have the anchors, larger growers who offer a large volume of products, and smaller growers who bring in exotics which generally aren't grown on larger acreage."
— Jack Gerten, Pres., St. Paul FM Assoc., MN

Large-scale grower sets up a "wall of oranges" at the Davis FM, CA

The Los Angeles Times has weighed in on the subject (Melinda Fullmer, May 7, 2000). One of California's largest fruit growers, with 650 acres of fruit and 232 varieties, uses a refrigerated warehouse, a fleet of trucks, four supervisors and a small army of helpers to cover various southern California markets. In Torrance alone the operation moves more than $10,000 worth of fruit on a Tuesday.

An organic apple grower gets $40 a box for Granny Smiths instead of barely covering costs with a normal $12 wholesale price. Many large growers estimate their returns at 40 to 80% more for their crop, often selling higher than chain store prices.

Of the 5,000 California growers involved in farmers' markets, the great majority are small producers. As large growers become more prevalent and take home big incomes, the people who built the system are feeling the pinch.

Managers need to be careful not to see their markets overwhelmed before they realize it. Large farms often can create huge displays and sell volume at lower prices, out-competing smaller growers. A grower doing $3,000 in a market may displace five or more local producers. As a manager, you don't have to give up. Limit the display space, no matter what size the grower. Any space limit is fair for everyone. Managers sometimes get lured into huge spaces for growers because they want to fill the market or they receive revenue based on footage. Find a proper balance.

Smaller growers should accentuate their small-scale advantages. As Ali Edwards of Fan Tan Farm in Santa Cruz, CA, says, "I see the farmers' markets and CSAs as an alternative to industrial agriculture. The market is one place where small farms have an advantage." If you are sitting on your tailgate, you have no right to complain about unfair competition from a large grower. Create colorful signage, build first-name relationships with your customers, re-arrange your display periodically to create visual interest, provide superior service with written and verbal recipes, and sample your products aggressively. Use photos of your farm on each price sign inside a plastic sleeve or enlarge one farm photo to 2x3 feet to set a tone for your display.

Any market has a difficult time excluding larger growers. It seems difficult to define small farm and fairly exclude the large producer. USDA's definition of a small farm is sales below $250,000 annually. While that may seem excessively high to some, how would you preclude someone using that standard and avoid litigation? The more successful your market, the more likely that larger growers will try to get in unless there are strong social and peer pressures for them to stay out or the customer base is substantially educated to small farm preservation and willing to purchase accordingly.

"Some people feel that the markets are for smaller growers because larger growers have other outlets. People have different shopping tastes. I feel larger growers can add to the market if they don't come in and cut prices and go for volume over quality and uniqueness. That creates a problem in the market. Some markets work very well with large producers. Our vendors voted to have a sliding scale for all vendors rather than a flat fee for booth spaces. The bigger growers voted also to have a sliding scale fee even though they pay $40 to $50 a day, because a flat fee would bring all big growers to the market and invite fiercer competition for them."

— Randii MacNear, Mgr., Davis FM, CA

Managers want farmers with quality and consistency throughout a season. Farmers in turn want assurance that managers won't let in competitors with the same crops, or at least not without warning, so they can scale back their load.

If growers are selling out of a certain product, it's natural for a manager to be concerned for the consumer. Ask if they can bring additional product; if not, let them know you may solicit other growers with that product. A manager doesn't want a grower always trying to finish the market day sold out. That can create a downward spiral as consumers at the end of the day find little product and stop coming, the grower cuts back even more on volume, and other customers get disenchanted. Instead, we need to remember that the consumer has a choice of markets to shop. If we don't offer quality, volume, selection, atmosphere and personal service, we may lose the consumer altogether.

Farmers' market managers, just like supermarket managers, should know all the products available. That means they need to know when a grower wants to bring in a new item or one that duplicates what others have. It is a great challenge to decide the total mix and competition levels that lead to the best growth for the market. Managers must be sensitive to the concerns of individual vendors, yet maintain an overall focus on their customers. Ultimately, they are governing what many would characterize as organized chaos.

"We have a large-scale grower at our market, and in my opinion they are not a threat to the other growers. Their stuff just isn't that good! Our Association's membership recently voted for more stringent regulations regarding farmers being at the market. As it stands now, the farmer has to be there in person once every quarter and growers feel that it should be more often. This ruling might nip the corporate farmer right in the bud, because they often can't be there more than once a quarter."

— Mark Sheridan, Santa Barbara FM Assoc., CA

Backyard Market Gardeners

For any grower a backyard gardener may be like a fly on the nose — a constant irritant. Worse yet, in the minds of some Davis Farmers' Market growers a few years back, was a local dentist who wanted to do something positive for the community. He brought in some tomatoes from his garden, sold them at 10 cents a pound and donated all the proceeds to his church. Local growers felt he was undercutting them unfairly.

> "It's not all pie in the sky at the farmers' markets from a larger grower's perspective. You can't compete on prices with hobby or backyard growers that don't depend on the markets for a living."
> — Rick Noffke, Collins Produce LLC, Neenah, WI

In most cases, however, it seems that tiny producers are contributing to their own income while bringing a specialty product to the market and giving it an extra dose of personality. They have much more time to spend with customers, and that's good since some customers want the attention.

> "We love backyard farmers. Growing is a hobby or a passion for them and they give us a variety at the market that is not available otherwise. At our market you can find orchids or hardy banana trees, all grown by hobbyists. If someone has what I want and if they have the proper licenses, I let them in. The commercial growers don't seem to complain because they know it's variety that brings people to the market."
> — Ginger Rapport, Mgr., Beaverton FM, OR

If your backyard gardeners step on the toes of growers making a living, establish a minimum price. Growers can barely survive, if that, selling to the wholesale market, so a figure somewhere over the wholesale price seems reasonable. The Yakima Farmers' Market recently set that minimum price at 60% over wholesale.

> "I have no problem with the market grower, because there's people that have an eighth of an acre, and they're serious about making a living from it. But then there's the person with a lemon tree and some rhubarb and they want to sell at the market. They often have seniority from having sold at the market, and they do lend character to the market, but they can be a problem for other growers who need to make a living."
> — Mark Sheridan, Santa Barbara FM Assoc., CA

Most farmers' market managers realize the importance of keeping gardeners involved — for the character of the market, the customer care, the unusual varieties and to provide a way for people to test their ability and interest in starting to farm more seriously. Numerous markets include community gardening groups who share a table as in Hillsboro, Oregon, while others host community tables where farmers and gardeners can drop off product and have it sold for them by the market. Down in Eugene and Corvallis a considerable quantity moves at the community table, which charges about 30% commission. That's another way to make sure it's not too cheap.

Market Mix

Garth Veerkamp

As with the farmer-only proponents, there are those who believe a farmers' market should have only produce, without any processed goods, crafts or other non-agricultural items. They argue that customers only bring so much money that rightly should go to farmers. They may feel that "crafts can be a cancer" which

Wool spinner in booth during fall craft days at the Auburn, CA, market.

spreads until they overrun the farmers. Especially with processed goods, what they may truly want is some assurance that any of these other products are produced with the same family labor as they put into their produce.

> "If you allow crafts in a market, it becomes a crafts market and overruns the market. Non-ag producers try to come in and get rich quick, and if they don't, then they leave and you're stuck."

A second group favoring inclusion of crafts and processed foods, if not more, argues that we need to give customers more of a one-stop shopping experience. The market suffers if a florist manages to prohibit the market selling cut flowers or if it doesn't have oranges that are farmed locally. By the same token, we should allow — nay, encourage — other small businesspeople who happen to work with local foods, fibers or other materials to make a living.

This still can be a purist approach, as long as the market requires that everything be produced by the seller. Some require that you grow the fruit or berries for your jams, others say all ingredients must be lo-cally produced. These standards mean little without enforcement, including inspections of records. Standards vary with breads, oils, vinegar and more. Whether through dried products, processed nuts, hand lotions or floral bouquets, the key is to keep farmers in agriculture by diversifying their product line and extending their market season.

"We don't sell T-shirts and trinkets at our market. Customers know they can find a great variety of food products here, from trees and perennials to herbs, fresh flowers and produce of every kind, as well as gourmet items like herb vinegars, fresh pasta, and excellent bakery and dairy items. Growers do

How One Manager Makes Issues Look Easy: The Dane County Farmers' Market Story

The Dane County Farmers' Market (DCFM) is the largest farmers' market in the U.S. with over 300 vendors stretching all around the two-block, state capitol square in Madison, Wisconsin. About 25,000 people come to the market each Saturday in a city of 200,000, and recently-retired market manager Mary Carpenter attributes the market's phenomenal attendance to several factors. Its customer base is "middle class to affluent," and the market is close to the University of Wisconsin at Madison, one of the largest universities in the country. "It's a very health conscious city," Carpenter says. "The university was one of the most radical campuses in cities in the 60s, and I think the market has bloomed into a great farmers' market."

Another factor in the market's success is that its customers include a wide variety of ethnic groups. For example, about 10% of the market vendors at the market are Hmong. Carpenter says she feels the market's vendor base should reflect people who are growing and producing crops and reflect local agriculture.

There is a two-year waiting list for qualified persons wishing to join the market. After about ten years as "daily vendors" members may graduate to "season stall" status which allows them to have the same assigned spot each week. Only about 40% of vendors have "season stalls"; thus, more than half the vendors must arrive by 6 a.m. to line up by seniority. At 6:30 these "daily vendors" drive onto the square in an orderly manner and claim any open space, including any "season stalls" vacant that day. "We have 20 to 30 new vendors coming in each year from the wait-

ing list," Carpenter adds. "They help bring fresh ideas to the market."

The DCFM is strictly foods, flowers and fibers; no crafts are allowed at the market. Even flowers can be sold only as flowers, not with bows or ribbons. "Variety is what brings customers to the market," Carpenter says. "One vendor brings 200 different kinds of herbs."

The market is run on a free-market basis, rather than having a lot of rules and regulations about product quality. Carpenter feels market competition encourages and even demands that growers bring their best, what customers want. "You don't get away with bringing seconds or poor produce because so many growers have great produce at the market."

One market rule that is enforced firmly is the strict "farmer-grown" really well at our market because customers come here to buy produce and not jewelry for Aunt Jane's birthday, or whatever."

— Ginger Rapport, Mgr., Beaverton FM, OR

The main problem for the above two groups is with those who favor the extreme open market where anyone can enter with any product. Carved wood from Africa and baskets from Thailand go right alongside bananas from Costa Rica and mangos from Brazil. Throw in Mary Kay Cosmetics for good measure. These advocates say, "Let the customers decide."

Solutions

"Markets might want to consider that no more than 25% of the display area be taken by value-added products. I feel it's OK to sell value-added, where the main ingredient is raised and grown on the farm. This helps balance things if you have a crop failure."

— Caryn Robertson, Kitsop Food & Farm Alliance, Ollala, WA

There are countless ways to treat artisans, craftspeople (or "crafters"), processed items, hot foods or other categories of vendors.

---

policy. Resellers are strictly forbidden at the market; everything sold has to be raised by the vendor, and they can be booted out of the market for violations. Each vendor is required to sign a contract that allows the market to do a drop-in inspection at any time, for any reason. If the vendor refuses to allow an inspection, they are automatically expelled. "If a person is selling eggplant and they don't show me the eggplant in the field, they're out," Carpenter says. "It has been years, however, since a grower refused an on-farm inspection. In fact, they are always very proud of what they grow and are anxious to show off their operations. We've had only one or two expulsions a year of people reselling product."

When asked if such a strict farmer-grown policy could work in a small-town, start-up market where some managers claim the need to relax the farmer-grown rules in order to diversify the market, Carpenter has an interesting answer: "Personally I wouldn't

manage any other type of market. We started with 11 vendors. They would get demands and they would do whatever it took to grow it. They could not depend on bringing it in from somewhere else. And the market just grew naturally."

The DCFM has developed a unique solution to the "big vs. small farmer" issue when small growers feel outgunned by big growers renting multiple booth spaces. Each vendor is given a 16-foot maximum frontage, which levels the playing field. "It also encourages vendors to be very creative in their marketing," Carpenter says. "We don't want someone's bank account dictating how much space they have — 16 feet is the absolute limit."

Another factor that contributes to the market success, Carpenter feels, is that the organization has a board of entirely vendor members. "We're an independent, self-governing, nonprofit organization. When it's a self-governing body, you listen to people. We're dealing

with our own problems and we don't have to explain them to people who don't understand what we're doing. The board is very independent and responsive to vendor needs, and active people tend to attend board meetings."

Bounty from bounty, the market supplies 11 food banks every Saturday. "At 11:30 a.m. the food bank people come by with carts, and a lot of growers say 'take the table' and some even bring some extra for that purpose," Carpenter says. In addition, every fall a large charity dinner is held to support the food bank. The market donates the raw goods, top Madison chefs cook the food, food bank volunteers serve, and all the proceeds from a $14 dinner go to the food banks.

Does Carpenter have any management tips to pass along? "Only that you deal with things with a sense of humor," Carpenter laughs. "And it doesn't hurt that I was a teacher." ✿

- You can separate them from your farmers.

- Limit the percentage or number allowed, just as with socio-political groups, non-profits or downtown retailers.

- Allow any individual no more than two weeks per month or require a pre-season application for desired dates.

- Permit only one sales day per month as the Ferry Plaza market does with most hot food vendors.

- Allow them during any slow periods when crops are lighter such as the beginning and end of your season.

- Allow only hand-crafted items or home-processed foods (in a licensed kitchen).

- Establish a minimum number of days per year to discourage hobbyists.

"Non-agricultural attractions can enhance the farmers' market if they're complementary. I like the producer-consumer philosophy. It has to be well regulated, so the image that you're presenting is a farmers' market. Crafters do add a lot of variety and expand the market, but if it goes too far can turn it into a bazaar or flea market... Put an ag theme on crafts. Jewelry, for example, or earrings and hair clips or pins, should have a farm theme such as fruit and vegetables, and you have to be the producer of the craft. This presents an image of integrity for the market. We have 65 farmers, 12 processed food sellers, and 6-8 crafters. We place a strict limit on the number of crafters and processed foods; otherwise they would dominate the market and take away from produce sales."

— Randii MacNear, Mgr., Davis FM, CA

Including crafts, processed foods, plants, dried flowers, and cut boughs will allow you to extend your market more than a month in either direction. You can gain extra income, but make sure you don't tarnish your more bountiful image of mid-season.

"Since produce is the backbone of any market, we try to keep our membership with at least 80% produce and the remaining 20% comprised of plants and crafts. Produce always has priority over plants

Albuquerque Area Farmers' & Growers' Markets, Alameda NM

and crafts and is given first available space for new members. Our policies are: you grow/make what you sell and YOU sell what you grow/make. All items on the market must be produced and sold by the members. We do not allow bought items to be resold on our market. All craftwork must be original, handcrafted items which comply with the set of craft guidelines and are juried by a craft committee."

—Sara Pollard, *Do's and Don'ts of a Successful Farmers' Market*

Farmer Needs vs. Downtown Rejuvenation

We are experiencing the mallization of America. Whether a downtown is dying or dead, its downtown association and the city frequently are clamoring for farmers' market relief. While it's wonderful to be in the catbird seat, we in the farmers' market arena need to inject some realism into the view that we can be a panacea for downtown economic ills. Farmers' markets have brought thousands of pedestrian customers into countless downtowns, but when they are used without proper care, they can fail. We need partners in the process who will prioritize the survival of the farmers' market above all else.

It is critical that government and local business associations appreciate the bottom line for dozens of businesses within the market, because they can withdraw very quickly in favor of other markets. Every farm sees itself as an important business, equal to each downtown business. With the proper promotion program farmers can entice crowds to downtown streets; it's up to downtown businesses to draw them into their stores.

We need joint strategies to re-build downtown and the market together. If the market does good presentation and promotion, local businesses should be doing the same. Businesses in San Luis Obispo, California, have put live manikins in their windows, painted footsteps from the sidewalks into their stores, declared farmers' market day "specials," opened their doors and come outside to join the Thursday Night activities. There is a strong promotional attitude that permeates most businesses; they want to be associated with the success of market night. In this city of 70,000 population, a chain music store had its largest opening day ever — that's right, on a Thursday. Truck deliveries to the region invariably happen on Thursday afternoon or Friday morning; people just love the excitement and energy of the market. Critical to its success — much like the Knott's Berry Farm empire — are weekly meetings of business and market people to resolve issues and plan strategy.

Numerous cities have invested thousands of dollars to start markets, realizing the attraction will benefit merchants. Sometimes, however, they push the market into a location that looks like a ghost town and ask the market to survive while they see if other businesses can be attracted. Many consumers do not want to enter a depressed zone. While markets can help with crisis management, they should not be left alone on a desolate battlefield. Planning is essential to ensure others are making an investment in redevelopment.

There are other cities that say they love the farmers' market but don't spend the time, staff or money to build or support it. As with any relationship without active love, the market is doomed to failure or a less-than-stellar performance. Another corrosive impact results from a merchant view of the market as competition. Instead, when merchants see the market as a special event with a powerful draw, they give the support necessary.

The farmers' market should be seen as complementary to established and new businesses. To gain that downtown perspective, they can:

◇ Cooperate on various projects, including parades, street fairs, and all-important transportation and parking strategies;

◇ Attend downtown association meetings to share ideas and responsibilities;

◇ Conduct regular merchant surveys to assess impact on stores and improve customer circulation;

◇ Participate in cooperative advertising programs to promote a family ambiance;

◇ Promote a marketing plan with a spillover effect on the neighborhood, especially since the market; and

◇ Maintain the integrity of the market by following rules and agreements which show respect for other businesses.

For example, Santa Barbara's TV ads try to influence the public perception about the safety of one of its six market locations by emphasizing their markets as the "chefs' choice."

It is essential that we be good neighbors, since we cannot have a positive impact on every business. Any business counting on quick in-and-out customers dependent upon nearby parking may look disapprovingly at the farmers' market. While the market day may hurt their sales, the farmers' market can make efforts to improve the overall desirability of the local shopping district so that downtown visits are increased even on non-market days. ✿

PROMOTING THE MARKET 11

"Advertising is like standing in a cold shower and ripping up dollar bills. You spend the money and think: 'I don't know where this has gone.'"
— Karen Durham, Mgr., Bellingham FM, WA

MARKET EXCELLENCE

Studies show that customers come to farmers' markets for quality, freshness, locally grown food, reasonable prices and a fun social and shopping experience. And let's not discount the importance of vibrant farmer personalities!

Nothing in promotion we can do compares with the impact of each farmer's product, presentation and personality. We could eliminate all our promotional efforts if every farmer in the market were committed to great customer service! Of course, our communities still want everything else as well!

TOMA is an acronym for top of mind awareness, the concept that people generally buy from the place that first comes to mind. It's why Campbell's commands 85% of the U.S. soup market. Such dominance in a product category is unusual. Within any local or national market for a product, there are often profound shifts within a period of several years. This is good news for farmers' markets; we can change people's shopping patterns as we become first in their minds. Like Westinghouse we need to realize that, "The quality goes in before the name goes on." So first we need to develop our farmers' focus on quality in every aspect. Then the market must combine those efforts into a collective statement of what we are. This requires an advertising and promotional strategy that will allow us to lead the TOMA category for produce in our area.

"What are the consumers' expectations when buying food? A successful food seller offers cleanliness, quality, variety, and good prices. Convenience, accessibility and what the competition offers are particularly important questions when planning a market. They are also important concerns from a service feature standpoint. Although not commonly considered to be promotions, how a market or any retail food operation deals with these features influences how the consumer will respond to the market. The basic expectations that consumers have for buying food are not an optional consideration. Without meeting these fundamental demands, all additional promotional efforts will fail."
— *To Market! To Market!*, U. of Mass. Cooperative Extension System

Pick up any advertising or promotion book, and it will say that word-of-mouth is the most effective promotion there is. Yet the book *Word-of-mouth Advertising* makes the telling point that word-of-mouth promotion has something even more basic underlying it: product excellence. If your product is excellent, promotion will enhance sales. If your product is poor, all the advertising and promotion in the world will only breed negative word-of-mouth, which in turn will scuttle your business. So before you promote your farmers' market, take a good look at your product — your market. Is it excellent in all regards?

These painted gourds add product diversity and beauty to any market. Some gourd craftspeople specialize in gourd instruments. Value-added products add to a market's depth during the slower winter months.

Products

On the sign above his Olympia market stall, Bob Sullivan proclaims what needs to be a more common guarantee, "If you're satisfied with our product, tell your friends. If you're not, tell Sullivan's Homestead." An absolute guarantee of quality satisfaction will bring people back so that you can teach them why those raspberries got soft (in a 100-degree car for six hours) or the tomatoes lost their flavor (because 50 degrees will cause chill damage).

Are the freshness and quality of your vendors' products superior to that of local food stores and are prices competitive? Is there an adequate variety and supply of in-season products? Do your vendors offer a variety of purchasing options as far as quantity — bag to bushel?

Look at expanding your product line within the market. If you have fewer than 100 products in your market, try to increase that figure by 30%. Can you add painted gourds? Processed jams? Oils, vinegar and mustards? Fresh pasta and pesto?

Markets tend to be seasonal because they seem to lack product diversity in the off-season. Yet, in reality they often close because of a lack of vision of how to be a year-round market. Even with the short, 120-day, Alberta growing season, the Old Strathcona Farmers' Market in Edmonton is open year-round. In mid-November 176 stalls are filled with squashes, greenhouse tomatoes, stored carrots from four farms, carrot juice, honey from four apiaries, pasta, bell peppers in four colors, mustards, cheeses, and a few ready-to-eat foods. Of course, also interspersed are hand-crafted items which seem to occupy about half the space without overwhelming the pleasant food atmosphere. The colorful mix includes dresses and figurine candles, carved wooden hats and wood benches, etched stone and fine jewelry.

In the 1990s superstores have come from nowhere to garner a 33% share of all retailing. As they continue to grow, we don't have the financial resources to fight fire with fire, but we do have a combination of resources that they can't touch. To maintain TOMA strength with a growing minority within our communities, we need to promote our special attributes.

While there is often much truth to "Simply the steady supply, rain or shine, of the finest produce does it," we have to consider whether handmade crafts can stretch our season AND set us apart. We can't rest easily as our competitors add our product line to theirs. Farmers' markets often popularize organic produce, gourmet mushrooms, fresh herbs, specialty bread, heirloom tomatoes, unusual sprouts, goat cheese and whatever else local farmers are ready to produce and promote. As the competition catches up with us, we need to proclaim what the stores cannot: incomparable freshness and buying straight from the producer, with all the personal service that infers.

Friendliness

The vendors' personalities behind the booths are your market's greatest resource! Motivate vendors to talk to customers. In larger retail settings employees perfunctorily do their jobs and many customers are left without the kind of personal exchange they desire. In a farmers' market the customer may make five purchases from different vendors and share friendly greetings with more, including customers. Do everything possible to increase hospitality and friendliness in your market so peoples' social needs are fulfilled and they're excited to tell friends about this positive experience.

You, as a manager, need to feel comfortable coaching vendors. Work with them to improve their displays and salesmanship. If a farmer is sitting on the tailgate with a poor display and disappointing sales, you might help by suggesting an experiment: "Let me put out an idea that might work for you; I've seen it work with others." Then pull boxes off the truck, create a multi-tiered display with the products, and show the seller that marketing can be fun. Remind them that customers are more inclined to buy from a busy farmer than a resting farmer. Demonstrating enthusiasm may show the farmer the difference between the $200 and a $700 a day. Ultimately, it is often the difference between someone who gives up the market and one who becomes a consistent, healthy participant in your market.

Customer Service

Pike Place Market recognizes the value of giving awards to farmers for excellent display or superior customer service. This farmer received a framed watercolor for his loyal contribution to the highest display and service standards.

Constantly examine your market from the standpoint of customer service. Do you have good signage to help customers find the market? Is it accessible on foot or via public transportation? Do you make efforts to reach special segments of the population by providing senior shuttles and accepting government food stamps? Is your market wheelchair accessible? Are there "customer care" centers in your market such as a free hot/cold cider table for fall customers? Do you provide carryout services for shoppers, especially seniors? If parking is distant, do you have a loading zone with claim checks?

Consumers also appreciate good enforcement of quality standards. Insist on clearly marked seconds. Designate canning product as such so that people don't buy it for fresh use.

Locating vendors consistently in the same spot makes them easier for consumers to find. Offer a directory of farmers and vendors with a site map and each vendor's name, address, phone number and product list. This encourages special orders and restaurant sales outside of market day.

A 1999 study of three Oregon farmers' markets suggested that carts or wagons would be helpful since 10% of respondents said they stopped shopping when they couldn't carry any more. Give local businesses exposure by painting their names on the side of a set of wagons. The same can be done with business and market logos screened on either side of a canvas bag.

"Take care of your customers. Look at every aspect of your market, such as the traffic and parking situation. Can they get in and out easily?"
— Rose Munoz, Former Mgr., Torrance FM, CA

Keep an open ear for complaints and concerns. A suggestion box will help. Markets often make it too easy for the customer to justify going elsewhere.

Market Ambiance

Create an attractive market atmosphere. Decorate the entrance with flowers, vegetable displays, scarecrows or other seasonally appropriate themes. Use your logo or even a mascot to make the market a colorful, fun place to shop. Make the market a community center by soliciting non-profit participation, organizing theme events and festivals, and allowing activities suggested by community members. Encourage farmers to create attractive displays and ensure that the market grounds are clean. The market is highly visible and presents an attractive location for local residents and merchants. Thus, the site should be clean and orderly even when the market is not open.

If the market does professional signs or banners, farmers may follow suit.

MARKET DEMOGRAPHICS

Target your audience. Promotion and advertising strategies should be targeted to the type of customer to be reached. Know your market demographics. Are your customers local regulars, tourists, transients, walkers, bus riders, bicyclists or drivers? Do you know their age, family status and preferences?

What's unique in your town? Your market should be reflective of your community. If 30% of your population is over 65, is that group similarly represented in your market? If your community is 40% Latino, are 40% of your vendors and customers Latinos? And if not, why? Your goal is to create a true community marketplace that is reflective of all elements of your community. Determine what population segments are missing and why; then create a targeted marketing plan with written goals and strategies to attract them.

The more you find out about your customers, the more you can cater to their wishes and increase sales. If you find you have a high-end community, direct your advertising to that market. Or perhaps your market has dense housing nearby where door hangers might work, if you have a church youth group to distribute them. Color code your flyer — yellow on apartment buildings, green on duplexes and blue on single family residences — with a coupon to check the response rate from each.

"What to do about declining, white, traditional customer base (they are aging, eat out and eat like birds)? Today's young couples don't know how to cook from scratch and therefore are not volume customers. The answer is in the exploding immigrant population which comes from vegetable- and fruit-eating and cooking cultures. Develop PR materials in their languages and encourage vendor participation from these groups whenever possible."
— Tony Evans, Maryland Dept. of Agriculture

Getting to Know Your Customers

Market research is generally divided between primary research — where you research your customers yourself — and secondary research — where you find available research that has already been done about your intended market. You will find a good deal of secondary research available through your local library, universities and colleges, Cooperative Extension in your state and elsewhere, and studies done by other markets. Be careful not to assume that all this research will reflect your local customer base. It may give you a good idea of the general characteristics and priorities of farmers' market shoppers. It will provide a number of questions for you to ask in your own primary research.

For primary research a residential phone survey is a good investment. Before starting your market you may want information that will determine the market's character. Ask about their preference for day, hours, location, products of interest and media outlets — "What type of music do you most prefer? What radio station do you listen to?"

Market surveys. After you open you need to continue surveying to learn how to keep customers coming back. Find how customers feel about prices, quality, presentation, friendliness, access, parking, ambiance and other particulars.

You also need help in attracting people not coming currently. Survey residents via phone or intercept interviews at key locations. If you ask and listen, you'll learn what's missing that may be keeping people away from the market.

As a good manager you constantly listen to customer conversations in the market and elsewhere. You also engage customers about desired additions or changes. Through these indirect or direct casual contacts, you gain valuable insights to make market improvements. Thus, you show customers you care and want to maintain their loyalty. In periodic vendor meetings managers can hear more impressions of subtle customer desires. This feedback loop is critical in making market adaptations.

Surveys are a much underused, yet very essential, part of a promotional campaign. [Please see and study "Customer Surveys" in the Appendix]

Are We Reaching Our Entire Community?

— Diane Eggert, *Farmers' Market Forum,* Farmers' Market Federation of New York

Most farmers' markets are located in areas with diverse populations. That is, senior citizens, professional people, blue collar workers, ethnic groups, impoverished, and affluent. But are we reaching all of these people and giving them a reason to shop our markets? It is important that we do not leave anyone out.

Seniors living on a fixed income can benefit greatly from shopping at a farmers' market. Many of the seniors living in retirement centers would love to shop at a farmers' market if they just had the means to get there. Make arrangements for transporting seniors from these centers to your market. If public transportation cannot accommodate this, check into school buses or private bus companies. If you have a "Friends of the Market" organization at your market, maybe they can organize drivers.

You can reach more of the elderly by contacting Senior Citizens groups. These seniors are mobile, but they have to know about you. Offer to speak about your market or local agriculture at one of their meetings. Offer product samples from your market while you're speaking. Then follow this up with a tour of your market facilities or a personalized visit at your market. Introduce them to the farmers and send them home with a free gift of apples, tomatoes or whatever you can arrange.

Young professionals are the ones with money to spend. But they don't always know about us as much as we think they do. How can we do something about that? Try reaching them through organizations, such as Rotary, Lions Club or professional associations. Tell them about the economic benefits of a farmers' market to them, to the farmer and to the community as a whole.

Speaking at union meetings about your market and supporting local agriculture may help you to reach some of the blue collar workers in your market area. Or try speaking at PTA meetings and to women's groups. Posters in local grocery stores and other neighborhood stores may also help you to reach out to more people.

Most market areas have impoverished neighborhoods, those requiring extra assistance to make ends meet. These people can benefit greatly by shopping at a farmers' market. That's why the Farmers' Market Nutrition Program is so successful. But there is still a number of these people that are not making use of farmers' markets. Is it because they don't have access to transportation? Can we arrange bus service for the poorer neighborhoods as we did for the senior citizens? This may bring a new group of people to your market and while they may not have a lot of money to spend, they do have food stamps, FMNP checks, and a need for our services.

Almost every community has one or more ethnic groups, people that maintain their heritage from their country of origin. But do we adequately reach and support these ethnic groups? First, we need to identify the different groups in our area and determine what foods are unique to their culture. If farmers are not already raising the produce they prefer, can we convince some of our farmers to grow them to offer at the market? Now you need to communicate to these people that your market offers what they are looking for. If there is a club, association or church that is unique to their ethnic group, make arrangements to speak with them. It's a great opportunity to reach out with information about your market and to receive feedback from them on what it is they would like or need from the market and its farmers.

Children are the consumers of the future. Yet children are not impressed with the freshness of vegetables — they want to have fun. Make your market appeal to kids. Offer petting zoos, hayrides, balloons, or whatever you can to make going to market with mom and dad a fun experience. Remember: This has a two pronged effect. The kids not only will continue to shop at farmers' markets as adults, but mom and dad also will come! ❧

ADVERTISING

Some farmers' market managers say that advertising works for them; others report disappointing results. This is consistent with an old Madison Avenue saying, "Fifty percent of advertising works, and 50 percent doesn't. The problem lies in figuring out which 50 percent doesn't!" Evaluate results constantly, so you can avoid spending money on ineffectual ads or promotion campaigns, and use all the free publicity and promotion you can get.

Since very few people react to just one ad or news story, effective marketers often use both publicity and advertising to increase the odds consumers will see or hear their message. A campaign that repeatedly places your message before your audience gets results. Remember, Campbell's dominates the soup market because of Top Of Mind Awareness (TOMA). People will buy their produce somewhere; your advertising helps determine where.

Both publicity and advertising are useful in introducing your market, building a reputation, announcing new products or services and promoting specific events. If you can't count on free publicity when opening a market, you had better advertise. Don't take chances with all that work and the market's future health on the line.

Ad Message

Advertising gurus advise to stress benefits. For farmers' markets that means "farm-fresh," "locally grown," "organic," "buy direct from the farmer," etc. Keep a consistent look with your logo but change the message to encourage shoppers to look for it. Farmers' markets also mean "fun" to most shoppers so don't repeat the same ad every week. Try a corny phrase like, "You'll be 'peased' at what you find."

Something new in the ad catches the eye in a fresh way — a chef demonstration, a cookbook signing, free shortcake on the market's birthday, an apple for every 50-year-old, a melon for anyone on a birthday. Have fun with this and get your growers involved.

Stress the availability of tree- or vine-ripened fruit, just picked vegetables, all from local farmers. Your press releases can address the average distance of your farmers compared to the 1300 miles typical of fruits and vegetables in the traditional marketplace. Customers are learning through media about the need to keep their local food supply viable. Your ads should reinforce that message with "Support Your Local Farms and Protect Your Food Supply."

Always put "Rain or Shine" in ads and brochures. People won't assume you are open in a downpour, but once they know they can count on you, they are more likely to come out even if it means getting soaked.

Joanne Neft, developer of the Foothill markets east of Sacramento, reinforces, "Develop an ad theme and then use it in display ads throughout the year. Keep posters consistent from year to year."

Budget

When you know what you want your promotion and advertising to do and whom you want to reach with your message, decide how much you should spend.

For each project draw up an expenditure list. Advertising costs include media space or time, special help fees, copy writing, design, layout, photographs, illustrations, typesetting, artwork and printing. When figuring expenses for events or festivals, consider the time spent in meetings, planning, research and phone calls as well as the hard costs of postage, shipping, delivery charges, telephone and office supplies.

Utilize free promotion before spending money. For low-cost promotion strategy, read books like *Advertising Without Money* by Salli Raspberry, *StreetSmart Marketing* by Jeff Slutsky and *Grassroots Marketing* by Shel Horowitz. Every promotion you do represents your market, so allocate enough money in your promotion budget to produce a promotion or advertisement that communicates quality. Without it you may be creating a negative image about yourself.

When defining your target audience, do not overlook your existing customers. Remember the 80/20 rule: 80% of your business comes from 20% of your customers. Always promote to your best audience on a regular and thorough basis before spending money on your second-best audience. Your existing customer base is your most important and easily targeted group. Spend the bulk of your advertising and promotional dollars in areas where current customers live rather spending promotional money in an effort to draw customers from new areas. Similarly, focus your advertising on certain income groups if you know they are strongly represented in your customer base.

A budget campaign of $50,000 a year for advertising may be appropriate for a strong market, while an ad budget of less than $5,000 may be too high for a very small market. Much depends on how much time is dedicated to free publicity opportunities, including special events. If the market has revenue of $100,000 per season and clocks $7,000 to cover market operations, it may spend less than $1,000 on promotion and advertising. That's 1% compared to many farm retailers who will spend 3-10% of gross sales.

So if your market is not growing, you might rethink how you can increase the budget to spread or reinforce the word or, better yet, create activities which renew excitement in coming to shop. Customers should enjoy you more than the competition.

> "We feel that our market's best advertising dollars are spent in a free Madison newspaper called *Isthmus,* a free-thinking, progressive, alternative-spirit publication. We do a weekly advertisement with what's new with the market. The progressive type of crowd is the very type that comes to the market. Our market customers tend to be very middle-class and into healthy foods and organic food options."
> — Mary Carpenter, Former Mgr., Dane County FM, Madison, WI

Market Logo

One of the most essential tools for any size market is a logo. An attractive emblem builds market recognition and consumer awareness and helps promote a professional and cohesive identify for the market. A logo can be put on virtually anything from stationery to trucks.

You can raise money as you build enthusiasm for the logo with such promotional items as hats, aprons, T-shirts and sweatshirts. You also might consider distributing free or low-cost items simply to reinforce this image. Buttons, pins, bumper stickers, and small posters are options. If your logo is a fun image, you might attend your county fair or city parade to apply water-based stickers to kids' arms and cheeks.

Involve market customers and the community in developing a logo. A market logo contest allows you to build interest and create publicity for the market while achieving a result.

Your logo should become the central, unifying element within your overall publicity and advertising plan. Don't print anything without it.

Fruits & vegetables make up this fun logo in Hollywood, CA.

Banners & Signs

Let people know the market is there. Set up A-frame sandwich board signs directing traffic to the market. Banners are cheap publicity in your market throughout the season. With your logo they announce market days and hours and a sense that this is the best place to be. Hang banners and place sandwich board signs for several blocks in every direction on each market day to notify approaching traffic. Especially effective is a huge, permanent sign that reminds all passers-by on a 24-hour, 7-day basis.

Wall Drug in South Dakota is famous because of its ability to draw tourists with signs. Think of all the places you can put them. Pasco, WA, and Ithaca, NY, have them on their open, shed structures, but you can use someone else's building, too. Phoenix, AZ, has them on bus shelters. Why not right on the buses? The rule-of-thumb is to tell a visual story and keep it to six words if you are attracting motorists. Work with a professional who knows size rules, e.g., six-inch high letters are readable at sixty feet. What about a farmer's barn with five-foot high letters?

A permanent, colorful sign advertises your market 176 hours a week. Using a city parking lot is extra guarantee of potential customers being regularly reminded and gives the city a reason to be extra proud of its use of city property. (Tamzen Corum, daughter of author Vance.)

Permanent sign in Beaverton, OR

Banners front two sides of a Prosser, WA, park, each displaying the logo and name of a different market sponsor.

Cathy Jones, manager of the Fearrington Farmers' Market, said, "We arranged with the North Carolina Dept. of Transportation to erect directional signs on a nearby highway, routing customers to our site. We also use banners that alert drivers that there is a farmers' market down the road." Ask your local legislator to intervene on your behalf with the state transportation department. There may be a charge, but it's well worth it. The Soulard Market in St. Louis paid less than $4,000 for a ten-year sign placement including maintenance.

Don't forget your customer base. Retailers across America spend literally billions each year on indoor signs that trigger the impulse purchase. Use your market space, not just local streets. Set up a permanent sandwich board in a highly visible part of the market, attaching laminated sheets that advertise your vendors, special events, service volunteers and promotional items. Your customers are the best market. Use signs that direct, inform and motivate. Encourage your farmers to do the same.

Banners across Main Street give immediate credibility. Placement and removal can be major costs, especially if the city limits such space to one or two weeks at a time; thus, ask the city or signage company for a donation. While similarly costly, billboards along freeways can be well worth the investment.

"Banners can be purchased from a variety of places. I chose a tent and awning manufacturer who had a long history of making canvas signs and banners. They are silkscreened with the market logo and information on both sides. They were $150 each seven years ago, but they have held up beautifully," says Chris Curtis in Seattle.

Get on the local marquee with a large electronic sign. The Hillsboro Tuesday Marketplace in Oregon uses an abandoned theater for equipment storage and the marquee hosts the name of the band playing each market night. Or use reader boards with changeable letters in front of businesses and community centers.

"The local YMCA, community centers, grocery stores and churches have helped us get the word out about the markets by letting us have the use of the reader board for a few days before the event begins. In one instance, I made a $100 donation for a week's use of the board."
— Chris Curtis, Mgr., University District FM, Seattle, WA

Flyers, Brochures & Posters

Many markets find that "guerrilla marketing" tactics with flyers, brochures and posters work great with farmers' markets. For example, you can have a flyer about the market with a 50¢-off coupon or a "something extra" coupon. Place brochures, flyers or posters wherever there is a collection of people who would be interested in hearing about you: store windows, schools, malls, churches, clubs, historical attractions, restaurants, museums, service stations, bed-and-break-

Tip sheet, Santa Barbara FM Assoc., CA

2-fold brochure, Santa Fe, NM

Support Our Farmers
Staunton Augusta Farmer's Market

Bumper sticker, Staunton Augusta, FM, Staunton, VA

Foothill FARMERS' MARKET

AUBURN   TAHOE CITY
ROSEVILLE   TRUCKEE
ROCKLIN   GRANITE BAY
SQUAW VALLEY
Celebrating Our 10th Anniversary!

Poster, Foothill FM Assoc., Auburn, CA

fast inns, campgrounds, hotel and motel rack card displays, laundermats, convenience stores, fire stations, travel agencies and fairs. You can even ask farmers to take flyers to their roadside stands! Guerrilla marketers never stop considering opportunities for exposure.

> "Look for places wherever people are encouraged to eat fresh fruits and vegetables and live a healthy lifestyle such as senior centers fitness centers, hospital cardiac units and weight loss centers."
> — Rose Munoz, Former Mgr., Torrance FM, CA

Ask local, civic-minded organizations to send your flyers with their mailings. Contact your chamber of commerce, visitors' centers and the state department of tourism for suggestions about where to place your printed material. If they offer to help distribute your literature, check to find out their guidelines for brochure size or weight, etc. before producing your printed pieces.

An 11x17-inch color poster can be a great investment. The Santa Monica market started in 1981 with $4000 spent on 1000, 4-color posters. Because the poster was professional and attractive, most were put up in local businesses and the last 400 were sold in the market to recoup over one-half the expense. This high-quality poster reinforced the city's intent to have a high-quality market. It quickly became one of the top markets in the U.S.

The same capital resources were not available in Astoria, Oregon, in 2000. Yet, when a printer offered a free ink color, the market suddenly was able to produce an eye-catching, red-on-yellow, 11x17-inch poster for only 15 cents per copy. With matching flyers next to many retail cash registers, the market's identity was established without an overblown, expensive approach. You don't need full color to have visual impact. Your goal is to attract the eye; when you want to give them loads of information, write a brochure instead.

The grassroots approach often requires people power to distribute leaflets at shopping malls or on parked cars. New Mexico Farmers' Marketing Association president Esther Kovari knows word-of-mouth is more effective because the personal touch works best. She says, "We still do radio, TV and print ads, but we're adding more direct methods like leafletting."

It simply comes down to the most cost-effective methods.

> "We've been utilizing flyers, direct mail pieces and less standard media advertising such as print ads. Market managers are trying to reach the customer directly — like doing direct mailings or putting flyers, brochures and posters on community bulletin boards and literature tables at churches or other community outlets. This seems to be most effective. Traditional advertising hasn't had the response that the managers would like for the amount of dollars spent."
> — Jeff Cole, Exec. Dir., Mass. Fed. of FMs

Direct Mail & Piggyback

Many markets find direct mailings effective, both for adding a personal touch and targeting a very specific audience. You can mail a flyer with a $1 coupon to homes in the vicinity of the market, for example, or to certain zip codes where you want to target a particular income shopper. Even if you don't get a high response rate, the reader is likely to spend more time considering your advertisement because of your coupon. You become more memorable.

Postcard, Foothill FM Assoc., Auburn, CA

A *visitor book* is effective in building a mailing list. Computerize this list and keep updating to contact market-goers with seasonal openings or special events. Have customers sign a pre-paid postcard that you mail to remind them of next season's opening. Create a "friends of the market" membership group and mail them periodic special offers at the market. Help promote word-of-mouth with "Tell A Friend" brochures. People fill them out, put them in a box at the market, and the market provides postage.

Newspaper inserts are inexpensive but they only reach those getting the paper, or specifically people who read the paper and check out your insert. A colored paper may be worth the extra cost for your ad to stand out.

Utility inserts are less costly still. City-operated public service utilities and banks are required to reinvest in their communities. You pay only the cost of printing an insert with their mailing. This is the least expensive outreach to every household in your community; the downside is that utility mailings are mailed over a 60-day cycle. Find the requirements — deadline, size, paper weight, count — so it doesn't raise their postage. This may be the same vertical 3-up form (3 copies on 8 1/2 x 11, cut) that you use for hotel and visitor center rack cards.

Postcards are the least expensive way to mail first class and allow you to delete old names when returned undeliverable. Use postcards to promote special events — they stick out in the mailbox and are cheaper! Portland, Oregon, uses color photos to entice people to their Summer Bread Festival, Tomato Fest, Fall Harvest Festival and other events.

The Santa Barbara Certified Farmers' Market Association uses full-color postcards to announce the opening of the market season and stocks them at info booths at all six markets. It is a great personal touch for customers and newcomers, more effective and much less expensive than brochures.

"Take-one" tear-offs. The Santa Barbara Market's postcards also make great "tear-offs."

Postcard/tear-off, Santa Barbara FM Assoc., CA

"Blow-ups of our postcards also make great poster boards, which are displayed at each of the markets. Postcards in padded sets are placed on the poster boards so that the customers can read the schedules written on the poster board, and then tear off a reminder postcard to take with them.

"The postcard is about a third of a letter-size page — longer than a normal post card — so the association is able to fit the schedule, a map and logo, as well as some sales copy including 'open rain or shine, six locations, certified farmers.'

"The postcards are made to fit in tourist racks and they're also effective as a brochure. What customers are really after is the 'where and when.' They don't really need to know about things like the history of the market. We do have a four-color brochure as well, but we print these in a limited edition for people who want more information."
— Mark Sheridan, Santa Barbara FM Assoc., CA

Coupons. Peter Jankay, administrator of the San Luis Obispo County Farmers' Market Association, CA, adds:

"This year the SLO organization tried something different that worked well in promoting the markets by mailing coupons to each person in a mail route within a two-mile radius of the market. We found this much cheaper than going door-to-door trying to hang them on doorknobs. The block mailing required that the mail pieces be prepared, packaged and assorted in a certain way, which a mail service helped to do. Each coupon was good for a free basket of strawberries, and this at a time of season when strawberries were at their best, so customers were really getting something of value. The promotion didn't cost the association too much money. The coupons could be redeemed with any grower who was selling strawberries, and the growers handed in their coupons to the market for redemption at market value. Whatever their price was at the market for their strawberries, that's what the market paid the individual grower."

If that sounds too costly, have your growers join in the promotion. After all, you're promoting their berries, not carrots or feijoas, so they should be willing to help cover the cost from their increased sales.

Radio

Radio is a very personal, low-impact medium so when the Yakima market started in 1999, it bought five spots a day for ten days and opened strongly. Ten daily commercials would not be too much, cutting back to three or four days per week, so listeners sense the frequency and assume they missed it the other days. The repetition is critical since people usually are doing other activities at the same time. Verbal commercials on a news, sports or talk show will get more attention than on a music format.

Because of its "act now" nature, radio is good for bringing people out to events such as festivals or grand openings. Since you can get a message out quickly, radio is particularly helpful when you have an oversupply situation. You can literally call a radio station on market day, tell them you're loaded with oranges or asparagus, and see an impact within the hour. Nothing can compare for immediate response.

Regular market day reports give customers a status update.

"We do a market report on a local radio station each Saturday at 9 a.m. We tell people what is at the market that day."
— Karl F. Schaefer, Mgr., Chapel Hill-Carrboro Farmers' Market, NC

As with all forms of advertising and publicity, determine the impact of your ads through a customer survey. Ask how they first heard about the market and what forms of promotion have reached them.

"Radio has worked better than newspaper for us."
— Charlie Springer, Mgr., Richmond FM, IN

"The association does do one radio program, called 'A Matter of Taste,' for which they are one of five sponsors. I go to the studio each week to talk about what's up and coming at the market, and other times the programmers come out to the market to interview growers live."
— Mark Sheridan, Santa Barbara FM Assoc., CA

"Radio is the best media for special events or sales, but keep your message simple. Use the best stations available that cater to your audience. Purchase the best times available. The ads cost more but for a good reason; they are reaching more listeners. Radio can be used to advertise your niche crop. The ad might be for a specific market, Saturday morning. Don't confuse listeners by listing your entire schedule. They won't remember it anyway."
— Dan Haakenson, *The Small Commercial Gardener*

Television

Television is obviously the mammoth powerhouse of communication. It may be within your reach. It touches emotional people with friendly farmers, colorful produce and unusual items and performers. It reaches intellectual people with a logical set of benefits including fresh-from-the-farm and great values.

Remember that sound frequently goes off with remote controls, so make sure the visuals are followed by your logo, site, day and hours in case viewers are listening only with their eyes.

Mark Sheridan outlines a television strategy:

"Last year the association put together an ad campaign called 'Chef's Choice' in which Santa Barbara's leading chefs come and shop the market. This theme is tied throughout all our print, radio and television ads. Local celebrity chef Julia Child acts as the voice-over, saying: 'The finest chefs shop at the farmers' markets.'

"Most of the association's advertising dollars are going into television ads. Television just seems to have the greatest reach, it has more 'eyes.' Advertisements are placed on local stations and mainly in the news slots, such as the 6 a.m. morning news, as well as a few women-oriented programs during the day. Ads are run two weeks on, and off two weeks, to maximize dollars. It costs $250 a commercial for a prime time, 6 p.m. spot, but it's worth it! People watch the news, and they know our different commercials. We get feedback like: 'I like the one with Julia at the market.'

"Commercials get stale, so you need to make more than one commercial, highlighting what's happening in the market. Showing a grower shucking corn, for example, should happen only when corn is in. You can leave certain elements in the ad and change just certain parts of the commercial. The programmers can help you with this. We also try get different appeals with different commercials. We're currently trying to stress the convenience of the locations and times, and we're also stressing that carryout help is always available. We let people know they can buy that extra bag of oranges and someone will be there to help them take it to the car."

"You don't need to know anything about filming because the production crew handles all of this, but you do need to hire them at about $250 an hour to come to the market and film. We take lots of footage so we can go back to the studio and go through the archives and say 'Yes, that corn,' or 'Yes, cherries.' We might be using last year's cherry shot in a commercial. Because we own the footage, we can use it at any time."

The rates will vary widely depending upon your television ratings, whether the camera crew is unionized, and how the station responds to your request. You may be paying for editing, voiceovers, scripting and other costs.

You may think cable TV is the way to save on TV advertising because it's cheap, but remember that they know the value of what they're selling. Many cable viewers are channel flippers and you will have no guarantees on the numbers. Sheridan continues: "I wanted to go with what was guaranteed. Go through the ratings carefully and find out which shows people are watching. Many markets would probably balk at spending $250 for a 30-second ad, but we found it works. You can spend $250 on a newspaper ad and not see any difference at the market." Mark Sheridan has pushed sales at his six markets over six million dollars annually. The strategy seems to be working. But that doesn't mean cable won't work for you if you are in a high-cost, urban media market and only want to advertise to a small, localized cable viewership.

"Television provides spectacular visual impact because of the sharp contrast between the colors of fresh vegetables. We use television to increase the customer base late in the season. Purchase the best times on your best station. It works. Cost: One 30 second spot on the 10 PM news cost us $95. Other decent times were about $50 each."
— Dan Haakenson, *The Small Commercial Gardener*

Newspaper

Newspaper ads benefit from at least once a week consistency over the long haul. Given your food focus, you should advertise with the food pages on Wednesday or Thursday if your market day soon follows. If you operate early in the week, you may prefer a Sunday ad when people have more time to read. Try to place your ad on the right margin of the right-hand page above the fold. Use a distinctive border unless your logo attracts the eye and reminds people of your news in today's ad. A coupon also helps make the ad memorable even if it isn't clipped.

Place classified or display ads in local papers to alert customers of days and hours plus a list of products available. Look for "Penny Saver" type free newspapers that can exactly target your zip codes and do a half- or full-page insert — this makes a very effective low-cost newspaper advertisement. However, Sandra Zak, manager of Soulard Market in St. Louis, warns that the Penny Saver may be useless in larger markets because people receive so many throw-away pieces and it's expensive because of the number of copies. Utilize newspaper ads as posters and handouts to get the most use of the money spent on the ad. Better yet, getting your newspaper signed on as a co-sponsor of your market or a particular event gives you some free ads.

To be effective with a classified ad, use it regularly knowing that the reader is just that, not a browser. Use bold capital letters in your headline. Speak factually as if you were telling the market's benefits to a trusted friend, using words like fresh, free, fun, you, meet farmers, guaranteed and great values. Communicate your sincere enthusiasm without overdoing it.

"We spend $160 each week on advertising in local, well-read newspapers, and 40% of our customers come because of an ad in the paper."
— Joanne Neft, Former Mgr., Foothill FM Assoc., Auburn CA

"Since it's expensive to advertise in major city papers, we advertise to target the organic shopper. Puget Sound has a large network of natural grocery stores and we advertise in their newsletter and also in weekly alternative papers that tend to be read because they have a more sophisticated food shopper."
— Chris Curtis, Mgr., University District FM, Seattle, WA

When you are consistent with your ad placement, the customer may look for your ad to see what is special this week, so vary the content to hold their interest. Use clip art to feature a new item each week or push the special event. The more advertising you buy, the lower the rate.

Rates

Demand of your media sources that they give you some free publicity for your paid ads. Don't be afraid to ask for something you deserve! You're working with a non-profit group and you're speaking for a large number of people representing a genuine civic interest. Be sure to ask for non-profit advertising rates and one-paid-one-free if you are purchasing a substantial quantity. You may also get a special rate by taking out a classified ad for the entire season, changing weekly as items come into season. Your biggest concern

should be frequency. If you can't afford weekly ads, keep them consistent as a reminder.

Don't forget to consider that media outlet as a potential sponsor. Hipfish, a cultural monthly in Astoria, OR, provided the poster layout and a substantial sized ad for several months in return for major sponsor listing on the market poster. Both the monthly and the market gained visibility without a hard cost. Each reinforced the alternative nature of the other.

Coupons

Coupons can be included in newspaper display ads, flyers or direct mailings. By offering the customer a free "bonus" or savings ("two for one") for bringing the coupon into your market, coupons act as an incentive to act. Coupons also serve as a loss leader; when customers bring in coupons for a free or discounted item, they usually purchase other items as well. Code your coupons according to different outlets and weeks so you can track your readership redemption.

Co-op Ads

Develop a group ad. The Medford Growers and Crafters Association in southern Oregon takes out a display ad stating the locations and hours of operation. Growers tack on individual ads at $20 each, 25% less than individual rates because of the organization's contract.

"We developed a 'Friends of the Market' map. It identifies libraries, schools, phone booths, parks and — for a fee — merchants' sites posted also on the map. We distributed 5,000 of the maps and had 24 ads on the first map at $35 an ad. Be sure to have the merchants proof the map to be sure their locations are correctly identified. List town events as well as the market's yearly activities on the back of the map. Since the maps can be used as restaurant placemats, they were distributed free to restaurants that were glad to put them on the tables for a captive audience!"
— Grace Richards, Arlington FM, WA

THE NEW FARMERS' MARKET

If you were selling washing machines, you would probably ask Maytag if they had cooperative advertising funds available. In the farmers' market realm, we often fail to realize how many companies want to be associated with our fresh, positive, community focus. Look at how many companies sponsor Little League Teams. A soft drink manufacturer may just as easily give your market a free tag on their TV ad because it shows them to be supportive of your great community event. Local car dealers may cover your ad costs in exchange for the right to place a car in the market periodically. In Modesto, CA, the market covers all its advertising costs through co-op ad funds.

Think about what ad program you want, how much it will cost, who might like to fund it. Then start to make the calls, write the proposals and meet with the people who want to help you as they help themselves. Be flexible in responding to their interest in one specific event or aspect of your market.

Chris Curtis suggests, "Go to the business community to do a co-promotion on a chefs' series. Local businesses put their ads around our ad about what chefs are coming to the market. They also help sponsor a local radio gourmet program called 'Mauny Kaseburg's Food Bites.'"

Movie Theatre Ads

Making a movie ad can be expensive if you want to show live scenes from your market. You might approach your local film instructor or ask a student filmmaker. Otherwise, your best bet is to shoot slides at the market and create a collage of all the various facets that intrigue customers and make it a people place. Keep the ad very upbeat.

The market in Beaverton, OR, tested the movie theatre world. It had difficulty justifying the high cost given that the theatre complex served a larger area than their primary market draw and they developed no concrete evaluation methods. In Davis, CA, the farmers' market has felt the theatre to be an effective reinforcement, perhaps because it is directly in the downtown area, blocks from the market.

Movie theater ad for Davis FM, CA.

Yellow Pages Ads

If your competition is listed under retail grocers, retail produce or elsewhere, you can gain instant credibility as an equal with the same size ad as your biggest competitor. If others aren't advertising you probably shouldn't. You might start with a listing before experimenting with a small ad. If you really want to stand out, pay for red ink.

PUBLICITY

Most farmers' markets soon realize that expensive advertising is not the only nor the best way to bring people to the market. Effective promotions don't require big budgets.

Local TV stations often are searching for new program ideas or may provide community service programs concerning nutrition and food. They often need material for "shorts" at the end of newscasts. Ask if a reporter is interested in doing a news story on an event or a colorful personality at your market. They might do the weather shot with your market as a backdrop.

Cable TV. Try to find a volunteer willing to create a weekly cable TV show featuring market products. Other stations are responsive to 30-second, public service announcements. Many stations have lots of hours to fill. Look especially for a channel that features local activities. Give viewers an update of vendors in the market and what's new in the market that month. Do a mini-documentary on your market.

Boy Is It Hot!

Contact the weather stations about doing weather remotes at your market. Weather people are always looking for colorful new filming locations. For example, on a hot summer day suggest they tell the weather from the booth selling peppers, clowning around: "You know how hot it is today?" (Bite into pepper) "Boy is it hot!" ✿

PSAs. Radio stations are required by law, as is television, to designate a certain amount of airtime to worthy community events. Public service announcements are the way to apply for these spots. Write a 15- and 30-second PSA on a separate sheet and attach it to your press release or a letter requesting airing of your PSA. Be sure to mention that you are a non-profit organization.

Practice reading each PSA to make sure they can be read in the allotted time.

Try to get free community service spots telling what's to be found or products coming on strong. Investigate sponsorship of a radio program. Give your local DJ a tantalizing basket of fresh produce at season's opening to tell his/her listeners how good it is!

As a festive, community-oriented group, your farmers' market has lots of things going for it when it comes to getting news items into the local media. Markets are highly visual and full of potentially newsworthy stories. Your market represents a genuine community interest. Media staff are very eager to find positive local stories and they have lots of print space or air time to fill.

Play on your particular local history and tradition. Celebrate your growers and emphasize new products. Play up your special events at the market for what they are — fun, educational, community events.

While some people believe special events tend to detract from market sales, remember that you are after media coverage in general to bring more people to the market. Special features are good. Strive to find new and different items that will intrigue the media and ultimately your customers.

"The main purpose is to get the press out: If we get 100 new people out to the market, OK, but if we get the press out, it means 10,000 new people. Always feed the press!"

Media List

Compile a media list of reporters and editors who might be interested in your stories. Target individual editors — especially food editors. Note the names of those reporters or editors who write for sections of the paper like Food, Leisure, Lifestyle, Agriculture, Business, etc. Learn to tailor your stories for their specific needs, i.e., one angle for the business section of the paper, another for the features editor, etc. Study articles and see which might be of interest to you. Look for different types of radio, TV shows or newspaper columns featuring topics or programs related to food, home and garden, agriculture, health.

Develop a strong media list, including newspaper, radio and television editors and writers. Other contacts in your database might include horticultural, agricultural or herb associations and organizations; co-operative extension personnel; and "friends of the market" or interested persons. Expand and update your media list yearly. One way to do this is to mail out postcards with "address correction requested" stamped on the postcard.

Get the name of the contact person and proper deadlines for the community calendar or events listing section. When you have a special event, your market can be listed. For TV and radio, get the names of the news directors and the names of producers for talk programs.

Look for senior citizen and freebie newspapers that have a calendar of events section. Add weekly news magazines and church bulletins to your list.

"We send a copy of 'What's Fresh at the University District Farmers' Market' regularly to about 70 food writers and specialists and to about 40 chefs as well."
— Chris Curtis, University District FM, Seattle, WA

News Releases

One of the most effective low-cost promotional methods is the publicity available through local newspapers, radio and TV stations. You should be sending out a fairly steady supply of press releases to get news articles, interviews and media exposure. The ability to write a simple release and establish rapport with the local media will often result in much better coverage and results than you can achieve through advertising.

> "The Marin market has probably gotten as much publicity as any farmers' market in the nation. It came from constantly sending out press releases and never letting up."
> — Lynn Bagley, Golden Gate FM Assoc., Novato, CA

An industry rule-of-thumb is that editorial coverage is seven times as valuable as paid coverage. Readers may not believe you when you say in a paid advertisement that the golden raspberries are incredibly tasty, but they will believe it when a reporter writes an article stating that your raspberries took her to food heaven! A good piece of publicity can be worth hundreds or even thousands of advertising dollars. So before spending money on advertising, first utilize all the free publicity and promotion available. Publicity is a boundless opportunity. Use it every chance you get. And that means you had better make sure your farmers realize the importance of high quality, good displays and fantastic customer service because a self-respecting reporter can only do so much to make you look good.

The key to getting news releases accepted is to send information about something that is unique or new and is of real interest or usefulness to the readers. Remember that a press release must be newsworthy. Editors want news, not advertising. If you expect to be taken seriously, analyze the writing style in the section to which you are sending the release. If they have to do a total rewrite, you're not likely to get ink.

An intriguing press release may focus on a unique, humorous event which has human interest. Be sure to set the scene with a specific reference to the visuals that a photographer or news team can capture as at this individually oriented, all-you-can-carry pumpkin contest (Santa Monica FM) for $5.

If there is no other farmers' market in your area, it may be relatively easy to attract the media initially. But after your opening, don't count on freebies coming your way so easily. You will have to work for their attention, creatively, unless you're a media darling. Even that takes work, whether it's socializing or getting media releases on their desks.

Get in the habit of thinking "possible PR story." Write your ideas down and file them. As you develop media contacts, this allows you to offer them several suggestions for stories about your market. Free or community service events, such as a food-tasting, demonstration or lecture by an expert, may be of interest for the community bulletin board slot in a small media market, but you need to get more imaginative in a larger market.

> "Marcia Halligan, manager of the Viroqua market in Wisconsin, says that the Saturday morning radio spots that list the items available at market are the most important promotion for their market."
> — Sara Pollard, *Do's and Don'ts of a Successful Farmers' Market*

While special events which are not food related may detract from the market, one has to balance the drawing power of the event and the follow-up media coverage against whatever negative impact some people may impute to the event. A strawberry shortcake giveaway may hurt impulse sales of pies and turnovers, but it should spark strawberry sales and, more importantly, give the media a reason to cover your market.

No matter what the media, the editor will expect you to present the "story angle" in your press release. This can be a simple announcement of a market opening, the logo contest results, the manager being hired, the site being chosen, farmers getting organized, the board being elected, or a profile of chefs that shop at the market. Continue compiling a list of "angles" available for market use as well as a list of which angles have been used and the results.

Uniqueness. Ask yourself: What is unique about our market, about our vendors and their products? Does our market offer unusual food items not normally available in grocery stores?

Human interest. There's a great human interest story behind every booth at your market! Feature a "farmer of the week" in your newsletter and encourage your community newspaper to carry it as well.

Humorous events are also great for publicity: How many pumpkins can you carry? What about the juggling contest with strawberries, cabbage and eggplant?

Recipes. Offer recipes and cooking tips to local food editors for the types of produce that are coming into season in your market. Food editors, and their readers, have an insatiable appetite for recipes!

Current events. The season's first strawberries or corn are timely issues and the editors especially like

News Releases Get Results — Free!!

— Diane Eggert, *Farmers' Market Forum,* Farmers' Market Federation of New York

A press release is one of our most useful and powerful marketing tools. The press release serves two purposes. First, it gets the information of our market before the public. Secondly, because a press release is a news story and not an advertisement, it gives the story, and therefore your market, credibility. News reporters and the public will see you and your market as important and newsworthy.

Your press release should tell how the community will benefit. Include anything going on at your market: the opening for the season, any events scheduled for the season, the number of farmers participating this year, any renovations or changes made to your market, any new products offered at the market, or anything else the public should know about. If your press release reads like an advertisement rather than as a news story, your news story won't be printed.

Include all the contact information. A reporter may want to ask you a few questions or do a more complete story.

Give your press release a clear and concise headline. Your first paragraph should include all the basic information. You can go into more details in following paragraphs. Also, send along any photographs you might have. These often make the story more interesting and more likely to be printed.

Send your press releases to specific media contacts if possible. Call the papers, radio and television stations to ask who your press release should be addressed to. These could be special interest news reporters, food editors, farm reporters, business reporters, or any reporter that you have found to be interested in farmers' markets or agriculture, in general.

Send press releases to local daily newspapers, local free papers (i.e., Pennysavers), tourist papers, regional papers, college newspapers, organization and association newsletters, corporate or industry newsletters/newspapers, local radio stations, local television stations, and local cable stations.

Once you have sent your press releases out, follow up with a phone call. This will give you an idea of how much coverage you will get. Sometimes you can add a little more information in your phone call that might make the difference in getting your story printed. ✿

to know this. Consumer concern about pesticides is big news; send the newspaper a story about the pesticide-free products offered in your market. When the Department of Motor Vehicles threatened to push the San Fernando market off their parking lot, the Southland Farmers' Market Association contacted media throughout Los Angeles.

Business news. Look for possible business angles about your market that might make a newsworthy story such as expansion or relocation of your market, how your market is helping downtown businesses, unusual accomplishments of market growers, or local businesses gaining visibility at the market. In Pasco, WA, there was an incubator story as many market vendors graduated to permanent retail space in a building across the street.

Market activities also make interesting news stories: special events, contests, fund-raising events, festivals or educational events. A chef cook-off or a barbecue contest provides great copy and photo opportunities.

Often, you can find market volunteers with journalistic interests who can help you supply a steady stream of great news releases to the local media.

> "Concentrate on what's fresh and what's in season and highlight interesting items that the customer won't find in Safeway, e.g., we have 45 kinds of tomatoes or 12 kinds of melons and 17 kinds of peppers this week."
> — Joanne Neft, Former Mgr., Foothill FM Assoc., Auburn, CA

Media Relations

Back in the 1980s we had a successful 30-minute program on Ag-USA, a nationally syndicated television program for farmers that aired early Saturday morning. Vance wrote the script so that each of six or seven farmers would be asked different questions to direct their remarks. We lined them up at the Long Beach Farmers' Market so that when the director walked down the aisle, it would look like he was naturally interviewing every farmer. While it was a slight interruption having television cables throughout the mar-

ket, everyone seemed to accept it given that we gained national visibility for farmers' markets. Sometime later they asked us to produce a similar show at the Santa Monica Farmers' Market, which we did.

Cultivate quality relationships with local press people. Then send your press releases directly to their attention. This is much better than sending out news releases blindly. Give personal releases to members of the media. Call to make an appointment with the food editor of the newspaper or the assignment editor of a local TV station or public service director of a local radio station. Get to know them!

Be selective; don't barrage the media with non-newsworthy events or news releases. Keep them supplied with news according to their capacity and receptivity. Keep them well supplied, but don't become a pest. Earn their trust by sending news releases that are timely and newsworthy.

Once you get to know a media person you can just call them, "Hey, I have a great idea. How about a 'Women in Farming' story? Would you like me to gather some information for you?" Or call the food editor, "Would you like me to put together a list of foods not available in the supermarkets?"

Rather than pushing your market happenings as agricultural or profit-making events, promote them as citywide, social events. Agriculture and self-promoting entrepreneurs are low on the media totem pole. Let the media know you have something important for the community!

Press kit. Prepare a press kit about your market, with a fact sheet about the organization, the number of farmers, when the market started, the locations and hours, the types of products featured, and any reprints of past coverage. Provide an updated press kit once a year or when a new person fills a media position. Be careful not to cause an editor to think his/her angle would be old news. You might want to put a list of story ideas in the pack.

Follow up your news releases with a phone call and call again the morning of an event because media often decide each morning where to send reporters.

"I'm so-and-so from such-and-such market and we just wanted to remind you we're having this event today. We feel your readers/listeners/viewers would be especially interested because…" Be brief and business-like. If it's a slow news day your call may make all the difference!

Organize farm tours for media and customers and send them personal invitations to events. When you get a reporter out to an event, stay with them as a host, if they are willing. Think about what you want to emphasize — consumer economic benefits, the organic food available, freshness and quality, or the tremendous labor by local producers in getting products to market. Point out these facets as you guide the reporter through your market. In this way you can help guide the story!

Co-op news releases. Local weekly or monthly newspapers may find having a feature on area farmers' markets more appealing if each of several local farmers' markets writes up a description of its particulars and submits them as a packet to be included alongside the feature article.

> "Any time you can make a news story out of a happening at your market — festival, demonstrations, ethnic produce — you're more likely to be covered by local media. Always take the time to talk with reporters and make your market available for the press to come down. You won't be sorry."
> — *Farmers' Market Forum,* FM Fed. of NY

> "Make sure you have lined up some vendors for media interviews. They may not speak to them all, but you have covered your bases. This also eliminates the possibility of them contacting the vendor who never has a positive thing to say or who may have an agenda of their own."
> — Sandra Zak, Mgr., Soulard Market, St. Louis, MO

Editors love getting free food samples, so at the beginning of every market season take a basket of fresh market produce embellished with flowers into your local newspaper, radio and TV offices, and put one on every food editor's desk. Especially with major city, larger newspapers, however, reporters or editors may not allowed to accept gifts.

Articles/Columns

Send educational articles to the media about the benefits of shopping locally, eating fresh foods, in-season calendar, etc.

Approach your food editor about supplying them with a regular weekly "What's new at the farmers' market" column. Include how to tell when ripe, the different kinds of varieties and how they taste. You might also write a gardening column with tips submitted by grower members.

Do a recipe of the week for the newspaper's food pages, and mention that the ingredients are in season and plentiful at the market along with sellers' farm names.

Offer a profile of farmers at the market, what they sell, a short bio about the grower and their family and farm, and where they can be found when they are not at the market. In addition to promoting each grower, consumers learn about the people who grow their food.

> "The Albuquerque Journal agreed to do a biweekly column called 'This Week at the Farmers' Markets' featuring different markets and what's up-and-coming at the markets. It's better than an ad!"
> — Esther Kovari, President, New Mexico Farmers Marketing Assoc.

> "The papers like a regular column because it's something they don't have to cover. We supply them a lot of material; we have a retired farmer who likes to write and has a degree in home economics. The key is to be consistent and give them something complete and ready to run and meet their deadlines so they don't have to call us up and ask for it."
> — Karen Durham, Mgr., Bellingham FM, WA

> "Write a news release each week and focus on a farmer. The farmer is the most interesting thing at the market, plus what's new and fresh, e.g., a woman who raises oyster mushrooms; or a woman who raises plants on land that belonged to her great grandfather; or a raspberry farmer who had increased business 2000%; or someone converting successfully to organic produce."
> — Joanne Neft, Former Mgr., Foothill FM Assoc., Auburn, CA

Visuals

Newspapers often won't print an article but will print a great photo, so send them one! Keep a multiple-copy collection of slides and prints, including overhead shots, good farmer-customer interaction, crowd shots, special events, seasonal berries or pumpkins, or people in shorts or coats on a fall day. You need to be the source; don't count on getting photos returned. When they print a photo or article, send a thank-you letter.

Send a news release to the local television stations highlighting the visual angle of your story. Television editors want a visual story to entertain their audience, especially weekend visual events.

Create a market video for cable TV.

Talk Shows

Let TV and radio talk shows know you can supply them with great material for their shows, and suggest special interviews with different growers or a regular interview to review what's fresh this week. Tape farmers even during off-season and send the tapes to a local radio or TV station. The Southland Farmers' Market Association has done regular programs with a major Los Angeles network, focusing on the nutritional value, history and growing practices of one crop, then developing a dish.

"The Central New York Regional Market in Syracuse has a weekly interview on a local noon-time television news program. The farmers' market director, Ben Vitale, talks about what's new in the market that week, and what's going on in agriculture and how it's affecting the food that's coming to the market. Right now we've had a solid month of rain, so he's talking about how that's affecting the crops. The local news anchor brings up a new topic every week, and we're on for several minutes. And that's worked very well as a promotion for the market. Luckily for the market, the TV station's news director, as well as the local news anchor person and news director for the station, all happen to be regular customers at the market."
— Diane Eggert, Exec. Dir., FM Fed. of NY

Tourists

Capture the tourist dollar. Network with tourist entities, get listed in their directories and summer entertainment guides, and see if they will distribute market flyers. These usually are on heavy-duty card stock with good graphics at the top, easily visible while sitting in a card rack.

Contact state, county and city tourism agencies or offices. Place brochures at interstate information booths. Call visitor and convention bureaus, your state travel director, bus tour companies, state and county fairs, chambers of commerce, bed and breakfast stops, motels, hotels, restaurants and other tourist attractions such as ski resorts, historic sites, and museums. Distribute flyers at major festivals.

You may want to take your entire market directly to the tourists as at some East Coast turnpike rest stops. Or consider a tourist destination. At the least, tourist hotspots recognize the importance of numerous attractions helping to draw people back to the area, so they generally will help spread the word if your market is a colorful addition to the area.

Once the tourists are in your market, make sure your farmers are ready for them. Consider what quantities tourists may want, what container will keep the berries from becoming a mess, and what gift pack may be perfect for that house gift they need. Expect low sales per customer if, like the Soulard Market, you are attracting senior bus tours sponsored by banks.

A "Where in the World Are You From?" sign & global map inviting customers to identify their hometown with a stick-pin is a great idea for tourist-heavy markets. Eventually, the map is filled with stick-pins and shows graphically the market's connection to the world.

Tourists can be a double-edged sword but few markets will come to see them that way. By the time they have impacted you like Pike Place Market, they may have alienated your primary, local trade. By that time you may be past the point of no return, with vendors depending on a different type of sale.

Miscellaneous

Billboard companies may loan your market unrented space for free. Be prepared with graphics and money to cover the production cost. Perhaps a corporate sponsor could be approached to help pay for design and printing. You need to act fast on this one.

Your *answering machine* can work for you. Outline market days and hours, locations, special events, free parking, and basic vendor requirements which reassure the consumer that they are buying from producers. During the off-season, promote next year's dates and readiness to accept new applications. Provide a list of "Press 1 for market hours, 2 for directions, 3 for vendor information, …" so callers don't hang up on your long message.

Business cards carry more weight with market times and a map on the back. Use a different color when your printer is doing a special color for free.

Colored *refrigerator magnets* sent to residents with the utility bill are more likely to go on the refrigerator than a flyer. They hold someone else's flyer, and the next and the next.

Evening-in-the-park concert series are popular in some towns. You might advertise there or host a market night in conjunction with the music if there is enough parking. If so, open the market an hour or two before the concert to piggyback on their advertising.

Parades. Years ago markets in Los Angeles teamed up to sponsor an entry in the Doodah Parade along with a briefcase drill team and other wacky entries. Managers passed out 40,000 fliers while pulling a cart laden with produce and tossing lemons to the crowd. Dress up for the 4th of July parade, with someone in a carrot or tomato costume wearing a sign 'Come to the Farmers' Market today.' Get a farmer to drive a tractor and wagon in the parade. Know your audience; if it's a drunken Mardi Gras crowd, your fruit may come back at you like softballs in an out-of-control batting cage.

Chef testimonials. If you don't ask, they can't say yes. Only Santa Barbara has a Julia Child, but Port-land, Oregon found two restaurant chefs who take turns as market chef. Bradley Ogden has helped make the Marin County markets famous. Working with your local chefs is a good way to check that you are on the cutting edge of a sustainable, regional agriculture.

Politicians. Invite a council member or county supervisor to a special event and hang on their coattails. Other markets choose to keep politicians at arms' length; only you know your local politics. (Paid petition gatherers can be rather aggressive.)

Invite a local TV weatherman to the market to talk to the public about how the weather affects gardens, and about weather forecasting in general.

Public presentations offer tremendous opportunities, including service clubs, senior centers, civic and women's groups, churches and garden clubs. Use good graphics, including computer-generated or 35mm color slides. You may inspire sponsorship by the American Association of University Women, which sponsors a market in Fullerton, CA.

Buyers' and consumers' guides. Many states publish directories of farmers' markets. Check with your state department of agriculture or local extension agent to find out how to be included.

Welcome wagons provide newcomers with local business directories. Ask your chamber of commerce how to be listed.

County fairs and home shows provide an excellent venue for flyer distribution. Make those long days fun by handing out samples which gives you something to talk about, a longer period of contact. Get addresses for your mailing list. Set up a farmers' market trade show booth at your local emporium with a little mini-tasting of the different products you have at the market.

Websites are increasingly common for farmers' markets. If you are owned by a city, use theirs. You can often piggyback on a community or neighborhood website and want to be cross-promoted on as many as possible. Go on various market websites to see what you like best: Fresh this week, Market chef schedule, How to rent a stand, Entertainment, General info, History, Neighborhood info. Keep the levels limited so that people don't wait long periods for another color screen to pop up. [See also "Embracing the Market" chapter]

Decorate the market with balloons, flowers and vegetable displays. These decorations in the perimeter and inside the market add a festive element and a sense of cohesion. Try a balloon arch over the entranceway, especially for a special event.

Information booth. In addition to educational material such as consumer buying tips, recipes and organic information, you can publicize upcoming events and related markets, provide your market newsletter, sell promotional items and solicit new vendors.

Feature vendor. Each week feature a different farm/vendor, putting them in the center in a reserved spot or placing a large ribbon on their booth. Numerous markets give various annual awards for the best display, most improved farmer, friendliest vendor and similar categories.

Weekly makeover. Customers want constant changes that we can demonstrate with new vendors, improved displays and other visual effects. A good, on-site manager continually evaluates and listens to the customer perspective and communicates valuable ideas for improvement to farmers and other vendors. Post new signs that point out the chef of the week or list new products or specials.

> "Announce vendor specials for vendors who wish to have their weekly specials announced on the PA system. Have them bring a written list of their specials to the market office after 7 a.m. on market day!"
> — Mgr., Kitchener FM, Ontario

Malls. Move inside to the centor court of a large shopping mall.

Farmers' Market Week

Approach your state legislator or governor's office to issue a proclamation.

> "Farmers' Market Week was established by the Federation in the state of New York in the first week of August primarily to enhance public awareness of the markets and their benefits. We use that time especially to educate the public about the foods that they're eating. We use a pamphlet put out by Cornell University that discusses the nutritional benefits and values of the fresh foods customers can find at the markets."
> — Diane Eggert, Exec. Dir., FM Fed. of NY

NEWSLETTERS

A personalized newsletter offers a soft-sell approach that allows you to keep in touch with your customers and build a close relationship with them. A newsletter make customers feel like part of the market "family." It saves postage and printing costs by compiling all your news, sales bulletins, classes offered and announcements into one mailing rather than several small mailings or numerous advertisements.

Newsletters also can be used for educational and recognition purposes. The more you educate people about food, agriculture and farming, the more they will understand and support you.

> "A newsletter makes people want to get involved in the market. After the initial start-up of the farmers' market, it may pay to put most or all of your advertising budget into the newsletter instead of paid newspaper ads."
> — Rose Munoz, Former Mgr., Torrance FM, CA

Make it two pages and zippy, with a calendar of events and news about tastings and product festivals coming up. Include tips regarding food storage, recipes, craft projects and gift suggestions. Your Extension home economist can supply you with educational articles about food and nutrition.

Other ideas for newsletter articles or features include: Farmer Profiles — where they are located, size of farm, growing practices, what they bring to market, and something personal; Tips on Storing and Cooking Seasonal Produce; Meet Our Market Volunteers — profiles about volunteers serving the market; Editorial: e.g.: "How You Can Help Protect Farmland." Have a focus with each issue, e.g., Spring Planting, Summer Recipes and Fall Preserving.

NEWSLETTER

Market Newsletters:
Making customers feel like part of your market family

— Diane Eggert, *Farmers' Market Forum,* Farmers' Market Federation of New York, Spring 1999

A newsletter is an inexpensive means of communicating with your existing customer base. It provides a personal touch that makes readers feel a part of the market family and therefore encourages loyalty. This loyalty translates into regular shopping at the market and increased sales.

What makes a good newsletter? There are a few simple design elements that you should follow. First, begin with a banner. The banner should include the name of your newsletter, your market name, your logo, and date. You should also include a contact name and phone number, although it doesn't have to be a part of the banner.

Newsletters provide information, but they should also be simple and easy to read. Therefore, articles for the newsletter should be short. Sentences should not be long and the vocabulary should be simple and easy.

Your newsletter needs to grab the readers' attention and draw them into the text. You can start attracting attention by printing on colored paper. Use bold headlines to spark interest in the article. And to break up the monotony of text, intersperse graphics, charts, diagrams, and quotes pulled from the text of the article. But be careful; there is a fine line between effective use of these techniques to break up text and overkill that actually hinders readability.

Be consistent. Use the same banner each time you publish. Also, be consistent with the number of columns, the font, and the overall look of the newsletter. Also, be consistent with publishing. It doesn't matter how often you send your newsletters, just as long as you are consistent about it.

Information to include

Include all the news of the market. If you have a full-scale festival, be sure to promote it to your existing customers through the newsletter. Also include the small, every-week kinds of things — demonstrations, musicians, etc.

Personal news adds to the feeling that the reader is a part of the market family. Announce any births or weddings or notify readers when one of the farmers or vendors has retired or died. Also use the newsletter to introduce new farmers and vendors. It'll help the newcomer to be more easily recognized and reduce the time it usually takes a new market vendor to build up their own customer base.

Information: Use the newsletter to educate your customers about the food they eat and the agriculture they support by shopping at a farmers' market. Feature stories on different types of produce or products offered at your market. Talk about how the product is grown, produced, or made. For example, how many of your market customers know how honey is extracted or know that tomatoes were once considered poisonous, and that the U.S. Supreme Court ruled on whether the tomato is a fruit or a vegetable?

Developing a mailing list. Where do you come up with all those names and addresses? How do you target only those with an interest in the market so that you don't waste money and resources?

One way to develop your list is to set up a table for signups at your market. Provide forms for customers to put their name and address on. You may even want to ask a few survey questions on the form. Offer a thank you, either an outright gift or as an entry into a contest. Use the signup sheets to enter them in a weekly drawing for a free prize, which you can have donated by a different vendor each week. (Be sure to give the vendor credit on the gift!)

The most important thing is just to send out a quality newsletter. By quality I mean a newsletter filled with good information and interesting news, with a personal feel to it. If people enjoy your newsletter the word will spread and the mailing list will continue to grow. ✿

Assign different columns or spaces in the newsletter to different volunteers. Farmers may want to contribute or take turns, e.g., "How to Grow Potatoes," or "How to Cook with Herbs."

Newsletters are great, but they can be time consuming! Try to get volunteer help.

"Put up a sign at the markets looking for volunteers. Often you will find volunteers who have graphic arts, public relations or computer skills. Journalism classes are another way to find help. Students get their name in print and gain some valuable experience. A Garden Club member might write a column about gardening. Your water department or a city agency may have an article to contribute, and Cooperative Extension often has lots of informational papers they are willing to contribute. State and county agriculture newsletters often have articles or interviews about issues such as pesticides that can be reprinted with permission."
— Rose Munoz, Former Mgr., Torrance FM, CA

Mailing. If you have 200 or more of the same item you can bulk mail for about half the price of a first-class postage, but you need to do all the sorting and bundling. This works if you have more time than money. Have a collating party with volunteers. Be sure to send stacks of the newsletter to community groups and local agencies. Remind customers to pick up their issue at the market to save mailing costs. You might also require them to fill out a form each year to stay on your newsletter mailing list.

 ## SPECIAL EVENTS

Special events bring out a lot of new faces! Even if it's a rainy day, growers may see their sales rise. If weather cooperates, you may witness two or three times your regular customer count. The key is to use many of the same principles used in starting a market: strong farmer volume, intense publicity, increased signage, and many elements to create a sense of fun, excitement and community spirit.

Early in its history, the San Bernardino market, CA, was small, with $2,000 in weekly sales among 12 growers. Hosting a Strawberry Festival, they did that much in berry sales alone and total sales more than doubled. That increase was sustained following the festival because new farmers were solicited and the expanded customer base had more selection to keep them pleased.

Special events done successfully are an opportunity to take your market to a new level of operation and volume. Organizers need to work constantly on getting new farmers and customers. To boost growers' sales, they must have more products with them. If they're going to risk harvesting more perishable product, it makes most sense for them to do so in conjunction with a strong promotion and advertising campaign connected to a special event.

The market should be fun and educational. Using the themes of fresh, locally grown foods, there are numerous special events that can be created to stimulate interest in the market. Events that are part of a market's promotion create reasons for people to come and explore possibilities.

"For several years, the Pasquotank County Farmers' Market in North Carolina, has promoted itself and the nutrition benefits of eating five or more servings of fruits or vegetables a day by holding seasonal 'Taste Festivals.' These are regularly anticipated events, especially amongst upscale citizens more prone to be health consciousness and apt to experiment with new foods. Patronage was increased by two to four times when the festivals were promoted heavily."
— Thomas M. Campbell, Pasquotank County FM, Elizabeth City, NC

TASTINGS

"At the 'Grill Crazy' Tasting, we take a lot of new products, show the shoppers how to grill them on the barbecue and give them out as samples. I'm not a vegetarian, but to me, eating a Japanese eggplant is like eating a New York Strip steak!"

Tastings are an excellent way not only to move a glut of products in mid-season but to introduce the public to the taste subtleties of unfamiliar varieties. Comparing the flavor and texture of 10 tomato or peach varieties gives the customer an experience unmatched in supermarkets!

Coordinate tastings with special events. A cherry or pastry tasting go along with a Cherry Festival. Get bakers at the market to contribute examples of pastry products. Check with your health department.

Special Events at Your Market
by Lynn Bagley

— Lynn Bagley is founder of the Marin County Farmers' Market, director of the Golden Gate Farmers' Market Association and a consultant with Bagley & Associates, Novato, CA

Events can hurt sales if they draw people who are not coming to buy. Events should promote the farmers' market concept which is to re-establish communications between rural and urban culture. Lots of people are looking for their rural roots again. We celebrate the seasons, for example, and in grocery stores there is no season.

Keep the focus on food! The purpose of special events is to promote the market. You want the attendees to come back, so before having special events, make sure your producers are providing high-quality products and services to build customer loyalty and bonding. Help keep customers coming back with constant new excitement, educational, food-related events and thematic entertainment, but don't get too far from "who you

are" such that special events detract from food sales. Events that have nothing to do with food or agriculture may promote sales for that one day, but in the long run they attract a different customer base and hurt sales.

When you have a glut of one thing (cherries, peaches, etc.) have a tasting! This turns a not-so-good-situation into a better situation. With each tasting event that you do, emphasize the quality and variety of produce to be found at the market. Studies show this is what draws the people to the farmers' markets. Whatever products you have that the supermarkets don't have, e.g., heirloom varieties of apples, a tasting helps show them off and highlights your competitive edge over the supermarkets.

In April or May flower-glut time, bring in the nurseries to talk about flower care, the local water district to talk about water-saving techniques, or chefs to do a demo on cooking with flowers.

Plan special events around what your target customer may want. Synergy begins to build and expands with diversity. With seniors, for example, you can do a "Senior Health Fair," including a range of senior health services and nutrition counseling. Involve local businesses; get employees out at lunchtime by serving some special lunches. Each person you hook may tell 10 people.

You want your market to serve as many different types of the population as possible. Target special events to attract population segments, e.g. certain ethnic groups or a wealthy clientele. If your demographics allow it, go after the "green consumer," and you'll have a repeat customer. At the markets they can find foods grown without pesticides and a chance to help farmers preserve farmland and the greenbelt around the city. Green consumers tend to be very loyal and often have more money and tend to better educated — they are a "natural" for the farmers' markets.

While it may be tempting to charge up to a dollar for a shortcake, a few hundred dollars income is far overridden by the value of community goodwill. Media coverage is also more likely if you do a give-away or allow another nonprofit organization to benefit.

Schedule tasting events around products as they come into season. Strawberries are great for festivals — 98% of Americans like strawberries! In Georgia a peach cobbler may be the perfect treat.

"Offer 8 or 10 different peaches and show a jillion different ways to use peaches, make peach juice, fry peaches, poach peaches."
— Joanne Neft, Former Mgr., Foothill FM Assoc., Auburn, CA

A Pumpkin Festival might include a carving demo and contests. Sell pumpkin or squash soup and identify varieties or make a contest of it. Have customers guess the weight of a giant pumpkin or the number of seeds in a jar. Host a scarecrow contest with prize money and judging by the public and a panel.

One way to attract the the "green consumer" is with Earth Day and organic events. Help celebrate Earth Day with a festival and also have a year-round sign describing how farmers' markets are ecological and thus a celebration of every day as earth day. An Organic Tasting Event allows you to educate people on what is "No Spray," what is "transitional," what is actually organic, and to show people how good organic products really are.

Another way to plan great special events at your markets is to look for businesses or community groups you can network with. Look at a Calendar of Events in the newspaper for upcoming events and call the organizations to see if they'd like to come to the market to promote their organization. Read the paper and look for food, garden or agriculture-related events or experts to find people who may contribute to the market. You might find someone who can provide a gardening or cooking demo or even teach a series of classes at the market.

Take advantage of the schools. They love coming out to the markets for Farm Day. Invite teachers and classes, and invite school boards to participate in planning. Invite the Farm Bureau and Cooperative Extension. Have a mural contest, an essay contest, a photo contest. Have a live story: "Where does lunch come from?"

Prepare a teacher packet that explains where food comes from and talks about the diversity of fruits and vegetables, etc. Have agriculture exhibits about food, where clothes come from, a recycling center, and Peter Rabbit's garden. When we get children thinking about where their food comes from, we create our future.

In conjunction with the Marin Community Food Bank around Valentine's Day, for example, the Marin County Farmers' Market held a "Have a Heart Day." A big red heart with lace around it was placed on a table, suggesting that people buy food at the market and donate for the Food Bank. To promote heart-healthy fruits and vegetables, market volunteers put little hearts on all the fruits and vegetables that are beneficial for the heart. A xeroxed list was passed out of "Heart Healthy Fruits and Vegetables."

Start out small and simple with special events, and build on it more and more. Don't plan so many events at once that you can't do them right. Don't try to do it all yourself. Have a special event coordinator and develop volunteers, partnerships and collaborators to help. Don't call it a special event unless you're really doing something special.

Don't do the same "special events" over and over. Build on them! Build fund-raisers in conjunction with special events to promote the market in general. In the beginning when you have little or no money to spend on advertising, spend money on special events instead of large paid ads and promote these with press releases, PSAs, signs at the markets, etc.

Plan for getting maximum coverage from media. Get last year's photos to print prior to the event and shoot new photos to send the newspapers for printing after the event as well. Send out press packets early and repeat releases two weeks before the event. ✿

Santa Monica received donations of shortcakes from Hostess, berries from their market growers, Redi Whip from the corporate headquarters and a local store, plus posters from the California Strawberry Commission. With only $50 spent on bowls and spoons, the Santa Monica Beach lifeguards served free strawberry shortcake to 1000 people in 74 minutes. This "berry kid" added to the fun.

"Tomato Day occurs on the last Saturday of July each year at the Kansas Grown! Farmers' Market in Wichita. The day is full of tomato and gardening seminars, tomato contests, diagnostic clinic, youth activities and tomato tasting. It receives free promotions from the media and draws the largest crowd of the season. Winners in the tomato growing and salsa contests receive 'Market Bucks' to spend at future markets."

— Robert I. (Bob) Neier, Extension agent, Wichita, KS

"When we have a glut of sweet corn, we get a permit from the city to have a corn feed. We hold it in conjunction with our Heritage Days celebration and everyone selling at the market dresses as in the olden days with long aprons and long dresses and skirts and gentlemen have bibbed overalls, boots and straw hats. Many of the vendors utilize containers to display items that have a link to the past like an old bushel basket with wooden handles. So often people get caught in the day-to-day business they forget to have fun at the market!"

— Bonnie Dehn, President, Central Minnesota Vegetable Growers

Organizing A Tasting Event

There are many forms of tastings. Generally, markets set up sampling tables in one central location. Put out samples on plates with identification signs or card

Tasting of Summer Produce directional signs at Oakland Museum, CA.

tents stating the variety, farm name and farmer's location in the market. Also have a map beside the tasting tables showing where participating farmers are located in the market. Clear your process with the health department.

If you host a tasting without a centralized location, you might have large signs and a map of tasting participants at key market entry points and encourage people to visit vendors giving samples.

In addition to slices so people can taste new products, display the whole fruit or vegetable so customers can see how it looks in the market. Have farmers contribute to a recipe sheet. Place your information booth in the sampling area where general questions can be answered, leaving the farmers more free to sell their products.

Have the public vote for their favorites and include a short survey. Make sure you gather addresses on the voting ballot to build your mailing list. A focus on one or more items each month is a great way to build customer interest and keep your volunteers excited about seasonal changes in your market. Volunteers can collect products donated by farmers, cut and display the items, answer questions, direct customers and do clean-up.

This kind of product focus deserves extra advertising, a postcard mailing, signage in the market for two weeks in advance and as much attention as you can give. With all the increased interest in specific products that are part of a tasting, make sure the growers are stocked extra heavy. Sales should be up considerably from the product focus as well as the additional customers that a tasting will draw.

The Tasting of Summer Produce was originally organized as a way to connect top Bay Area restaurants and small producers in the early 1980s, and evolved into an annual one-day tasting event and farmers' market. As a major event it demonstrated the interest among the public in comparing tastes of exceptional produce and led many California farmers' markets to incorporate the concept on a smaller but more regular basis. The challenge was to find sufficient corporate funding to staff the months-long planning process; with a farmers' market you already have the ongoing venue within which to host a successful tasting of any size.

Chef In The Market

On-site cooking demonstrations, along with tastings, are a sure draw at many markets. Each week a different local chef comes to the market and receives product free from farmers or is given $10 or more to shop for ingredients. After cooking a dish the chef answers questions and may give tastes and recipe cards to customers. In some markets this may last less than 30 minutes while elsewhere they spend 90 minutes or more constantly cooking if the customer interest is high.

Chef In the Market event at the University District FM, Seattle

Local restaurants find this a great exposure for the restaurant, and their food helps educate customers and entice them with the quality products. There's no better way to teach market-goers how to prepare seasonal produce and use combinations of foods.

Send letters inviting chefs to sign up for the chef demonstration series. Point out the opportunity to introduce or remind customers of the restaurant location, distribute menus or business cards, do a drawing for discount certificates and demonstrate some signature dishes.

In Beaverton, OR, a patio and barbecue company donated the use of a barbecue cooking unit for the season. A sign and business cards demonstrated their support for the Market Chef program run for 15 weeks. In Portland two restaurants regularly share the chef demo, sponsored by a major retailer or the major newspaper which donates half the advertising.

If local regulations prohibit handing out cooked samples, ask the chefs to prepare the dishes at the restaurant and prepare a demo at the market, showing people each step as they do them.

"We do 'Farm to Fork' events every two weeks where chefs buy fresh products from farmers and cook on the premises. Farmers experience their best sales ever on those days."
— Dana Plummer, Downtown Waterloo FM, IA

"Ann Yonkers, who manages our markets, is also a professional chef by trade. She makes sure that the recipes submitted by the chefs are usable by everyday people and not just for restaurants in mass quantities. They need to be recipes that everyone can use in their own home. The idea is to get people thinking seasonally and preparing food that is grown locally.."
— Bernadine Prince, Dir. of Public Education and the Freshfarm Markets, American Farmland Trust, Washington, D.C.

Contests

Contests stimulate excitement and interest and bring attention to the market. They can be useful for expanding community spirit, involving new individuals or organizations, creating memorable good times and providing photo opportunities for the media. Sponsor baking, gardening or music contests. When you hold a limbo contest or salsa-making contest within a Salsa Festival, you give the media the chance to focus on an average citizen within the market.

Create a contest around virtually any item in the market, challenging your growers to see who has the best corn, melons or peaches, especially if there are several vendors of that product with different varieties. Try a peach cobbler contest, a watermelon eating contest or a pumpkin seed-spitting contest. Provide small prizes for all entrants.

For your market anniversary offer a free trip, certificate or other prize for the best vendor display or friendliest vendor. Encourage vendors to decorate booths with flowers or ribbons. Take photographs. Consider having a theme. In Davis, California, vendors have competed in a dress-up contest, one year won by a garlic grower who wore a full headdress and necklace made of garlic.

Give pumpkin-carving classes with a free pumpkin and judge according to age categories. Involve local celebrities in teams where they compete in one-handed corn shucking, orange juggling, and "no-hands" grapefruit passes (neck-to-neck). Ask chefs to compete in a cook-off or a lunch-for-two. Hold an Easter Bonnet Contest among vendors with a celebrity judge.

"Salsa contest: We have both customers and farmers make homemade salsa, and we encourage customers to buy products at the market and go home and make salsa and bring it back next week so they can win farmers' market bucks (1st prize $15) that they can spend at the market. The farmers redeem these and get repaid from the market."
— Mary Lou Weiss, Mgr., Torrance FM, CA

In Virginia the Staunton/Augusta Farmers' Market sponsored an art contest to showcase the work of local artists, with the market as the subject. An anonymous donor funded the contest prize money with $350 for first prize. The artwork was displayed at a prominent downtown Staunton location and reproduced as a print that became a great market fundraiser.

Other Events

A Farmers' Market Breakfast or Brunch is another example of using food tastings to sell food. Instead of chefs or professionals, the growers themselves donate food and serve breakfast to market-goers. And hungry customers buy more.

Other ideas for special events include Ethnic Days, Farm Days for school children, or an April Flower Festival. The possibilities are endless!

Tie in with holidays, especially ethnic holidays. Host a Cinco de Mayo celebration for the Hispanic population. Later in the summer send a press release to the Latino paper with a chile ristra attached to announce a September 15 independence celebration.

Always have music at the market for ambiance. Invite local musicians to perform during market hours. Many will play if they can leave their hat or fiddle case open for contributions, others will simply volunteer for the exposure. Invite the growers to donate to a basket of produce for the musicians.

A big challenge is getting customers to the market in the winter. Your merchants' association can have a "Meet Me at the Market Week" in January and February.

Hold a Vendor Appreciation day with a free breakfast or lunch buffet or cater them with carts going down the aisles so farmers can eat food after they've set up for market. At the end of the season, have a potluck dinner where the market provides the main dish. The vendors really appreciate a chance to socialize outside the market atmosphere.

The Great Barrington Farmers' Market, MA, organizes a scarecrow-making booth for home gardeners. While vendors are selling seedlings, kids have a great time stuffing their old clothes with hay. This can easily be expanded into a contest or done later during fall harvest.

Go to bookstore or ask a local newspaper food columnist if there are any local cookbook authors. Invite them to the market for a day of sales and autographing.

Here's the formula for the spectacular Zucchini 500 at the Pike Place Market: Put up a 4x16-foot plywood ramp, two sheets end to end with a 1:5 slope (and a step at one end for small children) and one-quarter inch dowels running the ramp to create lanes. Give kids stickers, two pins or nails for axles and four wheels in a plastic bag for $1. Put out boxes of zucchini and invite a DJ to be the race announcer, dressed up in official costume. Kids have races and runoffs in the various age groups. "It's the 2-year olds!" and this gets a slew of photos on the front page!

Still more ideas for special events include:

✧ A Chilly Chili Contest. If it's regularly below freezing, use a tag line like, "It's really cold but it's really hot!"

This hot chili pepper eating contest at the Stowe Farmers' Market in Vermont found six hardy souls, initially. Only three were still sitting by the time they finished eating as many of four increasingly hot pepper varieties as possible. The winner: the man with the hat. When you're hot inside, don't be cool.

⬧ Scarecrow making. Have a balloon man for kids, a contest for the biggest tomato, and don't forget the home gardeners.

⬧ Soil testing day for gardeners. Advertise free or fee for Extension to test customer soils at the market. Invite the local flower/horticulture society to co-host.

⬧ Board of Supervisors invited to do a goat-milking contest.

⬧ Opening Market Day promoted as a Plant Day with giveaway of hundreds of plant plugs.

"We are having a multi-cultural entertainment series this summer to celebrate the diversity of the neighborhood in which the market is held."
— Belle Rita Novak, Mgr., FM at the X, Springfield, MA

"Herb Day. The Kansas Grown! Farmers' Market opens each spring on the first Saturday in May with Herb Day. Extension Master Gardeners plan the event including the Herb Society of South Central Kansas. Activities include herb and environmental gardening seminars, youth planting herb containers, demonstration garden seminars, Master Gardener plant sale, herb tasting and LOTS of herbs for sale. This gets excellent free publicity and the market is kicked off with a large crowd without paid advertising."
— Robert I. (Bob) Neier, Extension agent, Wichita, KS

"One thing we've been experimenting with more and more in promoting the market is having live music or other entertainment at the market. It's a little unclear how many of our customers really want this — some say they are there just for the food, while others seemed drawn by the entertainment as well. It does seem to attract a different clientele."
— Patty Brand, Exec. Dir., Friends of the St. Paul FM, MN

⬧ Offer hayrides around the market neighborhood. In Vancouver you can take an annual wagon ride to Washington's oldest apple tree.

⬧ Meet the Animals Day or Farm Day with animals for kids to see and touch, including sheep shearing and wool spinning. Focus promotion on children.

⬧ Apple Fest or Maple Fest. Bob for apples, apple/maple taste testing, samples, posters/banners, apple pressing with hand crank, maple syrup processing equipment.

⬧ Flower Day. Include dried flower wreathes and have bouquet demonstrations and classes for people to learn wreath-making for a small fee.

⬧ Harvest Festival. Have a huge salad sold by the dish, a large tent filled with corn stalks, corn, baskets, and a hay or corn maze.

⬧ Talk with Quilters Day. The quilters sell their items at no charge and make their own posters.

⬧ Corn Roast Day. Give roasted corn away, donated by the growers. People are fascinated by corn shucking, so do a contest.

⬧ Customer Appreciation Day. Give away cider, apple pie or shortcake. Ask farmers to give away some free items as random acts of kindness.

⬧ Market Mascot Day. Hold a naming contest. Invite a scarecrow-costumed person to the market to talk to the kids.

"We have a drawing every Saturday for a bushel basket of produce. Every grower contributes something to that basket and the growers and the customers really love it; all during the week they sign up."
— Connie Veselka, Mgr., Heart of Texas Farmers' Market, Waco, TX

Organizing Special Events

Any market may find that certain ideas work while others do not. If you think a musician or clown amounts to wasted money, let them perform as buskers, earning their pay from the public rather than the market. Try a different set of activities — roasting chilies or corn — until you find a mix that feels right to your customers. Keep trying new ideas. Marketing demands innovation.

Extra volume is critical so make sure your farmers are ready to back up the extra demand created by your special event publicity. If you make a quantum leap in sales you are creating a brand new market. How many people do you plan for? Get the growers behind it! You need to project a certain percentage increase in customers to buy their products.

Beaverton Farmers' Market:
How one market celebrated its birthday

In Beaverton, Oregon, in 1998, the goal for the farmers' market 10th anniversary celebration was to develop an event with various elements that would capture the imagination of customers, the local community and media.

The market hired a consultant, author Vance Corum, and the result was the "10th Birthday Berry Blow-out" which had as its theme "Recreating Community: Returning to Our Roots." Every element was designed to remind Beaverton residents of the history of agriculture and community activities. The Beaverton Modular Railroad Club set up a 10x26-foot rectangular track which drew several thousand onlookers, a reminder of the key role railroads have played in carrying products to market.

The March of Dimes was invited to provide volunteers who served berry shortcake to 1800 people for an old-fashioned dime donation to the March of Dimes. All items were donated including shortcake from Franz Bakery, whipped cream from a friendly supermarket and 38 flats of straw-

berries, blueberries, raspberries, blackberries, boysenberries, currants, marionberries and youngberries from (you guessed it) 10 farmers in the market. The March of Dimes was pleased to raise nearly $800.

Beaverton Bakery donated a sheet cake and a three-tier cake, both decorated with a railroad theme and marzipan fruits and vegetables which hundreds more customers enjoyed. The mayor cut the first piece for a front-page photo in the Capital Press.

Ten top area chefs took part in a "Chef Salute to the Market." Each was given a $20 bill to shop the market and then prepare a lunch for two. Five hundred people hovered around their circle of prep tables as they chopped and discussed their presentations in a non-competitive environment.

There were opportunities for fun as well as education. The Woodworkers' Store donated wheels and axles for the first 100 challengers to prepare their own Zucchini 500 racers. Heats were run down a 16-ft., five-lane,

wooden raceway. Fifteen nearby businesses gained visibility for donating prizes to winners.

The cherry pit-spitting contest drew another 150 participants, pitted against each other in seven age groups. Men, women and children took home prizes – from a bat house donated by a vendor to haircuts, music, shoe repair, travel certificates and dinners for two.

A budding, balloon-blowing clown, only 14, entertained hundreds of children in the celebration zone and collected donations as well.

The 10th birthday activities on the lawn next to the paved market space involved more than 5,000 marketgoers in one or more elements of the celebration, reinforcing the market's significant role in community-building. With three months of planning and 15 volunteers on the event day, the berry blow-out demonstrated market thanks to existing customers, while bringing in new customers and media attention to capture new ones in the future. ✿

Keep a seasonal focus with the festival. If you get away from food too much, it takes away from the farmer. Utilize things that will help sell the farmers' products like tasting or educational events — apple or cherry tastings, peach or asparagus recipe contests.

Tie special events into three-day weekends that draw a lot of tourists. Holidays often take customers elsewhere without bringing new visitors.

Organize a schedule of special events that will highlight the season and create special reasons for customers to come. Realize that each event builds its own history, so plan changes and growth in future years of each event.

Generally, many markets host events on good market days but there is nothing wrong with using an event to improve a market day late in the month. Check the effect from year to year at different times to evaluate the cost-benefit ratio.

A public bulletin board allows you to publicize special market events to customers and post your brochure and information from other community organizations.

Labor can be intense with any special event. Without a paid manager let different people play the role of coordinator for each different event to avoid burnout. Make sure you plan, pay attention to the details, and have the manpower to do it right, or don't do it! Have a Schedule of Events for the whole season with an event every week. Set up an event committee even to plan small events like a cookbook signing.

A back-up plan is a good idea in case your featured event doesn't fly. When a heavy rain hits, a great event can turn into a failure. What happens with hundreds of expectant kids when your event has to go indoors with limited space?

EDUCATIONAL EVENTS

Most markets view themselves as an educational site as well as a place for produce sales. Education comes in many forms: a market information booth, literature with recipes, nutritional information, posters from product commissions, and educational pamphlets from your state agricultural department, Cooperative Extension, and health and illness prevention organizations. You can invite groups to participate in market events or have an educational booth, such as master gardeners and food preservers, a nutritionist or a nurseryman.

Non-profit organizations like the American Heart Association may have a dietitian who can give people recipes and tips on how have to a "healthy heart" diet. Other organizations such as the American Cancer Society and 5-A-Day Program are good partners with materials to encourage intake of fruits and vegetables. Other ideas:

◇ Hospitals and county health departments can host mini-health fairs with glaucoma screening, cholesterol or blood pressure testing at the markets.

◇ Fire departments often do safety and fire prevention awareness education workshops at the markets, bringing Sparky the Fire Dog and letting kids climb on the fire trucks.

◇ Create a photo and information exhibit showing farm locations on a map with lists of crops produced by each farm.

◇ Print seasonal availability charts listing of vegetables and fruits at your market. Many customers post these at home to remind them of what is in season throughout the year.

Educators can influence in every way conceivable — kids raising gardens and becoming market sellers, a math class taught using local vs. global economics, a science class focusing on a market plant physiology, a nutrition class comparing local vs. distant products or fresh vs. frozen nutritional values. Invite local 4-H groups to educate customers about agricultural projects they've done.

"There are many educational programs you can do with the Master Food Preservers, including gauge checks for customers' pressure cookers."

"I have 200-300 school groups per year at the market, ranging from preschool to college. Teachers take the field trip for a variety of reasons: to get out of the classroom, history, math, exposure to fruits and vegetables, exposure outside their students' limited neighborhood, photography, drawing, architecture, marketing, entrepreneurship, etc. I do a 20-minute talk about the history of the market going back 200 years: how we ate with no supermarkets, prepared foods, nothing growing in winter, and a limited supply of what could actually grow in the region. I talk about transportation, refrigeration and how it changed the way we eat, ethnic foods, immigrants and refugees shopping at the market, and cultural differences."

— Sandra Zak, Soulard Market, St. Louis, MO

CHILDREN'S EVENTS

Kids' events are easy to plan and promote. Kids are your future, the ones who keep the market going! Have pony rides for kids. Sponsor special market tours for children. Wait until October so families have a chance to settle into the new school schedule. Offer yourself as a classroom speaker with a slide show or provide teaching materials to show how produce is grown. When kids get excited, they will bring their parents to the market.

Set aside a booth for kids who are farming alone or with their parents, or creating a craft. Or have a Kid's Day at the market, with kids selling in a special kid's section with spaces for kids. An annual kids' market in Vancouver, WA, adds immediacy and excitement for young shoppers to buy from other kids. They make a connection between work and income. This is also a good way to get kids into farming.

"We asked schools to give artwork done by children to display at the market. One school grew vegetables and we donated a booth for them to sell produce."

"We have a 'Dad's Day Olympics.' The father and son or daughter climb over bales, carry water together or have a watermelon seed spitting contest."

"The most successful event is the children's market, where kids sell produce or crafts that they've raised or made."

— *Do's and Don'ts of a Successful Farmers' Market*

"Flyers can be distributed through the schools if they are approved. If the kids can participate and the event is judged beneficial, the schools may even put them in the teachers' boxes."

— Rose Munoz, Former Mgr., Torrance FM, CA

SPECIAL PROMOTIONS

Promote to chefs. To increase large-order sales to restaurant chefs, mail a packet to all restaurants in the area. Include an invitation to shop at the market plus an "in-season items" flyer, and a "meet the farmers" flyer. Farmers sometimes combine trips, e.g., delivering to restaurants after the farmers' market. Elsewhere chefs call growers in advance to bring extra boxes and get paid that day. The chef can pick up from four or five growers, saving delivery costs. They're making several pickups simultaneously as they might at a wholesale produce terminal but without the middleman. Some markets allow chefs to purchase larger volumes one hour in advance of the public.

School kids' coupons. Started by an American Association of University Women chapter, the Fullerton, CA, market brings school classes through the market and gives a $1 coupon to every child, $1,000-$1,500 worth of coupons per year. Coupons are split in quarter pieces and farmers give at reduced prices, i.e., one farmer gives a couple of oranges for 25 cents, another some flowers, etc. They get the produce in the kids' hands, the children go home and parents show up the next week.

Postcards. Have customer sign a pre-paid postcard that you mail to them as a reminder of next season's opening. When trying to attract new shoppers, a flyer with real savings may make a difference.

Co-promotions. Attend a merchant meeting to present your ideas on how businesses can take advantage of the market's proximity. Be ready with specific examples of cross-promotional ideas. Encourage them to share possible strategies. Can a western wear shop put a live model in their window or have them do mime on the sidewalk? Will a shop give a discount during market hours to lure the farmers' market shopper into their store? If a local bakery doesn't want to sell in the market, will they provide discount cards for farmers to hand out to customers?

Try a cross-promotion with businesses in town. Connect each business with a grower. Have a strawberry grower pass out $1 off coupons for a shoe shine at the shoe repair shop and have the shop pass out 50¢-off coupons for strawberries from that particular grower.

"Market dollars. This is a cross-promotion with neighboring businesses where downtown restaurants give out market dollars to customers, good for a discount at the market and possibly vice-versa."
— Esther Kovari, Pres., New Mexico Farmers' Marketing Assoc.

Drawings and raffles. Fill a weekly or monthly food basket to raffle off. Give gift certificates to be spent in the market. Raffle tickets can be used to collect names and addresses of market customers. Work to build your database for future mailings.

"An hour before closing, we have a raffle. When people win they go to the farmer's booth to pick it up and that way they get to meet the farmer. Almost every farmer donates something, so there can be many winners — both the farmers and customers like it! I give a 5-minute talk before handing out the tickets, about new items, new farmers, who's out sick, etc. After the raffle is over — at 12:30 — all the vendors in the market have a sale, and the market closes at 1:00. Some customers come throughout the day and some come for the raffle and the sale only. It's not the mass shoppers that come for the raffle, but the bargain hunters, so you get them all that way. The raffles are a success at each of our four markets. Be sure to do the raffle near closing, because after the raffle the market is dead. Lots of work to do it but the farmers love it!"
— Nancy Caster, Mgr., Irvine Center FM, CA

"In New Bedford, market organizer Barbara Purdy has created a weekly market contest. Every time a shopper buys something, he or she is given a ticket to drop in a glass jar. At the end of the market, the number is picked and announced. The following

Food, Glorious Food

Food, Glorious Food is one way the St. Mary's Farmers' Market in Ontario, Canada, found to keep their market in people's minds outside the market season, as well as do some fundraising for the market. Food, Glorious Food consists of a series of six, two-hour food sessions given each spring, for which participants pay $10 an evening, or $50 for all six evenings.

One year Food, Glorious Food presenters included a local restaurant chef, a caterer and market vendors. People taking the classes taste different foods, take home recipes, see how food is prepared, and get information on how to use different foods, plus information on how the foods are grown or produced. (If you are interested in doing a similar series and would like more details, call Ann Slater at 519-349-2448.) ✿

week, the winner gets a beautiful basket of fresh market produce. Put out a sign at your market office booth announcing, 'Last week's fresh market basket winner was…'"
— *To Market! To Market!* Univ. of Mass. Coop. Exten. System

Coupon sheet. Participating vendors list a sale coupon and the market prints them all on a sheet and gives one to each customer. The Norwalk, California market solicited its farmers and printed a flier with coupons featuring 10-25% off at each farmer stall. Have the Boy Scouts distribute these coupon sheets once a month.

Promote holidays. Every retailer recognizes their importance. Since markets often represent the greatest ethnic diversity in a community, special holidays are an opportunity to celebrate diversity while educating and having fun at the same time.

Coordinate and plan with your farmers to prepare for each holiday. A holiday committee with vendors, community volunteers and staff can list every holiday, assign a budget figure to each and plan the marketing approach. Think of what is most appropriate for each holiday as far as music, market decorations, suggestions for farmers, gift pack ideas and even market gift baskets which include a mix of vendors' products. Your advertising should reflect your ability to celebrate every holiday in a collective way that others cannot replicate.

✧ Chinese New Year, late January - early February. Giant chrysanthemums may become the "must have" gift. Get growers to hang Chinese designs celebrating Year of the Snake in 2001, followed by Horse, Sheep, Monkey, Rooster, Dog, Pig, Rat, Ox, Tiger, Rabbit and Dragon in 2012. The 12-year cycle then repeats.

✧ Groundhog Day, February 2. Have a groundhog jump out of a farmer's pick-up and look for his shadow. Host a groundhog calling contest with prizes.

✧ Valentine's Day, February 14, is the perfect time for heart-shaped price signs and extra special gift packs. Apple growers can prepare by putting heart-shaped stickers on their apples just before they color on the tree. Think of how kids can buy small gifts to participate.

✧ St. Patrick's Day, March 17. This is the time for green everything, shamrock signs, and a best dressed farmer and customer contest.

✧ 1st day of spring/summer/fall/winter. Celebrate the changes with color, decorations and music. This is a wonderful time to experience transition by "tasting" seasonal products from new farms.

✧ April Fool's Day is a time for wild clothing and playful banter with customers. Make sure you have a jokester prancing around the market.

✧ National Day of Prayer, May. Invite various faith representatives to have a table and host an interfaith service to show thanks for the foods of our faith.

✧ Cinco de Mayo, the 5th of May. Promote cultural awareness with a dance troupe even if you lack a strong Hispanic clientele, much as the Mexican Independence Day in September.

✧ Mother's Day, May. Ask your farmers to help fathers and kids to find appropriate gifts for mom. Is this the time to host a special Mother's Day lunch or to kick off your market season?

✧ Memorial Day. Since everyone is barbecuing and headed on picnics, change grower signs from "sweet corn" to "barbecue corn." With barbecue on their minds, sell "barbecue garlic" as well.

✧ International Children's Day, June, is a time for celebrating diversity, acceptance and schools closing. Ask kids to dress in the native garb of their ancestors. Here's your last chance to get teachers involved this year and prepare for National Children's Day in October.

✧ Father's Day, June. Time for moms and kids to find those special "palate-pleasers" for dad.

✧ 4th of July. Organize a "picnic market" where customers can get everything they need for their picnic, from corn to watermelons. Invite unusual food purveyors just for the day to complement all your regular picnic products.

✧ Grandparent's Day, September. Coordinate a cross-promotion with local businesses to give a small gift to every grandparent coming to the market, including produce and gift certificates.

✧ United Nations Day, October. Invite global groups to participate in educating about various international concerns. Celebrate your international customers or a connection to National Children's Day.

✧ Halloween is the second largest holiday for retail sales. Vendors can dress up displays and sell healthy alternative giveaways.

✧ Christmas. As our largest holiday it causes even seasonal markets to re-open for a few weeks in December, especially if you have a crafts section to your market.

✧ Be aware of any special holidays of any ethnic or religious cultures that your market serves, and celebrate those at the market! Kwanzaa, for example, is an Afro-American holiday that falls on December 26.

Thanksgiving. "It's usually a soft market the weekend after Thanksgiving, because everyone has leftovers and refrigerators are full. But the tomato guys clean up, because everyone is making sandwiches and they like big slicing tomatoes. Learn to look for these little niches around holidays."

— Mark Sheridan, Santa Barbara FM Assoc., CA

PROMOTION EVALUATION

Consider ways of measuring the effectiveness of your promotions, just like your ad budget. With either you are spending valuable time or money. Shortly after each promotion and at the end of the year, evaluate your campaign. Keep a promotion book in a three-ring binder. For each event describe the promotion, budget and consumer feedback. Include copies of any paid advertising or free publicity. Then ask:

- ◇ Did we reach our target audience?
- ◇ Did we achieve our goals?
- ◇ Could we have prepared better for the unforeseen?
- ◇ Did we stay within the budget?
- ◇ How can we improve future promotional campaigns?

Promotion Evaluation Form

"After every promotional effort, use an evaluation form to ensure that every effort contributes to future promotional efforts. Have sections for planning, promotion, description of activity, time involved in planning, costs, implementation, ease of organization, factors which influenced success, unforeseen problems, time to set up and take down, vendor response, consumer response, approximate number that responded, and additional comments."

— *To Market! To Market!* Univ. of Mass. Coop. Exten. System

Coupons serve as an effective, low-cost way to test advertisements or promotions. Put a coupon on everything you print — a newspaper ad, a flier, even a brochure. Put in a 50¢-off, clip out offer on strawberries, for example. Code each coupon so you will know where it came from — this allows you to test the effectiveness of that medium. As each coupon is returned, reimburse the vendors at market value or have them share the cost. Don't count on getting a

That's Marketing!

1. If your farmers' market is coming to town and you paint a sign saying "Farmers' Market Coming to Town," that's advertising.

2. If you put the sign on the back of an elephant and walk him into town, that's promotion.

3. If the elephant walks through the mayor's flower bed, that's publicity.

4. If you can get the mayor to laugh about it, that's public relations.

5. And if you planned the elephant's walk, that's marketing!

lot of coupons (unless you're giving away big sums of money) but use the response level to compare results from different media so you can improve future ads and promotions.

Tracking promotion results may take the form of talking to customers, asking customers to fill out a short questionnaire, or sending customers a return-mail postcard. [See Appendix]

Keep and compare sales results and promotional expenses on a monthly and yearly basis — mapping seasonal and yearly trends helps you figure the impact of your promotional programs.

"Every farmers' market is unique. Each market organizer must assess the promotional ideas mentioned, and judge the best ones to be implemented. In the final analysis, only experience will answer the question, 'Which methods are best for my market?'"

— *To Market! To Market!* Univ. of Mass. Coop. Exten. System

FOOD COUPONS & FOOD STAMPS

WIC Farmers' Market Nutrition Program

USDA's Women, Infants, and Children (WIC) Farmers' Market Nutrition Program (FMNP) was established to provide fresh, nutritious, unprepared foods, such as fruits and vegetables, at farmers' markets to women, infants, and children who are nutritionally at risk and to expand the awareness and use of farmers' markets by consumers. The program requires a 30% match of benefits and administrative costs. In Fiscal Year 1999 the program was made available by 39 jurisdictions including 33 states, the District of Columbia, four Indian tribal organizations and one territory, Guam. Ten of those jurisdictions supplied their own additional funds to cover non-WIC clients, primarily the elderly and some serving older children and disabled adults.

FMNP coupons issued to eligible recipients can be used to buy from authorized farmers. The coupons are submitted to the state agency for reimbursement. During FY 99, there were 11,457 farmers and 1,560 farmers' markets authorized to accept FMNP coupons. Total federal funds just shy of $15 million were matched by $6.9 million of cash or in-kind, non-federal resources. Funds were distributed to 1,532,799 WIC coupon recipients and an additional 42,129 non-WIC recipients. Federal law established $10-20 as the range of coupons per person per year, but Iowa was highest at $28 among several states providing an overmatch to serve non-WIC individuals or to increase the benefit level.

For the 2001 season a separate $10 million senior FMNP program was established by USDA administrative action. The Commodity Credit Corporation felt this one-year program was appropriate under their guidelines for increasing the consumption of commodity crops. The jurisdictions receiving monies need only pay administrative costs.

This will add considerable impact to many markets. The average market in the FMNP coupon program felt $9600 of additional buying power aside from cash spent by those same customers. Some markets experienced a near doubling of sales for farmers and greater sustainability for the market. WIC-approved vendors are well identified to avoid confusion or embarrassment for anyone.

How does a farmer or market become authorized to accept FMNP coupons? According to the WIC Farmers' Market Nutrition Program section at the USDA website, "Each state agency is responsible for authorizing farmers and/or markets to accept FMNP coupons. Persons who exclusively sell produce grown by someone else, such as wholesale distributors, cannot be authorized to participate in the FMNP." The FMNP contact person for each State can be found at:

http://www.fns.usda.gov/wic/menu/contacts/farm/farm.HTM

You may also contact the USDA Food and Nutrition Service public information staff at 703-305-2286, or by mail at 3101 Park Center Drive, Room 819, Alexandria, VA 22302.

"The WIC program is one of the most cost-effective, win-win programs I've seen."
— Mariah Cornwoman, Wenatchee FM, WA

"The Farmers' Market Nutrition Program…was mentioned by 42% of managers in our survey as an important connection with low-income consumers. Studies have shown that WIC participants spend more than their WIC vouchers at the markets and are return shoppers."
— Farmers' Markets and Rural Development Project

One study showed that 40% of WIC recipients tried a new food item that season, largely because of recipes showing how to use new foods.

Food Stamps

Distinct from food coupons, the food stamp program helps nutritionally at risk families make wise food choices and supports family farms. The use of food stamps at farmers' markets nationwide is huge — estimates range from $75 million to $100 million annually.

"$19 billion a year is spent in food stamps in the U.S., yet most of it is spent in local 7/11s and food marts in gas stations, most of it on non-staple, non-nutritious food. Low-income people pay 10-30% more for their food than middle class Americans because supermarkets have fled the urban areas and so low-income people often do not have easy access to produce any longer. The small shops do not stock produce any longer. Low-income people not only have need of local produce outlets but can provide a strong base for farmers' markets."
— Kate Fitzgerald, Sustainable Food Center, Austin, TX

The application process for farmers' markets to accept food stamps is quite simple. To find out information and obtain an application for your market, contact your local USDA Food and Nutrition Service office. Your market has to reach out to the community to make low-income customers feel comfortable in farmers' markets. USDA has available signs, "We accept food stamps," so farmers can welcome customers to their displays.

Integrating the food stamp program can help your market become a mainstream, permanent, food provider instead of a niche food provider. While it does take time to process the food stamps collected by your farmers, the increase in sales from an expanded customer base and the sense of serving your entire community make the effort worthwhile if not downright necessary for your market's survival. One southern Oregon market redeemed $1,248 in food stamps its first year and tripled that the second year, income important to farmers and the market.

Manager Debra Osborne asserts, "The paperwork to receive eligibility is minimal, but you need to know your market's income. So if you charge per-day fees not based on sales, do an anonymous survey of the vendors at the market to obtain an estimate of the market's income." Totaling an estimate from all your vendors of their gross farmers' market income is sufficient for the annual application.

Post signs at the local food stamp office and at individual farmer booths to let recipients know that you accept food stamps. Educate vendors on how to handle them. Since growers redeem their food stamps at the end of the day, it's just like accepting cash.

"Be aware that eligible foods at farmers' markets also include seeds and plants. Food-producing plants that grow vegetables for your family's consumption are OK too. So seedlings can also be sold under the program," Osborne concludes.

"Work with your county social services department. Put together information packets that social services can hand out to all WIC and food stamp recipients. Include information about your market, what is in season, and general information about produce — how to choose, store, and cook it. Put on cooking demonstrations and classes that are free of charge to the WIC and food stamp recipients and include that in your information packet. You'll be providing a valuable service to the people that will benefit the greatest by shopping at your farmers' market."
— *Farmers' Market Forum,* FM Fed. of NY

FUNDRAISERS

There are many ways to build your budget or cover your operating costs other than space fees. Time and creativity are the major limitations. Your sponsoring group also may address a philosophical question of how much visibility to give other businesses or organizations. The issue appears with fundraisers or any promotional activity where another entity may contribute money or in-kind assistance to your market effort.

If a major beverage company is willing to print 2x3-foot signs in color but the bottom half of the sign with their logo overwhelms yours on top, you may have second thoughts about your market appearing to be owned by a large, private firm. However, they might put a tag on their television commercials or do other printing for you that meets your aesthetic standard.

So think about all the fundraising ideas possible in your community. What are the resources? Who would like to help? Ask farmers and customers for their ideas and a pulse on what is most feasible. List them and then start with several that seem to use your time and energy well, within your financial ability. Set clear goals and know how much you will spend to make your goals.

A *market cookbook* or other publication can be sold as a fundraiser.

A *market calendar* can be a fundraiser for your market and a reminder of market days. Other community groups may pay to have their activities or events listed. Find an artist through an art society and have them paint, draw or photograph market scenes or farmers' fields. The Davis Farmers' Market, CA, once did a calendar with 12 pencil-drawn scenes.

An *art fair* is a perfect way to involve a larger number of community artists who contribute a portion of all their sales, whether the theme is the market or otherwise. They might contribute to a market calendar or a raffle in conjunction with a dinner.

Brick sponsors. Seattle's Pike Place Market was able to re-surface the market while raising money. Customers or supporters were invited to have their names inscribed in a brick for $35 or a foursome for $140. Pike Place raised $1.2 million and the floor cost them $400,000.

Promotional items. Just about any promotional item can help you raise funds, whether a T-shirt, sweatshirt, apron, mug, hat, pin or jacket. There is a wide range of quality, styles, and prices among many national and local companies that handle this business, so do comparison shopping. Be prepared to spend money to make money.

Silk-screened *T-shirts* are relatively inexpensive at $5-8 each, plus a one-time set-up charge of about $25, depending on the shirt color, quality, the number of imprint colors and the quantity and sizes printed. Even a small market can probably afford a minimum run of 36 shirts, one-color, for about $200. If you have a popular logo and thousands of customers, you can probably do a gross (144) in four-color, instead, for a comparable price per piece. Continue investing once you see that your initial purchase is well received. Like farmers, you have to have substantial volume to sell; sales slow when you run low.

When you are more confident of your customer desires, you might invest in stitched items. You will pay $150-300 for an initial computerization of your image, depending on the color complexity and number of stitches, plus about $8-12 depending on shirt quality and stitch count. On a hat the maximum surface area is about 2x4 inches and you might use the same image on a jacket or denim shirt, as did the Santa Monica Farmers' Market for its managing staff. Stitched hats for sale at $12-18 can be hip for a youthful, fashion-oriented marketplace whether Santa Monica, CA, or Yakima, WA. If your customers are very price conscious, you may choose to silkscreen a $3 hat so everyone can join the fun for about $5. After all, it is a fundraiser, but like most fundraisers, be conscious that you are also gaining publicity through making someone a walking advertisement for your market.

"The Warwick Valley Farmers' Market promotes itself through selling promotional items and by offering premiums for joining a 'Friends of the Market' membership, ala Public Broadcasting TV memberships. Their biggest undertaking has been developing a Warwick Valley Farmers' Market cookbook. This was financed by selling advanced copies and done by professionals that volunteered a great deal of their services."
— *Farmers' Market Forum*, FM Fed. of NY

"At the beginning of each summer, The Marketplace at Buffalo gives its members sweatshirts with the logo for their farmers to wear. The market pays for the sweatshirts by printing the names of the market sponsors — one a media sponsor, the other a cash sponsor. The market also requires all vendors to wear special aprons that are designed to hold cash. The aprons create a consistent image for the market and also speed up the handling of cash."
— *To Market! To Market!* Univ. of Mass. Coop. Exten. System

"We issue 'market money' with wooden nickels, dated with expiration date at the end of the year, with a different color each year. We purchased

'10,000 at the beginning of the season, and sold them to customers, 10 for $1. We redeemed 500 the first year. They've become collectible items. Word-of-mouth kicks in, people see them and ask where they got them. We made over $400 in cash the first year. We also use the wooden nickels for our Produce Race in the fall — the nickels become the 'wheels' for the produce."
— Rick Castellano, Former Mgr., Olympia FM, WA

Shopping bags come in paper, canvas, plastic or string. They serve as a reminder to come again, and are an effective advertising tool for any market. Place a group-order for vendors' plastic bag orders, and print market information on the bags.

"One year we sold over $3,000 worth of 'Eco bags' and made $1,600. To fill up a bag with produce for display costs us $2.34 and we sell it for $5."
— Joanne Neft, Former Mgr., Foothill FM Assoc., Auburn, CA

Library bookmarks are a wonderful way to cross-pollinate ideas. Librarians in Great Barrington, MA, were happy to promote the farmers' market with every book that was lent out, using a bookmark that gave the library locations and hours along with the market logo and hours.

Dinner. With all the great produce and other foods available at your market, you probably can organize a successful dinner with less effort than a caterer, but it wouldn't be a bad idea to have the help of one. Consider other fundraising ideas once you have all those people there. Perhaps it's time for that art fair or local businesses may contribute items to be raffled to the highest bidder and your farmers can contribute as well. What about a weekend in a swanky hotel, a cruise on the paddle wheeler, a companion airfare anywhere in the U.S., dinner for four, a year of free movies or a bed-and-breakfast stay? Businesses want to help, especially if it doesn't cost them much.

The Reading Terminal Market makes a huge amount from its annual ball when Philadelphia's finest roam through the marketplace which includes farmer day tables. It is quite a high-brow affair, but not all dinners are so.

"Last year the Greenmarkets held a dinner dance called the Vegetable Heirloom Ball, for which some 150 folks forked out 300 bucks a pop. Held at the Judson Grill, an upscale, three-star restaurant in New York, the gala evening featured heirloom vegetables on display and as a part of the dinner, a barnyard auction and a bluegrass band. At the auction, the crowd bid on items like overnight stays at the Plaza Hotel. It was a high-end affair, but we asked people to dress down in country chic. The ball was a great fund-raiser, and it also brought awareness to the people about such issues as open-pollinated varieties."
— Tony Manetta, Dir., Greenmarket, New York, NY

"The key to fund-raising is to hold special events and turn them into fund-raisers at the same time. A special event, through media attention, draws more people to the market. Have an annual Harvest Faire, invite artists and craftsmen to rent booths, and charge customers twelve dollars each for a country brunch, inviting celebrity chefs. Silent auctions also can be combined with special events and are one of the most effective fundraisers. You can collect contributions from the community as well as vendors. Another fundraiser is having a bakery at the market, in which different bakery goods are sold each day. Breads, rolls, pastries and bagels are purchased wholesale from local bakeries."
— Lynn Bagley, Golden Gate FM Assoc., Novato, CA

"We had a shoestring budget at start-up and we developed a coupon program that we took to local merchants. They paid us $10 and we printed coupons offering 10% off or 20% off redeemable at their store. The customers could only get these coupons at the market, and they could only use them on that market day. Most of the stores were within five blocks of the market. We had an article in the newspaper and flyers in the merchants' windows and advertised the coupon program. It was immensely helpful in increasing the traffic flow at the market and also gave us a small amount of funding."
— Grace Richards, Arlington FM, WA

COMMUNITY INVOLVEMENT

Your market should be intimately associated with the community in everyone's mind. Whenever people think of "community," "community spirit" or "community involvement," you want people to think "farmers' market," not the "Portland Trailblazers" (or whatever your local sports team!)

As author and motivational speaker Wayne Dyer says, "What you really, really, really, really want, you'll get." The four "reallys" stand for what you wish, desire, intend and are passionate about. If you "really" want to make your market the center of community, you will do many things. You will be ready for opportunities to open. You will be ready to speak before various groups without worry because your inspired focus moves you!

> "You have to plant the seeds and enrich the soil to build, through marketing, a community feeling."
> — Kirk Lumpkin, Mgr., Berkeley FM, CA

Becoming the Community Center

Your goal should be to make the market the focus of many community activities. Think of every possible subgroup of the local populace and determine how they can become involved. Create a win-win situation with them.

Speak at the Lions Club, the Rotary, the Optimists and every other club or organization willing to have a presentation. Invite them to do a fundraiser at your market. You want to be the center of fundraising in your community.

Tie in with local businesses. San Luis Obispo Market, CA, for instance, sponsors a "Meet with the Chamber of Commerce" at their Thursday Night market. Downtown businesses are often eager to have a farmers' market, especially as suburban malls are killing the downtown business. If you have a downtown market in a business district, encourage businesses to come out onto the street with a cart so they can join in the market spirit. The cart, in effect, says,

Some markets invite select restaurants to participate once a month to add a "special event" touch to the market. Here, the Napa Chefs Market involves a caterer weekly.

"We are part of the market" and it encourages people to come into the shop. Some shop owners have painted little footsteps going from the cart into their stores!

Alternately, you might host a "Business Day" at the market. Send out letters inviting local business people to the market. Extend the personal touch: walk them around the market; offer free coffee and doughnuts; give them nametags; and show them how one enterprise supports the other.

Banks are required to do a certain amount of community service by law. Encourage them to promote your market and themselves through sponsorship of your musicians, the food bank collection or the market chef program.

Work with HMOs (health maintenance organizations): talk to their clinic manager, feed them market news for their monthly newsletters, and give them handouts to place in their clinics. You can also:

- ✧ Install a community bulletin board at the market.
- ✧ Find out what's happening in the ag community and tie into local ag events.
- ✧ Inform leaders in the faith community about your market.
- ✧ Put up a display at your local library.
- ✧ Invite local cooking schools to purchase and perform student demonstrations.

- ✧ Approach elementary schools about market tours.
- ✧ Talk to the local cafeteria directors about featuring fresh, local crops on the school menu.
- ✧ Get a soapbox, and invite political candidates to speak!

"The SLO uses the markets as a place to elect the city council every year. They all give three-minute speeches at the market."
— Peter Jankay, Exec. Dir., San Luis Obispo County FM Assoc., CA

"Bring brochures about the markets to Assisted Living Facilities, which have small kitchen facilities. We've gone to senior centers and let the managers know that if they bring seniors in to the market, we will provide parking places for them as well as provide assistants and give senior discounts."
— Karen Durham, Mgr., Bellingham FM, WA

"Get the community behind you at the earliest date in developing or reorganizing a market — civic associations, environmental groups, churches, senior citizens organizations, etc. These groups have newsletters and hold meetings and can do wonders in helping with potential customer surveys, free PR, etc."
— Tony Evans, Maryland Dept. of Agriculture

Networking

Become an active participant in civic organizations like the Rotary Club or Chamber of Commerce. Your true goal should be to participate and contribute toward the common good and highest goals of those organizations.

Good managers are involved with their communities. It is not a one-way street. They keep reaching out to see what the community has to offer and what they can offer back. They often offer to help rather than wait to be asked. They consider how the news in the paper affects the market and work to build connections with those in the news and those who will be, because they have a good community cause.

"At a local Chamber of Commerce dinner, I sat next to the head of the City of Seattle's City Engineering Department and he ended up putting up banners for me, instead of us having to rent a cherry picker."
— Chris Curtis, Mgr., University District FM, Seattle, WA

"As a board member of the American Institute of Wine and Food (AIWF), I met a food writer and that's how our market (Marin County FM) got in the New York Times."
— Lynn Bagley, Golden Gate FM Assoc., Novato, CA

Co-Promotions

While we have touched previously on co-promotions with business, be on the lookout for potential partnerships with them or service groups. Align the market with merchant associations or service organizations that already have marketing networks in place, especially those that promote healthy eating. If you can, solicit drawing or contest prizes, or any other involvement, by speaking to a downtown business meeting. Then follow up by approaching individual businesses, many of whom don't attend meetings.

Connect with groups like the American Cancer Society or the March of Dimes who have staff and volunteers to help set up. People from such civic groups as parks and recreation or 4H or the YMCA may also help you with events. Ask the FFA to do a petting zoo.

The Beaverton, OR, market involved a fire station in its 1998 festival called "Salsa: Some Like It Hot." Several firefighters trained a water hose on the contestants in the hot chili eating contest, casting the firefighters in a fun, friendly light.

Be ready to donate. When other organizations are having a fundraiser, a delicious basket of fresh market produce can be a welcome prize. If the perishability of donating produce is a problem, create market dollars which can be exchanged at the market. This will expose the market to another organization's audience and bring more people to market.

Your promotion of another entity need not have a financial aspect. You both may simply want to provide a service and improve the public perception of your organizations. This happens when a health screening organization provides blood pressure tests or a transit organization provides rides such as the Grants Pass, OR, downtown trolley shuttling people throughout the downtown.

"In cooperation with local transit, offer a free ride to and from the farmers' market on market days. Anyone wishing to take advantage of the offer may pick up tickets from the transit company or from the market office. These free transit tickets are valid on market days only."
— Kitchener FM, Ontario, Canada

"My wife Robin proposed a business sponsorship program to our local chamber of commerce. For $150, a business could become a sponsor of the month for the Chelsea Farmer's Market. In return, the business would be mentioned in all advertising for the month they sponsored and receive a complimentary stall space during their sponsored month. They could use this stall space to promote their business. Within one week, Robin had sponsors for each of the six months that our market is open. The sponsorship program has allowed the market to advertise more frequently plus helped develop relationships with other area businesses."
— Scott E. Staelgraeve, Chelsea, MI

Art & Music

Build ties with the artistic community. A glass shop might like to sponsor an opportunity for kids to set colored glass pieces into colored cement bricks that make perfect door stops or garden gifts. A tile shop may build a welcome wall at your market site, having kids reflect with their tiles on the theme of peace as was done at Jack London Square in Oakland. Ask a photo studio or a local artists' group to co-host an art exhibit called "Food for the Eyes." You provide the food and they arrange, decorate, carve, photograph and paint food scenes.

Allied Arts in Yakima was selected in 2000 as Washington's winner of the Millenium Arts Project Award. Their project, led by a Massachusetts artist, has transformed a portion of a downtown parking lot into a new plaza celebrating water as the basis of life. Customers at the farmers' market on Third Street now can park and sit in a beautiful space, watching other market-goers shop in front of the Capitol Theatre. Under its canopy musicians play each Sunday. Thus, the food and art community blend together in wonderful complement.

"We partner with the Metro Arts Alliance event, Jazz in July, that uses the farmers' market site for several Saturday performances by Iowa jazz groups."
— Deb Burger, Mgr., Downtown Des Moines FM, IA

An enthusiastic busking musician performs in front of a sticky bun cart at the Davis FM. Irregular, surprise musicians are an important part of the dynamic chaos that all markets should strive toward.

There may be a blues or jazz club that promotes musicians in your area. If your market is on a weekday when musicians' fees are generally lower, their response may be better. Make it worthwhile; encourage buskers and pay them if you can. Talk to local clubs where out-of-town musicians may be playing on a weekend; they may want another gig in the morning before leaving for home.

Sponsorship

Corporations and local businesses look for opportunities to sponsor events. Hopefully, your market is a perfect site. Corporate sponsors are an excellent source of publicity and promotion for larger market festivals with substantial crowds. Look for funding of segments of the festival as well as goods in trade, i.e., advertising for festival exposure.

Co-sponsors inevitably have a different set of goals from the market; what you are seeking is overlapping interests that give them the chance to claim your market as their own. The more community segments you have owning the market in a certain sense, the more it truly reflects your community's uniqueness.

You might start with smaller events where you build experience and credibility in the eyes of the business community. For $300 a day, one corporation donates shuttle service with their sign on a trolley. A legal firm has a private lunch area for their employees for the day. A bank sponsors a major band for $1200 while a CPA firm puts their name on the music sponsor banner for $350 the following week.

The Portland Farmers' Market, OR, has successfully expanded its annual "Summer Loaf: A Celebration of Bread" in mid-July with Fisher Mills as the main sponsor. In 2000 the Northwest's top bakeries gave the city a celebration in the South Park blocks very different from the normal jazz and brew festivals along the waterfront. A bread baking competition and classes plus media attention doubled the normal crowd to 10,000 and gave bakeries a novel form of recognition.

Manager Dianne Stefani-Ruff says, "Events have two goals — to bring new vendors and bring new customers. A normal event takes 40-60 extra hours of work, but for Summer Loaf there is an extra 400 hours of my time, 200 hours of an assistant, plus a paid director and committee meetings for a full year." The event has its own $30,000 budget, roughly half from corporate sponsors, revenue from classes at $50 per person, and income from 17 bakeries at $250 each. Fisher Mills, which owns Fisher Broadcasting, Channel 2, provides free PSAs on television. The event, started as a celebration of Portland's wonderful baking community, has taken on national significance with well-known instructors flying in to conduct the baking classes.

With Provista, a specialty foods company, the Portland market sponsors its "Tomatofest" and "The Great Pumpkin Event." The company has a market booth at both major events. Typhoon, an Asian restaurant, also sponsors the pumpkin event, distributing free pumpkins and hot cider and showing off their exquisite pumpkin carving skills. A major local berry grower, Columbia Empire Farms, sponsors the berry festival and gives away thousands of free berry shortcakes in return for promotional prominence.

"We've built a community where there was none — on a college campus," says Stefani-Ruff. "We're a destination market. People leave voice messages saying, 'Thanks for what you're doing.' We don't have an immediate base of customers but have drawn people, overcoming our parking problems and our hard-to-describe location."

> "Align with other groups. Don't fight 'em — join 'em! Our Chili Cook-Off Day is held at the same time as the city's Harbor Days. So we got together with our state's chili association to make our event part of the Harbor Days, and it's helped us both."
> — Rick Castellano, Former Mgr., Olympia FM, WA

The Market As An Event Location

Look at the organizations and activities in your area. Those organizations with successful fundraisers may want to use the market as a new location for their event. Let the library or the high school orchestra know that your farmers' market is available as a fundraising site. This builds community support and also brings in publicity. As your market grows in size and stature, larger organizations will be interested in using your location to host events.

Look at your Yellow Pages for organizations, social clubs and business organizations. An interfaith bake sale may give many religious bodies new visibility. If you allow them to make money through you, they automatically will bring you money as well. You have a base of customers to which they are adding. Work with them to accentuate their publicity efforts.

Other organizations may want to create their own new events at the market. The Red Cross can do a blood drive and the garden club might do a bake or plant sale. The market can become a central meeting place for local groups and causes. Put up signs at market entrances announcing these events so customers get in the habit of checking to see what's special today.

In Davis, CA, the market provides eight spaces for organizations with a social, cultural, environmental, educational, political or religious focus.

they don't permit singing by church groups. Their board policies have city approval since the market is on the city's Central Park. They do not disallow activities but can regulate the time, place and manner of them.

"Get involved in the community and have non-profit booths. They can have a booth for so many weeks in the season and in turn they are required to send out a news release saying that they will be at the farmers' market and say what they're doing. We ask that they send out a minimum of 10 news releases and we ask them to take flyers and talk about them in their organizations."
— Karen Durham, Mgr., Bellingham FM, WA

"Even if it's not directly a food event, we try to encourage sympathetic groups to use our market locations, and of course encourage them to get the media there. Have the announcer slip in something like: 'By the way, we're at the Union Square Greenmarket, and they're here three to four days a week, but today we've taken this section to have (event).' This doesn't require any expense or much organization for the market, but we get some great exposure out of it."
— Tony Manetta, Dir., Greenmarket, New York, NY

Market Booths

Set aside a few free spaces for non-profit or educational organizations such as Master Gardeners, Master Composters, community gardening associations, or an organic association. Let them have a free booth in exchange for doing some educational demo for the public or an educational and fun activity for children. Include home economics and science teachers, and invite the local humane society to adopt out animals.

Habitat for Humanity, the CROP Walk, an American Heart Association chapter, and the 4-H club suddenly gain visibility, solicit new members or raise funds. Send them a photo of their volunteers to include with an article in their newsletter.

In Davis, CA, the market provides eight spaces for organizations with a social, cultural, environmental, educational, political or religious focus, although

Become a "Giver" Organization

"We encourage farmers and customers to bring canned goods or nonperishable items, or donate fresh produce. The market's donations help a local food group serve hundreds of people each week. In addition to helping others, charitable events help promote your market. When people find out what you're doing, it makes the community feel like rallying around you, that you're part of the community and you want to help."
— Rick Castellano, Former Mgr., Olympia FM, WA

Encourage and arrange for farmers to donate produce to local food banks. Support other organizations by giving products or a market basket to their fundraising event. Recognize that community values do not always match market values. Be ready to flex to show support at times even when the request doesn't exactly seem to benefit your market.

Develop a reputation for being a "giver" organization, making your market a vital part of the community that everyone else wants to help succeed. Providing a scholarship to a local agricultural student gives you the basis for a press release. Give produce baskets to visiting dignitaries. When you consistently give to other efforts, make a list of your contributions for the media.

Use the market as a finish line for a 5K walk or 50K bike fundraiser for breast cancer research, multiple sclerosis, Parkinson's disease or whatever cause someone brings to you. Provide the fresh fruit and water for rest stations where your logo is visible. Keep your market name in the public eye. Work with a radio or TV station or the newspaper to co-sponsor and help promote the event. When it is covered in the media, your market gains visibility and trust among people who are watching news about events of concern to them.

You can build your community reputation even through something as unorthodox as buying shoes for school children as they've done in Fullerton, CA. Generally ask the beneficiary group to take an active part in a festival instead of saying "here is the check." Have them answer questions at an information booth and require them to send out news releases about their participation, as well as publicize it in their in-house newsletter. In staging nonprofit events, look for goodwill, future sales and long-term promotion rather than immediate profit. It need not always be food-related in order to meet a need. And there's always a way to make it fun and festive!

Model for Change

Your market can be a model for change among your farmers and within your community. Change is not easy, but can be fun. The old saying "If it ain't broke, don't fix it," unfortunately keeps many people stuck in the same patterns while customer demands are constantly changing. Indeed, about the only thing we can be sure of today is that change is going to come.

In promoting your market, be fearless in trying different ideas. Determine what customer problems need solving and take incremental steps so that you can modify your path if change makes things worse or simply isn't effective. Present ideas to your board and to vendors. Maybe it's time for an updated logo, a new series of special events, a different promotional strategy or a workshop on display. Become a pioneer — show your own motivation by outlining a plan, the rationale, the skills to be learned, the risks and the potential benefits. ❀

EMBRACING THE COMMUNITY 12

"We seem to have lost our sense of community, opting for profits first and a survival of the fittest...I am a farmer and a good neighbor..."
— David Mas Masumoto, *Epitaph for a Peach*

America's demographic tapestry is constantly being woven with new and beautiful strands that offer complexity and opportunity. California now has a majority of minorities; other states will soon follow. Markets are being created that have a more harmonious mix of food and culture than we have ever known.

Each immigrant group is new to our cultural melting pot and each brings real food additions for America's gastronomic experimentation. Having tried bok choy and finger bananas, the consumer is now tasting tatsoi and baby kiwi, Chinese long bean and nopales (cactus).

Educating shoppers by providing samples and recipes for new products is a time-honored way to create future regular customers. What better way to convince a hesitant customer to try a feijoa or yellow beet than for a farmer to include a sample in a bag with other produce. "Free gift with purchase."

> "The key is to educate the consumer. You need to provide recipes, cooking tips and nutritional information about the product, because it's new to them."
> —Rose Koenig, Haile Village FM, Gainesville, FL

In healthy markets, educating customers about agriculture is a priority. Farmers can talk about the problems they face, describe product benefits, ask customers what else they want to see and promote visits to their farm. Both individual farmers and the market should take on the educational role. For some, that means we also need to take on the role of educating farmers.

EDUCATING THE PUBLIC ABOUT LOCAL AGRICULTURE AND FARMERS' MARKETS

Friends of the Farmers' Markets – Santa Fe

New Mexico has a fascinating state model Friends of the Farmers' Markets (FFM) program, directed by Pamela Roy in Santa Fe. Its purposes are to solicit broader recognition of the state's farmers' markets, foster increased support among consumers and institutions for sustainably grown agricultural products, enhance marketing opportunities for the farmers, and encourage family farming and the preservation of indigenous agricultural traditions.

Friends of the Farmers' Markets seeks to achieve these goals through on-farm research, workshops and conferences, and "Farm Connection." This bimonthly newsletter uses both contributed articles and farmer-to-farmer dialogue to cover national and regional policy issues, direct farm marketing and local sustainable topics.

FFM also provides conference scholarships for farmers, sponsors farm improvement clubs to give seed money for farmer group projects, and funds farmers' market projects like customer surveys and farmer education workshops.

Roy says, "Farmers need to think about their farmers' market venture as a business. Especially as markets grow and there's more a competitive environment, farmers need to learn business skills like writing a business plan and utilizing long-range cash-flow planning instead of operating out-of-pocket from day to day." Teachers from local Small Business Development Centers or other nonprofit organizations are perfect for Friends workshops.

FFM also educates the community, especially children, through programs such as: a Farm Tour throughout northern New Mexico; hands-on activities in the Farmers' Market Garden; Shop with the Chefs and food demonstrations; festivals such as Stone Soup and Corn Grinding & Tortilla-Making Day; as well as Taste, Touch and Smell days.

Kids' Education. The "Farm to School" fall program reaches 2000 students at 20 Santa Fe public grade schools, fairly extensive outreach in a town of 60,000. "The kids come to the farmers' market and participate in our programs; the teachers' love it," Roy says. "It makes such a great field trip, and one of the things that we are aiming at in our grant proposals is to institutionalize the farmers' market in the school system through our Farm to School Program."

The FFM helps teachers enrich their curriculum on food topics by offering presentations in the schools prior to the market tours. Farmers are provided stipends to give the presentations and host field trips on their farms. The program thus offers introductory presentations about the farmers' market, visits to the market and on-site education, farmer visits to the classroom and farm field trips.

The "Kids in the Garden" program involves hands-on activities in a small community garden, about 70-yards long by 8-feet wide, at the farmers' market. "Kids of all ages" are invited to: "Come dig the soil, plant seeds, identify common garden plants,

A farmer becomes one with her dried flower arrangements which will make perfect gifts or home accents, paying for those long hours of design work by the fireplace. Some growers offer classes on arranging to spur flower sales.

construct trellises, harvest the bounty and taste the fresh tomatoes."

"We use the garden as an alive, hands-on experience," Roy says. On Seed Planting Day, kids plant in the garden. When they come back to the farmers' market week after week, they can actually see and tend their plants. They also take home six-packs of planted seeds to cultivate at home.

Compost Critters Day allows kids to use microscopes and eyeglasses to inspect all the beneficial insects in the garden. They also prepare soil and make compost.

Farm Tours. In 1999 there were 600 people from New Mexico and out-of-state who visited 20 participating farms. "The farm tour is a great opportunity for experiential learning," Roy says. "People learn how the food is grown and how to connect with their local farmer." They saw wool spinning, compost making, and bread making by a local bakery. The bakery handed out their brochures about encouraging the revitalization of local wheat production in New Mexico. The demonstrations were all done at farms; similar exhibitions are done at farmers' markets.

Taste Festivals. "Fresh tastings enable you to expand your palate by sampling the many varieties of super-fresh fruits, vegetables and herbs available at the market," Roy says. "You get to know those small, sweet, yellow tomatoes perfect for salads, kids or salsa; which roasted chili variety has just the right amount of heat for you; and whose sweet apricots and peaches you will stuff yourself on this summer!"

Taste, Touch and Smell days are seasonal events to celebrate locally grown, regional specialties. There are at least 40 varieties of tomatoes at the market, so a tomato tasting is a natural. Similarly, at the Chile Festival market visitors can sample 20 to 30 varieties of chili and sweet peppers, roasted and raw. With the Apple Tasting they can sample a dozen or more varieties and pick up literature that describes which apples are tart and sweet, which are good for apple pie, and which make a better applesauce. Sometimes farmers

The AGROArt Festival
A Way To Promote Local Agriculture & Farmers' Markets?

Farmers who have done and seen it all when it comes to fruits and vegetables are in for a shock when they stroll down the aisles of the AGROArt Festival, a four-year-old celebration held in Penryn, CA, each October to celebrate and promote local agriculture and the arts.

Common foods such as apples, onions, cabbage, potatoes and plums are combined into colorful, edible sculptures and people take notice! It's not every day that you see a five-foot Statue of Liberty made completely from cabbage leaves; a Japanese geisha with white-radish flesh and eggplant hair, robed in shiny red rhubarb; a goldfish sculpted out of orange slices; a turtle with an artichoke-leaf shell; or a sun delicately fashioned from orange slices, emitting carrot "rays."

Once people see the produce at the AGROArt Festival, they can never look at the produce department of their local grocery store in the same way again. One comment heard repeatedly is, "I can't believe these are made out of fruits and vegetables."

Prize money totaling $3,000 is offered in various categories in the sculpture competition. Locally grown produce is encouraged. Entrants bring their own materials like a papier mache base or a framework out of cardboard or papier mache.

Competitors in the artwork contest are free to use leftover produce however they wish, and anything they don't haul away is composted or recycled. According to the AGROArt Festival's publicist Patty Neifer, "Some people re-use the produce in stews or veggie soups."

As well as the sculpture displays, the festival includes a hands-on Produce Playgarden where festival-goers can make their own sculpture. As many as a dozen tables are loaded with fruits and veggies plus thousands of plastic skewers and toothpicks. "We thought this area would be for kids," Neifer said, "but it has been as popular with adults as children."

"Especially for the younger crowd, this event exposes them to fruits and vegetables they don't know about," Neifer said. "Kids go to grocery stores on their next visit and say, 'Mom, buy me some acorn squash or kiwi.'

"The festival's focus is to showcase local produce. Placer County is a very fertile region; we grow about every kind of produce here except some tropical fruit!"

Angela Tahti, executive director of the Arts Council of Placer County, which sponsors the festival, said: "The agricultural booths are really important because few children today really understand how ag products get to market. They enjoy their tutti fruiti fruit cocktails or whatever, but the connection is no longer made between eating the product and how it was produced or where it came from.

"AGROArt is a really fun way to show what this county has to give agriculturally and artistically. There's been an erosion of farms all over America and we'd like to celebrate what we have so farms can grow rather than diminish."

In 1999 Jan Kapple, an artist and poster designer from Auburn, CA, won $500 in the adult individual division, a title she has won three out of the four years of the festival. What's Jan's secret, aside from her talent? "When we make people out of vegetables, it's something people can connect with,"

THE NEW FARMERS' MARKET

are paid for their produce or flour from grant funds while others make contributions.

Stone Soup Day revolves around a sweet children's fable. A pauper arrived in a community and went door-to-door asking for food. Unsuccessful, he decided to ask people for help in making a community stone soup. He asked each household if they could contribute some carrots or some tomatoes and each one was willing. The soup project snowballed. Just by saying "I have a stone" and "I'm contributing," he got the community to contribute to a pot of soup. At the market the fable is told and kids learn to make soup, starting with a vegetable broth base. Adults love it, too.

Kapple said. "If it's some abstract object, it's just salad! But if you do a person that has eyes, it's a living thing! Even the (prize-winning) fish I did three years ago had eyes!" Kapple exclaimed, referring to "Mandarinean Sea," which featured a fish with sliced Mandarin oranges as scales.

Kapple listed some of her other favorite examples of humanizing fruits and vegetables: an "African Queen" using eggplants for the face and body, adorned with golden, banana-peel necklaces; the geisha girl; an Indian chief; and another entry featuring a woman and man dancing with watermelon slices for the woman's dress, eggplant for the man's suit, and shoes made from avocados!

"Making people aware of local agriculture is what this festival is all about," Kapple said.

The AGROArt Festival was created by arts and agriculture advocate Joanne Neft to celebrate Placer County agriculture. The first year's festivities were held in a small space with 20 to 30 contestants as part of the Newcastle Mountain Mandarin Festival. "I knew we already had a crowd at the Mandarin Festival and we could get an idea if "AGROArt" was something that would interest people," Neft said.

Arts Council of Placer County

With the head and torso made of eggplant; a headress of cabbage, radiccio and kiwi; a banana-peel necklace; and a skirt made of cornstalks, kiwi and cabbage, "The African Queen" made a stunningly regal display one year at the AGROArt Festival and won a Grand Prize for artist Jan Kapple.

"There was an amazing response. People loved it and it's been growing by leaps and bounds since."

Could the concept of AGROArt be used to promote local farmers' markets across the country? "Farmers' markets could devote one market day a year to letting kids come play with their food," Joanne Neft says. "AGROArt is so unusual and quirky and that's what makes it fun!"

According to Jan Kapple, the question of mixing AGROArt with farmers' markets is mainly a question of space and parking. "There were 5,000 attendees at the AGROArt Festival last year," Kapple points out. "A typical farmers' market couldn't accommodate that many people. That's why it's better to have the farmers' market be part of the AGROArt Festival. Lots more people generally come to a festival than normally come to a farmers' market, and you need a big enough facility to handle that many people. This is actually good, because it extends the concept of the farmers' market to a potentially wider audience.

"Another alternative is to do the AGROArt on a smaller scale at the farmers' market, having someone do a demonstration while at the same time promoting the AGROArt Festival by handing out flyers to the farmers' market patrons. At the AGROArt Festival you can have a booth that promotes the farmers' market and also have a market right there with growers selling produce. AGROArt and farmers' markets go hand-in-hand," Kapple says, "and to promote one promotes the other because they're both about local agriculture."

— AGROArt's website is: www.AGROArt.org/. ✿

On the same day they teach corn grinding and tortilla making. Market corn growers contribute cobs of corn. Kids shuck and grind it and make tortillas, a great source of pride, from the cob right to the tortilla.

"We want people to be conscious about where they buy their food and why, and we want people to know that they have options," Roy says, explaining FFM's considerable efforts in educating the public about local agriculture. "This is important because the young people growing up now are at least one if not two generations removed from family farms. They no longer have a grandparent or an uncle or aunt who operate a farm. So a lot of these kids, along with many adults, really don't know much about farm life and they have no idea where their food comes from.

Researching & Getting Grants

It's great to educate your community about farmers' markets and local agriculture, but how do you fund the programs to do this? One answer is through grants. To finance the ambitious and far-reaching educational projects of the Friends of the Farmers' Markets, executive director Pam Roy spends an appreciable amount of time writing grant proposals, developing business sponsorships, and spearheading an annual fund-raising campaign. FFM is set up as a nonprofit 501(c)(3) and acts as an umbrella for several organizations to help fund and develop their educational outreach programs.

"You really need to research who you are applying to, what they want, and what their purposes are," Roy says. To find out who's giving grants, go to a library and look for a CD-ROM from the National Foundation Center; this listing is also available on their website at fdncenter.org. "On their website you can find all kinds of information about foundations that may be interested in your organization's mission and programs," Roy says. On both the CD and the website you can do searches under specific key words such as "sustainable agriculture," "organic," "local agriculture" or "farmers' markets." Try to let your initial search be as broad as possible. Then you might narrow your search by state or by more specific categories.

Also consider what the foundations' major interests are. Sometimes you may think they are not interested in your proposed projects when in fact they may be, and sometimes the opposite may be true. "Simply calling them will let you know for sure," Roy says. Usually their phone numbers and e-mail addresses are listed as well as their mailing addresses. Often the listings will give information about what kinds of projects they have funded in the last year and of course this is a good tip-off about their interests and potential for funding your project.

Did they fund large projects or small, locally oriented agricultural projects? How much have they given in the past and how much do they now have available to give? Be realistic about their potential to fund your project. Look at how much money they gave last year. Often they will list both the total and a minimum and maximum range of money per project. Also take a look at which regions they target. They may only donate to a city or state that doesn't include your area, so don't waste your time applying where there's no possibility.

Take a look at who their executive directors are and consider if you know anyone in that community. Check with them to see if you know any of the board members. "This research often takes a lot of time and can be grueling," Roy says. "In order to maximize your efforts, you need to be realistic not only about who to go to, but in how much you can do as an individual or an organization."

Local community foundations often provide either workshops or services on how to write grant proposals — look under "Foundations" in the yellow pages. Often City Hall will have directories of local nonprofit community foundations and services. Community colleges, farm conferences and Cooperative Extension often have courses or workshops on how to write grant proposals. ✿

"We recognize that convenience is one of the number-one things people are looking for now in the 21st century — consumers lead very busy, active lives, so we're recognizing that farmers' markets need to make some transition to a certain extent.

"Yet we feel we're also here to help people make decisions about their food, learn where their food comes from, how it can be prepared, how they can be involved in their local food system if they want to be, and that they can make a conscious choice. That supermarket tomato may not be the only tomato in town — the local grocer or farmers' market may provide a tomato that is grown locally in the community, and by buying that instead of the supermarket variety, they're supporting the local economy.

"That's why we feel the educational aspect of the farmers' markets is so important. I always expect that people look for the higher good, but I'm also realistic in recognizing that our world provides us with so much information overload that sometimes people have to make the simplest choices for themselves. If we can touch even ten percent of the community, we feel we are making an impact."

Shop with the Chef. This program especially highlights local, indigenous foods such as chili, squash, corn posole and frijoles (beans) and also focuses on seasonal varieties of fruits and vegetables. "There's a lot of local indigenous foods around here that customers might see at the market, but they don't know how to use," Roy says. "These are culturally traditional or ethnic foods that customers ordinarily wouldn't see in other parts of the country."

"The chef will talk about the goat cheese or rhubarb that she's using in a demonstration, and why it's important to buy seasonally — why you don't see oranges or bananas in the farmers' market in Santa Fe, for example, and why you'll find greens and peas early in the year in the market and not apples," says Roy.

Ferry Plaza — San Francisco

Sibella Kraus, who founded the Tasting of Summer Produce in the early 1980s, created a non-profit Center for Urban Education About Sustainable Agriculture (CUESA) to run the market, a favorite site for premier organic growers and specialty food producers. Now Frankie Whitman acts as the consultant, developing innovative, educational programs at the market.

Ferry Plaza does a "Shop with the Chef Program" in which a local chef is given a budget to shop the market for what's fresh that day. Then the chef does a demonstration about what they've bought and why, what the people can do with it, and recipes and samples are handed out. "We don't have any problem getting chefs to come to the market," Whitman says, "because it's a rather high-end market and many of the chef's restaurant customers are also shoppers at the market."

Meet the Producer. A recent tie-in to the chef program is a weekly half-hour presentation in which a producer or a panel speaks about why they grow certain varieties and what it takes to get their product to market. While incredibly informative with a loyal following, attendance is less than a third that of the chef program. "People want to be entertained by celebrity chefs and learn how to cook," Whitman says.

Ferry Plaza, too, has added its own wrinkle to the idea of festivals centered around what's in season. "Tasting festivals are a great way to move products that are in glut," Whitman says, "but we feel it behooves the market to come up with something a little more creative than just comparing one grower's products against another's. Some growers don't like comparative tastings because they feel it pits one grower against another. We feel that the Meet the Producer program accomplishes a little bit more than just having a product out on the table. It helps consumers understand why farmers' market products are different than supermarket products.

To close their season, the market held "a discussion around the production of olive oil, different harvesting schedules, and a tasting of the different olive oil products." Peggy Knickerbocker, author of a book on California olive oils, facilitated the panel discussion. "Selling books is a good trade-off for authors and it gives the people at the market something nice to bring home." Check with a local bookstore, library or publisher to find local food authors.

"There are incredible resource people in any community who are willing to participate in these kinds of events and you need to draw on these kinds of resources," Whitman emphasizes. If not professionally organized, these events reflect badly on presenters and the market. Have a working loudspeaker, chairs, cooking equipment and a chef's assistant who can run it on time, introduce the program, thank people afterwards and distribute samples.

"With panel discussions make sure the panel knows in advance the questions so they can be prepared. In the Meet the Producer programs, we ask the presenters to bring in things to make it attractive, such as photographs of their farms, and set up some kind of display on the table. The programs shouldn't go on too long, about a half-hour or 45 minutes maximum.

"Look for nonprofit groups who are doing educational work around such issues as food, nutrition or gardening. It's an opportunity for them to get exposure."

With weekly events, it's hard to do extra publicity outside market signs, but with other special events, extra efforts are called for.

Cooking with Kids

Cooking with Kids is a multicultural food education program in New Mexico, currently operating in the Santa Fe and Cimarron public elementary schools. The program seeks to improve child nutrition through hands-on preparation of foods from many cultures in the classroom. Trained food educators work with students to prepare foods that are healthy and appealing. According to CWK program coordinator Lynn Walters, "If you're trying to convince kids to eat flavorful, healthy foods, ask them to prepare it

Water is a valuable element in any market project. This child gets excited, or terrified, amidst the water jets timed for surprises at the Davis Farmers' Market, CA.

themselves. The experience of eating and enjoying good foods, rather than just hearing the message of what's good for us, is really important. Cooking is a fun and creative process. And when children eat well, they are prepared to learn. And as they become educated about different foods, they are more likely to make positive food choices."

In addition to helping children learn healthy food habits, CWK classes provide opportunities for children to learn math, social studies, language arts, agriculture, art and music. By studying and experiencing food from around the world, the children also learn about people of other cultures.

During the 2000-2001 school year, CWK is working in seven Santa Fe elementary schools and one school in Cimarron, providing over 1,000 food education classes to students from kindergarten through sixth grade.

Cooking Classes are taught by a CWK food educator with teacher and volunteer help. Each class lasts about 1 3/4 hours. The food educator provides a cultural context for each class, hands-on cooking instruction, age appropriate curriculum activities, discussion questions, and all materials, ingredients and supplies necessary for each meal.

One student commented on the recipe for Green & White Fettuccine with Tomato Basil Sauce: "It's great; it's not coming out of a package." After cooking and eating Greek Pastitsio with Mediterranean

Launching a Fresh Foods School Education Program
An Interview with Dr. Antonia Demas, author of "Food is Elementary"

Many of us would like to improve the school lunch program, but I believe it has to be done through educating the kids in the classroom first. If you are concerned about the quality of food served in schools, you need to get a group of people together who are also interested in this issue. Make sure there is public support. Look for parents, farmers and farmers' market people who are interested in the school lunch programs and having healthier and more nutritious foods for their children. Get a core group of people together and come up with a proposal.

Your proposal needs to be carefully thought out and well organized. Schools are stretched to the max. You need to offer a program that you can provide initially. If the school perceives the project as more work or another program that they have to incorporate, they will reject it. There should also be no expense involved for the school. Once the school has seen the value of the program they may be willing to buy into it.

Your proposed program should address both education and health issues related to fresh foods. The nutritional advantages of fresh foods should be emphasized along with introducing foods that are available at the farmers' market and teaching the students about the cultures of the countries where these foods are indigenous.

A school education program about fresh foods is a natural for farmers' market programs because farmers' market products are so much healthier than what the kids are being fed in the schools. If more people saw the quality of foods served to children in many of the schools in this country, they would perhaps mobilize into action.

When children are enthusiastic about eating more nutritious food, the school lunch program will have a reason to change. Kids will eat healthy foods when they know what they are through positive, sensory-based education. If you put food from the garden in front of children without educating them about what it is, it's unlikely that they will want to eat it. If you tell them: "If you eat this, then 20 years from now you might not get cancer," it's not a compelling argument for children.

Food education should be an enjoyable experience for the kids, where they also learn about math, science, and the cultures of the world. If possible, bring in food-related artifacts along with music from various cultures to allow the children to have a rich exposure to different cultures. Have the children keep a journal of what they've learned so they can record their food-based experiences.

Use food as a vehicle to teach the academic disciplines. Let the kids cook the food and then eat it.

They will be so proud of what they've created and that they've created something beautiful. If that same food is then served in the cafeteria, because the children have had such a positive experience with that food, they will be eager to eat it. Children will eat up to 20 times as much of a new food item if they have had prior positive exposure to the new food.

Some adults in food education programs have tried cooking food in front of the kids and expected the children would eat it. This generally is not effective. The children need to do the cooking and have the direct experience themselves.

School food education programs should focus on getting kids excited about cooking and eating fruits, vegetables and grains. School meals are often a child's best meal or the only meal they will eat that day. We must educate our children about nutrition so that they can protect their health through diet as they grow. We have a moral obligation to see that this happens.

— Contact info: Antonia Demas, Ph.D., Director, Food Studies Institute, 60 Cayuga St. Trumansburg, NY 14886 (607)387-6884, antoniad8@yahoo.com.
[See Resources, Chapter 12 to order Dr. Demas' book, *Food is Elementary*] ✿

Salad, another child said, "There is joy in my mouth now." The same meals are prepared and served by the cafeteria staff several times a month as lunch choices in the school cafeterias.

Tasting classes, taught by classroom teachers, alternate with cooking classes and are devoted to having kids explore the diverse varieties of particular foods such as tomatoes or apples.

"Forty-five percent of the children in the Santa Fe Public Schools receive free or reduced-price meals," Walters continues. "Studies show that school lunch is the only complete meal many children eat each day. Many children are no longer learning from their parents and grandparents how to make tamales or strudel. One student even thought that food originated in the refrigerator."

To further the students' food education CWK developed a Farmer in the Schools program, which is now coordinated by Friends of the Farmers' Markets. The program brings local farmers into the classroom to talk about what they do and how they do it. Some farmers bring slides to show during the 30- to 40-minute presentations as well as the fruits of their labor to share with the kids.

"The parents of children who are in the CWK program frequently talk about how enthusiastic their children are after cooking in the classroom and that they like to cook more at home. We're encouraged about the possibility of getting children excited about cooking. If they don't cook, they're definitely not going to know what to do with all of the beautiful produce at the farmers' market!"

An Integrated Curriculum Guide is being developed by CWK and may be ready by fall 2001. Write to Lynn Walters at Cooking with Kids, 3508 Camino Jalisco, Santa Fe, NM 87505.

Senior Nutrition Program

In Decorah, Iowa, the Farmers' Market Senior Nutrition Program provides senior citizens with coupons that can be redeemed at their local market for fresh produce. According to director Connie Burns, it is similar to the WIC Farmers' Market Program and is funded through a local United Way. "The farmers love it, as do the seniors!"

Burns coordinates the program as a dietitian at a local hospital which gives "in kind" support through secretarial time, supplies, and printing of pamphlets. Public health nurses are also involved in the distribution of coupons to their senior clients.

The Integrated Nutrition Project

The Integrated Nutrition Project (INP) is a 5-A-Day program that is currently reaching 750 Hispanic children in elementary schools in Denver, Colorado. According to Cathy Romaniello, an instructor with the University of Colorado Health Sciences Center, INP consists of 26 weekly nutrition lessons focused on fruits and vegetables and how they fit into the Food Guide pyramid. The lessons are linked to school district aca-demic standards and are integrated into literacy, science, and math. They are designed to be hands-on and include food preparation and eating fruits and/or vegetables at each lesson.

Evaluation of this program from prior years found that the INP achieved significant behavior changes in children. Compared to control schools, INP children consumed 0.4 servings more fruits/vegetables at school lunch than did control children at the year-end post test. INP children significantly improved knowledge and improved attitudes toward the school lunch program.

— For information, contact Cathy Romaniello, Instructor, Dept. of Pediatrics, University of Colorado Health Sciences Center, Denver, CO, 80262. 303-315-5401 or cathy.romaniello@uchsc.edu. ✿

A market may give seniors more meaning than we imagine as this accordionist assures in Long Beach, CA. Markets provide limited-time spaces where unplanned, social get-togethers are more likely.

"There is a significant percentage of senior citizens in Winneshiek County that have limited incomes," Burns says, "and the opportunity to include fresh produce in their nutrition plan may not have occurred without the program's encouragement. The social and physical interactions with producers and consumers, who are advocates of healthy eating, further promotes these healthy habits. The interaction and instruction provided by the clinical dietitian, both at the meal site and the farmers' market, also reinforces the value of having a greater intake of fruits and vegetables as part of the senior participant's diet."

The Decorah Farmers' Market has 21 vendors who served an average of 280 senior citizens in 1998. Besides providing seniors with a healthy diet of fresh fruits and vegetables, the program provides seniors an opportunity to socialize, get fresh air and exercise by walking the market.

The clinical dietitian from the hospital provides nutrition presentations at the Decorah meal sites to promote the inclusion of fresh produce in the senior citizens' diet plan and distributes coupons to encourage seniors to register for participation in the program. They are exchanged for fresh produce from farmers who provide product information including recipes, food preparation and storage ideas. The dietitian also is available at the market to monitor the program activities and to provide further education.

A participant survey indicated that 92% of the seniors increased their intake of fruits and vegetables as a result of the program, 72% used all of their coupons during the season, and 67% visited the farmers' market six or more times in the season.

"The acceptance of the program and its utilization by the senior citizens in Decorah has been excellent," Burns says. "The program has become popular even though we can only allocate two to four one-dollar coupons at a time to each participant. The education provided by the clinical dietitian at the meal site is a key to the success of the program in having the produce available from farmers in a local community."

According to Burns, "Any farmers' market could probably set up a similar program. In fact, I've been trying to get a 'how to' manual together. I've done this program for seven seasons so far and have worked out the major bugs." Contact info: Connie Burns, 903 Walnut Street, Decorah, IA, 52101, 319-382-0173.

[For other senior nutrition resources, see Resources, Chapter 12]

The Farmers' Market Salad Bar Program

"We never thought we would see the day when kids are clamoring for kohlrabi or daikon, but after they've tasted it at the salad bar programs, they want more and more," says Laura Avery, manager of the Santa Monica Farmers' Market. She is referring to a new program whereby local farmers' markets supply farm-fresh fruits and vegetables to school cafeterias. At district schools children are offered a fresh farmers' market salad bar as an alternative to the traditional hot lunch five days a week. "I can tell you," one sixth grader exclaimed, "that we are very happy!"

The farmers' market salad bar program is run by the Santa Monica Malibu Unified School District (SMMUSD) Food and Nutrition Services Department and the City of Santa Monica Farmers' Market. Many of the children affected are from low-income families where access to fresh produce may be limited. The school district has seen more than a 500% increase in kids selecting the salad bar choice once the district began buying fresh fruits and vegetables at the farmers' market rather than through local produce dealers. The program has evolved from a pilot program in one elementary school to a district-wide success story being implemented in all 14 schools, thanks to a strong lunchtime demand from students for fresh fruit and vegetables.

In 1997, Occidental College researchers launched a pilot program to encourage students to eat more fresh produce while simultaneously supporting local farmers. The high-fat, high-salt food school age children often eat have created a paradox: many children are overweight and/or undernourished and school food is often the only daily meal available to them. In the past, school food menus may not have emphasized sound nutrition. Food insecurity is a condition that far too many low-income children confront daily, both inside and outside the schools.

The salad bar is a particularly compelling idea, given indications that nutritional deficiencies may have a significant impact on learning capacity. School food services often have become a political football between shrinking budgets, a reliance on low quality, commodity-based food, and the new shift toward privatized food services, which often emphasize fast-food type items.

According to Avery, "Kids pile their plates high with bright crunchy, juicy produce and often return for a second plateful. Nutritionally, the salad bar exceeds the USDA minimum requirements."

Rodney Taylor, SMMUSD food services director, says, "Serving nutritious meals that are also appealing to students encourages them to make healthy choices at an early age. Observing these good nutritional habits can help prevent a lifetime of serious health problems including obesity, diabetes, heart disease and cancer."

The Santa Monica school district has seen more than a 500% increase in kids selecting the salad bar choice once the district began buying fresh fruits and vegetables at the farmers' market rather than through local produce dealers.

The items for the salad bar consist of what's in season, with many of the items picked the previous day. A typical week's menu will include two different kinds of fruit daily as well as four to six different kinds of vegetables. Since the program purchases directly from local farmers, items vary by season. There is an educational benefit as students become aware that certain foods only grow in the region during particular seasons. Students also learn about growing issues in a school garden and through farmers' market tours.

Taylor believes the salad bar program has paid for itself thus far. It costs the district just pennies per serving as compared to the hot lunch. The district's food budget pays for the market produce, but volunteers or others funded by federal grants bring the produce daily to the students at the salad bar.

Because of good volume, growers give bulk discounts. "We're supplying the district with organic strawberries at $8 a flat which might sell at the market for $12 a flat. It's a guaranteed volume and at a price the farmers are comfortable with," says Avery.

The Santa Monica School District spent $23,400 on the salad bar program in the 1999-2000 school year. One of the 20 farmers sold $4,260 worth of produce to the district, a new customer that had never shopped at the farmers' market. Sales are beneficial to the farmers even at or below wholesale price because they don't make an extra stop, don't have to make a hard sell and it's a standing order each week. "The farmers also enjoy knowing that they are nourishing and educating a new generation of consumers," Avery adds. "They figure that kids that start out eating good food will continue to eat good food."

How do you start a salad bar program?

The Santa Monica Farmers' Market was fortunate to have several supportive people to get it started: the director of Food and Nutrition Services for the district, the market manager, and SMMUSD food nutrition coordinator Tracie Thomas, who pulled it all together.

"The food services director for your school district is the first person to approach," Avery says. "In our case the director happened to have a son in the schools whom he was anxious to get on this program." Another requirement is access to a large volume and good variety of fresh produce — it takes a lot of produce to supply a salad bar daily for a school district.

With the help of grant funds, the market also sponsors a Chef in the Classroom program to partner with teachers interested in incorporating nutrition into their curriculums, even in elementary school.

USDA grant. Having helped to demonstrate the feasibility of the concept, Occidental College is now heading a national consortium of universities, school districts and non-profit groups to develop new "farm-to-school" programs in California, New Jersey, and New York and expanding nationally.

Funded by a $2 million grant from the federal agriculture department, the farm-to-school project is an innovative effort to improve children's health and give small and medium-sized farms access to part of the $16 billion school food services market. "This will enable us to provide the kind of outreach and training needed to help others create and institutionalize their own programs across the country," said Robert Gottlieb, director of Occidental's Urban and Environmental Policy Institute (UEPI).

"We can envision farm-fresh food and gardens integrated into literally every school district in the country," added project co-director Michelle

Mascarenhas. By expanding the market for local farm produce, farm-to-school programs can create a major new sales opportunity for family farmers as well as provide healthier food for school lunches and an effective means of educating children about nutrition, said Gottlieb.

For more information, see Occidental College's Pollution Prevention Education Research Training website at:

http://www.oxy.edu/oxy/news/articles/farms.and.schools.html.

[See also Resources, Chapter 12]

Similar salad bar programs have been operating in Berkeley and Santa Barbara schools. The Santa Barbara Farmers' Market approached a local school to establish a garden, applied for a grant, and the kids now grow food and come to the market. They also sell to the cafeteria which meets the rest of their needs at the market.

Kids notice fresh. This wave of the future may only be limited by the variety of products available locally. When highlighting the 5-A-Day program or simply hosting a school tour, notify farmers to have at least one item "on special" for kids. An apple or Asian pear for a quarter starts the habit and gets an idea home. Fullerton, CA, has hosted children's tours where everyone receives 50 cents of coupons to redeem with farmers. Make sure they go home with a brochure. Work with the school nutritionist to incorporate farmers' market items and education into their program.

Kids love to leave their mark through a mural or tile project which can be incorporated into a market building or nearby wall.

SOCIAL CONCERNS

Markets can address numerous social issues on a local or even international scale. Residents feel their market truly represents the community when they can have a booth and talk with market-goers about the Audubon Society, Rails to Trails Conservancy, Greenpeace, American Cancer Society, People for the Ethical Treatment of Animals, Multiple Sclerosis Society, PTA, Rotary Club International, school programs, candidates for office or the library book drive. A free booth may be provided for groups engaged in education only, whereas a fee may be charged for fund-raising activities.

Numerous other vehicles for social responsibility can be implemented at farmers' markets. It's a simple matter of how connected your market is to the world around you.

Hunger Programs

Invite a community food bank to collect unsold produce from farmers at the end of the day for distribution to low-income citizens. A market might also display donation barrels or a donation jar at the info booth so customers can join the effort. If the info booth serves as a produce donation collection point, farmers don't have to be bothered individually and the market can more easily document the volume collected to reinforce your tax status and include in your annual report showing your community contributions.

The personal connection between food bank and farmer may lead to a quick call when a future rain or hailstorm hits — better to harvest for the poor than waste a crop. Hunger is a complicated problem and the Portland Public Market, ME, recognizes its role in helping to solve it. Working with the Preble Street Resource Center and other organizations, vendors participate in a Share the Bounty drive that fills bags with breads and other fresh, locally produced market

Often visible at the U District FM in Seattle are groups like Seattle Tilth and P-Patch, created by homeless teenagers who garden next to the market site.

foods for needy area residents. Customers can make a cash donation at any market business toward fresh market foods for local hunger relief groups. Each fall 25 area restaurants and all market vendors donate their time and foods for over 500 guests at the annual Portland Food Festival, raising more than $10,000 towards the centralized food recovery program.

Homeless Kids' Program

At Seattle's University District Farmers' Market, manager Chris Curtis points out, "There is a separate program for homeless kids in our urban neighborhood. They tend and harvest a large community garden plot. They sell a portion of their harvest at a free booth. Most of these kids are terribly marginalized and have truly fallen through the system's cracks. This particular program has worked beautifully for some. It has given them responsibilities in a school-like setting and something to care for and nurture. At least half a dozen have gotten off the street and are back in school or working at real jobs. I don't think the farmers' market is the reason but a small part of the solution."

In too many communities there are youth who live on the streets, in abandoned homes, under freeways or in hidden places. Often churches and social service agencies are working to provide them basic food, shelter and encouragement to return to school. Farmers' markets can connect with these agencies to provide jobs with farmers, as market staff or becoming entrepreneurs themselves. The Los Angeles program Food From the 'Hood is the model for kids to begin a food business using farmers' markets as the test market for their products.

Urban Health

More than 60% of Americans are overweight and one in four is obese, defined as 30% overweight. Obesity is growing among all groups, but it is highest among the poor and lower-income minorities are at greater risk. While 17% of whites are obese, the figure rises to 21% of Hispanics and 27% of blacks. Nutritionists say that the problem is partly due to lack of nutrition knowledge and access to healthier foods.

There is a clear link between body fat and watching television. One study has shown that 26% of children ages 8 to 16 watch TV four hours or more daily, but for black children the figure is 42%. The effect is pernicious because TV-watching leads to inactivity and exposes children to an average of 10,000 food commercials a year, pushing a steady stream of snacks, candy and junk food. The result is that 28% of blacks, compared with 16% of whites, have poor diets.

As poverty increases, rates of obesity rise. People trying to pay bills do not prioritize their food choices. Diseases result as younger people confront diabetes, cardiovascular disease, hypertension, and asthma.

> "The true lethal narcotic in this country, the real killer, is not crack cocaine, not tobacco or even alcohol. It is cheap, subsidized, processed sugar and enriched starch that layer with folds of blubber the rear, the belly and the thighs of the American eater."
> —Victor Davis Hanson, *Fields Without Dreams*

Farmers' markets can become part of a circle of hope – for farmers and city residents. With help from foundations and nutrition organizations, we can revive blighted urban areas and bring quality, fresh produce to millions of lower-income residents. There is no need to segregate the wealthy and the poor. Especially minority producers and those who appreciate every person's right to food access will attend markets in poorer communities in spite of lower prices. In part, they continue because of appreciation shown by their customers and because they can relate to need themselves.

Market development is most feasible in areas heavily dependent upon USDA food stamps and food coupons. Farmers' markets should be ready to do aggressive advertising of their participation in those programs to attract recipients and they should link with the local food bank to provide excess food for the needy.

New markets also will appear in higher-income areas. As organizers plan in any community, they will study demographic patterns. The "traditional" family, where one spouse works and one stays at home with the children, represents less than one-fifth of American households; there are twice as many dual-income households. Consumers' lives are more busy, providing new challenges for organizers selecting market hours and new opportunities for value-added processors.

Low-income Communities

Although some people wonder how low-income people's focus on price is going to jive with small farmers' focus on sustainability, many farmers' markets do exist in low-income communities. There are several factors for farmers and organizers to consider:

✧ Just because people are low-income does not mean they won't spend money on food, even organically grown. Poorer people have traditionally spent a disproportionate amount of money on food.

✧ If consumers don't have health insurance, true for 40 million people in the United States, they may realize that a healthy diet is their best insurance plan.

✧ A market serving low-income customers may well reach middle- and upper-income groups as well.

✧ If the farmers' market has good support from the local WIC office, there can be thousands of dollars of food stamps and food coupons coming into a single market.

✧ Farmers can commit like anyone else to supporting a farmers' market in a low-income area based on their desire to contribute to the social well-being of that community and their customers' appreciative response.

⬥ Nutrition education is a valuable part of attracting and maintaining a younger customer base, inexperienced in preparing foods.

⬥ USDA's WIC Farmers' Market Nutrition Program (FMNP) coupons expanded from $12 to $15 million in 2001. Food stamp sales at farmers' markets are estimated at $75-100 million.

⬥ Immigrants, including those with FMNP coupons, may be especially receptive to specialty crops that farmers cannot move in other venues.

Vance Corum

The Milpitas FM is very successful in serving working class Asians and Indians. Prices are competitive and fancy foods are uncommon at this site, one of 17 farmers' market run by the Pacific Coast FM Association.

In January, 1999, the Community Food Security Coalition released a report, *Hot Peppers and Parking Lot Peaches: Evaluating Farmers' Markets in Low-Income Communities* by Andy Fisher. [See Resources.]

The Villa Parke farmers' market has operated since 1980 in a small park in an African-American part of Pasadena, CA, not far from the Rose Bowl. About 25 farmers sell here every Tuesday. Market managers Betty Hamilton and Gretchen Sterling attribute the market's longevity to the broad base of neighborhood support. Betty notes, "This is their market." Betty and Gretchen have fostered this integration of the market with the community by returning the market's modest profits back to the community. They have sponsored soccer teams, bought a wheelchair for local organizations and at one point even bought 50 local kids new shoes. Another key to Villa Parke's success is that the managers subsidize its operation with fees earned managing a highly successful, middle-income market. They realize that subsidies may be the only way a low-income market can survive.

Like Villa Parke, San Francisco's Heart of the City Farmers' Market was sponsored in the early 1980s, by the American Friends Service Committee, as part of an effort to improve access to healthy foods in the nearby Tenderloin district. With about 60 growers in summer and 30 in winter, Heart of the City has a mixed-income customer base: office workers from the area's many business towers, tourists, and the Tenderloin's largely poor southeast Asian and Latino populations. The middle-income customers are key to balancing market economics, providing farmers with a stable sales base. The product mix reflects the ethnicity and income levels of the clientele. While a few stands sell upscale products, most sell basic fruits and vegetables at rock-bottom prices because of the high volume. Vietnamese and Lao growers from the Central Valley predominate, selling Asian vegetables to fellow Asian consumers.

Across the country on the northern edge of Manhattan, amidst the hustle and bustle of a Dominican and Puerto Rican neighborhood, the Washington Heights Greenmarket does a fantastic business four or five months of the year. It redeems $800,000 in FMNP coupons each year, well over half of sales. Without these vouchers, Washington Heights and a network of smaller Greenmarkets in the city's poor neighborhoods would likely collapse. Threatening them as well, is the impending conversion of paper food stamps to a debit card system, or Electronic Benefits Transfer (EBT). Without the phone lines or terminals to process EBT cards, numerous markets will lose the ability to redeem food stamps, a significant portion of their sales.

As these examples illustrate, farmers' markets can be a valuable tool for improving access to affordable and healthy food for lower-income communities. However, low-income markets offer special challenges in addition to those facing all farmers' markets. Certain barriers are common among low-income markets. These include:

⬥ *Fair price, low cost.* There exists a fundamental tension between farmers' obtaining a fair wage and low-income consumers' desire for cheap food. Supermarkets can source produce more cheaply and undersell small-scale family farmers. Supermarkets often use produce as a loss leader, selling it at or below cost to attract customers. In addition, low-income households may have little money available for food purchases beyond staples.

⬥ *Transportation.* Low vehicle ownership rates in low-income communities reduce the cumulative purchasing power of the target market. Limited transportation options diminish the trade area and impede consumers' ability to get to the market and purchase large quantities.

⬥ *Convenience.* Low-income individuals generally have less time and fewer resources. Shopping at farmers' markets during designated hours is less convenient than elsewhere.

Given the many barriers present, the challenges of organizing a market in a low-income community are greater than in a wealthier neighborhood. Following basic market organizing and management principles and having skilled staff are just as important in low-income as in middle-income markets. Successful low-income farmers' markets have additional criteria however. These include:

⬥ *Community support.* In the most successful examples, the markets are well integrated into the community with citizen board members and profits donated to local organizations. Grassroots community organizing may prove more successful than

FARMERS MARKET

FM at Sandpoint, Sandpoint, ID

a publicity drive in building support for a new market.

⬥ *Subsidies.* Low-income markets may need subsidies in the form of FMNP coupons, middle-income shoppers or creative market management that allows a wealthier market to support a poorer counterpart.

⬥ *Product mix and prices.* Market managers should encourage a product mix of basic foods at affordable prices. Building a connection between minority consumers and growers of the same ethnicity can also help to strengthen consumers' loyalty to the market.

Health and Food Safety

Whenever there is some kind of outbreak of concern about pesticides or chemicals in food, there is a surge of consumers that go to the farmers' markets because they start thinking about who is producing their food. While certain natural foods and mainline supermarkets respond with country- or state-of-origin labeling programs, farmers' markets provide the ultimate guarantee: a grower's word. This makes it all the more imperative that farmers recognize and respect their place within a cooperative-styled organization. The saying, "An injury to one is an injury to all" holds true. A farmer lie or misrepresentation will come out eventually and hurt that farmer's sales; it also hurts the credibility of all others in the market. An aggrieved customer can cause the loss not only of other existing customers but of ones you will never meet.

Thankfully, most people do not have adverse physical reactions to food inputs. Yet, for those who do, their sensitivity to particular ingredients, additives or chemicals used in the production of food is of critical concern. They often depend on farmers' market products for a certain level of food cleanliness or absence of toxicity. They need to depend on our word; if producers declare that a product is organic, the market should stand behind that claim. We should clarify and standardize what is meant by "no sprays" so that customers do not believe they are buying "organic."

Try to promote the concept of knowing who's producing your food and what they're putting on your food. Also, work closely with your local and state health departments to determine acceptable practices within your farmers' markets concerning food safety.

> "Consumers are concerned about where their food comes from. In the scare about sprouts that had e-coli they found that the seeds were imported, which made customers think it's important to have a local food supply. Our county is the largest raspberry producer in the nation, and customers ask: 'These berries aren't from Chile are they?' In the off season I shop at one of our local grocery stores and they've begun to label the country of origin. They sell tomatoes from British Columbia, right across the border, as well as South American tomatoes. The owner of the store told me they sell a lot more of the BC products because people feel they can trust something more local."
> —Karen Durham, Mgr., Bellingham FM, WA

An awareness of food problems around the globe, including the deaths related to mad cow disease in Europe, have prompted a safety response. Health departments are increasingly focused on hygiene rules from farm to restaurant. Businesses may be required to log crucial actions under Hazard Analysis Critical Control Point standards, known as HACCP. They also may face new machinery and building requirements for processing.

Dangers are overblown and consumer fears manipulated. In protecting themselves from consumer lawsuits, government protection agencies are over-regulating artisanal production in favor of a homogenized food supply which favors large companies. The net effect of this regulatory environment is that larger businesses strictly adhering to HACCP become immune to prosecution for food poisoning, quality food is replaced by clean food (which doesn't mean it's good), and small businesses are regulated out of existence.

Ask the Dietitian. Not all health departments are focused solely on regulation. In a more productive vein, the Southland Farmers' Market Association teamed up during the 2000 season with the Los Angeles County Department of Health Services Nutrition Program and California Project LEAN/LA Region to sponsor an innovative program linking registered dietitians to farmers' markets. The goal of the "Ask the Dietitian" Program was to improve fruit and vegetable consumption at eight select farmers' markets in the county. It gave shoppers the opportunity to ask nutrition questions, learn about healthy eating practices, and get tasty low-fat recipes.

A 1999 study by the California Department of Health Services reported that adults are not following recommendations for healthy eating, leading to greater risk of heart disease, cancer, and diabetes. Only 30% eat the recommended five daily servings of fruits and vegetables. Almost 35,000 Californians are diagnosed each year with diet-related illness. If we increase fruit and vegetable consumption, we can reverse these trends and lead to improved wellness and reduced health care costs.

Community Food Security

USDA has a Community Food Security program with 100 new commitments to fight hunger and strengthen local food systems. Their gleaning program alone has helped direct 13 million pounds of excess food to faith-based and non-profit organizations that feed the hungry. They provide technical assistance to anti-hunger and community food security projects. One of their partnerships brought together Hewlett-Packard and Second Harvest Food Bank to update computer technology and match companies with non-profits.

The Community Gardening Initiative involves the American Community Gardening Association, the Garden Clubs of America and the Garden Writers of America Association. The goal is to increase the number of low-income Americans obtaining food through community gardens, school gardens and private gardens that "Plant a Row for the Hungry." A Utah 4-H program, Fresh From the Heart, has kids gleaning produce from urban gardens.

Their partnership with Share Our Strength, based in Washington, D.C., seeks to recruit chef volunteers to teach nutrition education classes. Even student chefs in Rhode Island are doing demonstrations at farmers' markets.

All markets can look at these types of initiatives to respond to a growing awareness of the need for food security in our own communities. There are grant programs available at many levels to fund these creative solutions.

 ## COMMUNITY OUTREACH

An essential part of farmers' markets success lies in making it a vital part of the community fabric. It's vitally important in maximizing a limited budget to piggyback your efforts with other organizations.

> "Market managers are exploring new community connections that may become important new markets for their growers. In one community, where the market is sponsored by the local Lions Club, market stall fees contribute to community service projects and organizations such as the teen center and the food bank. These relationships create goodwill between the markets and the community, contributing to a better business environment for farmers and other market vendors. In some communities, managers have made contacts with hospitals and senior citizen centers to explore institutional food purchases from the market."
> — Farmers' Markets and Rural Development Project

"Collaboration is very important for any non-profit," Pam Roy says. "When you work with other organizations, you get whole organizations as well as individuals involved and invested in your programs, and you also get invested in their programs. Involving the broader participation of the community is really imperative to farmers' market success."

On Seed Planting Day in Santa Fe, for example, Friends of the Farmers' Market works with the Master Gardeners as well as different local nurseries and landscapers. Presenters are asked to work with some of the farmers or plant producers in the market, and talk about the plants that they have found in the farmers' market, and also mention who they got it from in the market, just as chefs mention farmers by name while using their products.

Cooperative Extension Service regularly does food preservation and nutrition presentations at markets. The WIC (Women, Infants & Children) staff distribute farmers' market nutrition program checks at the farmers' markets. The idea is to build on the theme of health and nutrition and invite other groups' participation.

The FFM also works regularly with the Department of Community Services and the New Mexico Department of Agriculture on the state and local level. "We also look for non-profit groups that are working along similar lines or goals," Roy says. "The Children's Museum, for example, has helped us with equipment. We invite them to be part of our programs like the Kids in the Garden projects and we also go out to their activities to do presentations about food, nutrition and farmers' markets.

FFM works with a group called the Food Depot which runs a food assistance program, helping over 50 agencies in the Santa Fe Community that provide shelters, soup kitchens and cooking programs to seven counties and 30,000 people. The Food Depot has a booth at the Santa Fe markets and customers are invited to donate. At the end of the day, farmers also donate what hasn't sold. "All of the food is weighed out so that we know exactly what came from the farmers' market," Roy says. Farmers receive receipts for a tax write-off.

To expand cooperative efforts between the two organizations, the Food Depot hopes to act as a distributor for farmers, making pick-ups and deliveries for farmers when it goes to outlying communities as part of its regular pick-up and delivery routes. For now, The Farm Connection has a cooling unit behind the market office and helps farmers sell to restaurants.

Serving Your Community

Being a credible, major player in your community may require that the manager or board members serve on various boards, participate in other organizations' events and, in general, help others to succeed

The Fall Festival in Davis means loads of different activities for market-goers.

as much as your market. When a local parade is organized, get a grower to drive a tractor towing a wagon with a farmers' market display, as they've done in Pacific Beach, CA. When you are asked to provide baskets of products for fundraising events, be quick to respond with a gift or clearly define your policy.

The Springfield Farmers' Market at the X, MA, has a community information table featuring a different non-profit organization each week. Other markets allot two or ten spaces depending on the size of their market and the demand from the nonprofit or business community.

In Yakima, WA, the Volunteer and Career Center's new director volunteered to do outreach to hundreds of nonprofit organizations and coordinate their periodic participation in the market. It gave her center greater visibility with community groups and gave the market valuable community connections while saving the manager's time for other duties.

Elsewhere, managers send letters to local restaurants encouraging them to buy direct from market vendors and to promote their market and vendors' products at other community events and locations. A grocery store has been known to sponsor an annual benefit for the local farmers' market. Community gardens are invited to join as compatible organizations.

As the driving force behind the growth of the Davis Farmers' Market, Randii MacNear has worked with a strong board to expand the role of the market in the community. Their many activities and connections with hundreds of nonprofit organizations made

them truly appreciated as crucial to the city's social fabric. Greater recognition came in the form of a multi-use, open-air, clerestory, 35 x 280-foot building that the City of Davis built as part of a two-block Central Park expansion. Included are a youth center, an English garden, several water features, playground equipment and recessed open space. The market contributed an additional $18,000 for a wooden deck and seating area around the commanding oak tree.

A similar 2000 park expansion in Vancouver, WA, was accompanied by moving the downtown market six blocks to a street bordering Esther Short Park, the oldest in the state. A covered concert stage now provides protection for performers during market or non-market activities.

Parks are used as market sites from New York City to Salt Lake City, where they provide a quieter, relaxing environment, often displacing needle-carriers with baby-carriers.

One of the most historically interesting is a park in Long Beach, CA, surrounded on four sides by a farmers' market. Unfortunately, it was decimated in World War II, when more than half of its farmers were forced into internment camps along with more than 120,000 Americans of Japanese ancestry. The Alien Land Law of 1913 had barred "Orientals" from owning land, so first generation "Issei" could not own the land they farmed. Now, suddenly they could not even farm the land they didn't own.

After the war the market never recovered its momentum and slipped out of existence in the 1960s. We called our new effort in 1980 the re-opening of the farmers' market, though there was no organizational connection. We invited Japanese-American and other farmers to return and reminded longtime residents of the wonderful bounty of the past as we once again sought to serve the community. After twenty years the market has once again regained center stage every Friday in the central core of downtown Long Beach.

Surveys

In most communities we can only guess at the farmers' market impact on the lives and happiness of area residents. Surveys allow us to quantify our impact. In 1998 Cooperative Extension surveyed 18 farmers' markets serving some of San Diego County's 6500 farmers. They found 63% are weekly shoppers, travel four miles to market, purchase 47% of their fruits and vegetables at farmers' markets and spend a seasonal high of $19.25 per trip from five farmers (elsewhere $10-15 per person is more common).

Customers in inland, north county markets were 75.7% white, median age in their late 50s and income above $60,000. Those in central and south county markets were 80.9% white, late 40s, and below $50,000 income. In order, the most purchased products are vegetables, fruits, cut flowers, fresh herbs (one in two customers), organic produce (nearly half), followed by baked goods and precut vegetables (one in four).

Knowing demographic and values differences may cause your market to slant a direct mail or other ad piece. A thorough analysis may lead you to help farmers develop additional sales through value-added products. Surveys conducted at the market can help you find that customers want more kids' activities, regular chef demonstrations, a larger range of products, more sophisticated crafts, cleaner restrooms and more entertainment.

An on-the-street or telephone survey of non-customers may demonstrate frustration over poor parking, high prices, poor quality, narrow aisleways and lack of support for local nonprofits.

A farmers' market signpost directs customers to local businesses in Hayward, CA.

A survey in Portland, OR, showed that 28% of their customers were coming downtown on Wednesday just for the market, even though parking is an acknowledged sore point. The market is now keenly aware of its powerful pull on customers that has spin-off benefits for local merchants.

So what's most important? It depends on how you word the question. When San Diego customers said what factors influenced their decision to buy at farmers' markets, the order was: freshness, quality, taste, local (7 in 10), help farmers (6 in 10), followed by nutritional value, atmosphere, best value, convenience, selection and price. Asking their top reasons yielded somewhat different priorities.

When a survey tells you that 74% think quality is better than at local supermarkets, especially the tomatoes, you have the basis of your next advertising campaign. That's why Julia Child did a "Chef's Choice" commercial for the Santa Barbara markets — quality is #1 with customers so they wanted to reinforce that the choosiest chefs shop at their farmers' markets. Since convenience is a high priority there, ads and promotional materials emphasize the choice of six different market locations and the markets employ customer service assistants to carry purchases to customers' cars. [See also Appendix, "Customer Surveys and Public Opinion"]

Just ask. Every market knows improvements are possible; the question is where to direct limited resources. If we ask the right questions, there's a good chance that we'll find out how we can better attract and embrace our entire community. ✿

*E*XPANDING THE VISION   *13*

"...the care of the earth is our most ancient and most worthy and, after all, our most pleasing responsibility. To cherish what remains in it, and to foster its renewal, is our only legitimate hope."
  — Wendell Berry

Farmers' markets involve more than the simple transfer of tomatoes for cash. They are about the exchange of ideas. As agriculture faces the greatest threat to the survival of family farms ever known, farmers' markets have a chance to be part of the solution. Farmers' markets can serve as a leading forum, a place for civic discussion about the issues our local agriculture and communities face in this new millennium.

To do so may require our most creative response to the issues of the day — declining consumer health, declining farm health and a host of others. Much as a farmers' market often has a nonprofit section, our book's nonprofit section is this: ideas for the future. Whether it's through the electronic medium of a farmers' market website or using the market as the physical location for lectures, debates or workshops about community issues, farmers' markets have every opportunity of becoming the focal point of the "vibrant agrarianism" that the brilliant book, *Fields Without Dreams*, maintains is the very basis of a vital democracy — and the survival of small farms.

Public squares have long been farmers' market locations throughout history. Portland's Pioneer Courthouse Square, OR, gave rise to immediate success for a Wednesday market but after one year the market moved due to a dramatic rent request.

An exchange of ideas is the necessary basis of societal progress. Public debate in the best sense — maintaining civility and a sense of humor — can engender a spirit of openness and sharing toward the greater good of the community. Together, our general goals are to improve farm sustainability and maintain or enhance the quality and flavor of food consumed. With the loss of farms during the last century, we have jeopardized the fabric of rural life along with tasty varieties possible only in a local agriculture. We face the challenge of bringing back old varieties, re-establishing the prominence of small farms, re-invigorating a sense of mutual interdependence — in short, re-creating a local agri-culture.

Farmers' markets will continue to evolve as this period of market renewal comes of age. Markets come about through steps to sustain small, family farmers and the independence that lifestyle begets. Increasingly, they will take steps to deal with the health of their community as well. Both sets of action will encourage positive exchanges that can only benefit our local as well as national cultures.

FARMERS' MARKET WEBSITES

"Bill Gates meets Thomas Jefferson" is the world of our future where high technology intersects with farm culture — light speed with patient seed. In this new world of our fast-paced, convenience-oriented, "now" society, many people still find comfort in an anachronistic, slower-paced, "wow" marketplace.

Farmers' markets are the places where people test thoughts and ideas with each other. Yet Bill Gates' technology is inserting itself into these farmers' markets of Jeffersonian days as a Washington farmer gives away apples at Pike Place Market in order to build his computer mail order list. Even with the introduction of this new electronic communication, we have to treat customers as friends, just as always, if we are to build and keep relationships. If we can help people touch the past even as they have stepped into the future, we will chip away the seeming barrier of an impersonal lifestyle in the new economy.

Recipes Online: American Farmland Trust

One of the most popular features of the American Farmland Trust (AFT) website at www.farmland.org is its Chef at Market Recipes, where web travelers can click on a recipe menu indexed by ingredient and season to pick and download an enticing recipe.

Ann Harvey Yonkers, FRESHFARM Markets manager, estimates that many market customers as well as tourists and cooking enthusiasts regularly check the Chef at Market recipes on the website. "We found that a lot people who come to the markets also like to get information about our farmers and farmland issues from the website. We hand out about 200 - 250 recipes per market day at the chef demonstration and at our information booth, but customers also like the option of finding our information online." AFT's newspaper clipping service also reveals that the online recipes are frequently picked up by the food pages of newspapers across the country and reprinted with AFT attribution and mention of the website.

Yonkers, who trained as a chef, writes and formats all the recipes submitted by the chefs who appear at AFT's markets. Her goal is to make the recipes as simple and straightforward as possible so they will encourage the home cook to purchase seasonal and local produce at the market and bring it home and cook with it.

With a roster of 80 FRESHFARM Market volunteers, the market utilizes e-mail to communicate with them and recruit people for weekly scheduling. In addition, a weekly market e-newsletter goes out to about 500 patrons highlighting seasonal produce, market activities and the Chef at Market recipe.

Reaching the Consumer: Maine Food and Farms

The main page of the Maine Food and Farms website:

www.mainefoodandfarms.com

entices viewers to "find great Maine foods and agricultural products direct from the producer!" Clicking on the Farmers' Markets link takes the viewer to farmers' markets listings throughout the state, with contact information as well as the dates and hours of operation of the markets. It also links to any market that has either an e-mail address or website.

The farmers' market section has search features so that a customer can do searches by the name of the market, the town or county, day of the week or any combination of these. A customer might go to the website to find out which markets are open on Fridays for that area, for example.

According to Deanne Herman, marketing development specialist with the Maine Department of Agriculture, "A lot of farmers' markets are a taking a look at how they market themselves. Several areas are forming groups of farmers' markets to do co-promotions. By pooling their resources for group television or newspaper ads, they can get much more exposure."

Maine markets that don't as yet have their own websites can list the Maine Food and Farms website in their advertising, which in turn leads customers to their own farmers' markets.

Internet marketing is only one part of the overall marketing mix for farmers' markets, Herman stresses,

The Open Air Market Web Site

The place to be for farmers' markets on the internet is an incredibly rich and diverse website called Open Air Market at:

http://www.openair.org.

There is a wealth of materials and resources on the Open Air website both for anyone thinking about organizing or managing a farmers' market, as well as for farmers thinking of selling at a farmers' markets.

Described on its home page as "The World Wide Guide to Farmers' Markets, Street Markets, Flea Markets and Street Vendors," the Open Air home page links lead to:

✧ "FAQ" (Frequently Asked Questions") list;

✧ Discussion forum;

✧ Market websites links page;

✧ "Alerts: Vendors In Jeopardy!" postings;

✧ Books and book reviews on farmers' markets;

✧ Reports, guides, essays, articles, book excerpts, and poems;

✧ Marketplace images;

✧ Tips for designing a market website;

✧ Links to market websites;

✧ Website of the month;

✧ Archives section;

✧ Market listings;

✧ Conferences (some reports are available from past conferences);

✧ Market associations and organizations;

✧ Current research on markets and vendors; and

✧ Links to related market resources, such as e-mail discussion groups.

"Every open air market related resource on the internet should be accessible from here," says Steve Balkin, a professor of economics at Roosevelt University in Chicago and creator and proprietor, along with Alfonso Morales and John Cross, of the Open Air website.

The Open Air site is "aimed mainly at computer users and paradoxically encourages them to get off the computers and visit outdoor style markets. We try to make it friendly for consumers so that they can visit the market in person," Balkin says.

"Shopping for goods and researching tourism destinations are two of the top uses of the internet. By using the internet to let people know about farmers' markets, they might find markets to visit that they might not otherwise go to.

"Farmers' market managers and planners can find on the Open Air site substantial material to convince local government about the advantages of a farmers' market."

Shoppertainment

"The virtual community is good only if it leads to real community," Balkin points out. "Set aside a place at the market where people can sit down, have a cup of tea or coffee, and socialize. Unless farmers' markets have these congregating areas, they lose some of their value as a social asset.

"One idea is to provide an area of the market where people can enjoy music and entertainment and eat prepared food. Supermarkets are becoming savvy to this. The big thing now in some of the big supermarkets in the Chicago area is to have restaurants and sit-down areas within the supermarket. It's another profit center for the market, and it also enhances the aspect of shopping as a destination activity, and that's what farmers' market should be doing — making it a destination activity. I want to go to the market and shop for food and also have this social experience.

"Not only should the markets improve upon the quality of the produce, but they should also make the process of buying food a fun, social and entertaining experience. The malls call it 'shoppertainment,' combining shopping with an entertainment experience. A big trend in real-estate development is creating retail centers that have shoppertainment."

Wanted: Volunteer(s) to Take Over Open Air!

Open Air has been an all-volunteer, no-budget effort that Balkin took on as a labor of passion during a research leave from the university. Now that the leave is ended, he's finding it hard to find time to keep it updated and is looking for a replacement. Steve's contact e-mail is:

mar@openair.org. ✿

and it may not be the most important ingredient. "I would put traditional promotional activities like putting up a great roadside market sign or doing a great job with PR work with the local media ahead of setting up a website. Still, the internet is one more opportunity to reach out to the public and should be utilized if you have the resources.

"A market website takes time, of course, and a key factor is the administrative time in setting up the site and keeping it current," Herman says. "Hopefully your market will have a volunteer who can do a market website."

For another great example of a website that makes it easy for consumers to find farmers' markets, see the California Farmers' Market Websites at:

http://farmersmarket.ucdavis.edu.

[See also: Resources, Farmers' Market Websites]

E-Mail Power: Crescent City Farmers' Market

The website, www.loyno.edu/ccfm, of the Crescent City Farmers' Market in New Orleans averages about 1500 visits a month, a remarkable number, considering that when it first went up three years ago it got about 50 hits a month. Market director Richard McCarthy attributes the jump in website traffic to eMARKET, a weekly e-mail version of the market's newsletter.

"When we first set up our website, it was a typical nonprofit organization website with a nice logo and a few nice pictures, but very static and not a lot of information. When we started the bulk e-mails, our visibility on the internet grew remarkably." (A service called listbot.com, www.listbot.com, can help you set up an e-mail mass mailing).

"About 700 people get the weekly e-mail letter, so it's a highly efficient way to reach our customers on a weekly basis instead of mailing our monthly quarterly newsletter to 6,000 people.

"The market website also helps create a sense of community," McCarthy adds. In addition to events

Home page of the Dane County Farmers' Market, Madison, WI (www.wisc.edu/agjourn/dcfm/farmmarket/home.htm).

happening that week at the market, the website has a recipe and a question and answers section. One of the local cooperative extension agents posts a weekly gardening tip on the site.

The Crescent City market sponsors a yearly workshop to help vendors at the market set up their own websites, listing the products they bring to the market and a photograph of their farm.

"We haven't been able to tell exactly how many people come to the market from the website," McCarthy says, "but we do know that it includes a lot of tourists. Contact your tourist boards and let them know about your market website. Exchange links with local restaurants on your market website because people who are traveling often will look up restaurants in the city they are traveling to."

Market Fax is a food product report that the market sends out to area restaurants and farmers on a subscription basis. It is updated weekly to show current prices, availability, delivery options, and how to place orders directly with sellers. "We list how to reach the farmers and how much their products cost," McCarthy says. "It acts as a brokering service for information to bring producers and restaurants together."

Telling Our Stories: The Saturday Market

The Ditty's Saturday Market website:

www.saturdaymarket.com

devoted to the San Francisco Ferry Plaza Farmers' Market, is an independent project done by a fan of the Market, Deidra "Ditty" Deamer.

One area of the website features personal profiles of farmers who regularly sell at the market. The Profiles highlight the farmer's personal background, a description of their operations, types of produce and seasonal availability as well as some of Deamer's own observations. Deamer started the market website simply by interviewing six or seven farmers, asking about their backgrounds and how they got to the farmers' market. "I found that they had very interesting stories to tell," Deamer says, "so I started interviewing more and more farmers."

Deamer gets e-mails from appreciative website visitors from all over the country. "I originally set up the website so that all the e-mail to the farmers went to me, asking questions like, 'How can I buy 500 pounds of artichokes?'" Since a lot of farmers don't have e-mail, Deamer sends e-mails back to the people who are trying to reach the farmers, asking them to revisit the site and contact the farmers directly either by phone, fax or e-mail (if the farmer has an e-mail address).

"I've had a lot of feedback from the farmers that they've established ongoing contacts through e-mail inquiries. So that's been a great benefit for them. I also get a lot of inquiries from customers asking about the hours of the market and if it's open when it's raining, etc. The customers tell me that they love to read

Designing A Market Website

Vendors' page

Set up a Vendors' page to let people know who's coming to the market and the products they carry. List phone numbers, as well as e-mail addresses and webpage links for any vendors who have their own websites.

E-mail newsletter

Send out a weekly e-mail newsletter to your market patrons, with what's up and coming in food and events at the market as well as recipes for upcoming cooking demos.

Market discussion area

Create a market discussion area for customers on the website and find a market volunteer to maintain the site, answer questions and moderate the group. There are various places on the internet that will give you a discussion area for free (such as www.egroups.com), so you don't have to hire a consultant to set up one on your site. "Who sells the best tomatoes at the market? When is the best season to buy apples? Do you have crafts?"

For a good example of an interactive market website discussion area, visit the website for the West Side Market in Cleveland, Ohio:

www.westsidemarket.com.

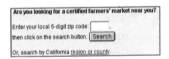

On the California Farmers' Market Websites page, consumers can search by zip code for a market closeby.

Links page

Create a Links page on your website with reciprocal links to complementary, related websites. Surf the internet and look for websites that have calendar listings or news about happenings in your area, such as nonprofit organizations, tourist boards or news media. County, city or other community calendar listings are especially helpful. Ask your city or state's official site to link to you. Suggest to state officials that all the markets in your state set up a single site.

Exchange links with local restaurants, hotels, historical societies and tourist attractions. E-mail them a letter asking to: "Please link us to your website."

Make sure your website is listed in the main search engines. (Check out your library or bookstore for a good internet marketing book.) Put your web address on all market literature, advertisements and press releases.

Make your website current and interactive

Encourage repeat visits to your website by keeping it current and interactive. In addition to all the What/When/Where basics in your market brochure, have parts of your website change from week to week, such as upcoming events at the market, new recipes, a kids' page, a vendor- or farmer-of-the-month, a Q & A section or e-mail discussion group for market patrons, and a weekly gardening tip.

— Check out also "Tips for Designing a Market Web Site" at Openair-Market Net, www.openair.org. ✿

about the farmers and that the website answers many of the questions that they would never dare ask the farmers, like how they got into farming and the history of their farms. They feel that the farmer is too busy to talk about these things during the busy market but they love reading about it on the web.

"The website is all about people with a common interest being able to communicate with each other," Deamer says.

FRIENDS OF THE MARKET

Friends of the Olympia Farmers' Market

In its 25 years of existence, the Olympia Farmers' Market has enjoyed a phenomenal success! In a town of 35,000 people, the market does more than $3 million in sales. The market operates from April through Christmas, nine months a year. According to Steve Wilcox, president of the Friends of the Olympia Farmers' Market (FOFM), the success of the market is due to several reasons: It is located in an affluent area whose "back-woodsy" environment has attracted a lot of environmentalists favorable to small-scale agriculture. These people are involved in the market both as landholders and producers/farmers' market vendors and as consumers who shop at the market for locally grown produce.

Another great strength of the market, Wilcox feels, is the self-governed, democratic manner in which the market is run. The member-elected board of directors is contracted by the city to manage the market. The membership of the organization is made up of 170 farmers' market vendors. The market itself has 80 stalls.

"We have a community here that embraces the idea of buying organic, locally grown produce," Wilcox says. "We also have people who want to grow the food, which includes many small families with children who want to get back to the land and raise their kids on a farm so they can learn farm-life values.

"The democratic structure of the market gives it a lot of flexibility in responding to changing customer demands as well as the needs of the vendors. The vendors feel they've had a voice in making the decisions that affect their participation and this makes them want to get behind the market and give it their support. They support the decisions even though they may not have agreed with them or voted for them in the first place."

About five years ago a partnership was formed between the City of Olympia, the Port of Olympia, and the market organization to build a permanent market facility. The city floated a bond to pay for the permanent structure and the port provided the land. The market pays a land lease to the port and makes annual contributions to the city to pay back the bond. The market does ongoing maintenance of the facility.

The membership is set up on a farmer-grown and crafter-made basis, with on-farm inspections and juried membership for admittance for crafters. The market admits up to 25% crafters. Farmers have to come locally, from a surrounding three-county area.

Given its considerable overhead, the market has very reasonable stall rental rates. Farmers and crafters pay 6% of gross sales, processors pay 8%, food trailers pay 9%, and contract fruit vendors pay 10%. "This ensures that only serious and successful vendors are at the market," Wilcox says.

The Friends of the Olympia Farmers' Market is set up as a nonprofit, tax-exempt organization with 501(c)(3) status. The organization has been granted tax-exempt status, Wilcox explains, because its stated purpose is to lessen the burden on local government. It provides facilities to the market, for example, that the city is not able to fund, such as brick walkways and benches.

According to the IRS, Wilcox explains, a tax-exempt organization like FOFM is not allowed to give directly to a "for profit" group such as the Olympia Farmers' Market. So that limits its activities to enhancing the market's facilities as well as public education about the market.

"The brick walkways have been a great way to both enhance the facility and raise funds for the market," Wilcox says. "In the last four years, 2,000 people have paid $30 for a brick with their name engraved on it." One of FOFM's current projects is building a commercial kitchen that vendors will be able to rent in order to prepare value-added products to sell at the market. If a grower has a lot of basil, for example, he or she can use the kitchen to make pesto.

Another project is to offer low-cost evening dinners which will be served at the market featuring market produce. "This adds another great reason for people to come to the market," Wilcox says. Other sources of funding for FOFM, besides the brick sales, are weekly raffles. The organization is also looking into applying for grants to fund educational activities. Some of FOFM's educational activities include putting out a quarterly newsletter, *The Market News,* and putting up a website for the market at:

www.farmers-market.org.

NETWORK OF FARMERS' MARKETS

American Farmland Trust and FRESHFARM Market in Washington, D.C., have taken the initial steps towards establishing a national Network of Farmers' Markets (NFM). The network's purpose is to educate the public on the economics of urban-edge farms and the role of these farms in countering urban sprawl and protecting open space.

In 2000 an estimated one million Americans shopped at their local farmers' market each week. At the same time the conversion of vulnerable farmland to housing subdivisions, roads and shopping malls continued at the rate of two million acres per year. Although it is clear that the American public values fresh food produced locally, this has yet to be translated into effective public policy to incorporate protection of farmland and open space into our planning processes. Most Americans remain poorly informed about the integral role family farms play in the local economy, preservation of open space, and protection of wildlife. Eighty to ninety percent of the

U.S. population is urban. For many Americans farmers' markets are the only place where they encounter agriculture. Thus, the many excellent farmers' markets throughout the country represent a unique venue for educating the public.

Initial participants in the NFM are: FRESHFARM Market, Washington, DC; Greenmarket, New York, NY; Dane County Farmers' Market, Madison, WI; Crescent City Farmers' Market, New Orleans, LA; Ferry Plaza Farmers' Market, San Francisco, CA; Santa Fe Area Farmers' Market, Santa Fe, NM; Santa Monica Farmers' Market, Santa Monica, CA; and University District Farmers' Market, Seattle, WA.

Education Programs Within the NFM

All network members' educational programs and materials have at their core an objective to reconnect people with the land. This underlying principle is the key ingredient in making a visit to a farmers' market more than just another way to shop.

Through educational programs developed by the NFM, patrons will understand that the act of shopping at the market has powerful implications for small farmers, the land, and the quality of life in their communities.

Market Brochures, Newsletters and Calendars

The most common materials are tri-fold or single-page brochures which provide market times and locations. Frequently, calendars are included to show when specific fruits or vegetables are in season, which encourages market patrons to keep the brochure. Some brochures provide background information on the farmers in the market, one even with a farmer group photo. Most network markets publish newsletters seasonally. One participant has decided to reach more customers through e-mail, especially after a poor mailer-insert response. A comparison of printed materials shows how extra effort and professionalism in layout, color, and design will increase their effectiveness significantly.

Special Events

Special events among network members tend to be food oriented; cooking demonstrations with guest chefs predominate. Other events include public farm tours hosted by the San Francisco and Santa Fe markets. These popular events are directly focused on raising public awareness surrounding farmland and open space issues. They are high profile and receive the attention of the media and elected officials.

Farmers can also be introduced to customers in a new way through these demonstrations. At the FRESHFARM Market in Washington, D.C., farmers give short talks about growing a particular fruit or vegetable, its season length, and useful tips on picking the best produce. Recipes are distributed which include facts about small farms, how to become a market volunteer, and related websites. Other markets have experimented with Meet the Producer style activities. Experience has shown that these are most effective when coupled with chef demonstrations.

Survey Tools

Most markets have used some sort of survey tool to determine the demographics and shopping habits of their customers. Some results are quite sophisticated, with extensive graphs and statistical analyses of respondents' answers. Not all information from member surveys can be put to use in developing an educational package which is applicable or adaptable to most markets. However, individual surveys do provide critical insight into the reason for farmers' market popularity. The Santa Fe survey pointed out several key reasons why people attend their markets:

✧ to purchase locally grown fresh produce and have a convenient location to find locally produced foods such as baked goods, honey, and processed foods;

✧ to support local farmers;

✧ to enjoy a sense of community; and

✧ to participate in a festive atmosphere.

It should be no surprise that farmers' markets provide a welcome relief from the pressure of professional life and they recall a time when life was less hectic and somehow more complete. Many successful markets cultivate this atmosphere and try to avoid creating a commercial environment. FRESHFARM Market in Washington, D.C., takes this approach. It permits only acoustic music by local musicians without amplification and farmers are encouraged not to play radios during the market. This has resulted in a welcoming atmosphere conducive to families. It also may result in patrons lingering longer at the market.

Policy Papers and Economic Studies

Two markets have policy papers specific to farming in their areas. The Crescent City Farmers' Market has two brochures, "Barriers to Growth: Problems Facing Small-Scale Agriculture in the Delta Region" and "1999 Report to the Community," as well as a detailed handbook, *From the Field to the Table: Suggested Food Handling for Open-Air Farmers' Markets & Fairs.*

The Ferry Plaza Farmers' Market in San Francisco wrote a "Public Market Strategic Plan & Feasibility Study," a planning document outlining the integrated market and education center proposed in conjunction with the San Francisco Public Market Collaborative. These in-depth resources are accessible to the general public in a variety of formats including seminars, brochures, and presentations at the market.

Children's Programs

As many network participants demonstrate, farmers' markets are an especially good venue for educating children. Yet children's education at farmers' markets remains a largely untapped opportunity, an arena that network members would like to develop more fully.

Market programs frequently have multiple benefits. One such example is the Santa Monica school salad bar program. Initially launched a few years ago to expand economic opportunities for farmers, it also has given teachers a way to present to students the issues of locally produced food, health and small business.

Market Volunteer Programs

Market volunteers play a crucial role in helping cash-strapped operations leverage limited budgets. For example, in the successful FRESHFARM Market volunteer program, volunteers staff the information booth, assist with set-up and break-down of the market, and help with special events. Volunteers are also one of the most important means of communicating with the public about the many benefits of farmers' markets. Santa Fe has successfully developed Friends of the Farmers' Market, an auxiliary organization that provides financial and volunteer support for the activities of the market, and more generally, encourages small-scale, sustainable, regional agriculture.

They are two of five market organizations — including Crescent City Farmers' Market, Greenmarket and Ferry Plaza Farmers' Market — that benefit from direct support or association with 501(c)(3) nonprofit, tax-exempt organizations.

THE FARMERS' MARKET FORUM: ISSUES FOR INTERNAL DISCUSSION

Market Integrity

We addressed integrity in the chapter on management, yet it bears repeating as an issue evoking considerable debate in the future. With farmers' markets becoming more attractive as marketing venues, other companies will want to take advantage of their success. Sponsoring boards will debate what range of products to include and whether national brands and franchisees should be allowed. The outcome may depend upon existing competition, alternative local outlets that might be approached first and the level of commitment to development of a localized food system.

Recently I watched a manager instruct a vendor on how her abuse of "no buying" rules undermines her credibility with other vendors. Trying to make some extra money on the side, she cast suspicion on her future actions. Market vendors serve rotating terms on a 10-person product review committee. With criteria totaling a possible 25 points, they approve with 15 points and the manager then has discretion on allowing approved sellers into the market based on space, competition, individuality and compatibility. A $25 fine may be imposed for minor infractions like late arrival, early departure, moving a vehicle into position before closing time, having a cart in the aisle during market hours, etc. Major infractions like buying product may lead to suspension of selling privileges.

More farmers should be actively promoting a guarantee for customer satisfaction with products where "if we sell it, we grow it — 100 percent." Valuing their participation in markets, vendors need to report suspected rule abuses to the manager, assist in inspections, support fines for infractions, and insist on adherence to the highest standards of integrity. Certain markets have already hurt themselves and tarnished the image of farmers' markets in general by having a loose or non-existent standard.

A push for reappraisal of state law, as in Maine and California, may be necessary in other states to clarify who can use the term and what producers should be allowed. We cannot take the consumer for granted; we have lost many would-be customers already. As produce consultant Mark Mulcahy says, "Perception is what determines consumer loyalty." Can we assure the consumer ours is not Mexican grown produce? Is the produce better at the supermarket or farmers' market?

By the same token, we may see markets defining themselves more frequently as "local" by having a 50-mile limit on producers. Others may use certain geographical boundaries, supporting producers within a watershed or "foodshed." As markets align with other organizations promoting a regional economy, these standards will evolve with individual variations.

Market Competition

As with individual farmers, managers are more aware of the need to improve when they have another farmers' market nearby. However, we usually have all kinds of competition close-by and those retailers will take our customers if we are not vigilant, creative and responsive to the local populace.

Good managers and good boards are people motivated to be the best, regardless of the competition. They look at other farmers' markets as friends, supporters and helpers in the overall drive to attract and hold customers as farmers' market loyalists. We share in common the goal of improving farmers' lives through educating local residents about the importance of supporting local agriculture. Without this active commitment — this partnership of those who believe in a regional food economy — our farms will continue to disappear as they have during the last century.

Strong markets do not hesitate to establish fees that reflect the real value that they provide producers. Jim O'Neill, manager of the Old Strathcona Farmers' Market in Edmonton, Alberta, explains the pricing of a corner space at $64 per day versus $53 for a regular aisle space, "People want the corners. They recognize the value of additional display space." With good oversight of additional income, the market can implement a promotion program to continue improving their market share vis-à-vis other competitors.

In 1997 the Portland Farmers' Market, OR, opened a new Wednesday market in the city's core to add to its Saturday market along the Willamette River. (Both relocated to two sites along the South Park blocks in 1998.) Despite objection, they decided to try a percentage stall fee to which they later added a minimum and a cap. They now clearly know that 2000 Wednesday sales increased 30% over 1999, whereas they can only estimate Saturday increases at 25% because of a fixed stall fee for their original market. The cap on the upper limit for farmer fees benefits larger growers and limits market income, yet the manager can track totals and individual incomes to be of help to farmers whose sales may fall off.

Market sales data will help markets retain good managers. A governing board has solid information on which to base personnel decisions. Portland manager Dianne Stefani-Ruff now receives a full-time salary plus an incentive bonus derived from gross sales and net market operations. Increasingly, markets are recognizing the high cost of manager turnover. A sign of sustainable farmers' markets is the evolution of salaries commensurate with a job well done. Markets that can't pay comparable wages need to provide learning opportunities, praise, recognition and a flexible work schedule if they are to keep good employees.

Welcome Farmer Competition

Many farmers are riding on the coattails of other vendors, failing to do their part in what has to be a collective effort at merchandising if they expect their marketplace to sustain itself. Seeing competition within a supermarket should give farmers reason to pause in their complaints. Encountered in a recent supermarket visit were three organic milks, five different soy milks and seven yogurts — all in six linear feet of refrigerated space.

When too many producers complain about the competition, it is a sign of their unwillingness to take a more pro-active role in creating their individual success. As an airport billboard advertiser proclaims: "Any fool can see where the competition is coming from. The trick is to outmaneuver it."

Strong markets recognize the critical role of substantial competition within many different product categories. One individual seller reminded this author how much she appreciated a new carrot grower — the fifth one — in pushing her to a higher standard of quality, value, merchandising, friendliness, customer service and the introduction of new product line. That response shows her sophistication in marketing and her positive view of her own product and selling ability. Unfortunately, many of us become lazy or unimaginative when we are too comfortable with our position.

We should welcome a competitor in the market who jolts us to realize we need to introduce new products. It's better to have a good competitor in our market reminding us what we need to do than to have him enticing our customers outside the market. We all know we are more complacent when we aren't staring a threat directly in the face.

Like it or not, small farmers should prepare for the continued entry of mid-sized and larger farms into farmers' markets, especially urban markets with substantial product movement. As the largest operators increase exports and sign more direct supermarket contracts, those in the middle are looking to replace sales lost to wholesale markets. They are part of America's farm heritage that needs protection by personal initiative.

Farmers' markets will satisfy the need of new farmers to enter the market realm, test new products and varieties, notice whether they are sufficiently people oriented and practice their customer relation skills.

There will be more pressure on management to be professional in dealing fairly with questions of access. Waiting lists will become more sophisticated including point systems focusing on prioritized crops and varieties, organic and specialty production, farm size, environmental impact, worker safety and other issues.

Across the United States several model programs are attempting to give farmers increased market access and higher price in the conventional marketing system. These will be used within farmers' markets as well. The Food Alliance (TFA), based in Portland, OR, has 44 farms approved with their 100-point rating system around reduced chemical dependence, protection of natural resources and care for workers. TFA-Approved farms selling in Portland-area farmers' markets help to fertilize the concept. In the process, markets may prioritize TFA farms in somewhat the same way many managers have encouraged and prioritized small and organic producers for years.

The competition, especially in good markets, will force farmers to clearly address how their products stand out from the rest. The question for individuals at farmers' markets is: If you were selling on your own, without any competition nearby, would people be attracted to stop at your stand?

Water features are an important feature at the Davis Farmers' Market. An $18,000 seating and performance stage surrounds the oak tree, directly before the marketplace pavilion. To the right of that multi-use, clerestory structure is a playground and park, with a $1 million youth center in the background. More is planned.

Premier Sites, Buildings & Sponsors

Every market does not need a structure, although sales rise to prove the benefit. Every market does deserve an attractive, consistent location which customers can depend on. Increasingly, boards of directors will focus energy on stabilizing their future by ensuring a permanent location. A market with good customer rapport over a lengthy period should qualify for consideration by the city, a foundation or service club to assist in this goal.

Quality of produce, displays and the overall character of markets will improve with the result that more farmers' markets will be asked to set up in premier locations. These sponsoring locations will seek higher standards to complement downtown Main Street programs, malls, parks and other retail experiences. Larger businesses will look to sponsor a farmers' market or elements within it, such as cooking demonstrations, entertainment and special events.

As they come to the fore, downtown business people will become better customers, their interest and involvement accelerated by market basket CSAs run by the market. Travel companies, hotels, leisure resorts and other businesses will seek face-to-face contacts with high-end customers through more tie-in promotions. Banks, restaurants, car sales outlets, hardware stores and other retailers will continue to be good partners in communities at all socio-economic levels.

Professional architects will more frequently incorporate design elements including issues of comfort, functionality and attractiveness, including public seating, heating, electricity, shade, public art, restrooms, telephones and color.

Where markets have existed for at least a decade, cities will seek to validate their importance by building or converting buildings for market use. Multi-use facilities with primary market use such as in Davis, CA, and re-use facilities such as Edmonton, Alberta's converted bus barn will become more prevalent.

These market buildings may be simple steel shed structures like the Cartwright Pavilion in Marshalltown, IA, or they may include a clerestory element allowing heat to escape the city parking lot in Pasco, WA. More architecturally complex is the pavilion element opening up the Davis structure. Based on a city bond, Olympia constructed a double row shed with a center pavilion and sliding, barn-like doors that allow airflow or close to keep the space warmer. Ithaca's open, clerestory, wood structure is T-shaped and, like Olympia, includes restrooms and an office. It was built largely through donations and vendors' sweat equity.

Ithaca also garnered state funds available through a farmers' market expansion program created by the legislature in the 1980s, inspired by Bob Lewis of the New York State Department of Agriculture and Markets. Similar programs should be developed in other states but each will need a leader and the active support and imagination of markets ready to create an environment more conducive to a lengthened season and a more secure future.

THE FARMERS' MARKET FORUM: ISSUES FOR PUBLIC DISCUSSION

Supporting the Local Farm Economy

Labeling programs are being recognized for their value in promoting a local region, as with the Puget Sound Fresh program (WA), a countywide program such as the Sonoma Select campaign (CA) or a statewide program such as Pick Tennessee. Farmers' markets can connect to these state or regional programs through mutual advertising and membership. Reinforce the local label at your market.

The Massachusetts Department of Food and Agriculture has done consumer focus groups and phone surveys, discovering that customers want to buy local but they don't know much about local agriculture. "Most people in the survey said if the quality was good and the price was fair they would buy local," says market bureau chief Susan Allan. "Most farmers could do a better job labeling their locally grown produce. Customers don't often know what's in season and they don't know whether or not produce in supermarkets is locally grown. A few counties are looking into the labeling of regional products, and our office offers the 'Massachusetts Grown and Fresher' logo, as well as signs and stickers and artwork for farmers to use in their advertisements or put on their trucks. A lot of farmers' markets, roadside stands and an increasing number of supermarkets use our logo."

"One of the advertising themes of our market is that if you spend your dollar locally you're supporting the local economy. Our market has participated with other local ag groups in the county to develop a farm map so people can buy direct from the grower on the days when the market isn't open. Part of our mission statement is to help the farmer make a living off the farm, and we think that if they're making a living from the farm, it will only help the market in the long run."
—Karen Durham, Mgr., Bellingham FM, WA

Diane Green of Sandpoint, ID, says that, "The strength of a farmers' market lies in promoting 'locally grown.'" In many communities the increasing diversity of farmers and farm products is making the local marketplace reflect how interconnected the peoples of the world really have become. With incredible variety of ethnic foods and faces, the global village has become local.

New immigrants are frequently providing the new generation of active farmers reinvigorating markets, whether at Pike Place or in New Orleans or various California markets. Often they are at a disadvantage, linguistically and otherwise, selling through wholesale channels, so farmers' markets offer a wonderful chance to make cash and learn English quickly. They help spread the word through their informal networks to increase the participation of more minority customers as well.

It is a great, missed opportunity that many markets have not built close associations with local agricultural organizations. As managers become more professional and have more time, farmers' markets will seek periodic visits from 4-H programs, petting zoos, pony rides, Master Gardeners, Master Food Preservers, Master Composters and those able to educate about agriculture in general. Managers need to engage organizations in conversation, suggesting programs in which they are interested, looking for sponsorship of special ag awareness days, and asking how they are most interested in connecting to market customers.

Farm Loss

"For one final moment in our evolution as a nation we still have a community memory of the family farm. Many still carry the personal baggage from our rural past, a history of family members who sustained the land, and the legacy of a community that worked the earth for generations. But this is the final generation holding an affinity with the American family farm. This is the generation that will control the destiny not only of my Sun Crest peaches but also of my way of life."
—David Mas Masumoto, *Epitaph for a Peach*

Among the many reasons for farm loss in this century are the industrialization of agriculture, processor and middlemen control, competition from imports, government policies and population changes.

In 1900, for every $1 spent on food in the United States, 20 cents went for marketing and 15 cents went to input costs such as land, equipment and fertilizer. The farmer received 65 cents of every dollar.

By 1990, marketing had tripled to 60 cents and inputs had increased by two-thirds to 25 cents. The farmer was left with just one-fifth what he had ninety years earlier, 15 cents on the dollar.

"Nothing in the last century has been more lethal to the American farmer than the accepted practice of processing and selling food. No other industry in America — not financial services, not used-car sales, not investment banking — has had such a sustained record of price gouging and outright theft, without regulation, without accountability or honesty to the farmers who make it all possible."
—Victor Davis Hanson, *Fields Without Dreams*

Much of the agricultural establishment and press has emphasized the need for producers to cut costs, but no matter how much they do, as other farmers do the same, they will be pinched even further. Like the corporate food barons, farmers need to vertically integrate; they do so as they take back control over marketing their products. They can't survive getting 15 cents of each dollar. They need to take that other 60 cents now eaten up by processors and marketers.

"Educating customers about produce comes naturally at the farmers' markets with the everyday banter with customers. We discuss just about everything with our customers. If someone says my prices are too high, I explain that the price of food is too cheap. A lot of farmers are going out of business because food is too cheap. The USDA for years has had a cheap food policy, 'Get big or get out.' We explain about the centralization of the food industry, and how produce is used by supermarkets as a loss-leader to battle each other for customers. Food is also cheap because it's grown by low-paid workers in Mexico and Chile with pesticides, or with federally subsidized water in California where they couldn't grow it otherwise. We also talk about buying local food and what it means for the local economy."

—Tom Roberts, Pittsfield, ME

U.S. Secretary of Agriculture Dan Glickman acknowledged in 1998: "I'm not afraid of running out of wheat or corn. I'm afraid of running out of farmers." The USDA considers farmers' markets and organic agriculture to be important economic vehicles for keeping folks on the farm. With six hundred family farmers going out of business each week, these alternatives need to be consistently re-thought. We need constant improvement to increase sustainability.

Between 1920 and 1992, African-American farmers collapsed from 14 percent to just one percent of American farmers. In 2000 the USDA admitted its complicity in that decline as it settled a class action lawsuit forgiving all loans to African-American farmers and providing each $50,000. Yet this was too little, too late for many who were denied USDA loans or given less than requested and thus had to depend on higher bank-rate loans. Many Japanese-Americans suffered a quicker demise, losing farms as they were placed in internment camps during World War II. These two groups are among the many minorities who have suffered various forms of institutionalized racism and prejudice. Hopefully, each can help create and find their place within a sustainable farm economy through involvement in farmers' markets. With customer feedback, immediate cash, receptivity to unusual crops and acceptance of cosmetically imperfect produce, farmers' markets represent one of the best options for an inclusive future.

America has shifted from being 75% rural to being 80% urban. That urbanization has concentrated retail power as independent grocers have been consumed by larger and larger entities, leaving people with farther to travel. The impact of the automobile cannot be denied; as people travel farther to go to big box stores for cheaper food, farmers' markets must compete on a different basis — quality and service.

As the 2000 U.S. census revealed, shifts among our 281 million population continue to impact the South and the West, making farmland loss a big story. Development threatens valuable farms along almost the entire West Coast, from Canada to Mexico. It is much the same in the South as people flood to the coasts. The Northeast long ago faced the pressure of overpopulation and struggles to maintain farms close to its cities. Once surrounded by rich farmland, Philadelphia new receives 70% of its food from out of state. Distant farms can easily compete since real transportation costs are subsidized. Thus, farmers' markets become essential in providing higher returns to cover the costs of farming close to cities.

"People should be educated to see the choice: support local farms and keep a balanced landscape or the land will sprout houses instead."

—Dean Bruschi, Martin County, FL

The farmers' market "movement," so-called given the dedication and enthusiasm of its foremost activists, has succeeded in slowing, and in certain areas reversing, the decline in the number of farms and of local, small and micro enterprises. We have provided an entry point into the world of commerce for many new businesses, including those owned by youth, minorities, immigrants and second-attempt farmers.

As various pressures force farmers and others out of business, many will re-tool their minds and re-invest in agriculture and other food enterprises with an entirely new focus. Unnoticed by statisticians, one business dies and a stronger one emerges — a process increasingly seen in farmers' markets.

Food Selection

Food business start-ups include the predictable to the novel — Grandma's molasses cookies to vegetarian sushi rolls. More delicacies are appearing as food connoisseurs recognize the opportunity to start micro-enterprises around their favorite old recipes or newest creations. Dessert cakes, cookies, fruit chutneys, teriyaki sauce, pad thai, pickled products, fudge, cheesecake, bagels, pestos, smoothies and salsas.

Natural light highlights honey and vinegar as a wedding party leaves the church in Barcelona's Plaça del Pi (Plaza of the Pines). This same farmer won the 1989 prize for the best goat cheese in Spain. He is one of a dozen professionals-turned-specialty-foods-producers who created this market where they sell the first Friday and Saturday of each month from 9 a.m. to 9 p.m.

In warmer climates entrepreneurs will consider opening juice bars. More hot and prepared food businesses will open within markets and nearby to take advantage of market pedestrian traffic. Markets will have "food courts" much as the Old Oakland Farmers' Market, CA, as businesses offer tastes of the familiar and the boutique to ethnically diverse consumers. Our food experiences and tastes will expand.

We will see an expanded array of products within farmers' markets. The challenge is to introduce new tastes to people. Tastings will continue to surge in popularity with new and old varieties of peaches, tomatoes and melons competing for customers' loyalty. The most progressive markets will attempt to lure people across ethnic lines by combining the familiar with the bold. Along with a fall tomato tasting where one can compare fresh tomatoes and tomato soup, they will offer bittermelon soup and bittermelon leaves braised in oil. These advances will be triggered in part by chefs who are constantly experimenting with cross-cultural innovations.

As a greater number of local, non-farm businesses take part, personal and political connections abound. The support and dependence of urban, non-farm businesses on farmers' markets heightens city interest in downtown markets. As a local market economy builds, a physical structure to house the farmers' market for an extended season becomes more realistic.

Certified Organic

With 275,000 people protesting the initial inclusion of irradiation, biotechnology and sewer-sludge fertilizer as acceptable for organic foods, the USDA reversed itself and banned all three methods under new organic standards enacted in February, 2001.

After an 18-month phase-in, completed in the summer of 2002, USDA is implementing the first standards ever imposed for the labeling and processing of organic foods, dividing products into four categories for labeling purposes:

⟡ "100% organic" — products must contain only organic ingredients,

⟡ "organic" — products must contain at least 95% organic ingredients,

⟡ "made with organic ingredients" — products with at least 70% organic contents, up to three of which may be listed on the package front, and

⟡ products with less than 70% organic — may list organic ingredients on the information panel but not mention organic on the front.

Domestic sales of organic products increased by 20% annually during the 1990s, topping $6 billion. Foreign sales should see substantial growth since there is now one USDA standard rather than those of 44 different state and private certifying agencies. Managers and producers may want to check with their state certifying agency to see if more stringent state standards have been approved by USDA.

The Organic Farming Research Foundation's 1997 national survey of 5,024 certified organic farmers found that 30% (360 of 1192 respondents) used farmers' markets to market 33% of their production, or 3,684 of their 11,183 acres. Compared to their 1993 study, there was an 86% increase in the total number of certified organic farmers and an 80% increase in those selling in farmers' markets in just four years.

By 2000 there were 6,600 certified organic farms, yet OFRF director Bob Scowcroft estimates an additional 15,000 farmers have organic production that is not certified. That changes with the new law. "Every grower using the 'O' word will need to follow all the requirements of the law, including a farm plan and recordkeeping," says Scowcroft.

Many small producers mistakenly believe they are exempt from the organic standards if they sell under $5,000 per year; not true. They are only exempt from the requirement to be certified by an accredited certifying agency and from submitting an organic systems plan.

Until now organic farmers selling at farmers' markets have been less likely to be certified because face-to-face customer contact allows them to explain their production practices. Within the conventional marketing system, by comparison, certification has been almost a necessity.

Managers need to ask organic farmers about their certification plans. After the law's full implementation in summer of 2002, if a producer claims "organic," he/she must be certified unless they meet the $5,000 exemption. Any organic processed products must be made using raw products from a certified source.

"Many farmers have spent years and thousands and thousands of dollars," said Scowcroft, "and it's not fair that someone else can scratch the word 'organic' on a piece of cardboard" and benefit from credibility and higher price.

At the turn of the century it is estimated that four to eight thousand organic farmers sell in farmers' markets nationwide, encompassing ten thousand acres of production or more. The organic presence will continue to grow, although some farms may continue to eschew certification and thus forfeit their right to use the "O" word.

The farmers' market industry needs to work closely with the organic industry to reinforce the organic standards for individual producers. This includes adding to their market rules to ensure that claims made to managers and consumers are valid. Not just "organic," but terms like "no spray" and "pesticide-free" as well as various eco-labeling terms need to be defined and have an enforcement protocol. When someone violates the rules, they lose their selling privilege. Either that or the market loses customer trust.

A similar high standard should be developed for any market presenting itself to the public as an "organic farmers' market." The People's All Organic Farmers' Market in Portland, OR, requires all sellers to be organic; other markets hopefully will meet that threshold in the future.

One other arena with tremendous organic promise is the Farm to School program (described in the previous chapter). Crops sold to school salad bars as well as hot food programs have great potential given that one organic trend has been the youth market and mothers looking for organic baby food. The Berkeley Unified School District, CA, already has specified that it wants organic crops. It appears that a new generation of parents with heightened food consciousness will influence school buying decisions.

Genetic Engineering and Corporate Control

With most of the producers in farmers' markets being organic and/or small farmers, there is considerable concern about large farmers. Thus, it is understandable that there would be real apprehension about the danger to our communities of a corporate agriculture that concentrates too much power in too few hands. This feeling prevails among rural and urban, rich and poor, Republican and Democrat, old and young, farmers and consumers.

Farmers have felt threatened on the commodity markets and even in specialty markets. Twenty years ago an olive farmer related that Prudential Insurance had planted 3,000 acres of olive trees in California's San Joaquin Valley. When Prudential sold their crop to the local processor for less than the harvesting cost alone, the impact on 50 small producers was devastating. The impact on the almond industry was similar years earlier when Mobil, Exxon, Superior Oil and others planted tens of thousands of acres of almonds in Kern County, California. Farmers' markets became at least that one olive farm's salvation.

Food and Agriculture Day. At the Food and Agriculture Day in Seattle on December 2, 1999, farmers from more than 30 countries participated in a church breakfast followed by panel discussions, press briefings, workshops and a noon rally at the Pike Place Market. The topics included genetic engineering, food security in a globalized economy, and food safety. As farmer liaison Mark Musick said, "The market is a magnet for pulling people together so it was logical that people gathered here."

Food and Ag Day finally brought the voices of small farmers and their supporters into the decades-old discussions about the world's food supply. Size, national rights and sustainability were at the core.

"In 1998 in Canada, farm income was $29 billion . Cargill's revenues that same year were $75 billion …We are the model the world is supposed to follow…and we're dying of it…It is not the levelness of the playing field, but the size of the player. If the rules are in favor of the big players and the field is level, they will roll over us."
—Nettie Wiebe, Canadian National Farmers Union

Doreen Stabinsky, of the Council of Responsible Genetics, contrasted the general European approach to genetically engineered foods using the precautionary principle with the U.S. approach of regulating only where sound science indicates proof of actual harm. "As a scientist, I resent this misappropriation of the word 'science.'" She reinforced the right of nations to determine their own environmental protection standards without fearing World Trade Organization (WTO) sanctions.

Farhad Mahzar, representing a farmer organization in Bangladesh, claimed, "We use only one calorie of energy to produce three calories of food. [Industrial farming] destroys 10 calories to produce one, and they want their system to take over… Agriculture is not a sector of industrial production. It is a way of life."

Farmers and consumers realize that farming as a way of life is threatened with extinction in many places. If free trade is a "rising tide that lifts all boats," one may ask why real wages are falling and 475 billionaires control assets equal to the annual income of 3,000,000,000 people, according to Jerry Mander of the International Forum on Globalization. While the level of corporate control is nearly absolute in many industries, everyone has an interest in assuring a safe and secure food supply based on a diversified delivery system. Farmers' markets are part of the solution in keeping tens of thousands of farmers on the land and connected to consumers.

Genetically engineered crops. Genetic engineering involves a set of very powerful tools that can change any life form on earth. Genetic traits that affect such factors as yield, hormone production, and cold or pesticide resistance can be moved across kingdoms — from plants to animals, humans to plants, animals to bacteria. In Edinburgh scientists have inserted a fluorescent jellyfish gene into a potato so that it glows green when it needs water. Unfortunately, genes used to modify crops can jump the species barrier and cause bacteria to mutate. A German researcher found that the gene used to confer Roundup resistance was found in the genome of yeast and bacteria in the guts of bees.

Scientific and public skepticism about the unknown risks of gene splicing has led companies like Frito-Lay, Gerber, Heinz and Nestle to go GE-free with some or all of their products. About nine of every ten North Americans want GE foods to be labeled, but it is currently optional. A strong majority see GE foods as a safety issue; they do not break down in the gut as previously thought. Genetic drift, now known to be up to 12 km. (7 miles), threatens virtually all organic producers since the definition of organic excludes any genetically modified organism.

Because farmers' market customers are significantly supportive of organic farmers, Mark Musick of Pike Place Market says, "A GE-free market is a real possibility. Who can you trust? Your local farmer. This [the corporate push toward genetic engineering] will be a shot in the arm for the organic industry."

In North America people are less connected than other world citizens to the politics of food, because we are separated from the producers of our food. We depend on government food regulators to guard over our food supply. Yet, in 2000 it was a coalition, Genetically Engineered Food Alert, which tested foods and discovered StarLink, a corn variety intended for animal feed, in taco shells intended for human consumption. The Taco Bell crisis sounded a consumer alert leading to a recall which may exceed one billion dollars in corporate losses.

This is only the tip of the iceberg when we look at the unknowns of inserting genes across species. Research is forging ahead with government approval, without heed for the precautionary principle in protecting human health and the environment.

Boulder Co. FM, Boulder, CO

Through farmers' markets the public learns about the impact of corporate policy on national and multi-national bodies. Farmers can present anecdotal evidence of depressed prices resulting from the North American Free Trade Agreement and the General Agreement on Tariffs and Trade. Nonprofit organizations can provide educational materials and presentations to spark increased debate and informed action.

Some leading farmers' markets have concentrated on having a majority of organic farmers. As the debate over genetically engineered foods heats up, markets are likely to declare themselves GE-free. They will be seen more prominently as the place to get straight answers from farmers about genetically engineered crops and demand they be labeled or prohibited outright.

Terminator and Traitor. Seeing the potential loss of seed as a right is one more reason for farmers and consumers to come together. Farmers need to maintain small seed companies and resist the temptation to purchase seed with Terminator and Traitor technology. Both are on a fast track to commercialization

according to a 2000 report by the Rural Advancement Foundation International (RAFI).

Terminator technology, the genetic engineering of plants to produce sterile seeds, is universally considered the most morally offensive application of agricultural biotechnology, since over 1.4 billion people depend on farm-saved seeds. Traitor technology, also known as genetic use restriction technology (GURTs), refers to the use of an external chemical to switch on or off a plant's genetic traits. According to RAFI, the goal of genetic trait control is industry-wide and the multinational agrochemical firms dominating biotechnology hold more than 30 patents.

Corporate commitments to disavow Terminator seem meaningless given the speed of corporate takeovers. Monsanto and AstraZeneca both pledged in 1999 not to commercialize suicide seeds, causing governments and organizations to think the crisis had passed. Yet by year's end, Monsanto had announced a merger with Pharmacia & Upjohn to create the new company Pharmacia with $17 billion annual sales, while AstraZeneca and Novartis had announced a spin-off of their agrochemical and seed divisions to create the world's largest agribusiness corporation, Syngenta.

"We've continued right on with work on the Technology Protection System [Terminator]. We never really slowed down. We're on target, moving ahead to commercialize it. We never really backed off."
—Harry Collins, Delta & Pine Land Seed Co., January, 2000

The Director General of the United Nations Food and Agriculture Organization (FAO) Jacques Diouf has declared his opposition to Terminator technology, defending the right of one-quarter of the world's population to save their seed for survival. It seems unbelievable that farmers could be forced to pay for seeds to which they have had free access for millenia.

The future of Terminator/Traitor technology rests with national governments and multinational corporations. Already the governments of Panama, India,

Ghana, and Uganda are working to oppose Terminator technology. Despite protests, the USDA defends its anti-farmer patent and research on suicide seeds. Massive political pressure on national governments and at key international fora will influence the debate just as boycotts will pressure elusive corporate decision-makers. (For a more thorough perspective, check "Suicide Seeds on the Fast Track" at www.rafi.org.)

Water. There is another dangerous trend toward privatization of water resources, which will result in a bidding war among the large corporations and ultimately affect small farmers. Trade rules may precipitate a global water crisis. "Wars of the next century will be about water," said Maude Barlow of the Council of Canadians and author of *Blue Gold: The Global Water Crisis and the Commodification of the World's Water Supply.* Access to drinking water will be determined by wealth.

Indian physicist and food activist Vandana Shiva agrees, seeing the contest as one of drinking water for the poor versus swimming pools for the rich. People don't understand how a natural resource like water, anymore than seed, can be owned. This is why Shiva, author of *Biopiracy* and *Stolen Harvest,* is leading a "five freedoms movement" to declare freedom for water, seed, food, earth and the village forests and pastures. She believes that if these freedoms can be protected — largely by women — we will limit "free trade."

In California people have long realized water's critical role. A century ago the federal government decided to subsidize water to encourage small, resident farms up to 160 acres. Unfortunately, larger corporations have controlled the political process, the water continues to be subsidized without regard for the acreage limits and the federal goal of helping small farmers has never been realized. It is generally small farmers without subsidized water who need and are selling at farmers' markets to get a higher price for their crops, while subsidized operations ship around the world competing with other more local farms.

NEW RELATIONSHIPS WITH HOPE

With articulate care farmers sample products, intermix flowers with vegetables, write 3x5 cards with recipes, laminate a Johnny's Seeds catalog description, remove yellow leaves, and protect the tendrils on mini-pumpkins. A curious question is met with an offer of an entire crisp Asian pear or a stem of mizuna; suddenly the customer feels befriended as an individual.

In displaying product and personality, farmers show themselves to be the characters they are. Through farming alone and then interacting with farmers' market shoppers, each farmer serves as an exemplar for responsible citizenship.

"If just 10 percent of our population lived on farms, did not move, never divorced, did not change jobs, and set the parameters of their day by dawn and dusk, the current madness could be stopped. Yet we lack that prerequisite reservoir of agrarians who might still arrest the itinerary of our present culture, of growing shiftlessness, criminality, and material banality."
—Victor Davis Hanson, *Fields Without Dreams*

Farms give our culture stability. Farmers' markets give farmers hope by providing an environment for meaningful experiences. In selling their crops, farmers notice customers' lives fulfilled, oddly enough, by some sense of connection to all their labor. Just as in every other marketing channel, they need to build relationships, this time with many individual buyers. The person who does this will survive, because relationships mean you are listening and responding to the other. No one is guaranteed or owed a future because of the past. Each day presents an opportunity to build trust through communication and a focus on value.

If we listen, communicate and develop relationships, we will travel to new places never imagined. An olive crop freezes and the grower starts making an olive oil soap with organic mint leaves. A farmer is trimming apricot and fig trees and the prunings go to Berkeley restaurant Chez Panisse for flavorful grilling.

Farmers should be doing periodic demonstrations at farmers' markets and constantly improving their presentations. Inviting customers for a farm tour each year — spring or fall — will spark a newfound loyalty and level of interest in their farms.

When you know your customers, you are more likely to treat your produce with greater respect. Show the best face of the food, stack less high, fill displays more often, avoid packing pint baskets too tight, leave it easier for customers to pick out their choice, and ask, "Does it hurt the food?"

Past and Present: Relationships in Community

"The Hellenic *polis* [city] and all which that institution implies — art, literature, notions of constitutional government, free speech, private property, direct vote of the citizenry, separation between political and religious authority, the right to bear arms, and the chauvinism of a middle class — *followed* from, did not precede, a vibrant agrarianism. Athenian democracy was a logical refinement of a prior two centuries of agrarian egalitarianism…(Aristotle) knew that the rural yeoman had created and maintained egalitarian government: 'When the farmer class and the class having moderate means are in control of the government, they govern according to laws… they have a livelihood, and they are not able to be at leisure, so that they put laws in control of the state and hold only the minimum of assemblies necessary.'"
—Victor Davis Hanson, *Fields Without Dreams*

Vance Corum

Oxnard farmer Jim Tamai, here with his granddaughter, still grows strawberries after more than 20 years in the market. His son has led the farm diversification into numerous vegetables. A daughter has started a bakery and sells her products in Los Angeles basin markets. Another daughter lives more than 300 miles northward most of the year to sell their produce at Bay area markets.

For thousands of years markets have existed as caravans met on various trade routes. Cities sprang from these fountainheads as commerce and culture inextricably intertwined and evolved. Even as goods were exchanged, ideas were carried from one people to another. Democracy flourished with the healthy exchanges of an economy based on agrarian values. The two have been intertwined in the history of our national development as well. It may be that our democracy has suffered in direct correlation with our shift from an agrarian to a corporate culture. It can be revived.

Today we still recognize the open dissemination of thought inherent in the exchanges among people from various backgrounds: rural and urban, local and tourist, established and immigrant. Food is an essential connector. It is a vibrant vehicle for sharing and celebration, holding within it the power to shatter barriers and build relationships.

Just as bards and troubadours passed through the markets of yore, we need to stay receptive to the unexpected — the artist or juggler drifting through town, the Andean band or the mime troupe performing at the local junior college the evening before market day. Music and other art forms give a sense of community; they are integral to bringing people closer together. Cultural activities are drawn to good markets, and good markets are a barometer of local culture.

Markets also reflect the temperature of the local economy. As farmers go out of business, we recognize the heat of corporate control and shrinking competition. With each farm loss we further risk the very structure of our local economics and, ultimately, our localized culture.

More communities will use farmers' markets as a tool to maintain or revive their local economy. New farmers' markets will express the goals of a new generation of young visionaries, market founders and farmers alike, who want personal, local relationships rather than an impersonal, world marketplace. Without becoming political in a larger global sense, people feel good about the politics of local food — taking a stand for maintaining small businesses in their own hometown. On that basis they increasingly will feel it appropriate to use the farmers' market as a vehicle for a public discussion about the issues of the day — how to determine water use policy, where to locate a new city hall, what to do about the homeless and underemployed, and how to creatively support the farms that beautify our local landscape.

Aspiring to be the community center will become a broad goal, not something achievable only by mar-

Vance Corum

A local theatre troupe promoted its Shakespeare play with one act at the Ithaca Farmers' Market, even as the building project was ongoing.

kets in Madison, Davis or New York City. It is within the reach of virtually every market than plans and works toward that goal. Farmers' markets will be a focal point for public debate and community action, where people easily socialize with neighbors and new friends, building connections through our common love for food.

Farmers' markets are sustained through numerous positive relationships. While egos cause separation, farmers' markets have the transformative potential of connecting people. If we collectively envision our highest goals for true community and economic sustainability, our farmers' markets will become the centerpiece of community activity and pride even as they sustain the farms that form the true basis of a democratic society. ✿

APPENDIX I

How Much Insurance Do You Need?

— Reprinted with permission, *Growing for Market,* Nov. 1999

One of the business matters that farmers must think about, like it or not, is insurance. There's not much enjoyment to be had in visualizing the possible disasters that could befall the farm, and nobody gets excited about spending money on insurance, but few would deny that insurance is a necessary evil for direct-market farms.

Working your way through the insurance maze is not easy. You need insurance, but what kind? How much? And how much should it cost?

There's no simple answer that will work for every farm, because every farm is different in the amount of risk it faces and the amount of assets it has to protect. But it helps to know what's available before deciding whether you've got the right insurance, and enough of it. If your business has grown or your marketing has changed since you bought your insurance, now might be a good time to reconsider whether your insurance has you covered.

There are four types of insurance that farmers need to think about (besides the personal insurance issues of health, disability and life insurance): farm liability, product liability, employee coverage, and vehicle insurance. Your best resource for figuring all this out is your insurance agent. Although he or she is in the business of selling insurance, if you've got a good one, you can trust the advice you'll receive.

The most important thing to know about talking to an insurance agent is that you have to be completely honest about every aspect of your business and make the agent understand exactly what it is you do. Neil Hamilton, director of the Agricultural Law Center at Drake University and author of *The Legal Guide for Direct Farm Marketing,* advises growers not to understate any aspect of their operations in the hope of saving money on the premium.

"If you don't disclose the full nature of your business, there is a greater likelihood that the insurance you buy will be inadequate," Hamilton says. "Then, if something happens and you ask the insurer to cover you (which is why you bought insurance in the first place), you may find out your policy does not cover the situation. Then you are in the worst possible situation: you have paid good money for an insurance policy that was not what you needed and now you have a problem for which you are uninsured."

Before you go to see an agent and explain your business, though, it helps to know some of the basics about direct marketing risks and policies.

How serious a risk?

Some farmers don't buy insurance because they don't expect to get sued. Their operations may be small, they may not have people out to the farm, or they may feel they know their customers and don't worry about them suing. That's the optimistic view, and there are two things you need to know before you decide to adopt it.

The most important thing to consider is that someone who is injured on your farm or by your products may be forced to sue you by his or her own insurance company. They may like you, even love you, but they have signed an insurance contract that allows their company to seek repayment from you if they get injured on your farm. This is known as "subrogation." Neil Hamilton describes how it works in *The Legal Guide for Direct Farm Marketers.*

Consider a situation like the one discussed in Chapter Nine, where a CSA member was injured on the farm. If Jimmy breaks his leg on the CSA, his family will go to their insurer who will pay the medical expenses based on the insurance contract for first-person coverage. But the insurer will also ask, "How did Jimmy break his leg and where did it happen?" Under the "subrogation" clause in the policy, the company has a right to seek recovery from someone else if they are responsible for what happened to Jimmy. If the company believes such recovery is possible, they could sue the owner of the CSA to recover from the owner's insurance (or sue the owner personally if there is no insurance). Under the subrogation clause the company can ask their insured to be a "use plaintiff," so the suit will be in the insured's name. Insurance companies usually don't bring suits in their own names because it might prejudice the jury. The insured is obligated to cooperate with the subrogation and to help with the case, such as by testifying. If the insured party refuses to sign or cooperate, because the third party being sued is a friend, the company can refuse to pay the coverage or seek repayment from the insured. For this reason you cannot assume that friends won't sue you if something goes wrong. In most cases they will not be making this decision; the insurance company will, and the insurance company is not interested in friendships.

That's probably enough to scare you into calling an insurance agent; but if you're a gambler, you might also want to know the frequency of lawsuits against direct marketers. Charlie Touchette, director of the North American Farmers Direct Marketing Association, studied direct marketing insurance for several years while creating a policy specifically for direct marketers (more on that later), and he says there's just no industry data on direct marketing claims.

Touchette has also managed the liability insurance coverage for the farmers' markets in Massachusetts, and in 12 years, with 50 to 70 markets covered each year, there have been only three successful claims. All three involved wind-related accidents — signs or canopies blowing over and hitting customers; all three customers went to the hospital; and the claims were settled for $12,000, $26,000 and $32,000.

In other words, the statistical risk of an accident is probably small, but accidents do happen and farmers and markets do get sued. Touchette says that for about a $300 annual premium, farmers don't have to worry about accidents or about defending themselves against a lawsuit, but he adds that it's a personal decision. "Sometimes it's just for peace of mind; it's hard to want to spend $300, but what kind of productive energy is lost worrying about it if you don't have it?" he asked.

Farm liability policy

If you've decided you had better have insurance, the first policy to consider is your liability policy. Many growers, when they first sell produce, assume that their homeowner's insurance will cover them both on the farm and at a farmers' market. That may or may not be true. Your homeowner's policy will cover an accident on the farm to a guest or visitor, but once that guest is paying you for your products, the relationship changes. For example, if you let a friend pick a bouquet on your farm, injuries would be covered by your homeowner's policy. If you charge that friend $20 to pick flowers, it might not be covered. Some companies won't quibble about small commercial transactions, but if you're making more than a few hundred dollars in farm sales, you'd better check to find out whether that business is covered. In some cases, you can just add excess liability coverage, called an umbrella policy, for your business activities. If you're currently buying only a homeowner's policy, read it carefully for mention of commercial activity, particularly the exclusions, and have a talk with your agent.

Once you start farming in earnest, you need a farm liability policy, which will cover all activities related to farming in addition to the usual liabilities of owning property. Whether your direct marketing activities are included in the company's definition of farming activities will vary, particularly if you're buying from a company that does most of its business with traditional farmers. Again, read the exclusions to find out if roadside markets, off-farm farmers' markets and pick-your-own operations are covered. Generally, PYOs will require additional coverage because the exposure, or potential for someone to be injured, is greater when there are more people visiting the farm.

Farm liability policies may contain two types of coverage: personal liability and medical payments to others. At the *Growing for Market* editor's farm, for example, our insurance company would pay up to $1,000 to any person who was injured on our farm if we had not been negligent. If the injured person decided to sue us, alleging negligence, we would be covered up to $500,000 and the insurance company would handle the defense.

How much coverage?

This brings up the point of how much coverage you need to purchase. The old insurance maxim is "Cover your assets." In theory, if someone was injured seriously because of your negligence (in the eyes of the court), the damage award could take everything you own and even attach your future earnings. In the Northeast and on the West Coast, where the price of real estate is high, and on farms with a lot of buildings and equipment, many direct marketers insure for $1 million. Farmers of more modest means might decide to go with $100,000 or $300,000 coverage.

The cost difference between $300,000 coverage and $500,000 coverage is relatively small — $25 a year on the premium, in our case. It would cost more to increase the medical payment for non-negligence accidents from $1,000 to $5,000 than it would to increase liability coverage to $500,000 because the risk of a small injury is greater than the risk of a big, lawsuit-producing one.

My insurance agent tells me it's unlikely that a court would force a farmer to sell the farm, but cash assets would be an easy target for the opposing attorney. And there have been cases in which defendants' homes, while not taken away from them, have been put in a trust that reverts to the injured person upon the death of the owner.

Products liability

Your general farm liability policy may or may not cover an incident in which your farm products made someone sick. Check to find out. If you're selling fresh produce only, you're probably covered. If you're doing any value-added products, you may need to purchase separate products liability coverage.

Some stores won't buy from you unless you have a products liability policy. Some insurance companies won't even insure for farm-made products like jams, salad dressings, baked goods and so forth, so you may need to shop around to find coverage. The company that provides our farmers' cooperative's products liability coverage (as well as our personal farm policy) is called Goodville Mutual Casualty Company. It's based in New Holland, Pennsylvania, and covers a lot of direct market farmers. You can call the company at 800-448-4622 to find an agent near you who sells their policies.

Farmers direct policy

If it's one-stop insurance shopping you're looking for, you might want to call the North American Farmers Direct Marketing Association for information about their new coverage written specifically for direct market farmers. It provides general liability of $1 million per occurrence or $2 million total per year. It covers all bodily injury and property damage claims resulting from direct marketing activities, on farm and off-farm, including farm stand and farmers' markets, hay rides, petting zoos, PYO, school tours, mazes, bakery, restaurants and festivals. It also covers losses up to $1,000 during a robbery, on or off your premises.

The cost is $3 per $1,000 gross receipts, or $300 minimum. Also, you must be a member of NAFDMA, which costs $75 a year and has other membership benefits. Call 888-884-9270 for information.

If you don't want to pay for $1 million coverage, find an independent insurance agent, preferably one recommended by farmer friends. You should be able to purchase a $300,000 or $500,000 farm liability policy, excluding products liability, PYO or vehicles, for under $200 a year.

NOTE: For insurance to cover empoyees and vehicles, see the original GFM article (Nov. 1999) or *The Legal Guide for Direct Farm Marketers*. [See Resources, Chapter 2] ✿

APPENDIX 2

"From an Empty Parking Lot to a Vibrant Social Center"
An Oregon Farmers' Market Study

According to a recent survey by OSU researchers Larry Lev and Garry Stephenson of consumers in the mid-Willamette Valley in Oregon, "Consumers are interested in purchasing local products because of their superior quality, because they want to support local growers, and because they just enjoy the buying experience."

Results of the Lev and Stephenson survey showed:

✧ Significant money is spent at these markets, and their presence benefits surrounding downtown businesses. The three markets attract about 4,500 adults and sell nearly $37,000 during an average week, even though they are open for only 13 hours during that time.

✧ Furthermore, up to 88% of the Saturday shoppers said the farmers' market was their primary reason for going downtown, but they often lingered to shop at other downtown businesses.

The markets are pulling people into the downtown shopping district rather than vice versa. That is welcome information to Rebecca Landis, the manager of three Willamette Valley markets.

Landis said that such information is invaluable when negotiating space and parking for the markets, which sometimes must move due to downtown construction or other changes.

Indeed, farmers' markets can serve as incubators for new agriculture-based businesses, serving as low-cost, low-risk places to try out new ideas and gain name recognition to increase sales through other outlets, including supermarkets and restaurants.

Their research so far has documented the significant economic development and social benefits that farmers' markets provide in certain areas.

"Our farmers' markets in Oregon are an amazing phenomenon," Lev said. "You take an empty parking lot and make it into a vibrant economic and social center, a meeting place for rural and urban Oregon."

Here are some results of their shopper surveys:

✧ Consumers spent an average of $12 to $15 a visit, with the amount increasing as more seasonal produce ripened and more flowers bloomed.

✧ Daily revenues for vendors varied widely, from $50 to $2,000.

✧ Eighty-eight percent of the visitors to the Albany Saturday market and 78% of the visitors to the Saturday market in Corvallis said their main reason for going downtown that morning was the farmers' market.

✧ Sixty-three percent of the Corvallis shoppers and 35% of the Albany shoppers said they also planned to spend money at other downtown shops or restaurants after their market visit.

— by Theresa Novak, based on research by OSU researchers Larry Lev, and Garry Stephenson. In *Oregon's Agricultural Progress,* Fall/ Winter 1998; Oregon State University Agricultural Experiment Station, Oregon State University. Available from the website: http:// eesc.orst.edu/agcomwebfile/Magazine/ ✿

APPENDIX 3

Customer Surveys and Public Opinion

There are several good ways to gather people's opinions, such as focus groups, informal conversations, written surveys and telephone surveys.

Focus groups are a way to delve deeply into the minds of a small number of customers. The process provides a more structured environment with people committed to a certain timeframe, such as two hours, to critique and give their honest, individual opinions. If you want to reach the elderly, for example, create a focus group with the elderly. Go to a retirement home and sit down with 8-10 people to address their perceptions. Do the same with housewives, househusbands, ethnic groups or any sub-group that may be an important segment of your market customer base. Ask a professional company or a community college professor to help in structuring the focus group discussion.

If you want less focused input from a larger group, you might hold a community meeting to get feedback on how you are doing or on a proposed expansion. This is possible even during a market day if you want only customer input.

Informal conversations. Many managers do a fairly effective job with various informal survey techniques. They regularly walk through the market eavesdropping on conversations among customers and with farmers. They purposely do some paperwork near a public seating area or a playground to overhear comments. They intercept customers to ask direct questions about what they'd like to see in the market. They build customer confidence that management really cares and is responsive to their desires. This process extends into the non-market realm; they have these conversations downtown and when socializing.

Board members, advisory committee or Friends of the Market members, farmers and others can do the same thing. They together act as eyes and ears to bring feedback and new ideas to the manager.

However, this technique may miss the more introverted customers or a wider range of issues among even extroverted but time-pressed customers.

How do you make sure you're getting all the radio signals from throughout your community? You can use surveys as a vital tool to learn about your customers and even your potential customers.

When you need interviewers, use market volunteers, high school students or college students studying sociology, marketing, statistics, rural development or a related field. Give clear instructions to reinforce your goal of getting more personal feedback on open-ended questions versus statistical feedback on multiple-choice or prioritizing questions. Since you may lose people if your questionnaire is too long, test the survey instrument with a few people.

Written surveys. As an incentive for your customers to fill out a questionnaire, hold a raffle with customer questionnaires as "tickets." Or, train your interviewers to intercept customers within the market or preferably at a market entrance point (before they have heavy bags). Set up a small table with a sign announcing "Customer Survey Here." Holding a clipboard, make a friendly, quick introduction so that the customer senses it will not be a long interruption in their shopping: "Hi, my name is… and I'm a volunteer with the farmers' market. We're doing a short survey of customer impressions of the market that will take about two or three minutes. Is that okay?" You may define the purpose in many different ways or simply say it's a customer survey.

To increase surveyor efficiency, invite the customer to complete the survey alone. You can keep three to six clipboards going simultaneously. This requires that almost all questions have answers that are checked off or circled rather than written responses. Make sure you remind them about the second side and when you collect the clipboard; check to see that they have answered all the questions before thanking them for their time.

What do you want to know? Brainstorm all the things that you may be curious about or that would be helpful to know. Then pare the list down to the essentials that allow customers to finish the survey in 2-4 minutes. Most people would prefer to answer questions on one side of a sheet of paper, although double-sided is realistic if the questions are easy and direct. Review the results of your last survey. There may have been customer comments you should pursue by inserting a question in your new survey.

Ask the easy questions first, like, "How often do you come to the market?," etc. Put the most sensitive question last ("What is your income?"), so you don't start a pattern of non-response early if they choose not to answer.

Use "Check all that apply" or "Circle" as instruction after every question. "Yes" or "No" is another option. If you want to have them rate elements, provide a scale of one to five out to the right side or have them circle "Poor, Fair, No opinion, Good, Excellent." Alternately, you may ask them to rank market aspects in order of importance (1 to 3). There are different ways to ask the same question to provoke thought – ask the same question in a different form later in the survey.

◆ Ask what advertising customers have seen or heard. List paid and free sources of advertising:
  ✧ unsolicited articles
  ✧ daily newspapers
  ✧ weeklies
  ✧ freebies
  ✧ phone directory
  ✧ radio station
  ✧ gardening program
  ✧ television
  ✧ magazine (women, parenting, gardening, active lifestyle)
  ✧ festival
  ✧ county fair
  ✧ state agriculture list

  ✧ parade
  ✧ Chamber of Commerce brochure
  ✧ hotel rack card
  ✧ web site
  ✧ church bulletin
  ✧ school flyer
  ✧ "drive by."

List a few places where you haven't advertised to check their memory.

◆ Why do you come to the market?
  ✧ freshness/quality produce
  ✧ organic produce
  ✧ variety of produce
  ✧ prices/good values
  ✧ support local growers
  ✧ crafts
  ✧ soaps
  ✧ flowers/plants/nursery stock
  ✧ fun activity
  ✧ ambiance
  ✧ people watching
  ✧ entertainment
  ✧ kids' activities
  ✧ proximity to other downtown shopping
  ✧ fresh-baked items
  ✧ hot food
  ✧ value-added/processed products
  ✧ honey
  ✧ goat cheese
  ✧ other (explain).

Since your list can be lengthy, you might ask people to check the top three or five reasons.

◆ What is your primary purpose in coming downtown on market day?
  ✧ farmers' market only
  ✧ primarily for market, but also shop downtown
  ✧ primarily for downtown shopping, but also shop at market
  ✧ fun place to be
  ✧ other.

Use these statistics to gain business support.

◆ How frequently do you come to market?
  ✧ every week,
  ✧ most weeks,
  ✧ twice a month,
  ✧ once a month
  ✧ occasionally.

See if you can determine what customers come more regularly. With demographic questions at the end you can appeal to them easier.

◆ Please give your opinion on the following aspects of the market:
  ✧ friendliness of vendors
  ✧ cleanliness of market
  ✧ parking availability
  ✧ seating
  ✧ restrooms/amenities
  ✧ day and hours
  ✧ variety
  ✧ number of vendors
  ✧ vendor signs
  ✧ no pets rule
  ✧ hot food concessions
  ✧ prices
  ✧ price signs
  ✧ number of crafts
  ✧ availability of specialty foods
  ✧ market layout.

You probably want to select no more than eight aspects to be rated.

◆ How long do you normally spend at the market?
  ✧ less than 15 minutes
  ✧ 15-30 minutes
  ✧ 30-45 minutes
  ✧ 45-60 minutes
  ✧ 1 - 1 1/2 hours
  ✧ 1 1/2 - 2 hours
  ✧ more than 2 hours.

(Or leave the question open for a write-in response: ___ minutes/hours.) If parking is a problem, you may want to have less entertainment to keep visits shorter.

✦ What is your age? (Open question.) When you categorize, break out into:
  ✧ 0-17 teens
  ✧ 18-22 college
  ✧ 23-29 20's
  ✧ 31-39 30's
  ✧ 41-49 40's
  ✧ 51-59 50's
  ✧ 60+ seniors.

✦ What is your zip code? Or provide list of towns nearby or clearly described areas of the city. You want to figure out the primary trade area, where 75 percent of your customers are from. Most of your advertising will be directed there.

✦ Is there any way you can help us spread the word? Provide them space and the chance to give you their name and phone, aside from just the idea.

✦ Always ask for comments. "Please tell us what changes or improvements we can make in the market!"

Put your market contact information at the bottom in case people want to contact you. Make sure your e-mail or web site address is easy to remember. For instance, "contact info@boulderfarmers.org" is pretty straightforward in getting information about the Boulder Farmers' Market.

You can find out many more characteristics of customers or issues important to them, if you ask. You may want to design a separate survey listing several optional responses. Be selective among these and other questions you may ask.

✧ What time of day do you listen to radio?
✧ Which else would you like to see in the market?
✧ Number in group?
✧ Do you come from home/work/school?
✧ What time do you get to the market?
✧ Would you prefer a market nearer to you at ….(location)?
✧ Do you shop at downtown stores while at the market?
✧ Which movie theatres do you attend most frequently?
✧ What magazines or other publications do you read?
✧ Which subjects do you read about?
✧ Which of these activities do you enjoy doing?
✧ Do you ever use food stamps/food coupons at the market?
✧ How do you usually travel to market? Walk, bike, bus, car, friend
✧ How many people live in your household?
✧ How much do you spend on an average trip to market? (Open question.)
✧ Do you own home/own condo/rent?
✧ What level of schooling have you completed? 1-16, Masters, Postgraduate?
✧ What is your household income range?
✧ Gender?

Surveying the General Populace

Many farmers' markets survey their customers, but they miss two population groups: those who no longer come to the market and those who never have come. For those groups you need to develop a different survey instrument through telephone, newspaper, focus group, or another vehicle.

Surveys can be done virtually anywhere. Analyze the limitations of the site – in front of a grocery store is better than a bowling alley. Where you survey will skew your results. You want to get a picture of the whole pie, not just a few market segments.

A *telephone survey* is one of the most objective surveys since the survey pool is not as tainted by interviewer bias. An interviewer, who may tend to intercept certain age people over others, is not biased when calling every tenth number in a reverse phone directory. You can readily give an introduction and tell the caller that you only have their phone number and name and the survey information is confidential.

These surveys will have an initial set of perhaps six questions for everyone, followed by separate questions for those who have been to the market (If "yes," go to Question #7) and those who have never been (If "no," go to Question #14). With those having attended market, you ask about satisfaction and what might lead to more frequent visits. With those never having been to the market, the interviewer jumps to question #14 to ask about food priorities, access (day and hours), parking, safety concerns or other perceptions. A positive side-effect of a friendly interviewer may be the resident's realization that you care about him/her as a potential customer. It can be a very personal form of publicity! ✿

APPENDIX 4

Are Farmers' Markets Profitable?

Editor's note: The following discussion on farmers' market profitability was taken from postings on a Direct Market internet discussion group.

In Nebraska in 1999 we had 38 regular markets and a population of 1.5 million people with two-thirds of those in the three eastern counties, essentially Lincoln and Omaha. The Lincoln Haymarket Farmers' Market on Saturday is the largest with up to 160 vendors (100 on average) serving 6,000 customers from a 150,000 population (225,000 in the county). Indirect assessment of cash flow is about $1.5 million per season, mid-May to mid-October roughly coinciding with frost dates. The highest volume sales are among established produce vendors averaging $500-1000, followed by fresh and dried cut flowers, bakery products including noodles, followed by crafts.

— Laurie Hodges, University of Nebraska Vegetable Specialist

Most markets in this area charge a flat fee to vendors, usually $20, but the Davis market charges 6% of gross sales. I'm sure there's lots of underreporting by sellers; even so the annual sales recorded are $1.5 - 2 million, netting the market $100,000+. We use this income to pay our manager, bookkeeping, liability insurance, cleanup service, live musicians, etc.

with some left over.

This is a not-for-profit market and the city provides the site and parking. There is a dicey management issue that is going to be tough in a for-profit market. The farmer wants to bring a load of product to market and by the end of the market have an empty truck and a full wallet. A for-profit manager wants the market to look well-stocked and diverse right up to closing time, so he will want to have twice as many farmers, who will go home at the end of the day with their trucks half full and their wallets half empty. The farmers don't like this. It's a constant source of friction, even in a market like ours that is run by farmers for farmers.

— Mike Madison, Winters, CA

Your question on the "profitability" of farmers' markets must first be clarified. Profit is generally not the motive of the market operators but hopefully is what motivates vendors to sell there. Most markets hope to be able to cover operating costs. Many are subsidized by city government or other institutions.

There are many examples of markets that operate profitably covering the cost of manager salaries, advertising, events, general operations, facilities or rental fees, maintenance (trash, etc.), and office expenses. I would say that "profitable markets" are those that

are able to cover operating costs primarily from vendor fees with no overhead or subsidy from public or private sources. The California markets are probably the most successful in terms of vendor fees covering operating costs.

The Ithaca Farmers' Market is able to successfully cover most operating costs from vendor fees. Fees provide the main source income to pay for a full-time manager, bookkeeper, traffic assistants, and all operations. Fees for 2001 include a $100 annual membership application fee (dues), a $100-300 reserved stall fee (sliding scale depending on numbers of markets attended/season), a daily fee of $18 or $22, and a $300 lifetime equity fee to a become member. This is what IFM lives on, plus a lot of volunteer work from the board of directors and the market membership. Our annual operating budget is around $95,000 of which about $16,000 is advertising, $33,000 for staff, $23,000 is rent and the balance is operations. Over the years, the market has had a goal of putting money away for capital projects.

As a result, we have a beautiful roofed, open-sided clerestory pavilion with room for 90 vendors built for approximately $200,000 with vendor labor and grants amounting to $85,000. We have added a dock for $20,000 (half of which was paid by a private donation) to enhance our waterfront location. In total, we have received over $120,000 in grants and donations in the last 12 years since we have found a permanent site which we lease from the city. The city does not subsidize the market in any way. In fact, IFM had to extend their own water and sewer lines, and pays the city about $20,000 rent each season for use of the 3-acre parcel. We are able to generate a little money on the side by subleasing the site to other groups (it is becoming a popular location for weddings).

The Ithaca Market is also successful in terms of vendor sales, which is what allows the market to operate profitably. We generate over $1.3 million in annual sales (1997 customer/vendor survey).

Annual gross sales per vendor range from $1,000 to $50,000 (average $11,500). Vendors need to make enough money in order to justify the fees they are required to pay. Some vendor fallout has been occurring because of high fees; as a result the market has started an entry program for new vendors who sell on Sundays.

A challenge for farmers' markets is to come up with the right location that attracts enough customers to satisfy the income needs of vendors so that they can afford to pay the fees needed to cover operating costs.

A new market often needs to be subsidized until vendors sales can support fees large enough to pay for all operating costs. Sometimes this happens rather quickly with the right location and customer base; other times it is a slow building process. Outside support helps markets survive. Most markets operate on a shoestring which impact their potential success. When seeking outside public or private support for starting a market, the secondary benefits of markets need to be promoted including their ability to draw customers to urban locations, generate sales for nearby business, serve to incubate businesses, provide jobs, improve food access in low income neighborhoods, preserve farms, etc. These can help justify the public or private investment in establishing or operating a farmers' market and help it realize its potential.

— Monika Roth, Agricultural Extension Educator, Tompkins Cornell Cooperative Extension ✿

APPENDIX 5

Benefits of Farmers' Markets for Vendors, Consumers & Communities

Why Farmers Markets Are Growing

Food imports

With the flood of produce imports coming into the country from overseas, even larger commercial growers are taking a second look at high-return marketing outlets like farmers' markets. Felix Fly, manager with the West Tennessee Farmers' Market in Jackson, Tennessee, says the number of farmers applying to sell in their farmers' market blossomed in 1999. "Normally we have 12 or 14 new vendor applicants each year, but this year we've had 51 by August," he said. "Due to the low prices this year in cattle, cotton, soybeans, hogs, and corn, we've found a lot of growers trying something new. I just got a call from someone growing pumpkins who had never grown them before."

Urban growth

According to Rose Koenig, Mgr., Haile Village Farmers Market, Gainesville, FL, "The agricultural economy is changing drastically in the U.S. What was profitable 50 years ago may not be profitable tomorrow. As land gets more expensive because of urban growth, small farms of 100 acres or less will get more and popular. This leaves growers with the choice of selling the land to developers or getting into higher value farming such as direct marketing. Some growers will sell out, and some will reduce acreage and start growing for a local market."

Health, taste & local food

The growth in farmers' markets is fueled by public awareness on how to eat better. Customers want to know where their food is grown and who grew it.

"People are following a healthy lifestyle, and are putting more attention into what they're eating.

—Charlie Haney, Mgr., Olympia Farmers' Market, WA

Farmer Benefits

Sellers at farmers' markets often get a larger cash return for their product than through wholesale marketing and get paid cash-in-hand, instead of waiting 30-90 days or longer. There is also the pride and fun in selling to the people who enjoy eating your produce.

[See also Chapter One, "Advantages, Disadvantages"]

Consumer Benefits

Most farmers' market customers come to the markets for the superior quality and freshness, unusual varieties, and a chance to support local agriculture and meet the farmers who grow their food. And if these shoppers can get much higher quality at a competitive price, they're getting a lot better value for their money!

"American consumers want several qualities in their food baskets beyond those provided by factory farming with its stress on volume, uniformity and price. They want local or regional, and hence fresher, food. They want varied food—no iceberg lettuce but more heirloom tomatoes. They want food with fewer health risks from chemicals. They want food produced with methods less likely to harm the environment. And they want to restore contact with the actual producer of the food."

—Susan Planck, Wheatland Vegetable Farms, Purcellville, VA

Taste and freshness

Farmers' markets offer shoppers the opportunity to purchase fresh-picked, good-tasting, seasonal produce from the farmers who grow it. Direct-from-the-farm products are often picked at the peak of maturity only a day or even hours before they are sold at farmers' markets. Once people taste what's available at the farmers' market they don't want to go back to the taste they get from the supermarket. Nothing substitutes for a vine-ripened, fresh-picked tomato, or a peach, corn or baby bok choy.

"Commercial fresh tomatoes epitomize the shortcomings of modern produce, but many fruits and vegetables also suffer from reduced flavor. One study showed that the typical peach is 2 1/2 weeks old by the time it gets to the grocery store. By contrast, that same peach found at a farmers' market was probably picked in the past two days."

—"Taking It To the Streets," *Farmer to Farmer*

Variety

At farmers' markets customers are able to sample new products and varieties not ordinarily found in supermarkets. While supermarkets usually offer only one or a few varieties of a product, direct markets may sell many different varieties of one product, such as apples, peaches, peppers or tomatoes, as well as exotic and heirloom products, organically grown produce, and ethnic foods.

Value

Many markets have been established to provide customers with fresh produce at lower prices than local supermarkets. In other cases the goal has been to provide fresher, superior product at competitive prices. Either way, the customer finds better value, which is defined by the relationship between product and price.

Social

Farmers markets are fun! Farmers markets are important social events. People run into friends and talk, or meet new ones including farmers to exchange recipes. In fact, some markets have adopted the slogan: "Come for the freshness; stay for the fun!"

Some say that the attraction of farmers' markets is fundamentally a human one. Shoppers at farmers' markets have seven times as many social interactions in a farmers' market as they do in a grocery store! Certainly, they are a return to a form of business and social interaction common for thousands of years, where consumers purchased goods more directly from those who produced them.

Customers come to trust farmers. Other customers intuitively follow that trust. The relationship one has with a produce clerk who doesn't know what country the tomatoes come from simply can't compare with a friendship with a farmer who can tell you what his soil tastes like, why she doesn't irrigate, how the Ace compares with a Zebra, the recipe for her best sauce, or how many weeks before he says so-long for the season.

Urban/Rural Connection

Many farmers as well as consumers report that the farmer-consumer bond is the heart and soul of the markets. An article in *NW Health* (May/June 1995) noted: "These stalls of sustenance may be the last place where many people can reconnect with food and its sources. The growers' offerings, which vary week to week, remind us that there is a season for everything."

Community Benefits

A successful farmers' market can be a tremendous resource for a community, large or small. Fresh food is available at a reasonable price, the local agricultural economy as well as the marketplace area receives an economic boost, and a festive and community-enhancing social center draws people together. Farmers' markets, in addition, help fight hunger through their participation in food recovery programs and federally funded subsidy programs.

Gathering place

When Shakespeare comes to the Ithaca Farmers' Market alongside central New York's Cayuga Lake, people are reminded of the market's role in integrating economic, social and cultural activities in one place.

"To visit a Greenmarket is to realize the power that a farmers' market can wield in transforming an urban space into an exciting and vibrant community. The more that Greenmarkets become fixtures in city neighborhoods, the more they resemble the proverbial backyard fence where neighbors meet to exchange recipes and gossip and concerns about their streets."

— *Barriers & Opportunities for Direct Marketing,* Farmers' Market Trust

Barriers bridged

Whenever people from various walks of life cross paths, there is an opportunity for learning. Stereotypes are broken. Voters no longer look dispassionately at rural issues when farming friends may be affected.

In many communities a politician cannot be elected without campaigning at the farmers' market. In San Luis Obispo, California, every candidate is given three minutes on a flatbed trailer festooned with red, white and blue bunting. "Thursday Night" is about more than simply food transactions; it is a community event.

"At first farmers' markets sales were viewed by town fathers as inconsequential. But now they're really beginning to understand the vital camaraderie that exists between the farmers' market seller and city folk."

—Jim Jones, FM Representative, Texas Dept. of Agriculture

Economic revitalization

Farmers' markets transform cities. City planners nationwide now recognize the value of the farmers' market. They have evidence that it revitalizes a downtown area like nothing else, by creating an active meeting place and income-producing community. More and more cities are viewing farmers' markets as a positive addition to their cities. The National Main Street Program has incorporated markets as a vehicle to rejuvenate declining downtown areas.

"Most managers felt that farmers' markets and the farmers who attend them are viewed positively by their host communities. The majority of market managers (78%) felt that their markets positively affect local businesses, primarily by bringing customers from both inside and outside the community. Several managers gave examples of businesses located in the vicinity of their markets that had expanded their hours to benefit from the increased customer traffic. This revitalization function is commonly used by downtown merchant associations and redevelopment agencies as a rationale for starting a farmers' market."

— Farmers' Markets and Rural Development Project

"The downtown merchants are behind the markets because restaurant owners realize that people don't buy produce at the markets to eat, but to take home. Having the markets nearby gives people more reasons to come downtown. As an inducement to sell at the market, many restaurants guarantee that farmers will sell out—if they don't sell out by 3 p.m., the restaurant will buy the remaining produce for their next few days' needs. They encourage the farmers to bring a wide variety. There also has been a shift in the make-up of downtown businesses. They don't have a lot of grocery stores, so in the downtown there is not a lot of competition. The merchants perceive the markets as complementary rather than directly competitive."

—Donald Coker, Florida Dept. of Ag and Consumer Services

Grocery impact

Ken Meyer, produce buyer for three Alfalfa's Markets in Colorado, says his chain has been a loyal customer to many of the growers doing business in the open-air market. "The markets get people excited about organics, and having them just down the street does mean some cross-over business."

"Farmers' markets probably affect grocery stores to the tune of less than one percent of their produce sales," says Jim Anderson of the Missouri Department of Agriculture. "Our markets - 55 statewide, most in rural communities - are only open between two and six days a week, six months a year, and they don't seem to have any impact on the grocery store's produce section."

For many years the family-owned Williams Brothers supermarkets in San Luis Obispo County, CA, allowed farmers' markets in their parking lots. It gave them a leg over their competitors and showed their support for local farmers.

"We're about a block from Alfalfa's Market and they were concerned about competition. Now 13 years later, they discovered produce sales went up 30% on Saturday when we were open."

— John Ellis, Boulder FM, CO

Improved identity

"According to Richard McCarthy, executive director of the Economics Institute, "The Market makes downtown safer because there are people on the street. It changes the feel of the neighborhood from that of a cold, impersonal urban environment to that of a community. Even vendors who once moved away from New Orleans now have a completely different experience of the city when they come to town for Market."

— Economics Institute, *1999 Report to the Community*

"Downtown businesses have also benefited from the Market's presence on Saturday mornings— which, otherwise, is not a busy time of the week for most of them. The AB Freeman study estimated that downtown businesses gain additional income of $450,000 a year as a result of the Market, and a 30%-70% increase in Saturday-morning traffic as a result of the Market."

— Economics Institute, *1999 Report to the Community*

Access

"Ironically, farmers' need for more and diverse markets occurs at a time when supermarket relocation to the suburbs has left many Philadelphians underserved. Inner city residents in particular have little choice but to rely on convenience stores that provide very limited access to fresh fruits and vegetables. The diets of lower-income residents offer poor nutrition, affecting the health and well being of individuals and their communities. Establishing farmers' markets in these low-income communities can serve the dual objectives of increased access to fresh produce for city residents and improved farm profitability."

— *Barriers & Opportunities for Direct Marketing*, Farmers' Market Trust, 1999.

The impetus for farmers' markets in southern California came from the Interfaith Hunger Coalition of the Southern California Ecumenical Council. Concerned about supermarket flight and inner-city residents' access to fresh produce at reasonable prices, they spearheaded a three-year, seven-market development program which exceeded its goals.

Donna Bryan vocalized similar concerns through Seeds of Hope when starting numerous markets in South Carolina. The faith community has been critical in developing countless markets by providing church lots as market locations, giving financial support and leading many organizing efforts.

Local food and greenspace

Lindsey Ketchel, horticultural marketing specialist with the Vermont Department of Agriculture, Food and Markets, reported on a recent department study of Vermont consumers. More than 60 percent were interested in buying local products and said they'd spend up to 10 percent more just to support local family farms. "Consumers are looking for ways to support the local greenspace," Ketchel said. "At the same time, it's a challenge for consumers is to find local products. They can't go to a Grand Union supermarket and find local produce. Farmers' markets are not just about buying food," she continued. "They bring farmers and consumers together in a community way. It's all about celebrating food grown in our own regions."

"From an ecological standpoint, shopping at farmers' markets helps support the greenbelt by enabling local farmers to become economically sustainable. It supports locally-based food production and distribution, thus reducing energy consumed on transportation. It also reduces solid wastes, by eliminating over-packaging of foods and supports environmentally sound and sustainable farming practices because family farmers tend to use fewer synthetic chemicals."

— Lynn Bagley, with the Golden Gate FM Assoc. in Novato, CA, quoted in *To Market! To Market!* University of Mass. Cooperative Extension System

"When you shop at a supermarket only 21% of every dollar spent goes toward actual food production whereas at the market more than four times that goes back to the growers."

—Ann Harvey Yonkers, Mgr., FRESHFARM Market, Washington, DC

ℬIBLIOGRAPHY

A Case Study of the Davis Farmers' Market: Connecting Farms and Community, by Heather Podoll, UC Sustainable Agriculture Research and Education Program, March, 2000.

A Case Study of the Laytonville Farmers' Market: A Rural Community Market, Christopher J. Lewis, UC Sustainable Agriculture Research and Education Program, March, 2000.

American Vegetable Grower, June 1994, "Open a City Farmers' Market!;" 1995, "Community Is Key to Market Success."

An Oregon Farmers' Market Study, by Theresa Novak, based on research by OSU researchers Larry Lev and Garry Stephenson, *Oregon's Agricultural Progress,* Oregon State University Extension Service, Oregon State University. Available from the website: http://eesc.orst.edu/agcomwebfile/Magazine/.

Barriers & Opportunities for Direct Marketing in the Philadelphia Region, Farmers' Market Trust, 1999.

Certified Farmers' Market News, Southland Farmers' Market Association, by Mark Wall.

Do's and Don'ts of a Successful Farmers' Market, Sara Pollard, Rural Mountain Producers Exchange, Inc., PO Box 3076, Fayetteville, AR 72702.

Dynamic Farmers Marketing, Jeff Ishee. [See Resources, Chapter 2]

Economics Institute, *1999 Report to the Community,* July 1999, Crescent City Farmers Market.

Farmer to Farmer, July 94, "Taking It To the Streets," by Lori Pottinger.

Farmers' Market Forum, Farmers' Market Federation of New York.

Farmers' Markets and Rural Development Project. [See Resources, Chapter 12]

Growing for Market: News & Ideas For Market Gardeners (newsletter), July 1996, "Farmers' Markets Need Rules on Reselling;" June 1999, "Crafts at Farmers Markets;" Sept. 1998, "Herb Grower Explains Why It Paid To Help Develop a Farmers Market;" June 2000, "What's Ahead for Farmers' Markets?;" May 2000, "Display Rack Keeps Produce Fresh and Crisp;" Dec. 1995, "With 300 Trips a Year..." [See Resources, Chapter 2]

New York Magazine, Aug. 16. 1999, "Amazing Tastes," by Peter Kaminsky.

NW Health, May/June 1995, by Molly Dee Anderson.

Produce Business, August 1992, "Greenmarkets and Farmers' Markets: Are They Cutting into Retail Sales?"

Rural Delivery (New Brunswick, Canada), March 1999, "How to Build A Successful Farmers' Market."

The New York Times, June 20, 1990, Elizabeth Schneider (interview with Lynn Bagley).

To Market! To Market! Promotional Ideas That will Bring Customers to Your Farmers' Market, University of Mass. Cooperative Extension System.

RESOURCES

Chapter 2 Getting Ready for Market

National Directory of Farmers' Markets can be accessed on the Internet (see below). A clickable map leads you to farmers' markets by state. Also has links to farmers' market websites. Farmers' markets listed at this site often are willing to share information on their by-laws, guidelines or mission statements. To obtain a printed copy of the directory, contact Velma Lakins at USDA-AMS-T&M-W&AM, Rm. 2642-S, 1400 Independence Ave., SW., Washington, D.C. 20250-0267. 202-720-8317; velma.lakins@usda.gov.
www.ams.usda.gov/farmersmarkets.

Farmer Direct Marketing Action Plan. Established to help small farmers sell their products directly to consumers. New direct marketing networks and a one-stop information clearinghouse will be created within the next three years, as well as training programs for market managers and small farmers. A copy of the plan may be obtained from Errol Bragg at 202-720-8317 or from the Internet at:
www.ams.usda.gov/directmarketing/
frmplan.htm.

Farmer Direct Marketing Newsletter (USDA)
www.ams.usda.gov/directmarketing/.

ATTRA's Direct Marketing Information Package, available from ATTRA, PO Box 3657, Fayetteville, AR 72702. 800-346-9140.
http: / /www.attra.org/attra-pub/
dirmkt.html.

Adding Value to Farm Products: An Overview — Value-Added Systems Guide
http://attra.ncat.org/attra-pub/
valueovr.html.

Add Value Through Marketing. A SARE publication.
www.sare.org/san/tipsheet/tip2.htm.

Barriers and Opportunities for Direct Marketing in the Philadelphia Region. Report from Farmers' Market Trust. The 63-page study documents the marketing options and barriers for small-scale farmers in a metropolitan region. $15.95 postpaid from Meredith Stone, Farmers' Market Trust, 1201 Chestnut St 4th floor, Philadelphia PA 19107; 215-568-0830 X10; fax 215-568-0882; fmtrust@libertynet.org.

Around the World at Farmers' Market: *A Handbook for Small-scale Grower-Marketers of Ethnic and Heirloom Vegetables, Fruits, and Herbs,* by Steve Salt. $34.95. Loaded with hard-to-find information for small-scale farmers on the very fast-growing markets for ethnic and heirloom produce. Presents aspects of choosing and developing a market garden site; selecting a product mix; raising, harvesting, and marketing ethnic and old-fashioned vegetables, fruits, and herbs. Special attention is paid to social aspects, problems, and techniques of dealing with customers of non-Anglo-American ethnic groups, such as language barriers, haggling, taboos, body language, gender roles, religious requirements and inter-ethnic conflict. Thumbnail sketches of hundreds of ethnic and old-fashioned vegetables, fruits, and herbs are given as sources of seeds or plants. Culinary customs, major holidays and festivals, U.S. and Canadian demographics, specialized periodical publications and associations, and other information pertinent to marketing ethnic and heirloom veggies are presented. An appendix gives terms and phrases useful for the small-scale veggie vendor in several major languages. Available 2001. [Contact New World Publishing, back page, for availability]

Sell What You Sow! *The Grower's Guide To Successful Produce Marketing,* by Eric Gibson. The definitive book on high-value marketing of farm products. Topics include: deciding what to grow, selling through farmers markets, roadside markets, pick-your-own, subscription (CSA) farming, mail order, grocery stores & restaurants, wholesale channels & cooperatives, developing specialty (value-added) food products, merchandising & customer service, advertising & promotion, pricing & more. 304 pp. [See New World Publishing, back page, for ordering information]

From Asparagus to Zucchini: *A Guide to Farm-Fresh, Seasonal Produce,* written by members of the Madison Area Community Supported Agriculture Coalition (MACSAC), features 46 different vegetable and herb sections which include nutritional, historical, and storage information as well as cooking tips and over 370 recipes. The beginning section of the book includes essays that address how our food choices fit into our economy, environment, communities, quality of life and agricultural systems. The last section has a number of local and regional resources. [See New World Publishing, back page, for ordering information]

An American Success Story, by Harriet Festing.
www.wye.ac.uk/FoodLink/
newpub.html.

Dynamic Farmers' Marketing: A Guide to Successfully Selling Your Farmers' Market Products, by Jeff Ishee. Bittersweet Farmstead, PO Box 52, Middlebrook VA 24459. 540-886-9394. See also Jeff Ishee's website for farmers' markets and market farmers:
httm://marketfarm.homestead.com/
start.html.

Growing for Market: News & Ideas For Market Gardeners. A must-read monthly newsletter for market gardeners, small-scale farmers, flower & herb growers, & greenhouse/nursery operators. It packs a lot into each issue: growing & marketing ideas, pricing information, management tips, networking updates, how-to stories & profiles. Often has articles pertinent to farmers' markets. List of back issue contents (by year) available on request. $30 postpaid per year. ($33 Canada) Growing for Market, PO Box 3747, Lawrence, KS 66046; 800-307-8949.

Missouri Alternatives Center
Extensive list of Extension publications on farmers' markets, available for free download, including:
Food Safety for Farmers' Markets (Kansas State University)
A Guide to Starting, Operating and Selling in Farmers' Markets (Kansas State University)
Weights and Measures Guidelines for Sales at Farmers' Markets, Roadside Stands and Other Commercial Outlets (University of Nebraska)
Food Safety for Farmers' Market Vendors (University of Nebraska).
http://agebb.missouri.edu/mac/links/
index.htm.

USDA Organics Program. Read the productions and certification requirements to sell products as "organic."
www.ams.usda.gov/nop/.

Small Farm Tip Sheets. Work efficiency and appropriate scale buildable equipment, i.e., harvest carts, packing shed, and high tunnels.
www.bse.wisc.edu/hfhp/.

Chroma Blockade Reflective Sunshade 2 sizes, 24 x 57 1/2 inches or 27 x 68 inches. You can find this in most auto parts stores and discount stores (such as K-Mart).

Reflectix Insulation. Jade Mountain Inc., 717 Poplar Ave., Boulder, CO 80304, PO Box 4616, Boulder, CO 80306. Orders 800-442-1972; Tech Support 303-222-3500; fax 303-449-8266.
www.jademountain.com.

Fruit Growers Supply Co. — now part of Sunkist Growers - CA
www.fruitgrowers.com.

Postharvest Home Page
http://postharvest.ucdavis.edu/
produce/storage/index.html.

Post Harvest Chlorination by Treavor Suslow, University of California. Publication 8003. E-mail inquiries to anspubs@ucdavis.edu.

Small-Scale Cold Rooms for Perishable Commodities, University of California. Publication 21449. E-mail inquiries to anspubs@ucdavis.edu.

Knott's Handbook for Vegetable Growers, by Lorenz and Maynard. Published by John Wiley & Sons.

Johnny's Selected Seeds offers a full line of vegetable, flower and herb seeds for the fresh market grower, including specialty crops. Cultural information on all their varieties in their commercial catalog. Contact Johnny's Selected Seeds, Foss Hill Rd. Dept 504, Albion ME 04910. 207-437-4395; fax 800-783-6314; commercial@johnnyseeds.com.

[See also Resources, Chapter 9, for further resources for selling at a farmers' market]

Chapter 3 Running Your Farmers' Market Business

The Legal Guide for Direct Farm Marketing — by Neil D. Hamilton, 1999. This guidebook provides clear answers to questions about the legal side of direct marketing. Covers liability, insurance, labor laws, advertising claims, zoning, pesticide drift, inspections and food safety. [See New World Publishing, back page, for ordering information]

ATTRA — Appropriate Technology Transfer to Rural Areas. Arguably the best appropriate scale and alternative crop sites on the web. This is THE site for posting apprenticeship and internship opportunities.
www.ATTRA.org.

Farmers' Markets — Marketing & Business Guide
http://attra.ncat.org/attra-pub/
farmmrkt.html.

Market Farm Forms: Spreadsheet Templates For Planning and Organizing Information on Diversified Market Farms by Marcie A. Rosenzweig with Bill Kaye-Blake. A 95-page manual and diskette containing Excel (tm) spreadsheet templates. ATTRA's Steve Diver says of this book, "*Market Farm Forms* is the best farm management spreadsheet I've seen to help organize and calculate a mix of vegetables and related crops raised by market gardeners, truck farmers, and CSAs." Non-computer growers can use the hard-copy forms in the back of the book with a pencil and calculator.
Market Farm Forms sells for $45, plus $5 S/H. Please specify platform and spreadsheet version. CA residents add sales tax. Order from Marcie A. Rosenzweig at Full Circle Organic Farm, 3377 Early Times Lane, Auburn, CA 95603. 530-885-9201.
fullcircle@jps.net.

Horticultural Business Management &
Marketing Journal Articles
www.cals.cornell.edu/dept/arme/
hortmgt/pubs/smartmkt/index.htm

Today's Market Prices — Herbs, Fruit
and Vegetables Prices
www.todaymarket.com/
tmplink6.htm.

Chapter 4 The Retail Storefront

Canopies, pop-ups and tarps

Cover Me http://tarps.com.

EZ Up
www.instantshelters.com/
booths.html.

Cover-It Shelters
www.coveritshelters.com/commer-
cial/com_market.html.

www.canopies.fiskars.com/
coolintheshade/index.html.

Elaine Martin Co. Replacement parts
for EZup and KD pop-ups including
replacement tops and snap joint parts,
anchors and ballast bags. 25685
Hillview Ct, Mendelein, IL 60060,
800-642-1043.
www.emartin.com.

Scales and cash registers

CCI Scale Co.
www.cciscale.com/scales/
dealers.html.

Precision Weighing Balances, 10
Peabody Street, Bradford, MA 01835-
7614, Orders 800-881-9570, 978-521-
7095, fax 978-374-5568
www.scaleman.com/mettler/mettler-
toledo.html.

ALL-PRO Direct, PO Box 235, Middle
Island, NY 11953; 800-773-4644; fax
1-413-625-6242. Battery operated cash
registers.
www.allprodirect.com/price-
computing-scales.htm.

Used scales

A&A Used Scales, 78 North 12th
Street, Prospect Park, NJ 07508. 888-
275-7991; fax 973-904-9777.
www.usedscales.com/
price_computing.htm.

**Healthy Farmers, Healthy Profits
Project.** Growers can download Univ.
of Wisconsin tipsheets on mesh bags,
standard containers, narrow pallet system, packing shed layout, rolling dibble
markers and the specialized sit-down
cart.
http://bse.wisc.edu/hfhp/.

Chapter 5 Display

Produce dry tables: to see how falls and
stacks are supported in the grocery store
see:
www.marketservicesinc.com/
produce/htm.

Portable sawhorses. Trojan Mfg., 9810
N Vancouver Way, Portland, OR
97217; 800-745-2120.
www.trojantools.com/products.htm.

Jer's Pattern Catalog of Templates. For
those with a skill saw and some time in
the off season. Barn & garage plans that
can work as packing sheds and roadside
stands, picnic tables for a convertible
bench/table, and the shop tools for folding work tables. Jer's Pattern Projects,
143 West Sherman Suite # 202,
Muskegon Heights, MI 49444. 231-
737-8746.
www.jerpat.com/catalog.html.

Folding display pegboards, white
boards, and quilt racks. Pioneer Products, 1625 N. Davis, Oklahoma City,
OK 73127, 405-789-1492.
www.bensproducts.com/index2.ivnu.

Table and Chair.com. Carries 2 types
of EBCO folding table legs so you can
build your own. Also has an interesting, albeit pricey, bi-fold table with
polypropylene top. Specs say it holds
500#.
www.tableandchair.com.

Folding Legs.com. 888-284-3395.
www.foldinglegs.com/index2.html.

HMC Display, 300 Commerce Drive,
Madera, CA 93637. 800-344-7371.
www.hmcdisplay.com/.

Cosco manufactures a wide variety of
tables that can be seen at:
www.coscoinc.com/products/
housewares/house2000/tables.html.

Advanced Display Systems, 20876
Maranatha Road, Tuolumne, CA
95379; 209-536-8677; fax 800-546-
4709.
www.displaysonline.com/
thumbnail_index.html.

Chapter 6 Merchandising

Floral Retailing On-line
www.superfloral.com/.

The Packer/Produce Merchandising
www.thepacker.com/welcome.asp.

Packaging Monte Packaging
www.montepkg.com.

Fruit Growers Supply Co. (now part
of Sunkist Growers - CA)
www.fruitgrowers.com.

Greenfield Basket Factory. Wood ve-
neer baskets for displays, gift baskets,
floral, craft and farm use. For a free brochure & price list contact 11423 Wilson Rd., North East PA 16428. 814-
725-3419 or 800-BASKET-5.
greenfieldbasket@juno.com.
www.greenfieldbasket.com.

Glossary of retail terms used in the produce industry. See Industry Terms
search function at:
www.supermarketworld.com.

Chapter 7 Sales and Promotion

5-A-Day website. Brochures, posters,
educational programs, lots of resources
for promoting 5-A-Day eating of fruits
and vegetables.
www.5aday.com.

USDA's The Food Guide Pyramid, published by the Human Nutrition Information Service, Home & Garden Bulletin #252, available from Consumer Information Center, Department 159-Y, Pueblo, CO 81009.

Nutrition and food composition books:

Nutrition Handbook, by Jane Brody; *Vitamin Bible,* by Earl Mandell; *Nutritional Almanac,* by John Kirschmann; and *Laurel's Kitchen,* by Laurel Robertson.

Chapter 9 Starting a Farmers' Market

USDA Agricultural Marketing Service. Guidance and advice for setting up a market. Contact Errol Bragg, Acting Program Manager, Claire Klotz, Economist, USDA/AMS/TM/WAM, Room 2642-South, 1400 Independence Ave., SW, Washington, DC, 20250-0269. 202-720-8317; fax 202-690-0031. E-mails:
errol.bragg@usda.gov.
claire.klotz@usda.gov.

Farmers' Market Survey Report. The 18-page USDA publication Farmers' Market Survey Report includes the number of farmers participating in farmers' markets, the number of sales days on a national basis, and the distance both consumers and farmers traveled to the markets. Call 800-384-8704.

Farmers' Markets and Rural Economic Development. A study of how farmers' markets contribute to local economic development. Available for $4 from: Cornell University, Educational Resources Program, 420 Kennedy Hall, Cornell University, Ithaca, NY 14853. 607-255-1837.

Establishing and Operating a Farmers' Market: A Manual for Sponsors, Boards of Directors, and the Managers of Farmers' Markets, by Robert P. Jenkins. Publication 847. Agricultural Extension Service, University of Tennessee. 24 p.

Agricultural Extension Service, University of Tennessee, P.O. Box 1071, Knoxville, TN 37901; 423-974-7271.

Step Manual for Organizing and Establishing a Municipally-Sponsored Retail Farmers' Market. $30 from: Michigan State University, Cooperative Extension Service, MSU Bulletin Office, 10-B Agriculture Hall, East Lansing, MI 48824-1039.

Starting and Strengthening Farmers' Markets in Pennsylvania. $4 from: Center for Rural Pennsylvania, Penn State Cooperative Extension, 212 Locust Street, Suite 604, Harrisburg PA, 17101; 717-787-9555.

Barriers and Opportunities for Direct Marketing in the Philadelphia Region. (See Chapter One Resources.)

A Guide to Starting, Operating, and Selling in Farmers' Markets. Free of charge from:, Cooperative Extension Service, Kansas State University, Manhattan, KS 66506; 785-532-6173.

Farmers' Market Guide. Send $2 plus $1 s&h to:, Extension Publications, University of Missouri-Columbia, 2800 Maguire, Columbia, MO 65211; 573-882-2792.

Direct Farm Marketing and Tourism Handbook. University of Arizona Cooperative Extension, Dept. of Ag. and Resource Economics, PO Box 210023, Tucson, AZ 85721-0023; 520-621-2581.
http://ag.arizona.edu/arec/pubs/dmkt/dmkt.html.

Guide to Developing a Community Farmers' Market: Step-by-step program for developing a successful farmers' market. Offers all the elements of establishing a steering committee, market research, management, set up, and promoting the market. It also contains sample rules and regulations, vendor applications, as well as sample surveys for farmer and consumer support for the development of a new farmers' market.

Farmers' Market Federation of New York, 2100 Park St., Syracuse, NY 13208; 315-475-1101.
diane99@dreamscape.com.

Missouri Alternatives Center
Extensive list of Extension Publications on Farmers' Markets, available as free downloads, including:
Feasibility Study for Kentucky Regional Marketing Facilities
(University of Kentucky)
Establishing and Operating a Community Farmers' Market
(University of Kentucky)
Farmers' Markets: Economics (Colorado State University)
Guides for Development of a Farmers' Market (University of Nebraska)
http://agebb.missouri.edu/mac/links/index.htm.

PPS Public Market Collaborative is a network of individuals and organizations involved in the planning, design, development and operation of public markets. The Collaborative conducts research and education programs and provides assistance to communities in market development, renewal, design and operations.
www.pps.org/publicmarkets/public_market_collaborative.html.

Chapter 10 Managing the Market

The Legal Guide for Direct Farm Marketing, by Neil D. Hamilton, 1999. Drake University Agricultural Law Center, Des Moines, IA. 235 pp. [See New World Publishing, back page, for ordering information]

Women, Infants, and Children (WIC) Farmers' Market Nutrition Program (FMNP). A federal program that benefits both vendors and low-income customers. The goals of the program are twofold: "To provide fresh nutritious unprepared food such as fruits and vegetables from farmers' markets to WIC participants who are at nutritional risk;"

and "To expand consumer awareness and use of farmers' markets." WIC participants are low-income, at-risk pregnant, postpartum, and breast-feeding women, infants, and children up to 5 years of age. WIC vouchers allow them to purchase fresh vegetables and fruits at participating farmers' markets. The FMNP is offered in 35 states and other jurisdictions. For details, please contact USDA Food and Nutrition Service, Public Information Staff at 703-305-2286, or by mail at 3101 Park Center Drive, Room 819, Alexandria, VA 22302.

http://attra.ncat.org/guide/marketing/wicfmnp.html.

Hot Peppers and Parking Lot Peaches: Evaluating Farmers' Markets in Low Income Communities, by Andy Fisher. $10 +$2 S/H from CFS Coalition, PO Box 209, Venice, CA 90294, 310-822-5410, fax 310-822-1440. asfisher@aol.com.

Chapter 11 Promoting the Market

Grassroots Marketing: Getting Noticed in a Noisy World, by Shel Horowitz. This book tells you how to get free publicity and cheap publicity, and how to spend your money for best effect. Covers creating an image, how to write ad copy and press releases, tricks of the printing trade to save money on brochures, ads, direct mail, selling on the internet, working with the media, and more. (See New World Publishing, back page, for ordering information.)

Missouri Alternatives Center
Extensive list of Extension Publications on Farmers' Markets, available as free downloads, including:
Farmers' Markets: Producers' Characteristics and Status of Their Business (Rutgers University)
Farmers' Markets: Managers Characteristics and Factors Affecting Market Organization (Rutgers University)

Farmers' Markets: Consumer Trends, Preferences, and Characteristics (Rutgers University)

http://agebb.missouri.edu/mac/links/index.htm.

Maine Federation of Farmers' Markets website includes free downloads of these articles: *Promotional Ideas for Farmers' Markets; Setting Up at Farmers' Market; Starting a Farmers' Market.*

http://members.mint.net/troberts/mffm/index.html.

To Market! To Market! Send $1.02 in stamps to: University of Massachusetts Cooperative Extension System, 44 Bank Row, Pittsfield, MA 01201; 413-448-8285.

The Northeast Regional Food Guide consists of a full-color information poster with food pyramid and seasonal lists, a seasonal produce guide, and a set of eight fact sheets providing additional nutrition information and tips on using seasonal produce. A set of eight fact sheets is $4.25. The poster and seasonal produce list is $4.50. The complete set is $8.25. Cornell University Resource Center, 7 Business & Technology Park, Ithaca, NY 14850; 607-255-2080; fax 607-255-9946.

www.nutrition.cornell.edu/FoodGuide/.

Chapter 12 Embracing the Community

Public Markets and Community Revitalization. A guidebook covering all aspects of the market development process, from simple, inexpensive farmers' and craft markets to large market districts. Includes sample budgets, staffing requirements, tenant mix plans, marketing strategies, cash flow analysis and cost projections. Project for Public Spaces, 153 Waverly Place, NY, NY 10014. 212-620-5660. $28 + $4 s&h.

www.pps.org/products/products_publicmarkets.html.

The Seeds of Hope Farmers' Market Project unites church groups and farmers to create and sustain local farmers' markets. Contact Dr. John O'Sullivan, Farm Management and Marketing Specialist, North Carolina Cooperative Extension Program, NCA&T State University, PO Box 21928, Greensboro, NC 27420-1928. 919-334-7957.

Farmers' Markets and Rural Development Project. The FMRDP project was conducted by U. C. Davis Sustainable Agriculture Research and Education Program (SAREP) in collaboration with the Farming Alternatives Program at Cornell University and Iowa State University. The project's purpose was to determine how farmers' markets promote community and economic development. This study is the first to explore how farmers' markets across the country function as small business incubators by providing a rich environment for establishing food and agricultural businesses.

www.cals.cornell.edu/dept/ruralsoc/fap/Farmersmarkets.html.

Food from the 'Hood teaches youth in Los Angeles entrepreneurship through producing and marketing value-added foods. Call 888-601-FOOD.

The Sustainable Farming Connection. Sustainable techniques for farms of all sizes and crops.

http://sunsite.unc.edu/farming-connection/.

Chef's Collaborative is a network of chefs, restaurateurs and other culinary professionals who promote sustainable cuisine by teaching children, supporting local farmers, educating each other & inspiring their customers to choose clean, healthy foods.

www.chefnet.com/cc2000.

Senior Nutrition Programs

Pennsylvania Department of Agriculture (PDA). In a program launched by the PDA in Fall 2000, 31,000 Philadelphia seniors who had limited incomes and were nutritionally at-risk received $20 vouchers for fresh fruits and vegetables to be redeemed at farmers' markets. Demand from seniors swamped some of the centers where vouchers were distributed. PDA officials report being bombarded by calls from state legislators demanding the program be expanded to seniors in their districts. The program was funded for the year 2000 only. If you would like the program continued, the Farmers' Market Trust suggests you call your state representative.

USDA Pilot Program for Low-Income Seniors — Senior Farmers' Market Nutrition Pilot Program (SFMNPP). The SFMNPP grants will be used to provide coupons to low-income seniors that can be exchanged for eligible foods at farmers' markets, roadside stands, and community supported agriculture programs. A total of $10 million has been made available by USDA's CCC to fund grants in 2001.
www.fns.usda.gov/WIC/CONTENT/SeniorFMNPP/SeniorFMNPP.htm.

Farm-To-School Project Resources

The Farmers' Market Salad Bar: *Assessing the First Three Years.* Booklet ($5 postpaid) from Community Food Security Project, c/o UEPI, Occidental College, 1600 Campus Road, Los Angeles, CA 90041; 323-259-2633; fax 323-259-2734, mm@oxy.edu. www.uepi.oxy.edu/cfsp.

The National Farm-to-School Program has nine partners including Cornell, Penn State and Rutgers universities. Programs are underway in New Jersey and New York. For more information, contact the CFSP website.

Also check the "Food and Nutrition Services" section on the Santa Monica Unified School District's web page at: www.smmusd.org.

Food is Elementary, by Dr. Antonia Demas, addresses both the reasons for having a health education program about food in the schools and also the nuts and bolts of how to start such a program. Weekly lesson plans are sufficient for an entire year in pre-school to adult classrooms. $20 + $5 s/h. Checks to "Food Studies Institute," Carolyn P. Landis, Food Studies Institute, 251 Crandon Blvd., Ste. 161, Key Biscayne, FL 33149; 305-361-5228.
cplandis@bigplanet.com.

Edible Schoolyard Project. Information can be found at:
www.chezpanisse.com/cpfoundation.html.

Farm Fresh Start: A guide to increasing the consumption of local produce in the school lunch program. 1997. Hartford Food System, Hartford, CT. Contact Elizabeth Wheeler, 800-296-9325.
www.hartfordfood.org/p/programs/p/project_farm.html.

The Food System: Building youth awareness through involvement. Harmon, A., R. Harmon, and A. Maretzki. 1999. Pennsylvania State University. Contact A. Maretzki, 814-863-4751.

Innovative Marketing Opportunities for Small Farmers: Local schools as customers. Schofer, D., G. Holmes. V. Richardson, and C. Connerly. 2000. Contact Daniel Schofer, 202-690-1170.

Summary of farm-to-school projects around the nation. Community Food Security Coalition School Food Campaign. Contact Andrea Azuma, 323-259-2566. www.foodsecurity.org.

Iowa State Extension offers info on direct marketing to schools:
www.extension.iastate.edu/Publications/PM1853A.pdf.

Chapter 13 Expanding the Vision

Organic Farming Research Foundation, PO Box 440, Santa Cruz, CA 95061, 831-426-6606; fax 831-426-6670, research@ofrf.org.

Farmers' Market Websites

California Federation of Certified Farmers' Markets. Great example of a website that makes it easy for consumers or farmers to find farmers' markets. Features a search engine that identifies local farmers' markets by entering a ZIP code, region or county.
http://farmersmarket.ucdavis.edu.

Homestead — Free websites. This is a good place to set up a free web page for your farmers' market if you're a computer novice.
www.homestead.com/.

General Resources

ATTRA — Appropriate Technology Transfer to Rural Areas. One of the best appropriate scale and alternative crop sites on the web. Loaded with publications and links.
www.ATTRA.org.

Audio Productions. Large number of cassette tapes available from farming conferences on a large variety of small-farm topics, including farmers' markets. 8806 S. Lake Stevens Rd., Everett, WA 98205. 800-356-2834 or 206-335-5223.

Campbell Creations. Desktop publishing and database support for agriculture and natural resource organizations. Books, newsletters, reports and databases. Nancy Jane Campbell, P.O. Box 632, Cool, CA 95614. 530-676-8144.

Openair-Market Net: Farmers' Markets, Street Vendors, Flea Markets and Street Markets.
www.openair.org.

Controlling the Chaos: Suggested Guidelines for Implementation & Management of a Retail Farmers' Market. Addresses issues like rules and regulations, job descriptions, organizational mission and other general operating procedures for farmers' markets. 50 forms are included that can be photocopied. 100 pages; $32 postpaid from Economics Institute, Center for Peace Through Justice, Loyola University New Orleans, 7214 St. Charles Ave., Campus Box 907, New Orleans, LA 70118-3565; 504-861- 5898.

The Sustainable Small Farm Information Network
http://ssfin.missouri.edu/index.htm.

USDA Direct Marketing Publications. For USDA publications or questions call 800-384-8704, or Velma Lakins, USDA/AMS/TM/WAM, Room 2642-South, 1400 Independence Ave., SW, Washington, DC 20250-0269; 202-720-8317; fax 202-690-0031.
velma.lakins@usda.gov.

Farmers' Market Coloring Book, from USDA, AMS. Limited supplies of hard copies, also available for free on the website:
www.ams.usda.gov/directmarketing.

Directory of Farmers' Market and Direct Marketing Associations. USDA publication, expected availability March 2001. Entries list contact information and each association's activities.

National Directory of Farmers' Markets. USDA also has an online listing of farmers' markets in each state at:
www.ams.usda.gov/farmersmarkets.

North American Farmers' Direct Marketing Association is a non-profit association dedicated to the needs of the farm direct marketing industry. Projects and benefits are targeted for farmers, market managers, Extension and other government agencies. NAFDMA resources include:

✧ Farm Direct Marketer's membership category: Provides farmers and farmers' market vendors with international fellowship resources to improve skills and profits.

✧ Farmers' Market Managers' membership category: Provides farmers' market managers with international resources, meetings, and fellowship with other market managers.

✧ Farmer's Liability Insurance: A general liability insurance program for farmers who sell on-farm and/or at farmers' markets covering marketing activities. Premiums are generally below $400 per year for farmers' market vendors.

✧ Annual Conference: The premier farm direct marketing conference in North America each winter. Many sessions and an annual workshop focus on farmers' market issues.

✧ Bus Tours: Bus tours of direct marketing farms in conjunction with the annual conference and in midsummer. Farmers' market tours are organized contingent upon interest and participation by farmers' market managers and vendors.

✧ Networking: Opportunities for members to network via website message services, conferences, and e-mail communications.

NAFDMA, Charlie Touchette, Executive Director, 62 Whiteloaf Road, Southampton, MA 01073; 888-884-9270; fax 413-529-2471.
nafdma@map.com.
www.nafdma.com.

Food and Health

Cancer Information Service, National Cancer Institute 800-4CANCER.
http://cis.nci.nih.gov/.

Produce For Better Health Foundation. 5-A-Day program. Recipes, nutrition info, selection tips for vegetables, fruits, nuts, herbs and much more. 1500 Casho Mill Road, PO Box 6035, Newark, DE 19614-6035; 302/738-7100; fax 302/738-4825.
www.aboutproduce.com/.

Mothers and Others aims to build demand for a better quality food system, to make the marketplace more responsive to consumer needs, and to create market opportunities for regional, sustainably-produced foods. 40 West 20 Street, New York, NY 10011-4211; 888-ECO-INFO.
www.mothers.org/.

Online Discussion Groups

DIRECT-MKT. A internet discussion group about direct marketing. To subscribe to direct-mkt, send the following message to:
majordomo@reeusda.gov: "subscribe direct-mkt".

SMALLFARM-MG. Serves small farmers and mid-size farmers to improve their income through a systems approach. To subscribe, send mail to majordomo@reeusda.gov. Leave subject blank. In the body, type "subscribe smallfarm-mg".

FARMERS' MARKETS discussion group. To subscribe, send an e-mail "subscribe farmers-markets" to lyris@franklin.oit.unc.edu. Archives of postings can be found at:
http://franklin.oit.unc.edu/cgi-bin/lyris.pl?enter=farmers-markets.

SANET-MG sponsors the Sustainable Agriculture Network from the USDA. Archives and subscription information can be found at:
www.sare.org/san/htdocs/hypermail.

Market Gardener's Forum
http://forums.gardenweb.com/forums/market.

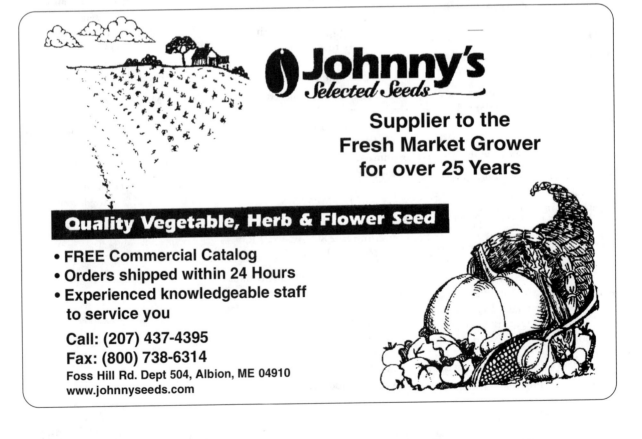

THE NATIONAL OUTREACH ARM OF USDA-SARE

Resources From The Sustainable Agriculture Network

SAN's print and electronic products cover a range of topics, from tillage tool selection to interpreting a soil test for your conditions. SAN books on CD-ROM or on the web are full-text and include the software you'll need to easily search for, copy and/or print out key sections of text. Many also are available at www.sare.org.

Managing Cover Crops Profitably explores how and why cover crops work and provides all the information needed to build cover crops into any farming operation. $19 plus s/h.

The entire text of *Managing Cover Crops Profitably, 2nd edition,* is available on CD-ROM. This great resource allows users to search for crops and download sections into new files for presentations and fact sheets. $10 plus s/h. Order with the book and save $5.

Building Soils for Better Crops, 2nd Edition, describes how to create a balanced soil ecosystem, which produces good harvests with minimal pest problems. Ecological soil management can raise fertility and yields while reducing environmental impacts. Print only, $19.95 plus s/h.

Steel in the Field: A Farmer's Guide to Weed Management Tools shows how today's implements and techniques can control weeds while reducing — or eliminating — herbicides. Print only, $18 plus s/h.

The Source Book of Sustainable Agriculture is a comprehensive guide to hundreds of free or moderately priced newsletters, brochures, reports, books, videos and software, and includes contacts and ordering information. Released in 1997. $12 plus s/h.

Informational bulletins

These free bulletins cover specific sustainable agriculture topics. Each includes a comprehensive list of more in-depth resources and how to get them. Download printable versions of the bulletins at www.sare.org/htdocs/pubs/

- *'Naturalize' Your Farming System: A Whole-Farm Approach to Managing Pests*
- *Reap New Profits: Marketing Strategies for Farmers and Ranchers*
- *Put Your Ideas to the Test: How to Conduct Research on Your Farm or Ranch*
- *Diversify Your Crops to Boost Profits and Stewardship*

How to Order SAN Publications

Please send your check or purchase order (payable to Sustainable Agriculture Publications) to: Sustainable Agriculture Publications, Hills Building, Room 10, University of Vermont, Burlington, VT 05405-0082. To order by credit card, or for information about bulk discounts and rush orders, contact (802) 656-0484; sanpubs@uvm.edu.

Add $3.95 shipping/handling for the first book or CD-ROM; for 1-9 books, add $0.95 per additional book; for more than 9 books, call (802) 656-0484. Please clearly indicate each item and the quantity, along with your mailing address and phone number. For the first book sent outside North America, add $6. For each additional book sent outside North America, add $2.

Vance Corum

My path started with organizing the Gardena Farmers' Market, the first in southern California. In over 10 years as a direct marketing specialist with the California Department of Food and Agriculture and 12 more years as a consultant, I have helped 65+ communities to establish new markets. My experience includes developing publicity campaigns, major tasting events, television shows, magazine articles, manager tours and seminars, consumer research, and economic development workshops — every aspect of market development in small towns and large cities. In addition to coordinating the North American Farmers' Direct Marketing Conference and regional conferences, I have spoken throughout the U.S. and Canada. After 22 years of visiting markets in Eastern and Western Europe, Central and South America, and Asia, I have 10,000 slides from 20+ countries and as many states and provinces.

I am available for speaking engagements and consultation in person, by phone, fax and e-mail and would love to help you better envision and reach your goals.

"The structure of the direct marketing industry in California is an ongoing tribute to Vance's creativity and foresight."
— *Les Portello, Board Mbr., Pacific Coast FM Assoc. and Ex-Mgr., Direct Marketing Program, California Dept. of Food and Agriculture*

"…a major draw wherever he is a featured guest…"
— *Rick Castellano, Exec. Dir., Olympia FM and Pres., Washington State FM Assoc.*

"Your keynote address…your slides of farmers markets around the world perfectly illustrated creative approaches to marketing in highly diverse communities…perfect tone for our two day conference."
— *Mark Musick, Pike Place Market Farmer Coordinator*

"In a lifetime we encounter few individuals that selflessly give so others may benefit. Vance has dedicated his life…"
— *Brent Warner, British Columbia Ministry of Agriculture, and Secretary, NAFDMA*

"He's as creative and energetic as a farmer."
— *Cheryl Boden, West Union Gardens, and Board Mbr., Beaverton FM, OR*

"I have frequently relied on his knowledge and experience to guide and inspire my program and policies…I regard Vance as a mentor and friend."
— *Laura Avery, Coordinator, Santa Monica FM, CA*

"He's a guide, a facilitator and an artist."
— *Bill Cook, Director of Community and Economic Development, Yakima, WA*

"Vance Corum offers the most diversified breadth of experience and exposure to all areas of direct marketing, including firsthand working knowledge of sites, organization, community development, marketing, and evaluation. He has worked up close and personal with markets all over the world, and has dedicated his life to the pursuit of the marketplace."
— *Randii MacNear, Mgr., Davis FM (18 years) and Co-founder, Calif. Fed. of Certified FMs*

✦ Farmers' Market Consultation
✦ Conference & Seminar Speaker
✦ Special Events
✦ Board Training
✦ Market Research & Development

Farmers' Markets America

Vancouver, Washington
(360) 693-5500, Fax (360) 693-5555
fma@pacifier.com

Marcie Rosenzweig

I wrote *Market Farm Forms* at the urging of other growers who had taken my workshops on using computers for recordkeeping on smaller farms and planning and production for CSAs. These are forms I developed to help extend my management time during the 12 years my husband, Lee, and I owned and operated Full Circle Organic Farm. Bill Kaye-Blake, who started as an apprentice and has become family, moved the book off dead-center. A change in my health leaves Full Circle fallow now, but I'm grateful to be able to write and to present workshops and trainings based on what I learned during that wonderful time. Hopefully, *The New Farmers' Market* reflects some of this knowledge. This coming year, I will be training producers in business planning as well as production and marketing. I look forward to meeting many of you who have been e-mail supporters these many years.

— *Marcie A. Rosenzweig, December, 2000*

"It worked!!! Thanks so much. I really appreciate it. I have already recommended it to lots of people. The templates are terrific. If you keep adding to them, I would love to purchase whatever you do - your work is top quality...I can just imagine how great your veggies taste!"

— *Blessings, Cheri*

"Since purchasing this from Marcie earlier this year for a conference session I gave on small farming I've incorporated it into my record keeping and can't begin to say enough how well thought out this resource is. I've had my own haphazard record keeping and other methods, but this is so VERY organized. It's worth every penny."

— *Michaele Blakely, Growing Things, Carnation WA*

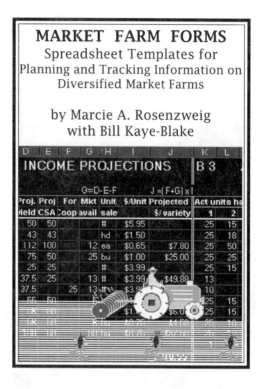

MARKET FARM FORMS
Spreadsheet Templates for Planning and Tracking Information on Diversified Market Farms

by Marcie A. Rosenzweig
with Bill Kaye-Blake

ATTRA's Steve Diver:

"Since it came to our attention here at ATTRA, some co-workers in vegetable production and agricultural economics have really been impressed at this genuinely useful and farmer-friendly book and spreadsheet combination. While a number of farm management spreadsheets exist, *Market Farm Forms* is the best one I've seen to help organize and calculate a mix of vegetables and related crops raised by market gardeners, truck farmers, and CSAs. On top of that, it supports the needs of certified organic growers with special features."

See further description of *Market Farm Forms* in Resources, Chapter 2. To order your copy, send check or money order for $45 plus $5 shipping and handling to:

Full Circle Organic Farm
3377 Early Times Lane
Auburn, CA 95603
(530) 885-9201, fullcircle@jps.net
California residents, add sales tax
Specify: Mac or PC

The New Farmers' Market

Thank you for purchasing *The New Farmers' Market!* If you like it, please tell others! **Quantity-order discounts:** *The New Farmers' Market* is available at group-purchase discount rates for organizations or market managers who want to make it available to market members, etc. See "Orders" below.

Sell What You Sow!

Sell What You Sow! The Growers' Guide to Successful Produce Marketing, by Eric Gibson. The definitive book on high-value marketing of farm products. Includes: deciding what to grow, selling through farmers markets, roadside markets, pick-your-own, subscription (CSA) farming, mail order, grocery stores & restaurants, wholesale channels & cooperatives, developing specialty (value-added) food products, merchandising & customer service, advertising & promotion, pricing & more. 8 1/2x11, 304 pp. $24.95

Orders: Credit card orders please call 888-281-5170 or from our web site at www.nwpub.net. Mail orders: Send to QP Distribution, 22260 "C" St., Winfield, KS 67156. Bulk quantity orders: call 530-823-3886. Book trade only for New Farmers' Market: Call Chelsea Green at (800) 639-4099. *Shipping:* $4.00 for the first book and $1.00 each additional book.

The Grower's Bookshelf

Look for other books we offer from our website at www.nwpub.net.

Wild Herbs In Your Backyard, by Brigitte Miner and Sean and Susan Shea.. This delightful pocketguide shows you how to identify and use more than two dozen wild, edible herbs which are commonly mistaken for weeds. If you are interested in improving your diet and health, in harvesting a bountiful natural resource, or in learning to identify useful plants on your next outing, Wild Herbs is simply a wonderful little book you can put in your pocket and head for the backyard! $6.95

From Asparagus to Zucchini: A Guide to Farm-Fresh, Seasonal Produce. This book features 46 different vegetable and herb sections which include nutritional, historical, and storage information as well as cooking tips and over 370 recipes. The beginning section includes essays that address how our food choices fit into our economy, environment, communities, quality of life and agricultural systems. 81/2 x11, $19.95.